John Cordy Jeaffreson

A book about the Clergy

John Cordy Jeaffreson

A book about the Clergy

ISBN/EAN: 9783743301412

Manufactured in Europe, USA, Canada, Australia, Japa

Cover: Foto ©ninafisch / pixelio.de

Manufactured and distributed by brebook publishing software (www.brebook.com)

John Cordy Jeaffreson

A book about the Clergy

NEW, REVISED, AND CHEAPER EDITION.

In 2 vols. post 8vo. price 24s. bound.

A BOOK ABOUT LAWYERS.

BY

JOHN CORDY JEAFFRESON,

B.A. OXON.; BARRISTER-AT-LAW.

PRINCIPAL CONTENTS:—The Great Seal, Royal Portraits, The Practice of Sealing, Lords Commissioners, On Damasking, The Rival Seals, Purses of State, A Lady Keeper, Lawyers in Arms, The Devil's Own, Lawyers on Horseback, Chancellors' Cavalcades, Ladies in Law Colleges, York House, Powis House, Lincoln's Inn Fields, The Old Law Quarter, Loves of the Lawyers, The Three Graces, Rejected Addresses, Brothers in Trouble, Fees to Counsel, Retainers Special and General, Judicial Corruption, Gifts and Sales, Judicial Salaries, Costume and Toilet, Millinery, Wigs, Bands and Collars, Bags and Gowns, The Singing Barrister, Actors at the Bar, Political Lawyers, The Peers, Lawyers in the House, Legal Education, Inns of Court and Inns of Chancery, Lawyers and Gentlemen, Law French and Law Latin, Readers and Mootmen, Pupils in Chambers, Wit of Lawyers, Humorous Stories, Wits in Silk and Punsters in Ermine, Circuiters, Witnesses, Lawyers and Saints, Lawyers in Court and Society, Attorneys at Law, Westminster Hall, Law and Literature, &c.

' "A Book about Lawyers" deserves to be very popular. Mr. Jeaffreson has accomplished his work in a very creditable manner. He has taken pains to collect information from persons as well as from books, and he writes with a sense of keen enjoyment which greatly enhances the reader's pleasure He introduces us to Lawyerdom under a variety of phases— we have lawyers in arms, lawyers on horseback, lawyers in love, and lawyers in Parliament. We are told of their salaries and fees, their wigs and gowns, their jokes and gaieties. We meet them at home and abroad, in court, in chambers, and in company. In the chapters headed "Mirth," the author has gathered together a choice sheaf of anecdotes from the days of More down to Erskine and Eldon.'—*Times.*

' These volumes will afford pleasure and instruction to all who read them, and they will increase the reputation which Mr. Jeaffreson has already earned by his large industry and great ability.'—*Athenæum.*

' The success of his "Book about Doctors" has induced Mr. Jeaffreson to write another book—about Lawyers. The subject is attractive. It is a bright string of anecdotes, skilfully put together, on legal topics of all sorts, but especially in illustration of the lives of famous lawyers. Mr. Jeaffreson has not only collected a large number of good stories, but he has grouped them pleasantly, and tells them well. We need say little to recommend a book that can speak for itself so pleasantly. No livelier reading is to be found among the new books of the season.'—*Examiner.*

' The present work is a meet companion for the cursory reader, to the author's "Book about Doctors," but it is something more. No work can give the reader a more comprehensive and accurate view of the characteristics of the legal profession than Mr. Jeaffreson's "Book about Lawyers." To illustrate his subject the author has brought to bear much legal and general erudition. He has produced a work genuine, full, and useful, which will be highly appreciated by the profession and the public, as well from the great ability which the author has evinced in its construction as from the importance of the information which it conveys.'—*Morning Post.*

' Scarcely any part of the work can be dipped into which will not yield something to entertain the reader, and it need hardly be said that a practised *littérateur* like Mr. Jeaffreson rehearses his stories like a man of understanding.'—*The Daily News.*

' These two very delightful gossiping volumes contain a vast amount of pleasing anecdote and interesting information. Mr. Jeaffreson has exercised considerable industry in the collection, and has displayed both taste and judgment in the arrangement of his materials.'—*The Sun.*

' The author of this "Book about Lawyers" has evidently taken immense pains, and spent a great deal of time, in collecting its contents. There is not a point of interest which he has omitted, and the amount of anecdote and information spread through the two portly volumes is enormous.'— *The Observer.*

' Mr. Jeaffreson is one of those writers who could not produce an uninteresting book; and being thoroughly acquainted with the subjects he handles, he is sure to obtain a host of readers.'— *Messenger.*

HURST AND BLACKETT, Publishers, 13 Great Marlborough Street.

NEW AND CHEAPER EDITION.

In 1 vol. crown 8vo. price 5s. bound.

A BOOK ABOUT DOCTORS.

BY

JOHN CORDY JEAFFRESON,

B.A. OXON.; BARRISTER-AT-LAW.

'THIS is a rare book; a compliment to the medical profession, and an acquisition to its members; a book to be read and re-read — fit for the study and the consulting-room, as well as the drawing-room table and the circulating library. We have before had folios of medical *ana*, of greater or less merit, but they all failed to accomplish what we had a right to expect from such literature. One collector is frivolous, a second ill-informed, a third inaccurate — all incapable of amusing and instructing at the same time. It remained for Mr. Jeaffreson to take a comprehensive view of the social history of the profession, and illustrate its course from the feudal era down to the present day, by a series of biographic and domestic sketches, the materials for which have been gathered from sources of information little known to any save historic students, and from the traditions of olden times, cherished as topics for choice familiar gossip amongst the elders of the colleges. The chapters on the Doctor as a Bon-Vivant, the Generosity and Parsimony of Physicians, the Quarrels of Physicians, and Loves of the Physicians, are rich with anecdotes of medical celebrities, provoking, over and above the boisterous laughter they create, not a little curiosity as to where on earth the author could have derived his stories of gossip. But Mr. Jeaffreson does not merely amuse. The pages he devotes to the exposure and history of charlatanry are of scarcely less value to the student of medicine than to the student of manners. On taking our leave of Mr. Jeaffreson, we thank him most heartily for the mirth and the solid information of his volumes. As we have already said, their appeal is to a wide circle. All the members of our profession will be sure to read them. During the winter evenings, when the firelight plays on the red curtains, and the day's work is done, and the young people range themselves round hearth or lamp, no more acceptable visitor will break in upon the scene than the "Book about Doctors," which suggests to the pupil new fields of inquiry, and for the veteran, whose diplomas were dated near half a century since, has those pleasant memories of the times and the men that have been, and are no more.'—*The Lancet.*

'A pleasant book for the fireside season on which we are entering, and for the seaside season that is to come. Since Mr. Wadd's details of his own experiences in the first of his popular works, there has not been so agreeable a book about doctors published as the one before us. Mr. Wadd, it will be remembered, chatted chiefly of his own experiences. Mr. Jeaffreson takes a far wider range. He has been into the medical garden, and gathered two armsful of herbs, and plants, and flowers, and everything connected therewith; and these he has classified and arranged, and out of hundreds of volumes collected thousands of good things, adding thereto much that appears in print for the first time, and which, of course, gives increased value to this very readable book.'—*Athenæum.*

'The republication of this work within so brief a period is but a natural and necessary consequence of its popularity. In its present cheaper and more complete form the work cannot fail to obtain a still wider circle of readers than it has hitherto had, and to become as it were a "household word" in all private libraries. Those who have not read the book may, perhaps, be informed in this place that it is one of the most instructive and at the same time one of the most amusing that has recently issued from the press. To those who have read it, this edition requires no additional recommendation beyond the facts of its cheapness and completeness.'—*Observer.*

'We have already spoken in high terms of the merits of this most entertaining volume, which became at once so popular that a new edition has been very rapidly demanded. In renewing our acquaintance with Mr. Jeaffreson, we find that we have not much to add respecting the merits of his performance, which describes the peculiarities, the rise and progress, and the system of well-known medical English practitioners, in a manner that is highly creditable to himself. Acting upon the great principle, "Nothing extenuate, nor set down aught in malice," he has done good service to the medical profession and delighted hosts of readers, whom his manner no less than his matter has attracted.'—*Messenger.*

'On many matters of interest pertaining to the profession a great number of curious particulars are mentioned, and the book will be found altogether one of the most amusing, and at the same time most instructive, that has issued from the press for a long time past.'—*Morning Advertiser.*

HURST AND BLACKETT, Publishers, 13 Great Marlborough Street.

A BOOK ABOUT THE CLERGY.

VOL. I.

A BOOK ABOUT THE CLERGY.

BY

JOHN CORDY JEAFFRESON,

B.A. OXON.

AUTHOR OF

"A BOOK ABOUT DOCTORS," "A BOOK ABOUT LAWYERS,"

&c. &c.

IN TWO VOLUMES.

VOL. I.

Second Edition.

LONDON:
HURST AND BLACKETT, PUBLISHERS,
13, GREAT MARLBOROUGH STREET.
1870.

The Right of Translation is reserved.

PREFACE.

TWELVE years have passed since difficulties, encountered in a course of reading, determined me to endeavour to supply a want of English literature by writing a book that should commemorate the usages and characteristics of the followers of Divinity, Law, and Physic in past times of English story,—a book that, without arrogating to itself the dignity of history, should be useful to historians, and, whilst affording diversion to all readers of general literature, should be of special service to artists bent on illustrating the life of our ancestors with pen or pencil. For the accomplishment of this undertaking I had made considerable preparations, when I altered my plan on seeing that it would be impossible to deal effectively with the affairs of the three learned professions in a single work of dimensions that would raise no obstacles to its attainment of popularity. Adhering to my original purpose, whilst relinquishing my first design for its achievement, I decided to produce three distinct works :—each of which should be complete in itself and altogether independent of the other two, whilst the three should together form an historic survey of the social progress and development of the three faculties.

To give effect to this project I began upon the profession with which my early training and personal associations rendered me most familiar, and in 1860 produced my memoir of medical men and their ways under a title that has been adapted by several writers to various well-known publications. After a lapse of seven years I published my history of legal usages,—the second instalment of a task that is completed by the volumes which I now lay before the world.

JOHN CORDY JEAFFRESON.

43 *Springfield Road*,
   S. John's Wood, N.W.

CONTENTS

OF

THE FIRST VOLUME.

PART I.—WYCLIFFE'S ENGLAND.

CHAP.		PAGE
I.	THE PIONEERS	1
II.	THE MONASTERY	13
III.	GOTHIC ARCHITECTURE	27
IV.	CLERICAL PREPONDERANCE	42
V.	POLITICAL DIVISIONS	53
VI.	DONS AND SIRS	67
VII.	CLERICAL MORALS	84
VIII.	MONEY AND LEARNING	98
IX.	THE POOR AND THE RICH	110
X.	THE BEGGAR PRIESTS	120
XI.	LOLLARDY: MANNERS AND SOCIAL ASPECTS	137
XII.	LOLLARDY: TENETS AND POLITICS	153

PART II.—PERSECUTION.

CHAP.		PAGE
I.	THE ANIMUS OF PERSECUTION	171
II.	THE LAW OF HERESY	180
III.	FIRE AND SHRINE	198
IV.	THE STAKE	210
V.	SECONDARY PUNISHMENTS AND DEGRADATION	227
VI.	THE DEATH OF PERSECUTION	237

PART III.—CLERICAL WOMEN.

I.	CLERICAL WIVES IN PRE-ELIZABETHAN TIMES	247
II.	CLERICAL WIVES IN ELIZABETH'S REIGN	256
III.	CLERICAL WIVES IN THE TIMES OF JAMES THE FIRST, CHARLES THE FIRST, AND THE COMMONWEALTH	272
IV.	CLERICAL WIVES, TEMP. CHARLES II. AND JAMES II.	287
V.	LIFE INSURANCE	299
VI.	ELIZABETH'S TWELFTH INJUNCTION	315
VII.	THE MODERN CLERICAL HOME	321

PART IV.—OLD WAYS AND NEW FASHIONS.

I.	GOD'S HOUSE THE PEOPLE'S HOME	336
II.	CHURCH PLAYS AND CHURCH ALES	347

PART I.—WYCLIFFE'S ENGLAND.

CHAPTER I.

THE PIONEERS.

FOR the educated mind, there is no more delightful pastime, or profitable exercise, than to meditate on those separate communities of religious persons, whose toilsome and pious labours were largely instrumental in reclaiming the British islands from primeval wildness, and converting their earlier inhabitants from Pagan superstition; and who, discharging at the same time the functions of the colonist and the missionary, were the founders of institutions that took deep root in the social system of our semi-barbarous ancestors, and through centuries of convulsion and change were of inestimable service to mankind as schools of civilisation and fountains of the true faith.

To realise the intellectual, moral, and material conditions under which these remote benefactors of our species achieved their fruitful work, is a task attended with many difficulties, arising from the fewness and inadequacy of the records, which are the only written memorials of their virtues and performances. But in the absence of fuller and worthier histories, we may well be thankful for the meagre chronicles which, at wide and irregular intervals, throw faint gleams of light athwart the otherwise unbroken gloom which covers these saintly actors from our reverential observation. For by the aid of those infrequent and uncertain lights something may surely be discerned of the simplicity and fervour, the mild submissiveness and superb daring, the exquisite tenderness and almost superhuman strength, that distinguished them from the inferior natures, for whose temporal advantage and eternal salvation they laboured with unselfish zeal and invincible resoluteness. And when this insight has been gained into the sources of their influence over their contemporaries, it is possible, though arduous for us—by a judicious and vigorous exercise of reason and imagination—to bring ourselves face to face, as it were, with the men and women of British or Anglo-Saxon race, who embraced Christianity in the earlier stages of its long war of numerous conflicts with the paganism of the Celtic and Teutonic tribes, and who, having thus adopted the faith of the Cross, retired in companies to the fastnesses of the forests, or the desolate spots of the thinly-populated land, in order that, whilst complying with the precepts of the gospel, they might contribute directly, and with effectiveness, to the conversion of that Pagan world from which they had withdrawn themselves for a time.

Conspicuous in the churches that furnished martyrs to the agents of Diocletian's persecution, and perished under the incursions of the German immigrants, these communities of Christian believers were still more numerous and powerful in the churches founded by those Celtic missionaries, who repaid the wrongs inflicted on their race by endowing its persecutors with the blessings of conversion to the one true religion. In times prior to the creation of parishes they sent forth the priests, who, upon the second overthrow of Pagan superstition in Albion, ministered to the spiritual needs of the scattered congregations; and growing in number and importance as Christianity gained more general acceptance amongst the Saxon peoples, they entered upon the dawn of their greatness, when they witnessed the completion of that parochial system which owed its origin to their priests, and continues to this day a grand memorial of their care for the interests of religion in every quarter of the land.

It should, however, be borne in mind that these ancient communities of religious persons in the Celtic and early Anglo-Saxon churches differed widely in several important particulars from the monasteries of later times. Until the tenth century, when Dunstan's zeal and irresistible will, effecting the work which Wilfrid was powerless to accomplish some three hundred years earlier, firmly planted the Benedictine system in the polity of the English Church, the monasteries of our remote ancestors were not so much colleges of ecclesiastics as associations of believers, who found it to be for their convenience and edification to dwell within a common home. We have called them communities of religious persons, but we should more exactly designate their constitution and functions by calling them associations of religious families; for they afforded shelter to the young and old of both sexes, to parents with young children in their arms, to widows and virgins. Comprising a clerical element, sufficient for the spiritual needs of its members, and the due instruction of its dependent churches, a Saxon monastery of the pre-Dunstan period consisted chiefly of lay-members, a considerable proportion of whom were females.

Nor was woman's presence a source of embarrassment, or an occasion of scandal, in these colonies of austere ascetics, in days when no edict of the Church imposed celibacy on her clergy, and social opinion had not yet discerned in marriage such a savour of sinfulness as rendered its estate incompatible with the sanctity of the priestly office. Frequently the feminine element, both in numbers and capacity, preponderated over the male in the British and Saxon monasteries, which not seldom obeyed the supreme control of the opulent and royal ladies, to whose munificence they owed their existence. The pious princess, who converted her residence into a refuge from worldly temptations for enthusiastic devotees, enjoyed a natural right to regulate the life of the guests who accepted her hospitality; and if she possessed the intelligence and energy to govern a numerous household, she soon came to exercise the functions of a religious superior by discharging efficiently the duties of a hostess. It was thus that the Deirian princess—whose beneficent career has given rise to so many unworthy jests—established her right to rule the monasteries, in which priests and bishops received instruction from her lips, and in the most famous of which she fostered the sacred genius of the cowherd, Ceadmon, whose rhythmical translations of the Bible stories charmed the ears and illuminated the minds of the rude Northumbrian converts: Thus also the Princess Ebba became the spiritual directress, as well as the temporal guardian, of her disciples at Coldingham. And whilst these Northumbrian ladies were thus spending their substance and lives in the service of the Church, Queen Etheldreda, after escaping from her husband's detested importunities, established in East Anglia the monastery in which she emulated the virtues and services of her aunt, the Abbess Hilda.

Whilst he meditates upon the incidents which must have attended the plantation of those early communities, the scholar of the nineteenth century surrounds himself with visions that strengthen whilst they delight the mind from which they have emanated. Looking down upon the minster of his native city from an eminence, that commands an uninterrupted view of the landscape, of which the antique tower is the central object, he gradually loses sight of all the marks which man's incessant industry has put upon the familiar country. No longer darkened by the factories that defile its waters whilst they utilise its force, the river flows clear and bright between banks, whose majestic trees throw dark shadows on its still and glassy surface. The ripening corn-fields, the green meadows, and pleasant homesteads of a hundred farms disappear, and are replaced by grand breadths of the virgin forest, that clothes the unoccupied valley and distant hills with every variety of greenness, and every diversity of curving lines. Far away, where the blue haze thickening the atmosphere deprives the outlines of their fineness, is just discernible the peak from whose summit may be seen, on the other side of a stretch of morass and moorland, the stronghold of the thane, whose goodwill to the Christian faith has recently borne fruit, in a grant of uncleared forest, to a band of religious enthusiasts, whom he has graciously empowered to live in the fastnesses of the conceded wilderness,— earning heaven by their prayers, whilst they enrich the earth by their labour.

And now, floating slowly with the river's steady current, there comes to the dreamer's vision a large, rude raft, similar in make to the smaller of those unwieldy floats, which, growing with the stream's width and the progress of their seaward course, move slowly down the Rhine from the interior of Europe to the ports, where they are broken up and sold for the benefit of the workmen, whose not unskilful labour felled their massive timbers in the forest, knit their cumbrous parts into monstrous floors, and then navigated them to the spot appointed for their destruction.

Just as each of those Rhine-rafts is seen to bear its company of workers, so the float of our scholar's vision bears a freight of passengers, whose hands made the vessel on which they are slowly gliding to their toil.

Perhaps the whole crew numbers fifty souls; and as they draw nearer to his point of observation, the dreamer observes them looking eagerly to the bank on which they are about to alight.

Amongst them are faces of every age, from the furrowed visage of the veteran, marked by the scars of battle, to the smooth cheek of the blue-eyed boy, who has embraced the sacred life with the fierce fervour of youthful enthusiasm. Beside men, whose garb and tonsure indicate their priestly rank, stand laymen, whose various pursuits have fitted them to endure the toil and hardships of settlers in the forest. Some of them have learnt in the courts of princes the emptiness of earthly honour; some are simple craftsmen, who from their earliest years have sustained themselves by the labour of their hands; and whilst most of them are endowed with natures that, under any circumstances, would preserve them from the commission of heinous offences, there are others, whose penitential air betokens the secret anguish of remorse for crimes known only to themselves and God. A brotherhood of rude creatures, in all of whom there is perhaps less of earthly learning than is possessed by any clever twelve-years' lad of our own time, who has had the training of a village school; and of them all, the one least familiar with the learning of books is the broad-shouldered, beetle-browed monk, whom they have made their chief—in unconstrained homage to his thorough goodness and proved devotion to the rules by which they have consented to regulate their lives. Such are the men who leap from the raft to the river's bank, bearing in their hearts the vital truths of the gospel story, and in their hands the few implements that will enable them to make a clearing and raise a Christian temple in the silent wood. Nor must notice be omitted of the patient women, who are sharers in the undertaking, and contribute to the plaintive sweetness of the choral strains with which the voyagers celebrate the close of their journey before the upraised cross.*

Then scenes follow each other in quick succession; scenes that, after the wont of dreamland's visions, compress the labours and events of years, generations, centuries, into hours, minutes, seconds.

Whilst the forest still resounds with the axes that lay its trees upon the ground, there rises from the soil a timbered church, whose roof is thatched with rushes. Dwellings spring up around it; and ere the colonists have reaped their first crop of grain, a town has been called into existence by the incessant industry of workers, who do and suffer for the love of God all that the backwoodsmen of this nineteenth century achieve and endure in American fastnesses for the sake of worldly gain. Each succeeding year witnesses a large extension of the settlement, and fresh arrivals of devotees, who are received into the community as soon as the abbot has satisfied himself that they have left the world because they are not of it, and desire nothing on this side of the grave but hard fare, hard toil, and the means of spiritual edification. No wonder that the work prospers; for what agents can be more fit for such an enterprise than men who prefer solitude to any kind of social recreation, and have learnt to delight in every privation that tends to deaden the sensual appetites by which Satan lures sinners to destruction? And whilst these pioneers of monasticism are thankful for the physical rigours of a lot that exacts from them continuous bodily exertion in return for the bare means of sustenance, they deem themselves no less fortunate with respect to all those details of conventual discipline, against

---

* Oswald of Northumbria has the reputation of having erected the first cross that ever stood in this country. 'The first cross and altar,' says Foxe. on the authority of Bede and the 'Polychron.,' 'within this realm, was first set up in the north parts of Hevenfield, upon the occasion of Oswald, king of Northumland, fighting against Cadwalla, where he, in the same place, set up the sign of the Cross, kneeling and praying there for victory.' Crosses became general throughout the country in the Anglo-Saxon period. 'A cross,' says the Count de Montalembert of this period, 'raised in the middle of a field, was enough to satisfy the devotion of the thane, his ploughman, and shepherds. They gathered round it for public and daily prayer.'

which unregenerate natures would rebel as vexatious insults to personal dignity, and unendurable encroachments on personal freedom. Instead of fretting at the restraints of its minute provisions for their daily conduct, they derive a delightful sense of spiritual security from a system which assigns a special duty to each of their wakeful hours, and allows them no periods of leisure, when, through want of occupation, they might become an easy prey to diabolical influences.

Spent in the painful discharge of duties, to many of which we attach notions of servility and degradation, the daily life of these laborious zealots presents us with spectacles that are apt to rouse a momentary sense of amusement, when they are put in sharp contrast against the ways and styles of ecclesiastical persons in more civilised and luxurious times. All our conceptions of the dignity and sacredness of the priestly office, and all our conventional notions of the clerical character, are so rudely disturbed by what is known of the humble industry of these earlier monks, that trivial minds are less disposed to admiration than merriment, when for the first time they are told how in the remoter periods of our ecclesiastical history bishops were habitual wielders of the woodman's axe and the ditcher's spade, whilst their clergy felt no shame in following the plough-tail, and performing the work of artisans or farm-servants. Nor can it be denied that some of the stories of monastic humility and diligence possess a grotesqueness which palliates, though it may not justify, the mirth which they stir in flippant minds. Even students, averse to jocosity, find it difficult to refrain from smiling at the thought of St. David—that prolific parent and wise ruler of monastic settlements—guiding the ploughshare, which his disciples draw through the clayey glebe. But inquirers, less ready to discern what is ludicrous in human action than eager to ascertain the sentiment which inspires it, dismiss their inclination to laugh over this strange spectacle of saintly zeal and clerical submissiveness, when they reflect how the scene,—to those who accept the legend as veritable history, —exemplifies the piety and fine devotion of the men who, having a righteous aim in view, were restrained by no vain care for their dignity from adopting the means by which it could be most readily achieved, and who were nothing loth to work like beasts of the field in the service of a Divine Master, who for their sakes had lowered Himself to the nature and condition of a man.

Thus it is with our dreamer's monks, whose axes are continually lowering the monarchs of the forest, whose spades are incessantly widening the tracts of cultivated ground, whose hammers are heard, far and near, from early dawn to late evening, and whose industry is covering the adjacent country with peaceful homesteads and churches, whilst it rebuilds and enlarges the central town.

The scenes follow each other more rapidly, and each new scene is a panorama of changes and improvements.

Three centuries of time have barely passed since the first settlers came down the river on their heavily-laden raft; and the wooden church—the earliest architectural achievement of the pioneers—has been replaced by a stone cathedral, whose massive tower, visible from the distant hills, summons worshippers by sound of bell, and mingles its clamorous music with the terrifying uproar of the thunderstorm.* In accordance with the larger proportions of the new cathedral, the spaces, that in old time encircled the wooden church, have broadened into ample courts and picturesque thoroughfares. Ecclesiastical reform has also effected material changes in the monastery, investing its occupants with a strictly ecclesiastical character,

---

* Noticing this superstitious use of church-bells, in connexion with the many accidents that occurred from lightning to religious buildings in days when artificial lightning-conductors were unknown, Thomas Fuller, in 'The Church History of Britain,' observes,—'Only we will add, that such frequent firing of abbey-churches by lightning confuteth the proud motto, commonly written on the bells of their steeples, wherein each bell entitled itself to a sixfold efficacy:—

" 1. *Funera plango* .... Men's deaths I tell
By doleful knell.
2. *Fulgura* } *frango* ...... Light and thunder
   Fulmina I break asunder.
3. *Sabbata pango* .... On Sabbath all
To church I call.
4. *Excito lentos* .... The sleepy head
I raise from bed.
5. *Dissipo ventos* .... The winds so fierce
I do disperse.
6. *Paco cruentos* .... Men's cruel rage
I do assuage."'

Part I.—Wycliffe's England.

drawing a broad line between the religious residents of the abbey, and the laity dwelling in the outer town, assigning separate residences to the two sexes of religious persons, and establishing scores of petty regulations, which tend to the aggrandisement of the clerical element of the community, whilst they manifestly weaken that sentiment of close, familiar fellowship, which used to knit all the inhabitants of the place into one compact family. In fact, the settlement of less than threescore religious persons has grown into a populous town, with an abbot for its ruler, residences for its clergy, a grand cathedral for its monastic celebrations, a parochial system for the instruction of its laity, a college for its nuns, and buoyant trades for the support of its increasing populace.

The life of the monastery has become less trying to monks of slender frame and delicate constitution than it was in the earlier years of its existence; but this change arises from the fact that the brethren are less frequently called upon to endure the rigours of a variable climate without adequate defence against the severity of winterly seasons, and is in no way due to any relaxation of the rules of their order. For though they have attained the fulness of such opulence and power as the age permits to the most fortunate of religious societies, success has produced in them no disposition to luxurious repose. From the abbot to the youngest novitiate they are zealous for the welfare of their house, the good of their fellow-creatures, and the glory of God, to whom they must one day render account of the use which they make of the talents committed to their stewardship. Loyal to his order, with a sentiment that combines the loyalty of the soldier with the devotion of the saint, each member of the sacerdotal college throws the plenitude of his energies into the performance of the work specially allotted to him,—whether his peculiar task be the care of any portion of the society's earthly estate, the pursuit of literary labour, the relief of indigence, the instruction of students, the primary training of children, or the cure of souls. And whilst they thus discharge their various functions to the best of their imperfect knowledge and defective powers, they are in perfect harmony with the spirit and aspirations of their time. In the celibacy which they have recently adopted as a rule of their lives, and in various minor arrangements which contribute more to the worldly influence than the spiritual efficacy of the monastic classes, shrewd observers can indeed see the first signs of the division which is destined to become a wide gulf of severance between monasticism and national interests. The contentions that have arisen betwixt themselves and the secular clergy also forebode innumerable humiliations and embarrassments in future days. But at present the monks are in perfect unison with every section of the laity,—with the nobles, from whom their novices are mostly drawn, no less than with the populace, who venerate them for their ascetic austerities and never-failing munificence. Whithersoever they journey, the needy and ignorant welcome them with blessings; and of the attachment and confidence cherished for them by the wealthy, there is evidence in the alacrity with which their schools are frequented by the children of thanes and princes;—children whose parents have in many cases sent them to the monastery and nunnery * from remote parts of the kingdom, not more for the sake of learning than for security from the incursions of the ruthless Danes.

Yet another vision in this dream of many visions.

The time has come when the Saxons must bite the dust or fly before the conquering Normans, and endure the anguish and shame which their Pagan ancestors inflicted on the Christian Celts. The decisive battle has been fought, and the victors are pushing forward the grim work of pacification with the headsman's axe and the hangman's cord; with proclamations

---

* Competent historians of the religious life of Old England concur in testifying to the importance of the services which the nuns rendered to society as teachers of children— services that began with the first establishment of conventual houses, and were continued till the destruction of the monastic system. But I am acquainted with no authority who is a more tender and vivid witness than Ailred of Rievesby to this particular usefulness of the religious women of remote times. 'There are some nuns,' says Ailred, 'who turn their cell into a school. She sits at the window, the child stands in the cloister; she looks earnestly at each of them, and while watching their play, now she is angry, now she laughs, now she threatens, now she soothes, now spares, now kisses; now calls the weeping child to be beaten, and then strokes her face, and catching her round the neck caresses her, calling her "her little daughter and darling."' This exquisite picture may be regarded as an illustration of conventual life during several centuries before, and many generations after, its execution by the pen of an abbot of the twelfth century.

Part I.—Wycliffe's England.

of bloody menace, and fires that cover wide tracts of country with the ashes of desolation. In every quarter of the land,—from the strongholds of princes, and the cloisters of the clergy; from towns, whose towers are visible to mariners at sea, and inland valleys bright with the evidences of careful husbandry,—companies of fugitives are hastening to the forests, in whose recesses the flower of the vanquished race will congregate in clearings, approachable only through tortuous glades, and altogether inaccessible to Norman cavalry. Made up of thanes and yeomen, priests and artisans, ladies of gentle lineage flying from nunnery or castle, and women with hands inured to servile labour, these fragments of a broken people comprise every man of Saxon blood, whose patriotism has rendered him a special mark for Norman vengeance, or whose proud heart forbids him to render homage to the insolent oppressors of his shattered race. In their disordered ranks, also, may be found every Saxon woman, to whose patriotic and affectionate heart exile in the forest—where the hardships of outlawry will be mitigated by companionship with kindred—is preferable to a shameful existence amid scenes where none of her race may henceforth linger, save those recreant abjects of a noble stock, who are ready to exchange freedom and honour for the bondsman's collar. And in this wholesale exodus of a nation, hurrying from peaceful haunts, which their labour has reclaimed from nature's inhospitable wildness, no braver hearts can be found than those which beat within the breasts of our dreamer's monks and nuns, who, after a last solemn celebration of their sacred rites in the temple, which will never again reverberate with the rich melody of their joyful voices, begin their rapid journey to the dark wood, through which, assisted by the companions of their banishment, they will hew a narrow and winding way to a central spot, where they may dwell beyond the invader's reach, and, outlaws though they be, may renew the pious labour and diverse trials of the founders of their brotherhood.

And now, like misty wreaths flying before the sun, our dreamer's visions pass away; and 'no longer surrounded by the fair imaginations and profitable fancies, by means of which, for one brief hour, he has heard the voices and seen the faces of men and women, whose flesh returned to dust in far-distant centuries, he looks down once more upon his native town, with eyes that can no longer see it other than it is,—abounding in the signs of recent enterprise, whose doings stand out in strong contrast against the memorials of a period which time has clothed with mist and silence. There stands the Gothic minster, on ground once occupied by a Saxon cathedral; and hard by its majestic towers, and lines of pointed windows, is visible the bishop's palace, flanked by ancient trees, from beneath whose black foliage the rooks are cawing out their social harmony. The eye can catch the tops of the canons' residence, and the ivy that runs in tumbled masses upon the parapet of the dean's garden wall. More might be seen of the Close and the antique Market-square, were it not for the highest of those tiers of stucco houses and trim villas, which interpose their dazzling and discordant whiteness between the sombre tints of the Upper Town and the black shipping that lies moored in the quay.

Descending from his point of observation, and, as he descends, musing on the moral of his long reverie—which has thrown light on many a page of history, and brought the results of disconnected studies into fruitful co-operation—he sees more clearly than before that the monasticism, whose earlier services are too often buried under odious memories of the abuses and vices of its decay, was planted and reared, almost to the plenitude of its perilous power, by men of prayerful hearts and toilsome lives.

CHAPTER II.

THE MONASTERY.

WITH reluctance, qualified by regret, I pause at the threshold of my task to guard against a possibility of misapprehension by stating expressly, that it may not be inferred from aught contained in the preceding chapter that I am in any degree disposed to palliate the corruptions which marked the decay of monasticism in this country, and which would have fully justified the wholesale suppression of religious houses, which was effected in the sixteenth century, even if no considerations of imperial policy and national safety had rendered their extinction an affair of obvious necessity. The evidence of those abuses is, at the same time, so conclusive and so notorious that I should lack the daring, even had I the inclination, to cover their gloomy and repulsive features with a veil of specious excuses and plausible extenuations. But whilst regarding the enormities engendered by those establishments, in their long and loathsome decrepitude, with the emotions natural to an Englishman, who, trained from childhood in schools of fervent Protestantism, has consistently striven to study his national history by the lights of liberal thought, I am of opinion, that the most valuable lessons deducible from the gloomy failure and unsightly decay of our monastic system are altogether missed by those who, either through wilful determination to close their eyes to the truth, or through any other darkening influence, are blind to the wisdom and beauties of its original design, and to the admirable efficacy with which it discharged its most important functions throughout a long series of dark and turbulent ages.

Its fundamental principle was an attempt to use, for man's spiritual needs and religious interests, that method of co-operation, which the merchants of feudal Europe employed so largely and profitably for the furtherance of their common objects; which modern society has adopted in almost countless undertakings for the promotion of learning, the attainment of philanthropic ends, and the accomplishment of political designs; and which, in these later generations, has conferred vast benefits on those of our artisans who have exercised it with discernment and fairness for the settlement of their disputes with the holders of capital. Originating in times when Paganism was an overwhelming force, and Christian converts were few and comparatively powerless, it was at first the faint protest of weakness against strength; the attempt of a minority in the right to range themselves for effective conflict with a majority in the wrong; the outgrowth of the natural, beneficial, and universal tendency of all holders of new truth to combine and act in concert for its establishment on the ruins of error. In this stage of its story, each of its supporters gave all that he possessed to the common fund, in imitation of those earliest Christians who had all things in common, not for mutual enjoyment, but for the attainment of their one and common aim—the conversion of those who differed from them in opinion. The rich man gave his riches to the uttermost farthing; the man of mental faculties devoted the whole of his learning and intellectual energies to the good cause; the man, whose material and mental endowments were so humble that he could contribute nothing to the wealth or intellectual force of the fraternity, followed to the best of his ability in the footsteps of rich and educated believers, and, like them, gave to the enterprise his whole heart, and every thew and nerve of his perishable body, —doing with alacrity, and thoroughness, and heroic patience, whatever service was imposed on him by his clearer-sighted comrades; and deriving an exquisite delight from the knowledge that the Church had need of such mean creatures as he, who could render no service but prayer and muscular effort, and that the man who gave to the Church with all his heart all the abilities of his body, and nothing more, made no valueless contribution to the joint stock of a Christian association. But, though the gifts differed in value, they were from one point of view equal, in being the whole which each contributor possessed in the entire world. The partners in the venture were also rewarded alike—with the consciousness which each received that he had given his all, and with the sure hope of eternal salvation. Thus, at its outset monasticism was communism of a nobler and purer kind than aught that our political philosophers have ventured to propose. Unlike, also, the projects of our political schemers, this divine and spiritual communism was destined to accomplish its ends, ere it perished of diseases that were in no small degree due to the completeness, or rather let us say to the extravagance, of its success.

Planted by native hands, and reared to maturity by the affectionate care of those whom it enriched, English monasticism was no foreign device, imposed on a reluctant or unwary nation, but the natural outgrowth of our needs and aspirations, at a period when Christianity was still only an experiment, and its adherents had no adequate organisation for giving practical expression to their principles in a society composed of conflicting elements, and recognising no finer rule of action than the assumed right of the strong to subjugate and tyrannise over the weak. Both before the extinction of Saxon ascendancy, and in later times, when the Conqueror's system had done much for national consolidation and unity, it contended with the gigantic evils of a community which, notwithstanding the theoretical subordination of its parts to a single supreme ruler, was little else than an aggregation of separate and often antagonistic governments, whose contentions were, in many cases, exasperated by the restraints that limited their independence, without moderating their disposition to despotic license. And in combating the ills of this condition of affairs, monasticism—learning its duty step by step, as it proceeded in the beneficial stages of its career—extended the benefits of domestic nurture to pious persons, who, outside the walls of the religious colleges, could find no abode where existence was compatible with obedience to Christian precepts; covered the land with schools for learning, and edifices for public worship; inspired men of carnal appetites and insolent tempers with a new reverence for woman, which became the promoter, if not the parent, of the gracious virtues of chivalry; and, having roused in all the sections of our fellow-countrymen the fierce enthusiasm, which resulted in the splendid madness of the Crusades, through the operation of those gorgeous and wasteful armaments broke down the barriers, which had hitherto divided the victorious Norman from the Saxon outlaw, making in several regions of the kingdom the descendants of the vanquished thanes a distinct nation, and a continual source of weakness to the foreign government that encircled the organised fugitives of the forest, without being able to punish or propitiate them. And whilst it thus illuminated the minds, and stirred the hearts of mankind, monasticism gradually mitigated the cruelty and insolence of feudalism; so that the lords relinquished their claim to powers, whose exercise inflicts scarcely less injury on the despot than upon the slaves whom he lowers—so far as human iniquity can lower any of our species—to the condition of mere beasts.

In fact, the triumph of monasticism was the triumph of order over anarchy, of knowledge over ignorance, of refining charity over brutalising selfishness, of civilisation over barbarism, of Christian light over Pagan darkness. For its earlier acquisitions of that real estate, of which it came in course of time to hold so exorbitant and dangerous a proportion, it could plead the best of all titles, that by which the colonist asserts his moral as well as legal right to soil which he has reclaimed from unserviceable wildness or bleak barrenness by sweat of brow and pain of muscle. And with respect to the inordinate possessions, which, in more recent times, rendered ' monk ' a bye-word for monstrous appetency, whilst the too-general indolence of the religious clergy was associated with luxurious sloth, and all the moral uncleannesses of which voluptuous ease is a hotbed, it should be remembered, that the widely extending lands and vast opulence of the monks came to them chiefly from donors, who, when full allowance has been made for the pernicious action of superstitious imaginations on the senile or the sick, were not without good reasons for believing that whatever they bequeathed to a religious house would be expended in ways conducive to the highest interests of mankind.

That the monasteries in later periods abused the confidence which had been reposed in them every one is ready to admit, though there is much difference of opinion as to the extent of their misapplications of funds committed to them in expressed or implied trust for the furtherance of religion and the good of society. But, however satisfied he may be that those misapplications were enormous and universal, no candid inquirer is likely to deny, that throughout a long series of generations the monks were sincerely devout and honest men, who discharged all their obligations to the world with scrupulous and conscientious exactness; and that they proved themselves upon the whole careful and efficient stewards of the talents for whose employment they held themselves accountable to their Maker. A system may perish prematurely, destroyed by an untimely combination of malignant influences; it may also be planted out of the right season, in which case it will die before it has struck its roots into the land on whose surface it has been set: but it is not in the nature of things that an institution should flourish, and bear fruit, and exhibit every sign of vigour throughout centuries, and yet all the time be growing upon ground that it merely cumbers. As soon as such a tree ceases to be useful there are usually men enough at hand to cut it down; or, in the cases where it is permitted to stand, its barren branches put forth no new shoots. Even if there were no other evidence of their usefulness and general rectitude, the confidence which society continued to place in them as good men and honest stewards of great wealth—a confidence abundantly demonstrated by the benefactions which unceasingly flowed in upon them from all classes of the community—would be satisfactory testimony that the regular clergy had neither lost, nor deserved to lose, their hold upon the affections and respect of the majority of their contemporaries, at a time when satirists—those brilliant but misleading lights in the obscuring shades of history—were exaggerating their peculiar frailties, and lashing their exceptional sins in elaborate lampoons and fierce declamations, in which justice and malignity, veracious portraiture and extravagant caricature, are so inextricably commingled, that it is impossible to separate precisely the truth from the falsehood of the piquant misrepresentations.

In order that we may form a fair judgment of the manner in which the monks before their general demoralisation discharged their duties to society, as citizens possessing large pecuniary resources, it is well that we should glance at the responsibilities attaching to wealth in our time, and at the way in which those responsibilities are fulfilled by right-minded persons of the present generation. And whilst making this survey, we should bear in mind that all thoughtful and conscientious men concur in the opinion, that no rich layman of to-day is less strictly bound than was the monk of old time to regard his riches as a trust held for the benefit of his fellow-creatures.

Let us take the case of any gentleman of landed estate, who, in consideration of generous birth, ample means, and corresponding culture, holds an honourable place amongst the gentry; and in doing so, we shall bring under observation a representative of a class that is not generally thought deficient in conscientiousness, or any of the qualities of meritorious citizens. If a man, placed in these favourable circumstances, takes ordinary care that the material resources of his property are so developed that they produce all which intelligent husbandry and judicious management can readily extract from them, and if, whilst thus carrying out prudent measures for the improvement of his worldly means, he exhibits a moderate degree of consideration for the feelings and welfare of his tenants and other persons concerned in the operations which utilise the productiveness of his estate, he enjoys credit for being a good landlord, and for discharging the most important of the responsibilities of his enviable position. Whatever more society feels that it may require of him, apart from the fulfilment of the duties of natural affection, is accomplished when he has shown himself a painstaking magistrate, a person ready to attend with promptness to all his legal liabilities to public or private creditors, and a householder not wanting in hospitality and good-fellowship to neighbours of his own social degree. If, in all these respects, he is an honest and kindly person, no voice ventures to whisper that he is otherwise than a meritorious trustee of the world's wealth. So long as he evinces no disposition to avoid his manifest liabilities to the tax-gatherer, he may, by all lawful and constitutional means, do his utmost to shift from his own to his neighbours' shoulders some portion of those fiscal burdens, which, in the opinion of most opulent persons, are the most vexatious of their responsibilities; and if he should succeed in his endeavours to lessen his share of the public expenses, by effecting a proportionate increase in the liabilities of another person, he is deemed a fortunate and sagacious fellow, and no one dreams of charging him with an inclination to shirk his social obligations. Provided he satisfies public feeling upon the points already enumerated, he may consult his own pleasure in spending on not scandalous objects, or in hoarding the surplus of his income over what may be called necessary expenditure; and whatever that pleasure may be, he is none the less held to have discharged the obligations appertaining to his property. But if his pleasure is to spend a tithe of that surplus on the acquisition of pictures, and another tithe on undertakings of benevolence, he is very often extolled as a munificent patron of art, and an exemplary philanthropist.

It is also desirable that we should see how societies, composed of several individuals, fulfil in our day the duties that devolve upon them as owners of considerable property, and that we should form some fair estimate of the benefits that accrue to the nation from the existence of such holders of wealth. And, in making this inquiry, we should pay less attention to those corporations that are notorious for remissness in the performance of their duties, or for scandalous perversion of the funds retained in their immoral custody, than to those collegiate institutions whose administration is characterised by such conscientiousness and efficiency that they are universally admitted to be highly advantageous to the community. Of those exceptional trustees of property designed for charitable uses, whose shameless action expends on luxuries for the rich the revenues that should furnish sustenance to the poor and aged, we will here take no notice. Nor will we waste regret over those civic companies which squander, on sumptuous and altogether profitless hospitality, the wealth that might be rendered conducive to the public good. Our more agreeable task will be to look at those institutions for the promotion of sound learning and religious interests, which continue to accomplish—imperfectly, no doubt, but still largely—the beneficent intentions of their founders and early supporters, and which are regarded by all cultivated Englishmen with reverential affection and grateful pride.

No one can make a sum of the benefits which flow to society from the affluence and action of any single college of Oxford or Cambridge, and put them against all the advantages that ordinarily come to mankind from the same amount of affluence in the hands of an ordinary private individual, without seeing that the balance of good results is prodigiously in favour of the learned corporation. For a moment, perhaps, this statement may rouse the dissent of those reformers, who, painfully impressed by the short-comings of our universities, which might easily be rendered much more serviceable to society than they are at present, may be likened to angry schoolmasters who, whilst wielding the rod, are mindful only of the offences which have roused their disapprobation, and are for the moment blind to the deserts of their peccant pupils. But, after a brief reflection, these dissentients will allow that, however much it may fail of excellence in design or practical perfection, the college enjoying a rental of 10,000*l.* a-year makes a larger return for what it holds of the world's wealth than any average squire of the same income. Whilst the private man's estate descends, in the usual course of things, to his eldest son, who gains it without any kind of elevating service, and too often without any ennobling sentiment of filial gratitude, the separate portions of the revenues of a college —the stipends attached to its fellowships and scholarships— are more or less open to general competition, and devolve upon those persons who, by certain invigorating studies, are furnished with intellectual and moral forces, which, at least, render it probable that they will be serviceable members of society. Thus, by a process, attended no doubt with many errors, but upon the whole fruitful of desirable selections, the college assigns the possession of its wealth to persons who possess a comparative immunity from the intellectual and moral imbecility, which is lamentably productive of mischief when it is united with the command of money. A fellow of a college may not be a person who can be classified with the wisest of his species; he may, in rare cases, be morally worthless; but anyhow, he is devoid of those congenital disqualifications, which, conjoined with large possessions, result in continual accessions to the ranks of those most pernicious of all social pests— men of fortune, who squander their means in profligacy and uncleanness. At the worst, he enters on his manly career with more than an average share of those mental and moral forces which are guarantees that their owner will not misuse his talents.

Moreover, through being attainable by industry exercised in certain fields of study, each separate share of an open collegiate foundation is a stimulus to learning in every part of the country: a stimulus which cannot be appreciated, until we think of the thousands of boys who, in our public and private schools, or in the homes of parents too poor to provide their offspring with the best initiatory training, are spurred onwards in the performance of their daily tasks by the hope of winning a share of the wealth as well as the learning of the universities.

And whilst the college thus stimulates intellectual activity throughout the length and breadth of the land, and exercises precautions for the transmission of its power to moral and highly intelligent men, it discharges with completeness its share of all those social responsibilities for whose adequate performance opulent private persons may be generally commended. Regarded as an owner of property, the college endures comparison with the average squire, whose personal residence amongst his tenantry is sometimes attended by evils that seldom exist on estates where the game is not too stringently preserved. The farms of our collegiate estates are certainly as well farmed as the land of the squirearchy; and, whilst their tenants are no less prosperous, their workmen are not more ignorant or wretched than the labourers on other properties. The college, it may be objected, is non-resident; but so, in a very considerable number of cases, is the squire for a portion or the whole of the year. And though the college may be an absentee, in respect to its lands, it has a locality where it permanently resides—the abode where it discharges the most beneficent of its functions, in forming the minds of young men during the most critical period of youthful life; and where it exercises a hospitality which, whatever may be its imperfections, equals in munificence and kindliness the hospitality of the squire's mansion. Its revenues may yield no contribution to a county hunt; but it maintains, at its own cost, a chapel, in which the services of religion are performed with care for their solemnity and effectiveness. And, though its income may add less to the brilliance and gaiety of fashion than the purse of a hospitable country gentleman, its wealth very frequently finds its way, through the operations of natural bountifulness, to humble cottages, where the necessitous kindred of college-fellows are supporting laborious lives on insufficient means.

The grateful admiration, which we entertain for the colleges of either university, is cherished in a still higher degree of fervour by all thoughtful men for the parent-association that gave birth to the separate corporations which she holds in her embrace, even as a benignant mother surrounds her offspring with fair arms, and draws them to the breast from which they have drained the milk of life. But all the services which the universities render to society in return for the riches with which it has endowed them are expressed by a cordial acknowledgment, that they contribute largely to the intellectual and religious life of the nation. To say more of their present achievements would be to offer our benefactors the insult of flattery. Valuable though they are, it cannot be urged that their overthrow would altogether stay our social progress, or change the course of our history. If, by some magical process, the academic buildings of Oxford and Cambridge, together with all the literary and artistic treasure which they contain, should be dissipated and utterly removed from us in a single night, England would have reason to mourn the loss of much that is at the same time most dear and useful to her; but, notwithstanding a regret that would only grow more poignant with the growth of time, the nation would pursue its onward way with scarce a transient interruption to any of its manifold activities. Not one science would be lost or retarded by the catastrophe; religious truths would not be less busily disseminated in consequence of the disaster; the culture of the young might for a while suffer from the loss of ancient stimulus to study, but no element of the national culture would be taken clean away. Literature, music, the fine arts, would be affected indirectly, but no book the less would issue from the presses of our London publishers; the directors of our musical taste would lose nothing of their influence; our painters and sculptors would be as busy as before; that the industrial arts would be paralysed by the incident no one can venture to suggest; the factories and the markets would be no less active because the ancient homes of scholarship had vanished; society would be shocked, but not disabled; and, in so far as she came to the conclusion that Oxford and Cambridge were needful to her, she would reproduce them in the third of a generation.

But the case was different with the old monasteries, whose sudden ruin, at the period of their greatest usefulness, would have been attended with utter destruction to letters and art; with confusion in politics; with stagnation in every department of industrial enterprise; and with social retrogression almost to the confines of barbarism.

For the religious houses discharged so many various and vital functions in the social system, of which monasticism may be regarded rather as the creator than the product, that they may be said to have contained at one time all the humanising forces of our national existence. In addition to their discharge of all the duties devolving upon owners of property, they were the instigators and directors of social progress, and the fountains of knowledge in every department of enterprise. At moments of supreme danger the abbot thought it no sin to don the soldier's mail, and lead his armed followers* to patriotic death. In times of ordinary tranquillity—that is to say, in the brief intervals betwixt sanguinary struggles—he gave his tenants and all residents within his government a degree of security seldom attain-

---

* Though it is but one of almost countless familiar facts, that illustrate the military fervour of the medieval clergy, a proclamation to arms of Edward the Third may be noticed, as affording testimony that the clerical proprietors of the feudal period could be relied upon to discharge gallantly one of the most important of the responsibilities attached to the possession of real estates—the defence of the land against foreign invaders. 'And besides this,' runs the record of this proclamation of a monarch in whose service Chaucer bore arms, 'the king commands and requires all prelates there assembled, that in respect of the great danger and damage which perhaps might happen to the realm and church of England, by reason of this war, in case his adversary should enter the kingdom to destroy and subvert the same, that they will put to their aid in defence of the kingdom, and cause their subjects to be arrayed, as well themselves and their religious men, as parsons, vicars, and other men of holy church whatsoever, to abate the malice of his enemies in case they should enter the kingdom; which prelates granted to this in the aid and defence of the realm and holy church. And so the parliament ended.'—*Rot. in Tur. Londin.* 37 *Ed. III.*

able on the lands of petty potentates, whose only means of defence and offence were earthly weapons. And, whilst the religious houses of his jurisdiction enjoyed exceptional immunity from the worst perils of a turbulent epoch, they were schools to the young, asylums for the weak and aged, taverns for the reception of wayfarers, fountains of charity to the indigent, factories where cunning artificers plied their hands with prolific skill, and centres of commercial activity, whither traders of every grade congregated for the transaction of business.

Whilst the labours of the monastic scriptorium multiplied copies of patristic divinity, the pious transcribers also preserved, by their patient and accurate pens, the remnants of a classic literature, which, but for the industry of their order, would have utterly perished. To the minster there was usually attached a school, in which the cleverer boys of the neighbourhood acquired the rudiments of learning under able instructors. From the earliest date of their existence the nunneries were academies for girls; and so faithfully did the religious women acquit themselves as preceptresses, even to the last, that the sudden dissolution of the 'shee-schools' was lamented by those who witnessed and approved of the suppression of the monastic houses. Agriculture was an industry which the monks may be said to have raised to the dignity of an art. As tillers of the soil and breeders of cattle they excelled so conspicuously, that ordinary farmers—then, as in later times, remarkable for their slowness of intelligence and averseness to change—became their imitators. It was in the workshops of religious houses that workers in precious metals made the gold thread for the gorgeous dresses of the priests, and produced the chalices that shone upon the altars of cathedrals. From the same retreats of labour came the brilliant glass,* at the splendour of whose hues we still gaze with delight; the specimens of illumination that charm the taste of the collector of missals; and those exquisite products of the chisel, which, after beautifying our churches for

---

* For the introduction of glass into this country we are indebted to the religious life of the Saxon period; Bede's patron and teacher, Benedict, surnamed Biscop, abbot of Wearmouth, having been the first person to use that material in England, *circ.* A.D. 670.

centuries, rouse the admiration of connoisseurs. Whatever medical knowledge existed in medieval England was lore that passed from monkish herbalists to the girls who gained their education in the nunneries. It was the same with surgery. If, in a moment of exceptional difficulty, the midwife, instead of having recourse to the repetition of superstitious charms or diabolical incantations, performed a timely act, that saved a mother's life and an infant's new existence, she acted upon anatomical instructions imparted to her directly or indirectly by a monkish teacher. From the same source also came the skill, valuable though imperfect, of the bone-setters, whose services were in daily requisition when an appeal to physical force was the favourite diversion of the idle, and the ordinary method of settling differences of opinion.

Nor are we at a loss to account for the successes of monasticism, when we reflect that the constitution of every religious house combined the principles of republican organisation with the principles of theocratic despotism. Within the sphere of his authority the abbot was supreme priest and absolute ruler, whose decisions had the force of divine as well as human authority over those who lived under his sway. No monarch was invested with more arbitrary power than the occupant of an abbot's throne; but the man thus raised to supreme authority derived his elevation from the free votes of companions, with whom he had passed the early years of life on terms of perfect equality and the closest familiar intimacy, and who were induced to give him their suffrages by an anxious desire to promote the welfare of their house, their order, and the whole Christian Church. That a system thus designed became greatly successful is less wonderful than that, after centuries of vigorous action, it should have degenerated to the condition of its later years, when, hopelessly vitiated by the enervating and poisonous influences of earthly power, it had exchanged asceticism for sensual license, industry for sloth, knowledge for ignorance, and retained no kind of energy that it was not prepared to employ for the humiliation of our country, and the degradation of its inhabitants. But to those who appreciate the excellence of its original design, and the grandeur of its earlier story, the spectacle of its downfall conveys a lesson no less valuable to persons of action than to students, by showing the perilous unsoundness of all institutions which endow individuals with enormous wealth and power on conditions that leave them unaccountable for their conduct to the social opinion of their contemporaries.

CHAPTER III.

GOTHIC ARCHITECTURE.

THE commencement of the generations, to which the first part of these sketches of the social story of English clergy directs the reader's attention, was a period in which the monastic system, after accomplishing the most beneficial and truly honourable part of its career in this country, had entered upon the fulness of its dazzling splendour and dangerous power. It was also a period in which the inmates of the monasteries afforded considerable justification for some of those charges of luxury and neglect of duty that were loudly preferred against them by their enemies, and were sustained by the less noisy expostulations of their wisest and best friends. The same also may be said of the entire Church, which, after rendering priceless services to mankind during the darkest centuries of our national existence, was teeming with corruptions that roused sentiments of antagonism to the clerical order in the breasts of patriotic laymen, whilst they drove many of the more zealous and devout of the clergy themselves to the painful conclusion that no measures, short of fundamental and even revolutionary change, could restore the ecclesiastical establishments to their original virtue, and make them once again universally conducive to the ends for which they had been created.

But whilst the deep-seated diseases of the Church were visible to the few observers whose exceptional sagacity enabled them to interpret the outward symptoms of insidious political disorder, there had never been a time when, to the eyes of ordinary men of conservative temper, the ecclesiastical system had seemed so uniformly triumphant and efficient, so sound at heart and vigorous in all its members. To persons of this common type—the self-complacent mortals who never look beneath the surface of public affairs, and misread all the superficial phenomena of politics in the manner that is most agreeable to their prejudices and private interests—the current whisperings and murmurs against the rapacity and dissoluteness of the clerical order were nothing more than the utterances of a few turbulent spirits, men for the most part of little name and no wealth, whose treasonable and blasphemous discontent with the existing state of things, springing from envy of the rich rather than from any desire for the public good, it would be well to check with a timely and unsparing use of the hangman's cord. And no inquirer into the social life of England in the earlier part of the fourteenth century, can deny that it abounded with facts which gave considerable countenance to the lethargic and contented minds that took this view of the Lollardy, whose earlier rumblings, ominous of the coming storm, had made themselves audible before Chaucer's birth, and whose course derived from the poet's pen a stimulus that contributed largely to the influence of Wycliffe's doctrines.

The thirteenth and fourteenth were the centuries which witnessed the erection of the most perfect specimens of that Gothic architecture which covered the land with sacred edifices, that are scarcely more admirable for the grandeur and harmony of their designs, than for the exquisite beauty and richness of the labour expended with lavish profuseness on the details of their structure. The hundred and forty years that intervened between the consecration of Boniface of Savoy to the archbishopric of Canterbury and the murder of Simon Sudbury, were years which, notwithstanding a succession of occurrences unfavourable to the interests and enterprises of art, saw no cessation in the labours to which we are indebted for the cathedrals, the churches, the colleges, the cloisters, that rebuke the clamour and feverish restlessness of our time by their solemn stillness and majestic loveliness, and will long remain sublime memorials of ages when all the artistic instincts and faculties of our ancestors were concentrated upon one worthy field of effort. Wheresoever we draw the finger over a map of England, it runs athwart spots associated with the architectural triumphs of the period in which our cathedral towns were seldom without the music of the sculptor's hammer and chisel: and not a few of them—such as London, Westminster, Wells, Lichfield, Ely, Gloucester, Worcester, Salisbury, Canterbury, Winchester, Oxford—witnessed in the achievement of new, or the restoration and extension of old buildings, the creation of those artistic beauties for which they are chiefly famous at the present time. Nor was this activity confined to the sites of our remaining cathedrals, and the most memorable of the religious houses which Henry the Eighth's despotic grasp deprived of injurious existence. The monastic dwellings that arose in this period could be counted by hundreds ;* and whilst some of them were grand structures, whose erection and adornment required the labour of many hands for a series of years, the least important of them comprised works that rendered their accomplishment a matter of keen daily interest to numerous persons besides the workmen employed upon them, and the proprietors at whose charges they were chiefly built.

Of the universality of the interest taken by the entire population in the general progress of these works, and yet further of the exact information which persons residing in one locality possessed concerning architectural operations carried forward in another and remote part of the kingdom, no reader can form an adequate conception who labours under the common but very erroneous impression that there was very little intercommunication between distant quarters of medieval England, and that the habit of locomotion was unusual amongst the subjects of the Norman and Plantagenet monarchs. To understand the social life of our ancestors throughout the strictly feudal period of our history, the student must thoroughly disabuse himself of this false and very misleading notion, and must never omit to

* In Catholic England, whilst Westmoreland had fewer monasteries than any other shire, Gloucestershire was the county most highly favoured, or, as Fuller expressed it, 'most pestered' by monks. 'Of all counties,' says the author of 'The Church History of Britain,' 'in England, Gloucestershire was most pestered with monks, having four mitred abbeys, besides St. Augustine's in Bristol (who sometimes passed for a baron), within the compass thereof: viz. Gloucester, Tewkesbury, Cirencester, and Wivelscombe. Hence the topical wicked proverb, deserving to be banished out of that county, being the profane child of superstitious parents, "As sure as God is in Gloucestershire ;" as if so many convents had certainly fastened His gracious presence to that place. As Gloucestershire was the fullest of, so Westmoreland was the freest from monasteries.'

remember that journeyings were more frequent amongst our forefathers of every social rank, before the Reformation, than in the times that intervened between the suppression of the religious houses and the middle of the eighteenth century.

One of the most noteworthy features of Old England was the wide dispersion of the estates in the possession of a single large proprietor. A great baron often held lands in a southern an eastern and a midland shire; or, whilst he had a castle and manors in a northern county, he would have separate properties in western and south-western regions of the kingdom. Roger Bigod's lands lay in Norfolk, Suffolk, Essex, Sussex, Berkshire, Gloucestershire, and in Ireland. The domains of Isabella de Fortibus were scattered over an extent of country that had the Isle of Wight for its southern extremity and a part of Yorkshire for its northern boundary. It was the same with the landed corporations. The property of a brotherhood often lay in a dozen or more different counties. For instance (as Mr. Thorold Rogers informs us, in his 'History of Agriculture and Prices'), Merton College owned, in the fourteenth century, estates scattered over 'Oxfordshire, Kent, Surrey, Bucks, Warwick, Wilts, Leicester, Cambridge, Hunts, Hants, Durham, and Northumberland;' to which the Wardens and Fellows of the association paid periodical visits, in accordance with the intentions of their founder, and the ordinary custom of the large landowners of the time, who were continually making progresses from shire to shire, to receive the rents of their numerous tenants and inspect their widely-separated manors. So long as the ecclesiastical and lay proprietors thus exercised personal supervision over their various distant properties, it was naturally a part of their policy to see that roads were kept in efficient repair; and whilst the legislature compelled the owners of real estate to maintain good roads throughout the country, the continual streams of wayfarers upon the highways called into existence a supply of hostelries sufficient for their entertainment, and insured to the unattended traveller a measure of personal security, the absence of which, in times subsequent to the Reformation, was one of the reasons why the custom of making journeys for mere pleasure was so very generally relinquished in the seventeenth century.

Part I.—Wycliffe's England. 31

Englishmen under the Plantagenets enjoyed great facilities for travel. There is also abundant evidence, that whilst they habitually availed themselves of those facilities for the transaction of worldly business or pleasure, or in the performance of religious exercises, they derived from their continual journeyings an extensive and uniform knowledge of all matters that were going forward simultaneously in the different parts of the country. The unanimity with which the humble people of remote provinces acted for the assertion of their political rights, would alone testify to the constancy of intercommunication between the inhabitants of the various shires; and though it is matter of certainty that the political correspondence of the disconnected populations of the kingdom was greatly promoted by the itinerant priests—a class of our countrymen who were incessantly on the march—it is no less certain on the one hand that the inferior laity, whom the mendicant orders inspired with the principles of medieval communism, did not wholly depend on the wandering friars for intercourse with men of distant counties; and on the other hand, that the action of those pious newsmongers and political agitators would have been far less fruitful of practical results, had not the usages of medieval life trained the ordinary Englishman to take a warm interest in transactions that occurred at places remote from his own threshold.

When I seek for the causes of the taste for travel which distinguished the men of Wycliffe's England from their countrymen of the seventeenth century, I am inclined to refer the prevalent fashion to the influence of the Church, which—partly through an enlightened design to stimulate the mental faculties of the inferior people by extending their knowledge of the world, and bringing them into close contact with each other; and partly through conservative adherence to practices that had their origin in the religious needs of a period when Christianity was in the hands of isolated families of believers, enjoying no adequate means of intercommunication—was the direct instigator and director of those periodic journeyings to sacred shrines, which contributed so largely to what may be called the locomotive habits of our medieval forefathers. Alike in Anglo-Saxon and Norman times, the powerful laity, when not acting under clerical influence, exerted themselves to bind the lowest classes of the people to the soil—to chain them to the huts of which they were the precarious occupants. Regarding his lowest serfs as mere cattle, the baron of the twelfth century liked to retain them, in their moments of relaxation, close to the fields on which they were required to labour; and whilst esteeming them as mere stock appurtenant to his soil, he was averse to every social arrangement that encouraged them to stray from their stalls and take liberties not allowed to other domesticated beasts. The influence of the Church was all in a contrary direction. To enter minutely at this point into the history and effects of the religious pilgrimages would be inopportune; but we may briefly notice how much they effected for the consolidation of the fragmentary system of the Heptarchy and the later Saxon period; how serviceable they were in amalgamating the Norman and Saxon peoples, and in diffusing sentiments of amity and familiar fellowship throughout the various, and too often hostile, communities of which feudal England was, even in its most harmonious periods, an imperfectly organised aggregation; and how greatly they encouraged that disposition for domestic and foreign travel—a disposition which not seldom became a deep and universal passion—which is one of the chief points of difference between the English of the Plantagenet and the English of the Stuart period.

The Crusades were nothing but vast pilgrimages; and it is not difficult to conceive how, on their return to the castles and towns, the villages and homesteads of their birth, the survivors of those expeditions must, by their glowing pictures of foreign scenery and distant cities, no less than by their narratives of martial dangers and exploits, have roused in the breasts of their listeners a burning thirst to see what the narrators had seen, even at the risk of death, and the certainty of suffering all that the marvellous speakers had endured. Nor let us forget that —whilst the stories of the Crusades were still the ordinary material of fireside tales told to eager children, even as anecdotes of the great fight at Waterloo still quicken the pulses of our schoolboys; and still later, when the episodes of the latest of those military excursions had died out of the memories of unlettered men, even as Ramillies and Malplaquet have become

Part I.—Wycliffe's England.

mere names to the grandchildren of those to whom they were romances—almost every English home had an inmate who, from having been either an unit in a vast company of pilgrims, or a servant in the train of a rich devotee, or a youthful adventurer with fellow-students for comrades, or a soldier in foreign wars, could tell of the wonders and beauties of distant capitals. These travelled persons of the middle ages, I doubt not, bore a larger proportion to their untravelled contemporaries than the English tourists, in these days of railways, and steam-boats, and circular tickets, bear to those of their fellow-countrymen who have never crossed the English Channel. And whilst their number was far greater than unreflecting persons are likely to imagine, their experiences were various. One could speak from personal knowledge of the beauties of fair France, whose rightful monarch, as all loyal men would swear, was his highness the King of England. Another could tell exactly of the commercial growth and marvellous industries of the Flemish cities; the delicate tower of Antwerp Cathedral, and the magnificent architecture of that splendid, glittering, overpowering Bruges, the desolateness of whose silent thoroughfares and neglected squares fills the modern tourist with a profound sadness, that is only varied by the mingled anguish and disgust with which he regards the loathsome mendicants whom he comforts with unavailing alms. And not seldom a group of neighbours would assemble round a medieval burgher's table, and drink a 'welcome home' to the burgher's daughter, who could tell them about the Holy City of Christendom, from which she had recently returned; and about the lovely towns of the Rhine in which she had tarried on her homeward route, with sisters of the nunnery in which she had received her education.* But however diverse

---

* The excellence of the schools for girls, or 'Shee-schooles,' down to the suppression of the conventual system, was so universally recognised, that even zealous Protestants of the seventeenth century regarded the extinction of them as one of the few evils attendant on the blessed Reformation. 'Nunneries,' remarks Fuller, in 'The Church History of Britain,' 'also were good Shee-schooles, wherein the girles and maids of the neighbourhood were taught to read and work; and sometimes a little Latine was taught therein. Yea, give me leave to say, if such feminine foundations had still continued, provided no vow were obtruded upon them (virginity is least kept where most constrained), haply the weaker sex (besides the avoiding modern inconveniences) might be heightened

the narratives might be, they all had the same result in fostering the sentiment that, whereas it was on the one hand agreeable and laudable for people to stir about and make acquaintance with life away from their own homes, there was on the other hand something contemptible in the torpor and dulness of men and women who were content to live and die in their native parishes.

By bearing these facts in mind, the reader is able to appreciate the concern and pride taken in the architectural activity of the thirteenth and fourteenth centuries by the 'general public,' as we should now term it, of the period, who responded to the judicious appeals of preachers by contributing liberally to the funds for defraying the cost of unusually magnificent edifices. To cover the expense of building Salisbury Cathedral, the prebendaries (as Dr. Hook tells us, in his admirable ' Lives of the Archbishops') having first given largely to the work from their private means, went through the shires of the entire kingdom, soliciting the co-operation of devout persons ; and such success attended this recourse to what we nowadays call the 'voluntary principle,' that the prebendaries returned from their mendicant circuits laden with money and promises of expensive materials necessary for the accomplishment of their devout purpose.*

---

to a higher perfection than hath hitherto been attained. That sharpnesse of their wits and suddenness of their conceits (which their enemies must allow unto them) might, by education, be improved into a judicious solidity, and that adorned with arts, which now they want, not because they cannot learn, but are not taught them. I say, if such feminine foundations were extant now of dayes, haply some virgins of highest birth would be glad of such places; and I am sure their fathers and elder brothers would not be sorry for the same.'

* In the 'Canterbury Tales' the Sompnoure opens his story with a satirical allusion to the manner in which the friars acted the part of mendicants for architectural purposes :—

> ' Lordlings, that is in Yorkshire, as I guess,
> A mersh contree ycalled Holdernesse,
> In which ther went a limitour aboute,
> To preche, and eke to beg, it is no doute.
> And so befell that on a day this frere
> Had preched at a chirche in his manere,
> And specially aboven everything
> Excited he the people in his preching
> To trentals, and to geve for Goddes sake,
> Wherewith men mighten holy houses make.'

Part I.—Wycliffe's England.

The same facts also, as I conceive, throw some light on the secret of that uniformity of speed with which Gothic architecture made its progress to perfection.

The neglect of the monkish chroniclers to communicate the exact circumstances to which we are indebted for our noble cathedrals, and their omission to name any persons who were conspicuous originators or teachers of Gothic architecture, have left a wide field for conjecture to those who would account for the rise and development of an art so prolific of sublime and lovely achievements. And availing itself of so favourable a ground for the exercise of its powers, the human imagination has ventured to assign the creation of our first ecclesiastical buildings to a numerous fraternity of masons, who are supposed to have drawn from the sages of a remote epoch, with whom they held mystic communion, the secrets of a science whose application to the material world resulted in the construction of our cathedrals. It is assumed that this singular brotherhood guarded with extreme jealousy the knowledge committed to it by occult agency; and that, when the power had achieved the ends for which it was entrusted to the masonic confederates, it was withdrawn from the members of the artistic corporation as mysteriously as it had been confided to them. So long as Gothic art flourished, no mason, not an initiate of the mystic society, could discover its recondite rules, or even comprehend its general principles; and when it vanished from the roll of living arts, no survivor or successor of the initiated masons, whose hands raised the temples in which we worship, could reveal its occult processes, which had become no less inscrutable to the freemasons themselves than they had ever been to the outer world. It is not wonderful that this tissue of fancies should find supporters amongst those who claim to be the corporate descendants of those magically illuminated artificers in stone; but it is matter for surprise that a theory, sustained by no facts that will endure for a moment the tests of historic criticism, should appear credible to writers not in league with the freemasons of our own time.

A few minutes' deliberation must satisfy any unbiassed inquirer that this mythical theory is one of the most fantastic crotchets ever hatched and cherished in the brain of man.

Experience teaches us how rarely a secret is preserved that is confided to half-a-dozen persons, even in those cases where the secret is of such a kind, that its revelation would cover all the participators in it with obloquy. And yet, in the face of this experience, the upholders of this marvellous conceit require us to believe that a special knowledge was successfully guarded from the intense curiosity of the outer world by a community which must have comprised many thousands of individuals, every one of whom would have gained largely in personal renown and individual influence by a prudent betrayal of the corporation's secrets.

That the processes of mechanical operations may sometimes be kept secret, will be denied by no one who remembers the several, though upon the whole infrequent, instances in which an inventor has contrived for a series of years to use his invention for the public convenience, and yet baffle the persevering attempts of his rivals to ascertain the peculiarities of his method. The inventor of the Ayrshire snuff-box was able for a considerable period to confine to himself and a few singularly faithful coadjutors the knowledge of the shape and nature of the tool by which he fashioned his novel hinge. Workers in glass and porcelain have at various times been lamentably successful in keeping from the world the secrets of their special industry. Chemical operators also have in recent times contrived to withhold their discoveries from general observation. But all the inventions which have been utilized secretly, for any considerable period, are of a kind that made it possible for a limited number of persons to carry out the new processes in strict seclusion. It is, however, seldom that an inventor's operations can be kept from the knowledge of those who are interested in ascertaining, and capable of imitating them. Even where the inventor's industry may be exercised in secret, its products tell the story of their workmanship. Were it not comparatively easy for clever workmen to imitate the productions of original mechanicians, there would be small need for stringent patent laws to secure to inventors the fruits of their ingenuity. It is in the nature of nearly all purely mechanical devices that to reproduce them is a comparatively easy task. When Mr. Hedley of Wylam had put his smooth-wheeled locomotive on the smooth rails of the Wylam tramway, it was no very arduous work that George Stephenson achieved when he produced those imitations of the Wylam steam-carriage that made him for a time regarded as the inventor of the locomotive. And of all mechanical arts, there is none less adapted to secresy than architecture.

The artificers of the first perfect specimens of Gothic art published their designs, by giving them permanent expression in a building open to the observation of every passer; and the means by which those designs were carried out were mechanical appliances, used openly in the broad daylight, before the eyes of hundreds of intelligent spectators. How was it possible to maintain secrecy for an art whose most important processes, no less than its most trivial operations, were thus performed in public?

Again, though it becomes none the less glorious or manifest, the excellence of medieval architecture appears somewhat less marvellous, when we reflect that it was the one really high art exercised during the period of its greatest vigour, and that the social conditions of the epoch brought to its sole service all those intellectual forces which, in modern times, are divided amongst the sister arts,—painting, sculpture, literature, and natural investigation. The painter's art can scarcely be said to have existed when Gothic architecture reached perfection. Salisbury Cathedral was begun before Cimabue's birth, and when the last stone was put upon its highest point the Florentine painter was still only a youth of eighteen years. Geoffrey Chaucer was a man in middle life, whilst Hubert Van Eyck and John of Bruges were still learning their primers; and when he expired, one hundred and seventy-seven years had to elapse before the birth of Rubens. It was much the same with modern sculpture, which, notwithstanding the interest that attaches to the separate pieces of older medieval carving, cannot be said to have flourished until the poet's ashes had rested a full century in Westminster Abbey. Till Michael Angelo's catholic genius raised it once more to its proper position amongst the fine arts, sculpture, rated at its highest, was merely an artistic industry subservient to the builder's aims. Hence, in the thirteenth and fourteenth centuries, architecture was the only art that offered an adequate field for the display, and liberally rewarded the exertions, of artistic faculty.

Yet more: apart from the conduct of public affairs, Gothic architecture was almost the only pursuit that furnished a congenial sphere of activity to men of the highest intellect and most refined taste. And to apprehend the full significance of this fact, the reader must remember that these centuries—whose imparted darkness is more applicable to the gloom that hides them from our sight than to the real life of the period—were literally surcharged with mental activity. Dark no doubt the epoch was in respect to the sciences, whose lights we rightly prize above all material possessions; but if 'dark' is used to imply mental torpidity and total absence of intellectual aspirations, no term more completely misrepresents a time whose scholars were eager and subtle, though unprofitable disputants, and the frivolities of whose crowded academies are a mournful spectacle to the historian of to-day, because they were characterised by ability, vehemence, and sincerity, that, rightly directed, might have been fruitful of vast and valuable results. And in these generations, so superfluously endowed with mental activity, there was such an absence of accumulated literature, of scientific resources, and of the means which the more vigorous minds of our time employ alternately for their diversion and profit, that a clever man—in need of a field of intellectual exercise, during some period of enforced retirement from public business—was compelled to choose between the barren disputations of the schools and activity in an art, whose allurements are so powerful to our race, that an Englishman is seldom seen to acquire wealth who is not also seen to expend some portion of it on the gratification of architectural fancies.

Hence it was in accordance with the nature of things that such men as Langham, and Sudbury, and Wykeham, occupied their leisure and abundant means in prosecuting the study, and encouraging the practice of architecture. And whilst the chiefs of the Church found, in devotion to the art of building, all the fine excitement and elevating diversion—which wealthy and refined persons of the present time vainly seek in a superficial dilettanteism over each department of the extended field of the fine arts, and in transient flirtations with letters and science—

the clergy of all degrees, from the inmates of superb monasteries to secular priests, toiling in humble poverty on ill-paid cures, made architecture an affair of daily consideration and study. To build in the Gothic style was the fashion of the time in every civilised part of the land,—in cities and modest towns; on sites where the chief mover of the work was an affluent abbot or far-ruling bishop, and on ground where the cost of building was defrayed chiefly by a municipal council, or a devout layman owning a manorial lordship. From the abundant intercourse maintained between the various parts of the kingdom, knowledge was everywhere obtained of the architectural doings in every quarter of the land, and wherever those doings presented a novelty worthy of imitation,—in the proportions of a window, or the spring and span of an arch, or a detail of adornment,—the new thing was adopted by the critical taste of scores of monastic designers and clerical committees, and was speedily reproduced in counties far distant from the spot where it first appeared. Hence Gothic architecture was the outgrowth of all society, instead of a single man or a single school. No one father, no score of fathers, could be assigned to a thing which was born of the entire nation; which was the product of the quick intellects of the epoch concentrated upon a single field of artistic enterprise.

Founded after the middle of the thirteenth century, Merton College was built, as we should nowadays describe such an achievement, without an architect. Designed by the fellows in council, it was reared by workmen who carried out their instructions. Mr. Thorold Rogers, in his 'History of Agriculture and Prices,' says, 'The fellows of Merton College were its architects. It may be that head-workmen were competent to carry out all the details, and very often to plan the work they had to do.' Some hundred and seventy years later, when the fellows built a bell-tower to their chapel, they employed a small number of masons, who received their weekly wages from the college-bursar, and worked slowly but soundly under the superintendance of Thomas Edwards. Mr. Rogers is of opinion that this master of the works was 'probably one of the fellows;' and whilst the facts of the case are decidedly in favour of this conjecture, there is no evidence whatever that the overseer was an architect in the modern and most restricted sense of the word.

Whilst the universality and magnitude of these ecclesiastical operations in architecture, during the thirteenth and fourteenth centuries, must have strongly impressed ordinary minds with a sense of the Church's stability, and have caused many persons to entertain exaggerated notions of its command of material resources, I have no doubt that this particular use of its wealth and influence conciliated persons in all classes, and rendered the commonalty less quick to discern the corruptions and resist the encroachments of the sacerdotal order, than they would have been had the power of the clergy been employed in a manner less beneficial to the classes in which Lollardy originated. When the reader reflects how much of injustice is patiently endured from every bad government by those who, upon the whole, gain by its existence, and still more patiently borne by those who are specially benefited by the healthier portions of its policy; when he reflects how prone every selfish man is to think well of the persons and institutions who contribute to his material prosperity; when, also, he thinks how ready the inhabitants of a small country town are to overlook the shortcomings and magnify the virtues of the rector, who, in any unusual degree, promotes the buoyancy of local trade, he will not think me fantastic in taking this view of immediate effects of the architectural enterprise of the medieval clergy. Bearing in mind how the religious sentiments of Lollardy were inextricably mingled with the political theories of medieval communism; how the Lollards combined a strong aversion for certain doctrines and usages of the Church, with a still stronger desire to dispossess the clergy of their superfluous wealth; and how it does not appear that any important section of our ancestors avowed the religious side of the Lollards' composite creed before they could cordially embrace the political side also, I cannot question that the architectural activity, to which we are indebted for the best of our Gothic cathedrals, effected in the Church's behalf what the French Emperor's architectural doings have in these later years effected for the contentment of the most revolutionary of his subjects, and for the stability of his throne. Anyhow, it must have produced a state of feeling unfavourable to the designs of the earlier Lollards, whether we regard their sincere and pious wish for religious reform, or whether we look at their less prudent and justifiable schemes for political change.

That any motives of mere worldly policy were the chief causes of the erection of our cathedrals, I would not venture to insinuate. But the storm of Lollardy was heralded by many premonitory signs, that must have occasioned deep anxiety to all thoughtful and influential persons responsible for the wellbeing of the commonwealth. And when I have endeavoured to realise the concern with which the more sagacious ecclesiastics must have watched the growth amongst the humble people of opinions antagonistic to their order, I am disposed—whilst attributing the development of Gothic architecture to religious enthusiasm and delight in art—to believe that the wiser of those energetic Churchmen, who were the chief controllers of medieval society, saw with satisfaction that the architectural labours, which redounded to the glory of the Church, tended also to promote material prosperity and contentment with existing institutions in the numerous population of artificers, that had been called into existence by the enormous demand for their particular industries.

CHAPTER IV.

CLERICAL PREPONDERANCE.

TO make a fair estimate of the clerical preponderance in this period of our history the student should endeavour to realise the proportion borne by the numbers of the entire ecclesiastical order to the rest of the population. The best authority[*] on the statistics of medieval society in this country is of opinion, that the whole population of England and Wales in the fourteenth century cannot have exceeded two and a half millions; and of this number he computes that the monks, nuns, and secular priests, amounted to between thirty and forty thousand. If we take the smaller of these numbers, and add to it the clerical men in orders lower than the priestly degree, who, in respect of those inferior orders, were ranked with the clerks, we cannot be guilty of exaggeration in calculating that the ecclesiastical persons were at least forty thousand; that is to say, that for every 62·5 of laity the nation possessed one ecclesiastical person.

This strong army of ecclesiastics comprised bishops, having control over the parochial clergy of their dioceses, and through their courts exercising a stringent authority, usually beneficial but often extremely vexatious, over the domestic life and personal property of the laity; abbots, who, within the jurisdictions of their abbeys, were invested with all the temporal powers accorded to bishops, though, unless they were of the episcopal order, they were precluded from performing the peculiarly episcopal offices of ordination, consecration, and confirmation; bishops *in partibus*—a class of episcopal personages, who, having received ordination in foreign parts, found employment

---

[*] Mr. Thorold Rogers.

in acting for bishops absent from their dioceses, and in discharging the functions of episcopacy within the jurisdictions of the monastic societies, who were amenable only to the chiefs of their orders, and, through them, to the Pope; the inferior monks, or 'regular clergy,' who, as monks, were not under the discipline of the national bishops; the mendicant friars,* whose influence, when full allowance has been made for the blinding animosity of their chief accusers, must have been most prejudicial to ecclesiastical discipline and social order; the various kinds of beneficed parochial clergy, such as rectors, vicars, and all other persons, who are now styled in common parlance 'incumbents,' and who in old time were generally known as 'curates,' from their having cures of souls; and the numerous body of unbeneficed secular clergy, who officiated as the assistants of resident, or as the deputies of non-resident incumbents, or who gained a mean subsistence by the performance in the parish churches of daily masses said for the behoof of particular individuals. Nor, in this enumeration of the more important species of the ecclesiastical order, must sight be lost of those colleges of canons or secular priests who were attached to the diocesan cathedrals, and who—as members of collegiate establishments, designed and governed very much after the fashion of monasteries—bore considerable resemblance to the regular clergy, from whom, however, they differed in two most important respects—their freedom from the *regulæ* of every monastic order, and their subjection to episcopal discipline. We must remember also the religious inmates of the nunneries.

But no adequate conception of the influence and activity of ecclesiastics of this period can be formed by the reader who thinks of them as employed only in the discharge of sacred functions and business directly appertaining to the clerical vocation. In every kind of labour, not actually servile, their hands were

* It is needless to say that the Mendicant Orders, in virtue of their obligations to special orders of peculiar stringency, were, in the exactest sense of the term, 'Regular Clergy.' But they differed so widely in character, aim, tone, and mode of action, from the older and more truly national organizations of monastic clergy, that it is desirable to speak of them by terms not common to the Mendicants and the Monks. To avoid confusion, the reader must never forget the many points of dissimilarity between the three species of clerical genus—the Monks, the Mendicants, and the Seculars.

engaged. If the king despatched an embassy to a foreign court, he chose its principal members from the clergy, from whom also he selected his confidential advisers on affairs of state. The visitor at the monarch's court found most of its highest offices, and a great majority of its inferior posts, filled by priests. The most powerful of the abbots and the most ambitious of the bishops were the dominant influence in the parliaments; monks and seculars thronged the antechambers and halls of the royal palace. The chancellor was always a supreme churchman, usually an archbishop. In the courts of common law priests occupied the judicial seats, and priests had the leading practices at the bar. When barons or inferior laymen sought special privileges from the Crown, they usually preferred their entreaties through the lips of a sacerdotal courtier; and when, in acknowledgment of favours received, or in politic gratitude for favours hoped for, they made customary offerings to the king's treasury, it was into an ecclesiastic's hands that they paid the timely fees. The business of the ecclesiastical courts—business steadily growing with the encroachments of the Church—was all in the hands of ordained practitioners. It was the same in every baron's court and household.* And, not content with engrossing all the most lucrative official business of the kingdom, they bestirred themselves in avocations still more incompatible with modern notions of clerical decorum. If required to do service in camps they donned mail, and distinguished themselves by military prowess. At all times they were seen to thrive as farmers, land-stewards, merchants, pedlars. The best markets in the country were the fairs held in abbey-towns; and, whilst the business and diversions of these gatherings were carried on in the immediate precincts, and even within the very walls of the minsters, monks distinguished themselves amongst the throng of dealers as the keenest, boldest, and most successful traffickers. Nor were the canons less sedulous than the regular clergy in the prosecution of purely

---

* Wycliffe, in 'The Office of Curates,' says of a certain section of the parochial clergy of his time, 'The tenth default is, that they haunt lords' courts, and are occupied in worldly offices, and do not take care of their parishes; although they take more worldly goods with them than Christ and His apostles.'

secular business;* and it was observed by envious spectators that whilst the ordained men throve as lawyers and tradesmen, they knew how to invest their accumulations to the best of lawful profit in land and houses.

It is usual with Englishmen of the present time to regard this omnipresence of the clerical order in every department of society as the result of ecclesiastical encroachment upon, and usurpation of, the proper privileges and functions of the laity. Looking upon medieval life with vision coloured by the sentiments, and perhaps the prejudices of the nineteenth century, our historians, scarcely less than their ordinary readers, are too apt to attribute altogether to the ambition and greed of the clergy a state of things that was, at least, partly due to the aspiring spirit and worldly designs of laymen. So far as the position was the result of intrusiveness, a minute's reflection will satisfy most inquirers, that, instead of being confined to one class, the intrusiveness was not less general amongst the laity than amongst the ecclesiastics. If the latter were willing to usurp the influence of the laity for the aggrandizement of themselves or their order, the former were no less eager to assume the

* Concerning the worldly avocations and greed of the secular clergy, the author of 'The Complaint of the Ploughman' sings:—

'Other they beene proude, or covetous;
  Or they been hard, or hungrie;
Or they been liberall, or lecherous;
  Or else medlers with marchandry;
Or mainteiners of men with mastry;
Or stewards, contours pleadours,
  And serve God in ypocrisie.

Soche priestes been Christes false traitours.
     *   *   *
Therewith they purchase have lay fee
  In londes there hem liketh best;
And builde also as brod as a cité,
Both in the east and eke in the west.'

In the same spirit railing at clerical lawyers, just as popular satirists lashed the extortionate lawyers of more recent times, the Ploughman sings:—

'For who so will prove a testament,
  That is not all worthe tenne pound,
He shall pay for the parchement,
  The third of the money all round:
Thus the people is raunsound,

They say such part to hem should assend:
There as they gripen, it goeth to the ground;
God for His mercy it amend!'

Whilst many of the secular clergy thus devoted themselves to the practice of law, to commerce, and to the conduct of worldly affairs, the friars, traversing the country in pairs, were the most energetic and successful—or, as their enemies declared, the most fraudulent and extortionate—pedlars and 'tallymen' of the period. The writer of the 'Song against the Friars' (published in Mr. Thomas Wright's 'Political Poems and Songs, accession Edward III. to ac-

clerical garb and thrust themselves into the religious orders for the attainment of temporal ends.

The true priests of the Church, that is to say, the clergy, who, after taking orders from purely pious motives, lived and laboured to the last in the zealous performance of sacred duty, may have been too quick to grasp temporal power, under the natural impression that the Church was the best utiliser of all kinds of not sinful influence. No doubt this was the case. But it is no less manifest that aspiring laymen were, for far less laudable ends, pushing themselves within the ranks of the clergy; assuming the dress and functions of the priesthood for no purpose but personal aggrandizement, and clutching at the wealth of the Church, for no end save the temporal advantage of possessing a share of the sacred revenues. Priests who entered the sacerdotal order for such considerations alone were

cession Richard III.'), satirizes the commercial doings of these priests in the following style:—

'Allas! that ever it shuld be so,
Suche clerkes as thai about shuld go,
Fro town to town by two and two,
    To seke thair sustynance.
For thai have noght to lyve by.
  Thai wandren here and there,
  And dele with dyvers marcerye,
    Right as thai pedlers were.

Thai dele with purses, pynnes, and knyves,
With gyrdles, gloves, for wenches and wyves:
Bot ever bacward the husband thryves
    There thai are haunted till.

    *   *   *

Some freres beren pelures aboute,
For grate ladys and wenches stoute,
To reverce with thair clothes withoute:
    Al after that thai ere

For somme vaire; and somme gryse
For somme bugee, and for somme byse,
And also many a dyvers shyse,
    In bagges about thai bare.
All that for woman is pleasand
  Ful redy certes have thai;
But lytel gyfe thai the husband,
    That for al shal pay.

Trantes thai can, and many a jape,
For some can with a pound of sape
Gete him a kyrtelle and a cape,
    And some what els therto.

Whereto shuld I other sware?
There is no pedler that pak can bere,
That half so dere can selle his gere,
    Than a frer can do.
For if he gife a wyfe a knyfe
  That cost bot penys two,
Worthe ten knyves, so mot I thryfe,
  He wyl have ere he go.'

The author of this ballad, some parts of which are scurrilously unclean, may have been, and doubtless was, guilty of unfairness to the religious orders, whom he regarded with abhorrence; but it is matter of certainty, that in Chaucer's time the Mendicant brothers were the chief purveyors of haberdashery and knick-knacks to the ladies and humbler housewives of England.

Part I — Wycliffe's England.

not true priests, but laymen who had thrust themselves into the clergy; and, in spite of their orders and vestments, they must be judged as mere men of the world, who combined in their own breasts the selfishness and ambition of unscrupulous laymen with the arrogance and acquisitiveness of unscrupulous clerks. When they have attempted to realise the number of these ordained laymen in the Church of Wycliffe's England, most readers will concur in thinking that the clerical usurpations and encroachments of the period were neither less general nor more reprehensible than the corresponding intrusions and assumptions of the laity. The clerical order was unquestionably dominant in every grade of the community, and never desisted from efforts to extend and heighten its power to the diminution of the influence of every other class; but its most reprehensible pretensions were chiefly due to those of its members, who had never taken aught of spiritual things nearer to their hearts than the sacred vestments with which ordination had clothed them. Indeed much sound argument might be made in behalf of the position, that the corruptions of the Church sprang from the admission of these ordained laymen* within the hierarchical body.

Hypocrisy can scarcely be charged upon these clerical men of the world, who seldom put any disguise upon the considerations which had induced them to become priests, and the nature of whose religious profession was as notorious to their contemporaries† as the fact is notorious to all educated Englishmen of our own time, that a majority of the nominal barristers entered in the Law List consists of gentlemen who never had any fixed purpose to practise at the bar, but who joined the Inns of Court at the instigation of fashion, or from a design to qualify themselves to hold offices which are usually given to members of the

---

* To this expression, 'ordained laymen,' some readers may object that it contradicts itself, since every recipient of holy orders ceased to be a layman at the moment of entering the clerical class. But I can think of no term that, better than these paradoxical words, would describe the nature and condition of men whose existence was a paradox, whose temper and aims were in open contradiction to their title and profession.

† The openness with which the more worldly of the clergy of Wycliffe's England pursued the pleasures of this life is certified abundantly by the reformer who, denouncing them in 'The Office of Curates,' says,—' The fifteenth is, that they haunt taverns out of measure, and stir up laymen to drunkenness, idleness,

bar, though their duties do not require that their holders should possess accurate legal information.

The ministry of the Established Church of to-day is a profession in two senses — a profession of sacred opinions and purpose, and a calling in which men of certain intellectual qualifications may attain to various degrees of social prosperity and eminence; and, whilst there is no need to insist that the majority of our clergy regarded it only in the former character, when they solemnly selected it as a sphere of arduous and momentous duty, no sincere and intelligent person would venture to deny that the minority consists of gentlemen who, with every honourable determination to discharge their obligations to society, and not without a grave sense of the heavy responsibilities of the clerical office, entered the divine profession because it offered them more worldly advantages than they could hope to attain in any other vocation. But the clerical order in the fourteenth century was so much more generally regarded as a profession, in the latter and less solemn of these two significations, than it is in our own time, that we cannot easily conceive the carelessness and levity with which young men of Chaucer's England would sometimes seek episcopal ordination, or the smallness of the scandal occasioned by a priest who was a notorious worldling. In our time, the mere thought of a young man taking holy orders whilst in an unhallowed condition of mind, is not more shocking to the piety of devout than revolting to the honour of worldly persons. A profligate priest, in like manner, is shunned as abominable by persons whose morality allows them to be very lenient judges of the delinquencies of laymen. But the social opinion of the fourteenth century was by no means unanimous in condemning the action of the young man who, designing to practise law, or push his fortunes at

and cursed swearing, chiding, and fighting. For they will not follow earnestly in their spiritual office, after Christ and His apostles, therefore they resort to plays at tables, chess, and hazard, and roar in the streets, and sit at the tavern till they have lost their wits, and then chide, and strive, and fight sometimes. And sometimes they have neither eye, nor tongue, nor hand, nor foot, to help themselves for drunkenness. By this example the ignorant people suppose that drunkenness is no sin; but he that wasteth most of poor men's goods at taverns, making himself and other men drunken, is most praised for nobleness, courtesy, goodness, freeness, and worthiness.'

court, or make his life's game as the land-steward and secretary of an opulent baron,* caused himself to be made a priest, in order that, whilst following a worldly calling, he might be the non-resident rector of a fat living.

Had some of our more recent ecclesiastical historians given a larger measure of attention to these ordained laymen of the middle ages, they would have been less ready to repeat a hackneyed apology for the mundane pursuits of the medieval clergy. Writing in a time when the ordinary man's conception of the clerical office differs widely from the medieval view, and when social opinion, distinctly traceable to the influence of Puritanism, cries shame on the ecclesiastic who, whilst holding spiritual preferments, devotes his chief energies to worldly matters, these historians urge apologetically that small blame attached to the medieval bishops for their devotion to the secular business of the country; since, in the feudal period, it was seldom that any but clerical persons were competent by education to discharge the functions of the secular offices generally filled by clerks in holy orders. Unquestionably the fact was so; but the way in which the apologists present the fact is likely to give rise to the erroneous inference, that the absence of highly-educated laymen was due to an universal neglect of letters on the part of the laity, who were, consequently, indebted in a high degree to the Church for transacting work which very few non-clerical persons could perform. Whereas the fewness of the educated laity arose not

* To the last day of his life Wycliffe, the vehement denouncer of clerical lawyers and benefice-hunters, was in a minority; and though he had adherents in the aristocracy, powerful enough to protect him from his enemies, his followers were for the most part of the lower people. Whilst the Wycliffites were abhorred for their opinions by the majority of the powerful or fairly prosperous persons of the land, they were also despised for their social meanness. The terms 'Lollard' and 'Londlese' were used by the current cant of the day as synonymous: it being a primary article of the political creed of the persons who constituted what may be termed 'good society' in the fourteenth century, that to be a Lollard was to be a pauper in fact, a robber in intention. The minority, however, of whom Wycliffe was the mouthpiece, were vehement censors of those clergy of whom 'The Office of Curates' says, 'They run fast, by land and by water, in great peril of body and soul, to get rich benefices . . . . They practise strife and plea. and gather envy and hate from laymen for tythes. They leave preaching of the gospel, and cry fast after tythes, and summon men to account, and by force take their goods, or else curse them seven foot above the earth, and seven foot under the earth, and seven foot on each side.'

so much from the intellectual dulness and indolence of their section of the community, as from the fact that, so soon as a worldly layman had mastered a certain amount of learning, and recognised his own ability to push his fortunes upwards in the world, he invariably took orders and joined the ranks of the ordained laymen, so that he might put his feet upon the ecclesiastical ladder, whereby clever climbers could most easily and securely effect an ascent to the higher places of the social system.

But when we realise the medieval clergyman's conception of the nature and functions of his sacred office, we see that there is small need to apologise for the zeal which he very often displayed in pursuits that men of our own time regard as altogether worldly. At present, offices of instruction are the only distinctly secular offices which we esteem as so appropriate to ordained men, that they may honourably and without any kind of offence devote the best energies of their whole lives to the performance of them. All other secular avocations are deemed so foreign to the sacred calling, that no clergyman ought to employ himself altogether, or otherwise than sparingly, in them. But the case was quite different in old time. The theocratic sentiments of the medieval Church taught the clergy to regard as sacred all work that was done for God's honour; and in their opinion all work, that tended to the stability and glorification of the Church, and that emanated from a desire to produce those results, was work done for the honour of the Almighty. So long as he laboured from this motive, and for this end, a priest might put his hand to any work not actually sinful. He might dig or work in the harvest-field, he might be a farmer or land-agent, and yet be toiling in an appropriate sphere. It was this sentiment that had spurred the old British monks to tug lustily at the ropes which fastened them to the plough which their abbot guided. To the same sentiment also must be attributed the fact that the friars of Chaucer's England could tramp the country as itinerant vendors of haberdashery, and yet regard themselves as in no way unfit to administer the sacraments of the Church to the same ladies whom they supplied with silk bodices and bobbins.* The clerical order,

---

* One of the devout pedlars of Old England attained the honours of canonization—a fact which must have heightened the general respect for itine-

as we have seen, abounded with men whose only object was to mount to the highest offices of state; but though those offices were often filled by such worldlings, it quite as often happened that the ecclesiastical occupants of these supreme places were bishops of untarnished morality and sincere devoutness. And when such a model of episcopal excellence sat in the marble chair, or journeyed on an embassy to a foreign court, it never occurred to him that he was less becomingly engaged than he would have been had he remained in his diocese and thought of nothing but its wants.

Carnal warfare is unquestionably the pursuit which, in our time, is deemed most incongruous to the clerical character; but in the middle ages it was not excepted from the avocations which priests might religiously follow. This opinion found expression in the military-religious orders, whose establishment recognised the sacredness of warfare—waged with muscles of flesh and weapons of steel—that had for its sole end the glorification of the Church. The distinctions between Holy and Secular warfare are plainly stated in St. Bernard's treatise in behalf of the New Chivalry. 'As often,' says the abbot, 'as thou who wagest a secular warfare marchest forth to battle, it is greatly to be feared lest when thou slayest thine enemy in the body, he should destroy thee in the spirit, or lest, peradventure, thou shouldst be at once slain by him both in body and soul. From the disposition of the heart, indeed, not by the event of the fight, is to be estimated either the jeopardy or the victory of the Christian. If, fighting with the desire of killing another, thou shouldest chance to get killed thyself, thou diest a manslayer; if, on the other hand, thou prevailest, and through a desire of conquest or revenge killest a man, thou livest a man-

---

rant packmen throughout Christian Europe. In one of the broadest and least presentable anecdotes to be found in 'The Actes of Englysh Votrayes,' Bishop Bale says of this holy man, 'Saint Godryche, borne at Walpole, in Northfolke, went first abroad with pedlary wares, and afterwards on pilgrimage to Rome and Jerusalem. On his return he professed the chaste life of an hermyte at Fynkale, in Durham, and became the great founder of dyspersed hermytes here in England.' The means by which Saint Godryche disciplined his body so that it should render obedience to his pious will were grotesque; but an enthusiast's habitual self-denial and courageous persistence in what he believed to be the path of duty did not merit the ridicule which the Protestant bishop cast upon it.

slayer. . . . . But the soldiers of Christ, indeed, securely fight the battles of their Lord, in no wise fearing sin, either from the slaughter of the enemy, or danger from their own death. When, indeed, death is to be given or received for Christ, it has nought of crime in it, but much of glory.'* This utterance of opinion in behalf of the Templars represented the view which the most devout of the medieval clergy took of carnal warfare—a view that survived the extinction of the Knights Templars, which occurred in Chaucer's childhood; that was universally accepted by the military prelates of feudal England, of whom Henry Spenser of Norwich was not the last ; and that after outliving, by many generations, the century in which Edward the Third ordered the parochial clergy to don armour for the defence of the realm, received its death-blow, together with sundry other medieval notions, in the successive convulsions which resulted in our Reformed Church. That it lingered amongst living opinions in this country to a still more recent date, we have evidence in the cases of the several Royalist clergymen of the seventeenth century, who felt themselves justified in rendering military service in Charles the First's forces. As soldiers, fighting against those whom they reasonably esteemed to be the enemies of their Church, these Caroline priests deemed themselves engaged in such warfare as St. Bernard commended.

* The Knights Templars. By C. G. Addison, Esq. of the Inner Temple.

CHAPTER V.

POLITICAL DIVISIONS.

GAZING at the majestic beauty of a Gothic cathedral, reared in the thirteenth or fourteenth century, and discerning in its stately and harmonious proportions a work that could only have resulted from the steady co-operation of many forces; or musing amidst the silent ruins of an abbey that has been slowly falling into picturesque decay for more than three centuries; an uninformed person is apt to attribute the solemn serenity of his mind to the period of which such objects are a tranquillising memorial, and to imagine that buildings, which alike in perfectness and in dilapidation are eloquent of unity and peace, must have been produced by generations ignorant of such divisions and warfare as distract and perplex the religious minds of our own time. A superficial survey of those centuries, however, dispels the agreeable illusion, and teaches the inquirer that the bickerings of our existing parties and sects are little more than the faint echo of storms that were rising to their full fury in those medieval days which fancy would fain invest with the charms of spiritual peace coexisting with spiritual fervour.

But though no minute and protracted investigation is needful for the discovery that the period, of which Wycliffe's career is a central fact, was pregnant with religious doubts and disturbances, a longer and more careful examination must be made of the principal religious phenomena of the epoch, before the student can appreciate the universality and violence of the contentions that occupied the minds, and consumed the energies, of the majority of our clergy in the centuries under consideration. Even when he has read all the evidence, the young inquirer is reluctant to accept the conclusion which it forces upon him, and to allow that the Church which perfected our ecclesiastical architecture was a Church rent and riven, from roof to basement, by intestine commotions. The facts, however, are so clear and decisive, that after a struggle he relinquishes pleasant misconception for instructive certainty.

Throughout the feudal period our clergy were divided into two political parties,—the Papal Party, consisting of the ordained persons who supported with various degrees of vehemence, but seldom with lukewarmness, the pretensions and encroachments of the Popes; and the National Party, who, whilst concurring in the universal sentiment of the Western Churches that recognised the Pope as an authority on matters of faith, were in continual indignation against his exactions, and in perpetual contest with the emissaries of the Papal court, by whose intrigues and unscrupulous employment of force the policy of the Popes was pushed forward in this country. To draw an exact line between these irreconcilable armies of politicians is difficult, because in the long series of their contentions it often happened, that on a particular issue large sections of the Papal party were found siding with the defenders of national privileges; and again, it often happened that ecclesiastics of the national party, whose natural position was with the Antipapal clergy, gave their influence to the Pope's friends. In political warfare, sections of parties are usually found to prefer the pursuit of sectional interests to a course of fidelity to supreme principles. But though each of the two great political parties of the medieval English clergy was constantly receiving help from individuals within the lines of its opponents; and though there were occasions when both parties would momentarily combine, with an appearance of almost unbroken unanimity, to protest against some especially obnoxious Papal exaction, the two sides were, upon the whole, marked by a solidarity and separateness which seldom characterise two large multitudes of political contendants. As soon as the momentary combination of irreconcilable partizans had effected its purpose, or (which was more usually the case) ascertained that its end could not be achieved by an unnatural coalition of implacable enemies, it came to an end; and its liberated elements returned to their old antagonisms and rivalries.

Due allowance being made for these incessant exchanges of

Part I.—Wycliffe's England.

force between the two divisions, the Papal party consisted of the regular clergy, whether monks or friars ; whilst the National party was composed of the secular priests. Though their influence in this country was fraught with ruin to the Papal dominancy, the mendicant brothers were the consistent supporters of those pontifical pretensions, to which they were largely indebted for their prosperity and existence, and from which came their mischievous power of interference with the parochial clergy. Since it sanctioned their insolence, and expressly authorised their extortions, it is no wonder that they loudly magnified the virtues and rights of the Papal supremacy. For awhile they were most serviceable agents of the Popes, in whose behalf they laboured with a success commensurate with their unscrupulous zeal—a success that, so soon as their purpose was understood and their temper revealed, earned for them the vindictive hatred of the secular priests.

Whilst the friars thus distinguished themselves by audacious advocacy of pontifical pretensions, and by proceedings that struck at the very roots of the authority which they strove to extol until it became their interest to degrade it, the monks were far less turbulent, but much more dignified supporters of the Papal throne. There was no feature of the monastic system which the monks regarded with greater complacency, and for the preservation of which they were more ready to contend as a vital principle of religious association, than their independence of the national bishops, whom they never permitted to exercise any control (in their episcopal character, *i. e.*, upon the strength of authority derived from the national episcopacy) within the monastic houses. As great landowners, they would support the Crown and contribute to the well-being of the community ; but the bishop of the diocese in which they resided was, in his character of bishop, no more to them than any bishop in the south of Spain. The Crown might select its own policy with respect to the secular clergy, and decide how far it should endeavour to control the national bishops and parochial priests ; but though for the most part of English birth, and participating to some extent in the patriotic sentiments common to Englishmen, they were not, in consequence, *of* the nation, in which they held rank as territorial lords. Amenable only to the superiors of their respective orders, who were most generally resident at the Papal court, and through those superiors to the Pope, they would suffer no English bishop to meddle with their affairs. This was the position of the medieval monks, who, priding themselves on their peculiar freedom from national authority, and the directness of their connexion with the successors of St. Peter, held themselves aloof from the strictly national clergy; disdaining them as their inferiors in learning and culture, no less than in opulence and political dignity. When an abbot required the services of a bishop within the limits of his jurisdiction, either to confirm, ordain, or consecrate, he usually had recourse to one of those bishops *in partibus*, of whom notice has already been taken. In every crisis of national politics, affecting the interests of his abbey, he obeyed the instructions of the superior of his order, whose command was in most cases the wish of the reigning pontiff. Occasions, of course, continually occurred in the factious life of the Papal courts, when the superior of a monastic order was at open variance with the Pope; and when one of these frequent cases took place, the superior's private instructions to English abbots directed a coalition with the National party to thwart the pontifical schemes, or left them free to pursue a personal object in the varying complications of the political game. But so long as the Papacy was not flagrantly inordinate in its demands on their pecuniary resources, the monks were disposed to sustain the foreign power, whose aggrandisement seemed to enhance the dignity of the religious orders, to the detriment of the parochial clergy and the weakening of the national bishops, who, if there were no Pope able to control them, would not be slow to assert their right to interfere in the affairs of the monasteries.

But the power, which enjoyed the varying support of the monks, whilst the itinerant clergy never ceased to agitate for its more complete ascendancy, was regarded with no cordial affection by the national bishops, who were continually called upon to submit to its ruinous exactions, without deriving from its policy any compensatory aid. However disposed the bishop of an English diocese might be to recognise the Bishop of Rome as the Church's sovereign, he could not shut his eyes to the

Part I.—Wycliffe's England.

fact that, whilst it never strengthened his hands for the efficacious discharge of his episcopal duties, the Papacy took every opportunity to weaken them by draining his coffers and contracting his patronage. Hence it came to pass, that so orthodox a churchman as Bishop Grosthead—whose devotion to the Pope's spiritual authority savoured of bigotry, and whose notions concerning the privileges of the clergy were altogether in favour of ecclesiastical aggrandisement—became the resolute opponent of pontifical claims. And men of Grosthead's order and opinions were not premature in entertaining alarm for the future of their church when, in the middle of the thirteenth century, 'the Pope' (to quote the words of Matthew Paris) 'sent in command to the Archbishop of Canterbury, and four other bishops, that provision should be made for three hundred Romans in the chiefest and best benefices in all England at the next voidance; so that the aforesaid archbishop and bishops should be suspended in the meantime from all collations or gift of benefice until the aforesaid three hundred were provided for.' The period at which the Pope made this intolerable attempt upon the privileges of the English bishops was a time when the abbots offered a general, though ineffectual, resistance to the extortionate demands of the Papacy for funds wherewith to prosecute its martial and exhausting policy. But when the immediate cause of irritation had passed away, the religious houses could resume their old friendliness to the spiritual sovereign who only struck them with whips of cords, whilst he chastised the secular clergy with scorpions, and whose greatness was after all, in a certain sense, their greatness. The case, however, was different with the bishops, who, notwithstanding the resoluteness and gallantry of their resistance to the invaders of the ancient rights of the national church, were usually worsted, and were never altogether victorious in the long series of struggles which resulted in their complete subjection to Rome.

The enmity, however, which the chiefs of the secular clergy cherished for the ecclesiastics who fought the Pope's battles on English ground, was hearty friendliness in comparison with the rancour that animated the inferior parochial priests towards the promoters and abettors of the Papal encroachments. To estimate the feelings of this humblest portion of the clerical army, the reader must understand the light in which the ordinary curates regarded the Pope's authority, apart from the vexations of which it was productive to their class. The high notions of the Pontiff's infallibility, that generally prevailed from the commencement of the fifteenth century down to Henry the Eighth's rupture with Rome, can scarcely be said to have existed amongst the clergy of Chaucer's England; but the secular priests concurred with all other Western ecclesiastics in regarding the Pope as their appointed chief, and with a lively sense of the advantages which resulted from unity they were affectionately disposed to the theory of the Papal control over the countries that acknowledged his spiritual sway. But consent to the theory did not reconcile them to the hardships which they endured from the mode in which it was put in practice. That the Pope's power was the result of worldly policy they needed no instruction; but however questionable, and even censurable, might be many of the measures from which it had derived its origin and vigour, his supremacy was a fact which they accepted as a thing of divine ordinance; regarding it with what may be called the theologian's readiness to believe that whatever is must, somehow or other, be the effect of providential design. So long as it was a fact they were ready to submit to it: just as ordinary men, reserving to themselves the right of privately criticising its operations, deem themselves bound by duty as well as prudence to obey whatever *ipso facto* government they may live under. The Pope had been permitted by Heaven to gain a limited control over the Church of England; and therefore it was incumbent on the national clergy of that Church to submit themselves to his rule. Whilst this statement cannot be charged with underrating the allegiance by which the National party of the Church deemed itself bound to the Pope, it makes it clear that the Antipapal section of our clergy deemed themselves free to canvass the acts of the Papal government, to inquire what good their Church derived from its connexion with the Papacy, and, when the evil seemed preponderant over the beneficial results of that connexion, to pray for the liberation of their Church from the maleficent government.

Part I.—Wycliffe's England.

When the average members of the National party began to sum up the consequences of the Papal supremacy to their Church, they soon saw grounds for grave dissatisfaction with the foreign ruler; and on striking the balance of the account, they generally came to the conclusion that his Pontifical Highness was an enemy to the religious interests of their flocks.

Through the connexion of their Church with the foreign bishop they saw vast sums of money annually withdrawn from the country, and from its impoverished people, who languished through insufficiency of capital, in order that the Church's sovereign might be enabled to carry on wars that were sometimes alike inexpedient and immoral. This abstraction of the national wealth for martial undertakings, from which the country could derive no benefit, was not rendered the less grievous to them from the fact that they had been recently compelled to surrender a fifth of their means to supply the Pope's needs. The hardship became all the more intolerable when they reflected, that very likely the Pope's collectors would descend upon the Church in the course of two or three years with demands for yet another fifth of the clerical livings. Had the Pope been content with the prodigious contributions that ordinarily flowed to him from first-fruits, Peter-pence, collations, reservations, and the score other exactions which had come to be regarded as his 'dues,' the poor seculars would have refrained from rebellious murmuring. But Christian humility and forbearance have their limits, though the Pontiff's greed had none. And when their endurance was exhausted, they asked one another what good the Pope did them that they should be required to do so much for him?*

But, even more than the Pope's exactions of their money, the secular clergy resented his interference with the rights of

---

* The most cursory perusal of any history that gives the details of the Popes' incessant withdrawals of money from England throughout the thirteenth and fourteenth centuries, will satisfy the uninformed reader that this brief notice of the general character and tendency of those exactions is in accordance with facts. From the time of Bishop Grosthead to the death of Wycliffe the English clergy groaned under Papal extortion. From the middle of the earlier of those centuries, when the Pope demanded a fifth of every ecclesiastical man's living for the cost of his war with the Emperor Frederic II., down to the last days of Simon

the patrons of English livings, who were required to appoint to the best benefices in their gift the nominees of the Papal court. Those foreign nominees were for the most part Italians, needy members of powerful families, who, in consideration of their kinsmen's services to a pontiff, were thrust into English rectories, or preferred to the most lucrative canonries of the cathedral chapters. The position of these foreign ecclesiastics, planted amongst a people whose language they could not speak, and who abhorred them as despoilers of Christ's Church, must have been very unenviable. It is not difficult to imagine how, in the cold fogs of a northern climate, they pined for the bright suns and joyous cities of Southern Europe; and how they sent to the homes of their early days doleful accounts of their exile in a land where they could find neither acceptable amusements nor congenial friends. Nor is it otherwise than easy to conceive the exertions which their relatives in Rome or Avignon made to obtain licenses of non-residence for the unhappy exiles, so that they might be free to spend the revenues accruing from their English preferments in the warmer atmosphere and brighter society of their native country. It is impossible to give the exact number of these Italian immigrants, but the ferment occasioned by their presence, and the frequent appearance of Italian names in the ecclesiastical archives of the period, indicate that their fewness could not be pleaded in extenuation of the wrongfulness of their intrusion.

In the thirteenth century, the indignation with which the ecclesiastics of the National party, and most of the laity, regarded the presence of these Italian incumbents of English benefices, expressed itself in one of those armed demonstrations which patriotic sentiment and respect for simple justice make us distinguish from ordinary rebellions against authority. An English knight, whose patronage of a benefice had been vio-

---

Sudbury's archiepiscopate,—in less than one year of which official tenure the Pope drew more than 60,000 florins of exceptional contribution from our countrymen,—the English clergy paid a heavy price for their connexion with the successors of St. Peter. The repeated resistances which our clergy during this period offered to the demands of the Papacy, demonstrate the exasperation to which those demands gave rise, and the spirit with which the national ecclesiastics could withstand their suzerain's encroachments.

lated by Papal agency, in order that an Italian might be advanced to the preferment, placed himself at the head of some eighty soldiers, who, accompanying their chief through the different shires of the country, broke into the tithe-barns of the foreign rectors, and distributed their contents amongst the poor, who were invited to purchase the provisions at low prices. Having commenced his campaign against the foreigners by sacking the tithe-barn of the 'Roman parson' of Wingham in Kent, the daring adventurer moved about the kingdom, committing depredations on the stores of other Italian rectors, who fled for safety to the nearest monasteries, whilst the soldiers scattered their corn amongst jubilant mobs of beggars and purchasers. When the strong arm of the law had put a stop to these scandalous doings, and caused inquiry to be made into all the circumstances of the riotous movement, it was ascertained that, besides possessing the sympathy of the populace and inferior landowners, the knight's conduct was approved by laymen of condition and several chiefs of the secular clergy. Bishops and royal chaplains, archdeacons and deans, were amongst the abettors of the principal transgressor, who was found to have such a hold on public opinion, that he not only escaped punishment, but, on making submission to the Pope, received the papal absolution and recovered the ecclesiastical patronage which had been wrongfully taken from him. The year of this droll and characteristic episode in our ecclesiastical story was 1232; but the grievance against which the insurgents protested was the affair of the fourteenth, no less than the earlier century.

An evil that repeatedly roused opposition to the Papacy within the ranks of the regular clergy, this grievance was felt acutely, and resented hotly, by every section of the secular priesthood; by the bishops, whose patronal rights it infringed; by the beneficed curates, who, though holding preferments, witnessed with displeasure the partial absorption by foreigners of the fund, of which they hoped to gain a larger share, and which, under all circumstances, they looked upon as the peculiar appanage of the national clergy; and still more by the unbeneficed clerks, whose chances of obtaining preferment were manifestly lessened by every fresh importation of Italian candidates for English livings. When, moreover, it is borne in mind that nearly every considerable lay landowner was possessed of patronal rights in the national church,—rights which, though less openly sold than at present, were direct or indirect sources of material advantage to their possessors,—it may be judged how cordially the landed knights and squires shared in the clerical disapproval of the Pope's usurpations of ecclesiastical patronage.

It is seasonable that we should here glance for a moment at another matter, which caused a considerable number of the secular clergy to regard the Papal rule with discontent, and in some instances with positive hatred. No popular error is more general or more fruitful of false inferences than the impression that English clergymen neither did, nor could, marry in the middle ages. The case was far otherwise. Both sections of the regular clergy, monks and friars, were absolutely precluded from marriage, by orders which they could not violate without incurring instant and condign punishment. The canons also enjoined celibacy on the members of the secular priesthood; but though the ecclesiastical law in this respect received an irregular support from the law of the land, and in the great majority of cases controlled the domestic lives of the seculars, a very considerable proportion of our parochial clergy had wives. Social opinion unquestionably accorded such sanction to these marriages, that no married parson was disesteemed by his congregation so far as to be thought a priest unfit to discharge the functions of his office, because he had a wife and a family of children. The bishops and higher seculars looked on these unions with disapprobation; and within the lines of his own division of the clerical order, it is certain that a secular parish-priest lost caste by marriage. By the act which gave him a wife, he greatly lessened his chances of professional advancement. But he was not regarded as an utterly disgraced man, nor was the stigma of bastardy affixed to his children. The law recognised the legitimacy of the offspring of married priests: women of honest parentage and fame, of gentle natures and pure lives, became the wives of beneficed clergymen; and not seldom these women saw their sons rise to honour, and their daughters accepted in matrimony by gentle houses.

Part I.—Wycliffe's England.

Reginald Fitz-Joceline, archbishop of Canterbury in the last decade of the twelfth century, was the son of a married bishop. But whilst social custom and common law took this view of clerical marriages, the Papacy persisted in regarding those unions as utterly sinful; as arrangements which combined the sin of uncleanness with odious profanation of a sacred rite. Consequently, the devout and zealous married priest of Wycliffe's England, amongst his other grounds for discontent with the Pope and his aiders, took note of the contumelious and revolting epithets that Papal law, and the agents of Papal law, were continually hurling at his beloved wife and innocent children. In the coarsest and most violent language, the regular clergy would openly declare that his sons were *filii nullius;* that their mother was a woman of shameful life. If any Englishman will imagine how he would respond to any persons who should venture thus to asperse his wife and offspring, he will be in a position to realise the feelings with which the married clergy of Catholic England, in the thirteenth and fourteenth centuries, regarded their Papal calumniators.

To those who are disposed to think lightly of the division between the Papal and National parties in the Church, on the ground that it was not attended with disputes on points of theology, it may be remarked that, though both sections concurred in holding the chief tenets of Catholic opinion, there were several minor questions, within the domain of polemics, about which the Churchmen of the period wrangled with the proverbial bitterness of religious disputants. And these matters of controversy were all the more productive of discord, from being not so much sources of difference between the two parties, as fields on which the members of each party waged wordy battle amongst themselves. When we come to pay special attention to the friars, we shall see that, detested though they were by the parochial clergy—whom they habitually insulted within the bounds of their parishes, and in the faces of their assembled congregations—they were even more cordially hated by the pro-Papal monks, against whose luxurious indolence they turbulently declaimed, and whose sentiments they shocked, by teaching the laity to prefer the utterances of Scripture before the declarations of the fathers and the traditions of the Church. No class of persons, in the fourteenth century, were more directly and terribly menaced by the rapid development of medieval communism than the inhabitants of the monasteries, who, with good reason, attributed the socialistic doctrines, daily becoming more popular amongst the poorer people, chiefly to the influence of the Mendicant Orders. In like manner, when we shall come to consider the growth of Lollardy, we shall find it fruitful of dissensions amongst the parochial clergy, compared with which the controversies of our clergy on matters of form and doctrine are affectionate and harmonious exercises.

Of course in the higher ranks of the two parties there was less of violent and discourteous disputation, less also of blinding animosity, than in the lower grades of churchmen. The mitred abbots and the bishops were men of the world as well as dignified ecclesiastics, and, as men of the world, they were superior to mere collegiate spites and parochial jealousies. Through mutual intercourse, and not seldom through common endeavours to bring their respective parties into co-operation, they learned to respect one another. Frequently, the bishop of a diocese had spent the greater part of his life in a cloister; and, where the sentiments of the two sections of the Church were thus united in a man, who, before rising to be a chief of seculars, had been a monk amongst monks, the most violent members of both parties found in him a common friend, whose influence was conducive to general union. So, also, amongst the inferior clergy, whether regular or secular, the animosities and rivalries of class were frequently subordinate to the generous instincts and amiable tendencies of human nature. Where this was the case monks and seculars lived on good terms with one another, exchanging the hospitalities of the table and the amenities of social intercourse, even as men of our time, holding extreme and diametrically opposite opinions on politics and religion, are very often agreeable neighbours, and sometimes are fast bound by the closest and strongest ties of familiar friendship.

But, under ordinary circumstances, the lower natures of the two parties were incapable of mutual forbearance and charity. If we realise the vindictive rancour which a narrow and harsh

Part I.—Wycliffe's England.

Elizabethan Puritan cherished for disdainful and unyielding supporters of the new Church, and the insolent pride with which such a Churchman repaid the animosity of such a Dissenter;—if we recall the sarcastic derision with which the typical fine gentleman of Charles the First's court expressed his contempt for the humours and eccentricities of the Primitive Baptist, and the air of spiritual self-sufficiency with which the Baptist prayed for his mocker's conversion;—if we imagine the boisterous malignity with which the free-living Royalist rector, whom the Parliamentary commissioners had in former time declared 'scandalous,' hastened, on the Restoration, to eject from his recovered parsonage the Presbyterian minister who had occupied it throughout the interregnum;—if, coming nearer to our own times, we remember the ineffable detestation in which our High-Church grandfathers held the ministers of conventicles; —if, lastly, we combine all the varieties of intolerance and pride, of passion and scorn, that animated these different politico-religious foes—the result will be the kind of enmity which the overbearing friar and the hot-tempered parish-priest of the commoner sort harboured and nursed for one another. It will also comprise the passions that continually broke out in abusive altercations when the mendicants and seculars of the fourteenth century were thrown together in a tavern, or encountered on their road towards the same shrine, like the friar and the sompnour* of the 'Canterbury Tales,' who furnished amusement for their fellow-travellers by their vituperations of the sections of clergy to which they were respectively attached. Lastly,

---

* Chaucer omits to state what orders the 'Sompnour' had taken; but as the office of an apparitor of an ecclesiastical court was one of emolument, and just such influence as a clerical busy-body, combining an extortioner's greed with a gossip-monger's love of scandal, liked to be invested with, an archdeacon's sompnour was very usually a clerk in priest's orders, who either subsisted by zealous attention to his office, or who was allowed to absent himself from his benefice in order that he might pursue the lucrative and congenial vocation of an ecclesiastical informer and summons-server. But whatever his orders, Chaucer's sompnour was an ecclesiastical personage; and in attacking him, as an official representative of the secular clergy, the friar gave utterance to his rancorous detestation of all persons and things pertaining to bishops and their courts. The tone of the sompnour's retaliation demonstrates the intemperance and sheer indecency which distinguished the language of clerical antagonists in the fourteenth century.

it will hold in suspense the malice and pungent spitefulness which monks wrangled with monks, and friars squabbled and fought amongst themselves.

But enough has been said of the political divisions of the Church that busied itself in producing our sublimest works of Gothic architecture. It is time that we should look at the contending factions from points of view that are social rather than political.

CHAPTER VI.

DONS AND SIRS.

THE popular conception of the monk of the fourteenth century is mainly derived from the pungent representations of his contemporary satirists, and the sprightly effusions of later humorists, who have combined to delineate the typical member of our ancient regular clergy as an easy-tempered and rather jocose voluptuary, chiefly remarkable for his dislike of bodily exertion, the breadth of his capacious paunch, the rubicund tinge of his jolly jowl, the twinkle of his merry eyes, and the peculiar slovenliness of his attire. A port-drinking rector of George the Third's time, thrown back into the feudal period, and slightly modified in garb and modes of action to meet the requirements of medieval society; this is the average monk of popular imagination, who lifts a black flagon to his lips in drinking songs, flirts with Margery, and consumes something more than his rightful share of venison-pasty. Whenever this worthy is seen at minster service he is tranquilly dozing, or loudly snoring, in a comfortable seat, whilst the choristers, controlled by the superb melody of a noble organ, make the vaulted roof of the cathedral reverberate with sacred strains. But away from the festive board, where he daily pledges the Pope's health in copious draughts of mellow wine, he is studied to best advantage whilst sitting under his favourite tree in the abbey-garden, beneath whose shade he delights to pass his summer mornings, munching succulent pears, and making the juniors of his brotherhood laugh till their sides ache by his quaint stories.

Created by more than twelve generations of satire, this jovial celibate has become to most persons an historic fact; and

I am by no means prepared to call him otherwise than historic, and true to the life of the period in which he is believed to have lived. Satire that has no element of justice and veracity quickly perishes; and, therefore, it would be most unreasonable to charge this humorous caricature of the ancient monk with absolute untruthfulness. I have no doubt that the portraiture is as reliable as most of the personal portraitures of fictitious literature —as truthful, for instance, as Fielding's Squire Western, or Sterne's Uncle Toby, or Theodore Hook's sketches of lord mayors and aldermen. But superficial readers need to be reminded that this typical representative of monastic jollity— worthy though he is of acceptance as a veritable historic personage—is at most only one character taken from the many strongly diversified types of human nature that found their homes in the religious houses of Wycliffe's England. Enough has been said in earlier pages of this work to show that medieval monasticism—which gave us statesmen, scholars, ambitious directors of ecclesiastical movement, and men conspicuous for activity in every kind of social affairs—was no system altogether made up of indolent, gossiping voluptuaries; and, whilst no competent historian on the Protestant side has ventured to deny, no intelligent inquirer into the facts of our religious story is likely to question, that, even at their most corrupt period, when their days were numbered, the monasteries of England comprised a large number of conscientious and devout men.*

Whenever the popular mind imagines monks of a less genial and more sternly realistic kind than Simon the Cellarer, it calls into being a set of ungainly and morose, or drivelling and bleareyed creatures, whose low brows, repellent visages, and unwashed

---

* On this point, in his 'Church History,' Fuller (whose Protestantism is beyond imputation) says, 'It is confessed by impartial people, that some monasteries of both sexes, being put to the test, appeared very commendable in their behaviour, so that the least aspersion could not justly be cast upon them. I read in one author that "some societies behaved themselves so well, that their lives were not only exempt from notorious faults, but their spare times bestowed on writing books, painting, carving, engraving: so that their visitors became intercessors for them." Amongst these, the nunnery of Godstow, near Oxford, must not be forgotten.' Throwing proper ridicule upon certain of the wild stories, affecting the morality of the last of our English monks and nuns—stories which had their origin, probably, in the heated imagination of honest people, though they were

Part I.—Wycliffe's England.

skins, demonstrate the qualities of intellect and taste which, it is presumed, must have distinguished men servile enough by nature to submit themselves voluntarily to monastic rule, which, it is also assumed, was chiefly influential on its votaries of finer stuff, by depriving them of self-respect and the dignity of manliness. Even our painters—a class of men, for the most part, superior to the blinding prejudices and degrading animosities engendered in ignorant minds by polemical contention—are so much under the spell of this general antagonism to the old religious orders, that, when they aim at representing scenes of monastic story, they seldom do justice to what must have been the prevailing facial and corporeal characteristics of our medieval monks.

In every stage of its story, from the period of Saxon consolidation to the present day, the English Church, considered as a profession of spiritual teachers, has been an eminently aristocratic vocation, with the exception of the hundred and fifty years immediately following our rupture with Rome. The Anglo-Saxon Church was enthusiastically supported by the nobles and opulent landowners, who endowed it with lands and tithes, admitted its chiefs to a preponderating share in the government of the country, and rejoiced at seeing men of their best families enrol themselves in the ranks of clergy, at seeing their noblest matrons and virgins assume the dress and life of nuns. The same was the case with our clergy under the Norman kings. The priests whom the Conqueror preferred to the chief offices of the Church, on the flight, or summary dismissal, or gradual removal (through death or political sentence) of the Saxon bishops and abbots, were of his own race; and be-

---

often repeated by partisans who must have known their falsity—Fuller observes, 'Here I cannot believe what is commonly told of underground vaults, leading from Fryeries to Nunneries, confuted by the situation of the place, through rocks improbable, and under rivers impossible, to be conveyed. Surely, had the Waltham monks had any such subterranean contrivances, they would not have made use of so open a passage; and such vaults extant to this day in many abbeys extend but few paces, generally used for the conveyance of water, and sewers to carry away the filth of the convent.' In fact, to accept these stories we must believe that the Thames Tunnel and the subterranean borings of our railways are little else than insignificant copies of the engineering achievements of the lazy monks.

sides being, in a certain sense, noble, by virtue of their foreign descent, in a state of society when to be a Norman was to belong to the ruling caste, they were usually of parentage that rendered them noble amongst Normans. And, throughout the succeeding generations of the feudal epoch, which lavished on the sacerdotal order every kind of splendour and privilege that could render its service attractive to men of high birth, the Church—the word being again used in its narrowest sense— was emphatically a profession for gentlemen. There is need to insist on this fact, since it often escapes due attention through the admiration with which students regard the truly Catholic policy, which caused the rulers of the Church to admit men of the humblest birth within the sacerdotal order, and to allow of their occasional elevation to the supreme places of the ecclesiastical system. Whilst taking note of the crowds of plebeian ecclesiastics who found employment in the Church, and of the numerous instances in our ecclesiastical history of men of the humblest origin rising to the highest clerical dignities, the student must always remember that, whilst the plebeian clergy for the most part ministered to plebeian worshippers, the most honourable ranks of the hierarchy were chiefly filled with men of honourable extraction. The same may be said, with limitations, of the existing English clergy, which comprises the sons of peers and the sons of farm-labourers, and whose most important hierarchs are usually men of good social extraction, though we are not unaccustomed to the sight of an honest tradesman's son taking his place upon the bench of bishops. But whilst, on the one hand, the plebeian element is much weaker in numbers and actual power in our modern clergy than it was in the ecclesiastical order of the middle ages, it must, on the other hand, be conceded that the medieval church had a larger proportion of the highest aristocracy in its ordained service than even the present highly aristocratic Church of England can boast. And of this feudal clergy—so catholic in its reception of men from every social grade—the best-descended and best-bred (or, to describe a thing of fashion, let me use one of fashion's favourite metaphors, and say the 'cream') were found in the colleges of the regular priests.

Composed chiefly of men of knightly origin, or, at least, of

Part I.—Wycliffe's England.

gentle birth — the brothers or sons of the gallant knights who fought at Crecy and Poictiers, the lineal descendants of fiery nobles who joined in the first crusade—an ordinary college of regular clergy in the fourteenth century contained a large proportion of monks whose lineaments and mien proclaimed their honourable parentage, and demonstrated the physical characteristic of the purest and finest types of the Norman and Saxon races, and of that still nobler race that had resulted from the fusion of the victorious and conquered houses. Whilst some members of the fraternity would exhibit signs of their Norman extraction in their proud brows, aquiline noses, and thin lips, others would be no less remarkable for the Saxon breadth of their foreheads, the Saxon openness of their frank countenances, and the ingenuous clearness of their blue eyes; and all of them by their gait, tone, bearing, would betray their consciousness of their social dignity and status among the ruling class of their fellow-countrymen.

The varieties of monkish type were no less numerous than the diversities of monkish activity. One type would consist mainly of studious men, who occupied themselves principally in controlling the labours of the scriptorium. The artistic monks, intently engaged upon architecture and illumination, carving in wood and sculpture in stone, and all the finer industries conducive to the perfection of cathedrals and the splendour of divine services, would constitute another species. Then there were the political monks, who watched, with attentive eyes and anxious prescience, the course of national and international affairs; the enthusiastic and ascetic monks, the medieval equivalents of our modern 'High Churchmen,' who entertained schemes for the regeneration of the priesthood, and the amelioration of all classes of mankind, through the fuller operation of the ancient powers of the clergy; the numerous keen-witted, critical, loquacious monks, remarkable for what may be termed medieval eclecticism and dilettanteism, who professed sympathy for, and accurate knowledge of, the whole range of monkish interests; and who, with something of the dash and recklessness of a nineteenth-century junior barrister, and something of the arrogant cleverness of the nineteenth-century journalist, presumed to judge the doings of their brethren, in the various domains of theological controversy, art, music, classic scholarship, patristic lore, politics, agriculture, horticulture, church-government, and social progress. Each of these too-generally-forgotten kinds of regular clergy had its characteristic varieties, all of whom have been thrust either clean off, or backwards to the dark corners of the historic stage, in order that the pot-bellied caricature of monkish joviality may have more room to shamble to and fro, and convulse the house with Falstaffian drolleries.

But the monks who played the most conspicuous part in the ordinary social life of the fourteenth century were a class of ordained gentlemen who, combining some of the characteristics of a world-loving Oxford or Cambridge collegiate 'fellow' of our own time, with the briskness and energy of a modern sport-loving country squire, were in their day the kind of personages whose nearest counterparts in existing society are our well-born and active 'county men.' Although monasticism forbade the individual monk to acquire and hold property for himself, it encouraged the accumulation of wealth in the hands of religious corporations; and the revenues accruing from monastic properties, after liberal contributions had been rendered to Papal needs, and due provision made for the material welfare of the house and order to which each source of income specially pertained, were distributed with greater or less fairness amongst the members of the regular clergy. Hence, these clerical celibates were amongst the richest persons of the land; and, obeying the instincts of human nature, the particular class of monks now under consideration made no attempt to conceal their personal affluence. Expending a large proportion of his ample means, and no less ample leisure, on field-sports, a monk of this kind kept the best-bred horses in his neighbourhood, and was known for the pluck and judgment with which he rode them across country; and, whilst his stud was the admiration of a county-side, he was noticeable for the excellence of his kennel, the vigour of his carriage, and the luxurious costliness of his dress. When he approached a tavern, on a journey through the country, his advent was heralded by the music of the bells that rang merrily on his hunter's bridle; and when he alighted at the tavern-door, loungers at the shuttered windows remarked the richness of his fur wristbands, the brightness of the supple leather of his riding-boots, and the delicate workmanship of the large gold pin that fastened his hood beneath his chin.* Whilst idlers gazed with delight on the bravery of his aspect and costume, the hostler, paying due obeisance to the rank of the newly-arrived guest, touched his forehead repeatedly, whilst taking 'my lord's' orders respecting the way in which the mettlesome steed should be rubbed down and baited. By the same respectful title the monk was addressed by 'mine host,' who, notwithstanding the high social esteem in which superior inn-keepers were held in Old England, and the familiarity with which they were consequently treated by travellers of high degree, would on no account have omitted the customary

---

* It is almost needless to observe that the materials for this portrait are taken from Chaucer; but those of my readers who have not the 'Canterbury Tales' by heart, or at hand, will like to have Chaucer's 'monk' put before them in the poet's own language, in a note:—

'A monk ther was, a fayre for the maistrie,
An outrider, that loved venerie:
A manly man, to ben an abbot able.
*Full many a deinte hors hadde he in stable;
And whan he rode, men mighte his bridel here,
Gingeling in a whistling wind as clere,
And eke as loude, as doth the chapell belle,
Ther as this lord was keper of the celle.*
 The reule of Saint Maure and Saint Beneit,
Because that it was old and somdele streit,
This ilke monke lette olde thinges pace,
And held after the newe world the trace.
He yave not of the text a pulled hen,
That saith that hunters ben not holy men;
Ne that a monk, whan he is rekkeless,
Is like to a fish that is waterless:
This is to say, a monk out of his cloistre.
This ilke text held he not worth an oistre.
And I say his opinion was good.
What shulde he studie, and make himselven wood,
Upon a book in cloistre alway to pore,
Or swinken with his hondes, and laboure,
As Austin bit? how shal the world be served?
Let Austin have his swink to him reserved.
Therefore he was a prickasoure a right.
*Greihoundes he hadde, as swift as foul of flight;
Of pricking and of hunting for the hare
Was all his lust, for no cost wolde he spare.
I saw his sleeves purfled at the hond
With gris, and that the finest of the lond.
And for to fasten his hood under his chinne
He hadde of gold ywroght a curious pinne.
A love-knot in the greter end ther was.
His hed was balled, and shone as any glas,
And eke his face, as it had ben anoint.
He was a lord ful fat and in good point.
His eyen stepe, and rolling in his hed,
That semed as a forneis of a led,
His botes souple, his hors in gret estat,
Now certainly he was a fayre prelat.
He was not pale as a forpined gost.
A fat swan loved he best of any rost.
His palfrey was as browne as is a bery.*'

appellation which defined the social dignity of the medieval monk.

Nor may it be supposed that the costume, appointments, and venatory taste of this hunting clergyman, were at variance with the social opinion of ordinary gentlefolk, at a time when field-sports were the universal and most eagerly followed of aristocratic diversions; and when the superior nuns of the country were remarkable for the richness of their jewelry and the fastidious daintiness of their costume, and ordinarily went on journeys with small greyhounds at their heels.* The same reliable delineator of contemporary manners, to whom we are indebted for this portrait of a fourteenth-century monk, introduces us also to an exemplary nun, who is pointed to as a model of feminine propriety, and an example of the exquisite refinement and spiritual worth of the religious ladies of the period; and the same verses which commend her exact observance of all the requirements of social decorum, and state that she was properly accompanied by a female companion and three priests, draw attention to the amatory motto on her brooch, and the hounds that sat beside her at table. Chaucer's hunting monk, moreover, is consistently represented throughout the 'Tales' as being a gentleman of considerable attainments and great worth, who reflected credit on his order, and was almost as bright an exemplar of monastic merit as the knight was a brilliant illustration of chivalric honour. Apart from the good-humoured banter about the proverbial unholiness of hunters and other like pleasantry, the poet betrays no disapprobation of 'hunting' monks; and yet he was so much tainted with 'Lollardy,' and so

---

* Chaucer's prioress was adorned with jewelry, that may have aided her devotions, but were also articles of personal decoration, and was attended by pet hounds.

' Of smal houndes hadde she, that she fedde
With rosted flesh, and milk, and wastel
  brede,
But sore wept if on of hem were dede,
Or if men smote it with a yerde smert:
And all was conscience and tendre heart.
Ful semely hire wimple ypinched was:

  * * *

Ful fetise was hire cloke, as I was ware,

Of smal corall aboute hire arm she bare
A pair of bedes, gauded all with grene;
And thereon hung a broche of gold ful
  shene,
On which was first ywritten a crowned A,
And after, AMOR VINCIT OMNIA.
Another Nonne also with hire hadde she,
That was hire chapelleine, and Preestes three.'

much in harmony with the clergy who strongly disapproved the venatory habits of the priestly order, that no tenderness to clerical delinquents can have made him improperly lenient to the hard-riding monk. Had my lord monk's zeal for sport caused scandal to the more decorous members of his acquaintance, Chaucer would most certainly have said so; but, instead of making any such intimation, he is at pains to show that the ecclesiastic was in thorough accord with the prevailing opinion of his time.

The customary application of the title 'My Lord' to the medieval monk is a respectful usage, that deserves some words of special notice, as it serves to mark the esteem in which the regular clergy were held as the social superiors of the secular clergy. Had the practice been confined to mitred abbots, who were lords of parliament as well as lords of abbeys, it could have been explained as an allusion to their political status, used as the same mode of address is still employed to bishops who are members of the House of Peers as well as rulers of dioceses. But the honourable designation was accorded to all monks. In familiar conversation this homage was rendered by the word 'Don,' an abbreviation of *Dominus*, which was customarily prefixed to the monk's Christian name, just as 'Dom' and 'Don' are still applied to monks in France and Spain. Hence the monk of Wycliffe's England was called 'Don John,' or 'Don Hubert,' by speakers who, for convenience sake, or from some other motive, omitted the more pompous terms 'Dominus,' or 'My Lord;' but it frequently occurred that civil speakers, in their anxiety to give a monk the fullest possible measure of deference, linked together* the abbreviation and one of the full forms of address; in which case the monk had the pleasure of hearing himself appealed to as 'My Lord Don,' or 'Dominus Don.' Sometimes the address became 'My Lord Dominus,' or

---

* In the Prologue to the Monk's Tale in the 'Canterbury Tales,' the host rings several changes on one bell. Thus:—
    'My lord Monk, quod he, be mery of chere;
    For ye shul telle a tale trewely.
    Lo, Rouchester standeth here fast by,
    Ride forth, *mine owen Lord*, breke not our game.
    But by my trouthe I can not telle youre name.

'My Lord Dominus Don.' Amongst other traces of monastic influence, that have survived more than fourteen generations of continual change at Oxford and Cambridge, may be found this piece of elsewhere obsolete courtesy preserved in the title 'Don,' by which undergraduates colloquially designate any Master of Arts, or academical person, equal in degree to a Master of Arts, who is invested with any university or collegiate authority over gownsmen *in statu pupillari*.

Whilst the regular clergy were thus addressed as nobles, no such deference was shown to the secular priests, who would have deemed themselves the object of ironical insult had any one called them 'Lords' or 'Dons.' The monks were 'lords;' but the most usual title of courtesy for a parish-priest was 'sire' or 'sir'— a designation which Chaucer applies indifferently to his knight, clerk, monk, and man of law, and which seems to have been accorded by medieval etiquette to all persons of social respectability, whatever their degrees. Of course, 'sir' thus used was no indication of knightly rank; and in this sense it was very generally given to the members of the inferior

> Whether I shal call you my lord *Dan John*,
> Or *Dan Thomas*, or elles *Dan Albon !*
> Of what hous be ye, by your father kin.'

In the same spirit Chaucer's Shipmanne ennobles the monk about whom he speaks. Thus:—

> 'This noble monk, of which I you devise,
> Hath of his abbot, as him list, licence
> (Because he was a man of high prudence,
> And else an officer out for to ride,
> To seen his granges, and his birnes wide,)
> And unto Seint Denis he cometh anon,
> Who was so welcome as my lord Dan John,
> Our dere cousin, ful of curtesie?'

The best editors of Chaucer spell *Don* with *a*—DAN. Whether Chaucer, or his transcribers or his editors, are chargeable with this peculiarity of orthography I have not troubled myself to inquire; but, however spelt or misspelt, the word is 'Don,' for 'Dominus.' No single letter has more frequently been changed for another particular letter, by transcribers of old MSS., than *o* for *a*. In small-letter writing, when the *o* appears in the body of a word, the stroke connecting it with the next letter usually makes it so much like an *a*, that it is often mistaken for the latter character. Perhaps Chaucer's Dan is Don miswritten or misread.

clergy, who, far from priding themselves upon the customary right to the title, preferred to be addressed by the mention of their academic status. In times subsequent to the Reformation, parochial clergymen, ignorant of the ancient disesteem for the clerical 'sirs,' sometimes insisted on their right to be 'sirred,' under the comically erroneous impression that the appellation was originally granted to priests as an indication that they ranked with knights. But in feudal England, when the custom first prevailed, every parson, vicar, or other curate, instead of regarding this 'sireship' as an honour to be stickled for, rather construed it as a sign of insignificance in the clerical person, who could be described by no brighter distinction than a title currently accorded to every person having even the slightest tincture of letters. The significance of 'sir,' as applied to clerical persons in the fourteenth century, does not differ widely from the meaning of the word when applied, at the present time, by epistolary etiquette to persons rather beneath the rank of gentlemen. Under these circumstances parish-priests rather avoided than courted the appellation; and whenever a curate, educated at a university, had attained any academic status above that of pupillage, he was addressed as Master or Doctor — or Sir Master, or Sir Doctor — according to his scholastic rank.*

Bachelors of Arts, being university students *in statu pupillari*, when in orders, seem for some time to have been designated 'sir' without any allusion to their condition of pupillage; but after the Reformation, it seems that Bachelors of Arts were addressed as 'sirs,' within the limits of their universities. Thus used as an academic distinction, the 'sir' had a more complimentary significance than when applied in earlier time to parish priests, who had either received no university education, or had not taken a degree; and it is most probable that the mode in which it was employed at Oxford and Cambridge was a chief cause of its retention amongst clerical titles* so late as the time of George the First. Indeed, it is more than

---

* The parliamentary records of the fifteenth century contain instances of the use of this title, as the formal mode of describing a parish-priest.

likely that this later and more honourable use of 'sir' at the universities—to designate the class of scholars intervening betwixt undergraduates and dons, who, though still *in statu pupillari*, had taken a degree, and therefore savoured of donship—led in some parts of the country to a revival of the clerical title, which in the days close before the Reformation had become a term of reproach. The lowest point of its general disesteem was reached in the sixteenth century, when to call a clergyman 'sir' was equivalent to denouncing him as an illiterate fellow, without university standing or scholarship, who was a discredit to the sacred vocation. At this period of its absolute ignominy, the title was commonly joined with the Christian name John—a name which, in past time, became, from unknown causes, a byeword for contempt in several European countries besides England. And when 'Sir' and 'John' had both become terms of contempt, 'Sir John' was the opprobrious nickname for untaught and disreputable curates.

It is a nice question of etymology whether the familiar title 'Mister' or 'Mr.' is referable to 'magister'—a person having *more* power than others, and hence their *master;* or to the Norman form of address, 'mon seigneur' from the Latin 'senior'—a person entitled to the homage accorded from the most ancient days by the young to their natural elders. Of course, it is from 'senior' that we derive 'seigneur,' in its numerous variations of spelling, and its abbreviation 'sir;' by the light of which familiar derivation we see that 'sir' was at its origin identical in force with the Saxon 'ealdorman,' still retained in the municipal title 'alderman,' and the more widely used appellation 'elder.' But it is open to discussion whether Mr. (mister) is 'mon seigneur' or 'magister.' My own opinion is, that each of the explanations is right; and that either history of the term may be upheld, according as the speaker chooses to use the title in a scholastic or feudal sense. Regarded as a

---

* Fuller, in his 'Church History,' says, 'More Sirs than Knights. Such priests as have the addition of "Sir" before their Christian name were men not graduated in the University, being in orders, but not in degrees; whilst others, entitled "Masters," had commenced in arts.'

legacy from the medieval schoolmen, the term is unquestionably referable to 'master;' regarded as a remnant of domestic feudalism, it is no less clearly traceable to 'senior.' This ingenious controversy about a word is of some small service to inquirers into the social life of old time, from the demonstration it affords that the scholastic 'master' (though something more honourable than 'sir' in the estimation of schoolmen) was almost the exact equivalent, as a measure of respect, to the 'monseigneur' and 'sir' of non-academic life, until the colloquial abbreviation of 'senior' dropped into disrespect, through its universal association with a disrespected section of the clergy.

The light, moreover, which a careful consideration of the clerical ' don,' 'master,' and ' sir,' throws upon the social relations of the medieval clergy is by no means unimportant. In the middle ages 'titles' were of far greater significance than they are now, though no one can urge that they have become mere idle sounds. The jealousy with which the superior members of feudal society insisted on the due recognition and observance of their claims to titles of honour, is of itself conclusive testimony of the great effect and importance of the distinctive appellations; and there is an enormous mass of corroborative evidence, showing that, far from being mere devices for the gratification of individual vanity, titles of honour in the feudal epoch were no less significant of the esteem in which their bearers wished to be held, than valuable as means for exacting social homage. The liberality of modern society has effected such a change in this respect, that whilst mere titular rank, disconnected from the possession of direct parliamentary influence, retains only the vestiges of its original favour and faculty in the circles of intellect, refinement, and power; though satirists are still not without justification in facts when they ridicule the proneness of our opulent middle classes to fawn with servile obsequiousness on the lowest representatives of hereditary *noblesse;* and though it cannot be denied that the splendour of an Irish or Scotch peer's merely titular nobility continues to daze the intellectual vision of provincial residents.

But whatever respect inferior persons now cherish for men of lordly style, was felt with tenfold force by the ordinary members of feudal society. The man by courtesy called 'my lord,' and the man to whom conciliatory deference could offer no grander title than 'sir,' appeared to the average feudal Englishman as persons belonging to two perfectly distinct social spheres. The gap between the two was at least as wide and clearly marked as the difference that exists at the present time between an opulent country squire and his chief tenants. When, therefore, we find medieval society habitually styling clergymen of one kind 'noble,' and clergymen of another kind merely 'respectable,'—addressing the one sort as 'my lords,' and the other as 'my good elders,' or 'my reverend sirs,'—we may rest assured, that whilst the more highly distinguished priests were esteemed very great personages, the clergy of the less honoured sort were held to be only a few degrees above commonality.

A proof of the social value set on the donship of the monks is found in the assumption of the title by the chief teachers, and subsequently by all the scholastically employed masters, of the universities, which became the chief schools of the secular clergy at an early date of the feudal epoch. 'Dons' became cheap and common at Oxford in the fourteenth century, when a famous occupant of the theological chair had established in the public mind a connexion between the honourable prefix and an university professor. This celebrated teacher was entitled in courtesy to the designation 'Don,' by virtue of his brother-hood with the Minorite Friars; and no sooner had he made his voice heard from his professorial chair, than rumours spread far and wide of his learning, subtlety, and eloquence. No one can state the nationality of this famous man. Some historians maintain that he was an Irishman; others are no less positive that he was a Scotchman; and whilst he is thus assigned to each of the sister kingdoms, the probability is that he was of English birth as well as English education. 'Myth' has been busy with his personal story, and at least one of the wildest achievements of his mythical biographers has obtained credence wherever his fame endures. Whilst his surname gave rise to the story of his Scotch extraction, its misleading prefix, 'Duns,' inspired an annalist to assert that the renowned dialectician was a native of Dunstance, in the parish of Embleton, in Northumberland. Another authority, working in the same fashion, assures us that the great man was not born at Embleton in Northumberland, but at *Dunse* in Berwickshire. Whether he was or was not born at either of these places I cannot affirm; but I have no hesitation in saying, that both of the personal stories are nothing better than manifest and ludicrous biographic fictions, in so far as they concur in representing that the teacher derived his first name from the place of his birth. His rightful Christian name was *John*, the popular byword for dulness and perversity; and, consequently, when Scotus became the famous Oxford lecturer, his disciples preferred to omit the opprobrious Christian name, when speaking of their profoundly learned and luminous instructor. Prefacing his surname with the title of lordship, which attached to him as a monastic person, they called him Don Scotus; and when thousands of clamorous and excited students shouted forth the name of their beloved teacher, with quick and reiterated utterance, the Don was soon softened into Dun, and Don Scotus became Dun Scotus,—whence Duns Scotus, and subsequently, by scornful opponents, Dunce Scotus. Hence 'dunce,' *i.e.* a fool, and 'don,' *i.e.* a learned teacher, are the same word, variously pronounced. That 'dunce' was derived from the derisive mention of Duns Scotus, is a matter known to everybody; but hitherto, I believe, all writers about Duns Scotus, and all collectors of etymological curiosities, have overlooked the true history of Scotus's first name, and the very singular fact, that, through its application to the most learned and brilliant scholar of the thirteenth century, the ancient and still retained designation of an academic professor became the distinctive title of a blockhead.

At the close of these remarks on ancient forms of clerical address, notice may be fitly taken of the recent discontinuance of a formerly universal use of 'sir'—a use so similar to its original and respectful application to parish-priests, as to be almost identical with it. Long before clerical 'sirs' dropped into contempt, and until they began to fall into disesteem, the 'sir' was accorded to the secular pastor as an expression of affectionate and reverential regard. In this sense the term was still often applied to pious ministers in Chaucer's period, when formal politeness also accorded it to all secular clergymen, without reference to exceptional desert, and to members of every social grade, from the king on his throne to the lawyer at his desk, or the apothecary in his medicine-room. Long ere it became the special appellation of knights, or had gained a reproachful significance from the peculiar demerits of one class of persons, the title was given to all whom courtesy recognised as social elders. In this sense it had much the same force as 'father,' which the Russian peasant still applies to the pastor of his village, and the Czar, whom he reverences as God's vicegerent; and which the Irish peasantry still accord with religious attachment to Catholic priests. Thus employed, the term was assigned to all persons supposed to be worthy of the tender respect felt by generous youth to honourable years,—as Sir Lord, Sir Monk, Sir Knight, Sir Priest, and, with especial emphasis, Sir King. From this signification the word derived a still closer and sweeter sense, in which it means 'nearest male progenitor.' With natural love of old usage, we still make frequent use of the word in its old sense. The king is still addressed as 'sire;' in letters we still use 'sir' freely to persons of widely different ranks, lay and clerical. But though 'sire' will always continue to be synonymous with 'father,' sons have very generally, if not universally, ceased to address their fathers as 'sir.' Very many, if not the majority, of Englishmen, now in the middle term of life, were trained in boyhood to appeal to their fathers, in oral conversation no less than in writing, by this old-world title. But at the present time I am not aware that I know a single family in which the boys are taught to call their father 'sir.' Sons in the last century almost invariably commenced epistles to their sires with 'Honoured Sir,' for which form 'Dear Sir' was substituted in the earlier part of the present century, as being less frigid and distant: and now the 'Dear Sir,' though not seldom retained in epistolary style, has very generally given place to 'Dear Father,' the term of address universally employed by sons in speech made to their sires. It is possible that a century or more hence, persons curious about past social usages will be interested in learning the precise time when this change occurred; and so that those persons may not misjudge their ancestors of to-day, it is well to record that the change was no consequence of filial disrespect, but was the result of the general desire felt by fathers for closer companionship with their offspring.

CHAPTER VII.

CLERICAL MORALS.

WHEN an historical inquirer endeavours to form an estimate of the mental and moral worth of the secular clergy of Chaucer's England he experiences no slight difficulty in dealing with a mass of conflicting evidence, and in assigning their respective measures of credibility to various witnesses who, speaking doubtless with a conscientious desire to tell the truth, testify strongly against or in favour of the parochial priesthood. Much of the testimony is drawn from satirical literature; and as it is the practice of satire to give prominence to the reprehensible, whilst taking only incidental notice of the redeeming, characteristics of the classes which it censures, the student is often at a loss to decide when the pungent invective of censorious scribes may be taken as protests against merely exceptional evils, and when it may be fairly supposed to indicate very general, if not universal depravity;— how far it is guilty of those humorous exaggerations, which endow satirical compositions with their strongest piquancy, and how far its statements are veracious in letter as well as spirit. Again, nearly all the contemporary witnesses were vehement partisans; and, even when thoroughly honest in purpose, vehement party-men are so prone to overstate the merits of their friends, and magnify the faults of their opponents, that, notwithstanding their simple design to be servants of the truth, they are very often most misleading guides. Hence it is that the reader, who would arrive at a fair notion of the parochial clergy of the fourteenth century, must trouble himself to weigh and compare nicely the conflicting depositions of Lollard enthusiasts and priestly advocates; to discharge the functions of a judge between satirists who saw little but corruption in the sacerdotal order, and recriminators who maintained that the accusers of the clergy were utterly mendacious vituperators, inspired by malignant animosity against holy men, and by rebellious discontent with all existing institutions. At first the labour of discriminating between the true and the false of the adverse testimonies seems hopelessly arduous; but, by vigilant and sedulous exercise of the critical faculties, the impartial investigator discerns, at least, something of the truth that lies midway between extreme statements on the one side, and extravagant assertions on the other.

Most persons, who examine the story of our feudal church in this spirit of intelligent and dispassionate inquiry, will come to the conclusion that, whilst the priests of the parishes were by no means so ignorant, and lethargic, and grossly immoral, as many writers have inferred from a hasty consideration of portions of the evidence respecting them, the clergy of all grades, in a very large number of cases, justified the praise poured upon them by monkish eulogists.

That a considerable number of the parochial 'sirs' were thoroughly worldly men I have no doubt; that a still larger number, perhaps a majority, of them were men who, without being absolutely depraved or devoid of conscience, were strongly tinctured with worldliness, I also regard as a definitely established fact: but it is also a matter of the clearest certainty, that the age in which Wycliffe lashed the vices of the curates,* whom he indignantly charged with avarice, gluttony, drunkenness, profanity, and childish delight in frivolous amusements, was an age that witnessed the pious, laborious, and spotless lives of

* 'The ninth error is, that they waste poor men's goods on rich furs, and costly clothes, and worldly array, feasts of rich men, and in gluttony, drunkenness, and in lechery. For they sometimes pass great men in their gay furs and precious clothes. They have fat horses, with gay saddles and bridles. St. Bernard crieth, Whatever curates hold of the altar more than a simple livelihood and clothing, is not theirs, but other men's.'— *Vide* Wycliffe's 'Office of Curates.' Further on in his indictment of curates the Reformer says, 'They take their worldly mirth, hawking, hunting, and doing other vanities, and suffer wolves of hell to strangle men's souls by many cursed sins. They should draw men from worldly vanities; .... but now, the more a curate hath, the more he wasteth in costly feeding of hounds and hawks, suffering poor men to have great default of meat, and drink, and clothes.—XV. The fifteenth is, that they haunt taverns out of measure, and stir up laymen to drunkenness, idleness, and cursed swearing, chiding, and fighting. For they will not follow earnestly in their spi-

thousands of village-pastors, any one of whom would, in the present time, be deemed zealous to a fault, and chargeable with puritanical averseness to earthly pleasures.

Like their brethren of the regular orders, the richer seculars of the worldly kind imitated the ways of the feudal aristocracy, and spent much of their superfluous means on horses, hounds, hawks, and equestrian accoutrements of costly materials and sumptuous workmanship. Living in a period that delighted in external display, when persons of every social grade were far more prone than the vainer folk of our time to 'pinch the belly for the sake of the back,' many of them were careful that their canonical attire should be made of the richest fabrics, and in the newest fashions of ecclesiastical millinery. Much of the gloom which the popular imagination attributes to medieval society arises from the erroneous notion that the feudal priests were, like our modern clergy, an uniformly 'black-coated gentry;' whereas the ecclesiastical persons of the thirteenth and fourteenth centuries were no less remarkable than the ecclesiastical ceremonies and the internal adornments of churches for brightness, warmth, and diversity of colour. Gorgeousness, and splendour akin to gorgeousness, were amongst the chief characteristics of their strictly sacred vestments; and, in addition to their sacerdotal raiment, which shone and glittered in the pompous processions with which the feudal church attracted and delighted its votaries, they decorated themselves with the gaudy hoods and flowing robes that indicated their varieties of academic standing and ecclesiastical preferment. Some of them wore

---

ritual office, after Christ and His apostles. Therefore they resort to plays at tables, chess, and hazard, and roar in the streets, and sit at the tavern till they have lost their wits, and then chide, and strive, and fight sometimes. And sometimes they have neither eye, nor tongue, nor hand, nor foot, to help themselves for drunkenness. By this example the ignorant people suppose that drunkenness is no sin: but he that wasteth most of poor men's goods at taverns, making himself and other men drunken, is most praised for courtesy, goodness, freeness, and nobleness.'—*Vide* 'Office of Curates.' This mention of the way in which 'ignorant people'—a term comprising gentle as well as simple persons—regarded the proceedings of the worldly and free-living clergy, is noteworthy, as one of the numerous pieces of evidence found in Wycliffe's writings, that, outside the growing body of Lollard precisioners, the social sentiment of the fourteenth century was not at all scandalised by the men who are now usually deemed the clerical delinquents of the period.

green gowns, others dazzled the spectator with their trains of scarlet silk; and, not content with their sufficiently showy canonicals and academicals, the clerical fops of the cathedral towns, risking censure and punishment, sometimes displayed jewelled baldricks and slashed clothes under the folds of their outward raiment, and exhibited themselves in the public streets with swords at their sides, and the most fashionably-pointed shoes on their feet.*

These extravagancies of attire were, doubtless, the exceptional excesses of our friends, 'the ordained laymen;' who, whilst holding two or three fat livings, resided chiefly in the cathedral towns, where they had no lack of congenial acquaintance, and busied themselves with legal practice in the ecclesiastical courts, with the fomentation of intrigues in bishops' households, or with the discharge of light routine duties in cathedrals. Still they are excesses that illustrate the general disposition of the world-loving curates to assume the tone, and to consort with the most frivolous members, of gay society.

---

* The author of 'The Ploughman's Complaint' has preserved for us many of the details of clerical foppery which Wycliffe denounced:—

'*Griffon.* What canst thou preach
    against chanons,
That men chepen seculere?
  Pelican. They ben curates of many
    tounes,
On earth they have great powere,
They have some great prebends and
    dere,
Some two or three, and some mo:
A personage to ben a playing fere,
And yet they serve the king also.

    *   *   *

Bucklers brode, and swordes long,
Baudriko, with basclardes kene,
Soch toles about hir necke they hong:
With Antichrist soche priests been.
Upon her deedes it is well seen
Whom they serven, whom they ho-
    nouren;

Antichrists they been clene,
And Goddes goodes falsely devouren.

Of scarlet and grene gai gounes,
That mote bee shape of the newe;
To clippen and kissen they counted in
    tounes
The damosels that to the daunce sewe;
Cutted clothes to shewe her hewe,
With long pikes on her shone.
Our Goddes gospel is not true,
Either they serve the devill or none.

Now been priestes pokes so wide
That men must enlarge the vestiment;
The holy gospel they doen hide,
For they contrarien in raiment.
Such priestes of Lucifer been sent,
Like conquerors they have been araied,
The proud pendentes at . . . ipent,
Falsely the truth they have betraied.'

His disapproval of the cardinal's hat (a gaudy covering similar to the headdress of a professional musician or stage-player in the fourteenth century,

The clergyman, who thus spent his substance on stables and rich housings, on kennels and mews, on furs and silks, was an habitual frequenter of taverns as well as of rich men's feasts. At the latter he took a not conspicuous place amongst guests of good estate and gentle lineage, who, though they were well pleased to exchange social courtesies with a hard-riding pluralist rector, never lost sight of the fact that he belonged to the inferior order of clergy, and, notwithstanding his many personal merits, was 'only a secular.' But at the chief ale-house of his parish he was a far greater man; and there he spent the greater portion of his leisure, gossiping with blunt yeomen and their outspoken wives, playing at chess or tables with persons either of, or not greatly beneath, his social degree, and sharing a stoup of wine with a landed squire, or the rector of a neighbouring parish. The ale-house was, in fact, his club, where he learned the news of the country from the constant stream of wayfarers, and where, when not out with his dogs and falcons, or in the pursuit of some rural sport, he was ordinarily to be found by persons seeking him either for business or for pleasure. It would be unjust to charge him with habitual sottishness because he thus constantly took his ease in the inn, which he more frequently entered in the pursuit of society than from a morbid appetite for strong drink. Still we are assured by Wycliffe, that the

and first assigned to cardinals by Innocent IV.) the Ploughman declares in these words:—

'For Christ made never no cathedrals,
Ne with Him was no cardinall,
With a redde hatle, as usen minstrals;
But falshed foule moute it befall.'

The insinuation that cathedrals are, to a certain extent, to be regarded as Satanic devices, because our Saviour never built a Gothic church, belongs to a family of arguments in vogue with those denouncers of ecclesiastical corruption who urge that the bishop who rides in a decent carriage must be a servant of Antichrist, *because* none of the apostles kept a coach and liveried servants.

With respect to clerical dress at this period, Mr. Thorold Rogers observes,— 'It does not seem that ecclesiastics and persons of gravity affected sombre colours, though the statutes of some monasteries proscribed russet or dark cloth. Bloxham, for instance, who was warden of Merton between the years 1375 and 1387, aff·cted green, white, red, and scarlet cloth, though he was certainly in orders, having graduated as Bachelor of Divinity.'— *Vide* 'History of Agriculture and Prices.'

Part I.—Wycliffe's England.

reverend gentleman often retired from the tavern with an unsteady gait; that sometimes he failed to complete his homeward journey through sudden incapacity to make another step; and that now and then, when his potations had not robbed him of the power of walking, he would startle his parishioners by trolling a stave, or 'roaring' in the streets.

At the risk of incurring a momentary suspicion of flippancy, I have spoken thus lightly of the most repulsive vice largely prevalent amongst the clergy of Wycliffe's England; but no attentive reader of these volumes will, I trust, find any difficulty in believing that my assumed levity has a grave purpose. I wish to put in the most offensive light the most revolting characteristic of these ancient world-loving priests, in order that the worst moral fault* that can be fairly charged on any large number of them may be seen distinctly, and remembered with proper resentment. Of another immorality, more degrading and abominable even than sottishness, which is generally supposed to have been scandalously common in every grade of the ecclesiastics of the fourteenth century, I am satisfied that they were comparatively, though not entirely, innocent. No doubt, amongst the monks, the mendicants, the seculars, there were black sheep, who were restrained neither by fear of God, nor respect for women, from habitual indulgence in the most odious of all fleshly sins; but such unspeakably scandalous persons were few. The strongest denouncers of clerical incontinence were Papal

* Most unjust inferences have been drawn from the words of annalists and official documents concerning the morals of the medieval clergy. Because William of Newburgh records that in the twelfth century social order was often disturbed by 'thefts, rapines, and homicides,' perpetrated by clerks, it has been inferred that such outrages were affairs of daily occurrence amongst priests, by writers who would have shown sounder judgment had they reminded their readers that the ecclesiastical class of that period comprised throngs of unappointed clerks, who were neither priests in rank nor religious men in any but a formal sense, and that the disorders mentioned by the chronicler were doubtless, for the most part, done by these obscure camp-followers of the clerical army. In like manner, because Edward the Fourth's charter, giving the ecclesiastical authorities jurisdiction over clerical offenders, enumerates with needful legal accuracy such crimes as treasons, murders, rapes, robberies, thefts, it has been supposed that archbishops, bishops, priests, deacons, and other persons in holy orders, were constantly engaged in the perpetration of the said enormities and breaches of law, and that the charter was extorted from the Crown to secure them from adequate punishment for their scandalous proceedings.

partisans, whose violent assertions against the domestic morality of ecclesiastical persons were directed at the lawful wives of married priests; and mainly from the misinterpreted language of these abusive censors has sprung the popular misconception, that it was a common thing, in the thirteenth and fourteenth centuries, for a village-priest to commit the crime which is most repugnant to virtuous women. The contemporary satirists were wont to stigmatise the friars as habitual breakers of the seventh commandment, but I am disposed to think, that on this point the satirists stated far more than they could have proved; and however just such charges may have been in the case of the mendicant orders, I am satisfied that they were totally inapplicable to the majority of the parochial ministers. But that sottishness was sadly prevalent amongst the worldly parish-priests is certified by the concurrent testimony of their friends and foes, their accusers and apologists.

From the commencement of the twelfth century, when Anselm, by one of his synodal decrees, ordered that 'priests should not resort to taverns or banquets, nor sit drinking by the fireside,' down to the earlier decades of the seventeenth century, when rectors were deemed wanting in loyalty to the crown and devotion to the church if they did not habitually drink a morning-cup, in the sight of their parishioners, to the confusion of the Puritans and all other enemies of good government, the great difficulty of every zealous bishop was to check the tavern-haunting propensities of his clergy. No peruser of our ecclesiastical annals can fail to see, that alike under the Plantagenets and the Tudors, the country clergy were habitual frequenters of ale-houses. In 1536, Henry VIII.[*] only repeated an injunction, that hundreds of bishops had vainly uttered before him, when he ordered his clergy to spend over the Scriptures the time which they daily squandered over

---

[*] The words of his highness's injunction on this point are, 'Also the said dean, parsons, vicars, curates, and other priests, shall in no wise, at any unlawful time, nor for any other cause than for their honest necessity, haunt or resort to any taverns or ale-houses; and after their dinner and supper they shall not give themselves to drinking and riot, spending their time idly, by day or by night, at tables or cards-playing, or any other unlawful game: but at such times as they shall have such leisure, they shall read or hear somewhat of holy scripture, or shall occupy themselves with some honest exercise.'

pots of ale. Using almost its exact words, Edward VI. renewed his father's injunction ;* and when the leaders of ecclesiastical reform had fled the country to escape the Marian persecution, Cardinal Pole ordered his bishops to make inquiry 'whether the said parsons, vicars, or curates, do haunt taverns or alehouses, increasing thereby infamy and slander, or no.'

It should, however, be borne in mind that, in frequenting taverns and ale-houses, the medieval clergy merely did what the most respectable laity of all social grades were wont to do. In our own time the village inn is no place of daily resort for any persons, except the habitually idle, the flagrantly dissolute, and the gossiping wastrels of the lower classes. But the case was very different throughout the feudal period, and the generations of the transition from feudalism to quite modern society. In Wycliffe's England, as well as in days long before and long after the Reformer's time, the tavern was the common club— literally the *public*-house—where the knight, the squire, the yeoman, the bailiff, the tradesman, met daily for the delights of neighbourly intercourse ; and though the Lollards regarded it as a place of carnal pleasure and temptation, public opinion, disdainfully opposed to the puritanical crotchets of Lollardy, was strongly in favour of the modest hostelry as a social institution, that contributed to the enjoyment of men of all degrees. When, therefore, the bishops ordered their clergy to spend less

---

* Of the tavern-haunting habits of King Edward's Irish clergy, Bishop Bale wrote.—'Upon Ascension Day I preached again at Kilkenny, likewise on Trinity Sunday, and on St. Peter's Day at Midsummer. On the 25th of July, the priests were as pleasantly disposed as might be, and went by heaps from tavern to tavern, to seek the best Rob Davie and aqua vitæ, which are their especial drinks there. They caused all their cups to be filled in with " *Gaudeamus in dolio* ;" the mystery thereof only known to them, and at that time to none other else. Which was, that King Edward was dead, and that they were in hope to have up their masking masses again.' Scarcely had these Irish priests gained their wish, when, in Queen Mary's first year of reign, some of the pious inhabitants of Maidstone were discussing the conduct of their curate, John Daye, concerning whom John Halle wrote to John Foxe,—' And thus in a furye he flung from them to the alehouse, whych he so much frequentyth that he veray often goyth home dronke, scant able to speak or stand on his legs : yea, drynkynge, bowsing, cardying, and table-playing is all his hole holy exarsyse all the weke from tyme to tyme. This brefely for this tyme, but I meane that ye shall shortely have a copye of owr supplycacion, whych we meane shortely to make to my lorde of Cantorbury, wherin ye shall more at large understand the lyfe and behaveour of this monster.'

time in ale-houses, it is not to be inferred that the bishops regarded those places of entertainment as necessarily vicious and scandalous; the fair inference from the episcopal injunction being, that the chiefs of the church wished to impress on the subordinate priests that the obligations of the clerical office required them to exercise forbearance with respect to social enjoyments. In like manner, drunkenness—which was unquestionably a clerical failing in this old stage of society—must not be regarded as the distinguishing and peculiar vice of parochial ecclesiastics. However much it prevailed amongst the world-loving clergy—who, notwithstanding their worldliness, retained as a class some sense of decorum and professional duty—inebriety was far more general amongst the laity.

The same view must be taken of the other failings of the priests, whose worldliness roused Wycliffe's indignation. Love of fine clothes, proneness to gluttony, inordinate devotion to the pleasures of the chase, were the almost universal characteristics of the society in which they passed their lives; and far from condemning the clerical sympathy with and participation in the prevailing tastes, respectable laymen were well pleased to obtain for their favourite diversions the ecclesiastical sanction that was implied by the presence of richly attired clergymen in the hunting-field and at the tavern-table. Instead of feeling that priests were out of place in such scenes, the laity were cordially pleased to see them there: just as the country squires and superior yeomanry of fifty years since cherished hearty admiration for well-mounted rectors, who could keep well ahead in a smart run across country; and for the vicar or curate who could play a judicious game at whist, or enliven a Christmas party with a comic song. In the last hundred years great changes have occurred in our social tastes and usages; and the somewhat coarser worldliness of our great-grandsires has been replaced by a worldliness abounding in elegant and graceful diversions, of which they knew either nothing or little. The keen appetite for three bottles of fruity port has disappeared, and been followed by the critical taste for a single bottle of a lighter, more costly, and more exquisitely flavoured vintage. Though hunting clergymen, like lay huntsmen, are much fewer than they were a century since, clergymen who kill grouse on the moors, or take out licenses to shoot pheasants, partridges, and hares, are not less numerous. The superfluous means which some of the affluent country rectors of Georgian England expended on inordinately large stables, costly kennels, and heavy banquets to all their nearest neighbours, many of the rich beneficed clergy of the Victorian epoch expend on greenhouses, the care of highly ornamental grounds, artistic curiosities, choice editions of quaint books, and delicate repasts to the most refined and graceful of their acquaintance. The bowling-green has been superseded by the croquet-ground; the seat of the hunting-saddle has been exchanged for the seat of a luxurious Long Acre carriage. But though it is more expressive of the qualities of a highly polite society, who can say that the New is less worldly than the Old Worldliness?

Let it not be supposed that I am slily preferring a charge of unworthy action against the wealthier and more aristocratic of our existing clergy. Nothing is further from my object than to raise any question that may be answered to their disfavour. For myself, I am so far a worldling, in a deliberate and philosophic sense of the word, that I am slow to discern evil in the kinds of worldliness against which nothing worse can be proved than that they are so agreeable as to be very general. What are ordinarily called worldly pleasures, though often productive of incidental ill, seem to my worldly eyes to be, upon the whole, largely conducive to the intellectual vigour and moral health of mankind; and, far from wishing to see the official guardians of religion and morality refrain with stern asceticism from the pleasures of this life, I hold that they are both acting within their proper sphere, and doing good service to their fellow-men, when, by open participation in social enjoyments, they proclaim the inherent innocence of worldly things, and when by their moderation in periods of social excitement they demonstrate the manner in which Christian people should regard and share in transitory pleasures. But whilst one section of our clergy expresses a general concurrence in this view of earthly enjoyment, there is another section, composed of men whose piety and usefulness are no less admirable than their opponents', that condemns even temperate participation in purely social and innocently frivolous amusements.

The members of this party, with greater or less unanimity and consistency, abstain on principle from all diversions that have no direct and close connexion with strictly religious interests. Whilst refraining from the perusal of nearly all imaginative literature, except tales and poems written solely to illustrate moral truths or special theological opinions, and regarding secular music as fraught with dangerous influences, they regard the amusements of the ball-room, the theatre, and the card-room, with such repugnance, as sources of moral hurt, that they do not hesitate to condemn all promoters and countenancers of the obnoxious diversions in terms of severest disapprobation. For the very many excellent clergymen who play whist, frequent theatres, and give dancing-parties, they express a righteous sorrow and abhorrence, identical in nature with the more outspoken hostility which Wycliffe declared for the clergy of the fourteenth century, who either loved the world immoderately or encouraged social arrangements that very often resulted in immoderate devotion to earthly pleasures. That this party does not monopolise all the goodness of the land it is needless to say: but no thoughtful or generous opponent can refuse to render homage to its sincerity and richness in virtue. Perhaps the majority of our educated classes are its conscientious adversaries, but the party is strong in numbers, organization, wealth, and intelligence; and as a party protesting against the worldliness of the period it bears strong resemblance to the Wycliffian party of Chaucer's England, although it has not the slightest tincture of, or respect for, the political tenets of Lollardy.

To attempt to define the influence and usefulness of this party, to show where it errs and in what particulars it is in the right, to hold the judicial scales betwixt its numerous members and its many opponents, would be an act of presumption, of which I am not likely to be guilty. But it may be permitted to an illustrator of past manners to urge, that by reference to and examination of the composition and relations of these two prominent sections of existing society, the student may obtain the light in which he should read much of what the ordinary orthodox Churchmen, and the zealous reformers of Wycliffe's period, have put on record about themselves and their adversaries. Just as we find that much real piety separated from excessive zeal, much active Christian kindliness expressed in other ways than those most acceptable to the philanthropic platform, and an abundance of jealous regard for social morality, may be observed in the ranks of those large classes whom certain moralists denounce, with at best only partial justice, as given over to worldliness, and whom the greatest satirist of our age has designated as one vast Vanity Fair, so I doubt not there were fine forces of piety, and good taste, and pure human affection, in that multitude of clerical persons and 'ignorant people,' against whose worldliness the Rector of Lutterworth very properly and nobly protested.

Turning at length from the darker aspects of clerical morals in the fourteenth century, and regarding the brighter features of the subject, we find abundant proof that Wycliffe's England had parish-priests for whom any land might be thankful. It is a strong fact for these parochial seculars, that their splendid fame for devoutness and zeal, for ardent love of their flocks and abundant learning, proceeds from the mouths of the boldest and most incisive denouncers of clerical lukewarmness. Since Wycliffe and Chaucer, the Lollard divine and the Lollard poet, concur in admitting the existence, and extolling the worth, of these exemplary pastors, we cannot overrate the excellence that extorted praise from such censors.*

---

* Stronger than his more direct testimony to the existence of much piety amongst the parochial clergy, is the force of Wycliffe's incidental admissions that the priests were not so totally given over to sloth and corruptness as many writers have inferred from the Reformer's indignant censures of prodigious evils. For instance, the opening words of his famous and violent arraignment of the ordinary priests contain a word of suggestive exception. 'The office,' began the enthusiastic accuser, 'of curates is ordained of God: *few* do it well, and many full evil. Therefore test we their defaults, with God's help.' Even in the fierceness of his wrath he could not be guilty of the injustice of saying '*None* do it well.' Again, in the 'Short Rule of Life,' the Reformer's picture of what a priest ought to be— read with reference to the other pictures, with which it is grouped—is seen to be a picture of many a worthy priest known to the author :—' If thou art a priest, and especially a curate,' runs the admonitory sketch, ' live thou holily, surpassing other men in holy prayer, desire, and thinking, in holy speaking, counselling, and true teaching. And that God's commands, His gospel and virtues, be ever in thy mouth; and ever despise sin to draw men therefrom; and that thy deeds be so rightful that no man shall blame them with reason, but that thy open deeds be a true book to all subjects and unlearned men, to serve God and do His commands thereby. For example of good life, open and lasting, more stirreth rude men than

Unlike the world-loving clergy, of whom enough has been said, the good parish-priest of Wycliffe's England was, for the fourteenth century, just such an example of simplicity, devoutness, and zeal, as the poor parson of the 'Deserted Village' was in the eighteenth. Content with the onerous duties and slender emolument of a single cure, he never left his home to seek additional preferment from bishop or lay-patron. Full of the learning of his university, he was well versed in the homely avocations of his parishioners, and gained their respect for his judgment by the knowledge which he displayed of husbandry and the employments of humble workmen. If his tithes yielded him an ample income, he spent on himself out of that income only enough for his sustenance, and distributed the surplus to the sick and needy. Not seldom the objects of his bounty were poor scholars, who required alms wherewith to defray the cost of residence at Oxford.* Whilst the hunting-clergy were

true preaching by word only. And waste not thy goods in great feasts of rich men, but live a humble life, of poor men's alms and goods, both in meat, and drink, and clothes; and the remainder give truly to poor men that have not of their own, and may not labour for feebleness or sickness; and thus thou shalt be a true priest to God and man.' Another instance from 'The Office of Curates,' a passage in which the Reformer may be thought to recognise a disposition, even amongst some of the world-loving clergy, to be good parsons, though he laments that this disposition is not strong enough to withstand adverse influences:— 'But the curate that gives himself to study holy writ and teach his parishioners to save their souls, and live in meekness, penance, and busy labour about spiritual things, and cares not about worldly respect and riches, is held to be a fool and destroyer of holy church. He is despised and persecuted by high-priests and prelates and their officers, and is hated by other curates. This makes many to be negligent in their spiritual cures, and to give themselves to occupations and business about worldly goods.'

* Chaucer says of this precursor of Sweet Auburn's pastor:—

'A good man there was of religioun,
That was a poure Persone of a toune;
But riche he was of holy thought and werk.
He was also a lerned man, a clerk,
That Christes gospel trewely wolde preche.
His parishens devoutly wolde he teche,
Benigne he was, and wonder diligent,
And in adversite ful patient;
And swiche he was ypreved often sithes.
Ful l th were him to cursen for his tithes,
But rather wolde he yeven out of doute,
Unto his poure parishens aboute,
Of his offring, and eke of his substance.
He coulde in litel thing have suffisance.
Wide was his parish, and houses far asonder,
But he ne left for no rain ne thonder,
In sicknesse and in mischief to visite
The ferrest in his parish, moche and lite,
Upon his fete, and in his hand a staf.
This noble ensample to his shepe he yaf,

following the hounds on their mettlesome horses, he denied himself even the luxury of a pony, and was daily seen walking on foot, with a devotional book in the breast of his girdled gown, and a staff in his hand, to visit bed-ridden or dying parishioners in the outlying townships of his cure. To sinners his reproofs were so eloquent of sweet, conciliatory pity for their perilous condition, that no one ever feared to lay before him the secret guilt of a burdened soul; but he was no such cautious time-server or timorous respecter of persons as to falter in rebuking his most powerful parishioners for misdeeds, in respect of which they had neither made atonement nor declared their repentance. Such were the parish-clergymen who may be termed the substance and salt of Wycliffe's party—that soundest section of the national clergy, that had been a power in the Church long before Wycliffe became its mouthpiece, and remained a stubborn and noble protest against Papal aggressiveness and ecclesiastical lukewarmness long after the ashes of Wycliffe's exhumed and charred bones had been cast into the crystal stream: —the party that rallied round Bishop Grosthead in the thirteenth, strengthened the strong hands of Henry in the sixteenth, and reached the fulness of triumph in the seventeenth century.

That first he wrought, and afterward he taught,
Out of the gospel he the wordes caught,
And this figure he added yet thereto,
That if golde ruste, what shuld iron do?
For if a priest be foule, on whom we trust,
No wonder is a lewd man to rust;
And shame it is, if that a preeste take kepe,
To see a shitten shepherd and clene shepe:
Wel ought a preest ensample for to yeve,
By his cleannesse, how his shepe shulde live.
He sette not his benefice to hire,
And lette his shepe acombred in the mire,
And ran unto London, unto Seint Poules,
To seken him a chanterie for soules,
Or with a brotherhede to be withhold,
But dwelt at home, and kepte wel his fold,
So that the wolf ne made it not miscarie.
He was a shepherd, and no mercenarie,
And though he holy were, and vertuous,
He was to sinful men not dispitious,
Ne of his speche dangerous ne digne,
But in his teching discrete and benigne.
To drawen folk to heven, with fairnesse,
By good ensample was his besinesse;
But it were any persone obstinate,
What so he were of high or low estat,
Him wolde he snibben sharply for the nones.
A better preeste I trowe that nowhere non is.
He waited after no pompe ne reverence,
Ne maked him no spiced conscience,
But Christes love and H's apostles twelve
He taught; but first he folwed it himselve.'—*Canterbury Tales.*

CHAPTER VIII.

MONEY AND LEARNING.

DIFFERING in tone and aim far more widely than the parochial clergy of our own time, the parish-priests of the fourteenth century were certainly not less remarkable than the ministers of modern time for the inequality with which the revenues of the Church were distributed amongst them. Notwithstanding the careful and methodical labour expended on farming, agriculture was still so far in its infancy that an acre of good arable land could not be made to yield more than a fourth of the amount of wheat that it nowadays produces with average husbandry; and in other respects the earth was proportionately less productive of things that had marketable value. So long as this was the case, the tithes of the most highly-cultivated and fertile parishes were of comparatively small amount. The tithes, moreover, small though they were in comparison with modern tithes, were frequently much in excess of what the officiating parties received. A considerable proportion of the livings, as we have seen, were held by non-resident pluralists — a very numerous class in Wycliffe's England; and wherever a living was thus in the hands of an absentee rector, his deputy — a priest who was at the same time a curate in the obsolete, and a curate in the modern, sense of the word — performed the chief ecclesiastical work of the parish, for a pitifully small remuneration. Again, of another very numerous class of parishes the tithes were either wholly or partly appropriated to the use of monasteries or other religious corporations. When the appropriation was complete, the religious house that absorbed the whole of the tithes usually provided for the spiritual service of the parish an indigent priest of the monastic or secular sort, who received from his employers no more than the customary stipend of a deputy-curate. When the appropriation, as was very often the case, left a small portion of the tithes for the maintenance of a parochial minister, who was termed the vicar, though the incumbent enjoyed a measure of independence, security, and consequent dignity, that made him, in a certain sense, the social superior of a curate-depute, he was seldom much richer than the ordinary clerical substitute for an absentee pluralist.

It is needless to remark, that these impropriations of tithes bore an appearance of injustice and injury to the parishes, from which considerable sums of money were thereby withdrawn for the benefit of more or less distant colleges. But in their favour it must be remembered, that some of these impropriations were effected by the original donors of the tithes, who, when endowing religion with gifts of their own free will, were acting quite within their right in naming the precise manner in which their donations of wealth should be expended. For the more numerous impropriations effected at later dates, through gifts of advowsons to religious corporations, a no less valid justification can be offered. It should be observed that, when judiciously made, as in most cases they were, these assignments of parochial revenues to expensive institutions, distant from the sources of revenue, tended greatly to the efficiency of the Church, and were, upon the whole, the immediate result of a policy aiming at a just, instead of a partial, distribution of ecclesiastical wealth. As institutions created for the good of the entire country, monasteries, cathedrals, and secular colleges with reason looked for support from remote districts. They were, in fact, the centres at which, for the spiritual good of society, it was desirable to expend year after year extraordinarily large sums of money on matters pertaining to religion; and in most cases the special localities, that were drained of tithes for the support of these central establishments, did not stand in real need of the whole of their ecclesiastical tenths for their own purposes. Amongst the present anomalies of our ecclesiastical system, perhaps the most conspicuous are the injurious inequalities which mark the distribution of the Church's revenues. Whilst the rector of a rural parish, on whose purse the claims of local indigence are trifling, has occasionally a thousand or two thousand a-year, the incumbent of a populous town very generally is hampered by want of funds for charitable use amongst the needy of his flock, or is even troubled by the insufficiency of his means to cover the expenses of his modest household. By observing the numerous evils that spring from this unsystematic disposal of our ecclesiastical revenues, which allows the Church to languish in crowded cities whilst it renders many of our rural and lightly-worked rectors wealthy beyond their proper requirements, thoughtful men have been led to extol the wisdom of that old method of impropriating tithes, which has been too unreservedly condemned by certain authorities. Indeed, our legislation has, in quite recent times, not only recognised the value of the principle of impropriation, but has empowered the Ecclesiastical Commissioners to act upon it, by applying to the augmentation of poor livings a portion of the wealth which accrues from preferments whose revenues from ancient sources are in great excess of their present needs. Every inordinately rich Crown living, whose surplus emoluments are thus redistributed by our ecclesiastical agents in Whitehall Place, is dealt with in the spirit that animated the old impropriators.

But though much may be said in favour of the impropriations of the feudal church, as arrangements just in principle and for the most part beneficent in result, the fact remains that they tended to the impoverishment of parish-priests, who, in the fourteenth century, were by no means a wealthy class of persons. A rector, in Wycliffe's England, if he had only one cure and no private means, was seldom 'better than comfortably off.' His tithes at best yielded him a narrow income, and, small as they were, he frequently had much difficulty in screwing them out of his reluctant parishioners, when he was of the worldly sort, and the farmers had imbibed the political principles of Lollardy, which encouraged men to think, if it did not expressly teach, that Christians were not bound to pay their tithes to unworthy priests, but might render them to any minister, who, though not officially appointed to receive them, proved his claim to them by works and doctrine.* That even Chaucer's mild and exemplary parson was sometimes compelled to wring his dues from the superstitious fears of intentional and contumacious defaulters, by cursing them, after the method or-

* Even the clergy, who sided with the Lollards, held and proclaimed views respecting tithes, that must have induced many a devout layman to infer that he might conscientiously withhold his tithe from a bad curate, so long as he paid the amount to a good one. Wycliffe says, in 'The Office of Curates,' 'The fifth default is, that they practise strife and plea, and gather envy and hate from laymen for tithes. They leave preaching of the gospel, and cry fast after tithes, and summon men to account, and by force take their goods, or else curse them seven foot above the earth, and seven foot under the earth, and seven foot on each side, and afterwards draw men to prison as though they were kings and emperors of men's bodies and goods; forgetting wholly the meekness and patience of Christ and His apostles, how they cursed not when men would neither give them meat nor drink nor harbour: but Christ blamed His apostles when they would have asked such vengeance, as the Gospel of St. Luke teaches.' With respect to tithes, like most other topics on which he disputed, Wycliffe's views changed as his vision became clearer and his enthusiasm for reform more ardent; but the evidence is abundant of his thinking that tithes might be withheld from unworthy priests, if they were otherwise devoted to God's service: a theory which most of the modern rectors, who applaud Wycliffe unreservedly without reading him, would certainly not approve, if they heard it uttered in the debating-club of a mechanics' reading-room. Another Lollard of this period, William Russel, commemorated in Foxe's 'Acts and Monuments,' maintained 'Personal dymes fall not under the precepts of God's law; wherefore, if custom were not to the contrary, it is lawful for Christ's people to dispose them to piteous use of poor men.' The words of the judicial indictment of William Swinderby, who was tried for Lollardy by the Bishop of Lincoln in 1389, express without exaggeration the views popular amongst the extreme Lollards with respect to tithes,—' That if any parishioners do know their curate be . . . incontinent, an evil man, they ought to withdraw from him their tithes, or else they be fautors of his sins. That tithes be purely alms; and that in case curates be evil men, the same may lawfully be conferred on other men. That for an evil curate to curse his subject for withholding tithe, is nothing else but to take with extortion, wickedly and unduly, from him his money.' To these charges, which unquestionably represent opinions largely prevalent amongst the Lollards, William Swinderby pleaded not guilty, and explained that he had only taught 'That it is leefull to kings, princes, dukes, and lordes of this worlde, to take awaie fro popes, cardinalls, fro bishops and prelates, possessions in the church, their temporalities, and their almes that they haue giuen them, vpon condition they shoulden serue God the better, when they verilie sene that their giuing and their taking bene contrarie to the lawe of God, to Christes liuing and His apostles.' Though the principle of this statement has been accepted by the legislature of even so Catholic a country as Spain, it must have seemed abominable to Swinderby's bishop.

dained by the Church, before the assembled congregation, 'seven foot above the earth, and seven foot under the earth, and seven foot on each side,' we may infer, from the terms in which the poet records the good man's reluctance to have recourse to so awful, and, as we should think now, so revolting and blasphemous a process of enforcing payment of a lawful debt.

The fees which the clergy received for special services—such as performances of duty at churchings, christenings, burials, and the saying of masses for the souls of particular persons—were an important addition to the incomes of the parish-priests; but, though these separate payments were considerable in cases where duty was done for persons of high social condition, they were more frequently of trivial amounts. In the middle of the fourteenth century the clergyman of Bucknell, near Bicester (Mr. Thorold Rogers tells us), received for service at the interment of a child, the offspring of affluent parents, so large a fee as two shillings; but he performed the same duty over the body of a child of humble rank for so small a sum as three farthings. Other burials were solemnised for fees varying from 9s., 3d., and 5½d. Wedding-fees at Bicester in the same period were high, the relative value of money being taken into consideration, ranging as they did from 5s. 3d. to 3s. The payments made for churchings were also very high, running as they did from a shilling (the fee paid for a poor woman's churching in most rural parishes at the present time) to tenpence and eightpence. Unless the Bicester accounts, examined by Mr. Rogers, record only the more notable fees (which does not appear to be the case from their mention of a three-farthings' funeral), the casual payments of the parish clergy in Wycliffe's England must be designated very liberal, if not exorbitant.

But it still remains to take into special consideration the material state of the lowest class of parochial priests—the unbeneficed clergy (the *curates*, in the modern and most limited sense of the term), who subsisted on payments made to them for saying private masses, or for acting as the substitutes of absentee incumbents. The general condition of these humble servants of the Church was certainly not devoid of hardship; the annual stipend for such a curate being 3l. 6s. 8d. when his work was confined to the mere discharge of the routine duties of a parish, and 4*l*. when, in addition to those routine duties, he performed daily private masses, the fees for which accrued to his employer. The social status implied by the possession of either of these poor incomes may be seen by comparing them with the earnings of farm-labourers at the same period. Before the Great Plague, usually called the Black Death, a good agricultural working-man, unassisted by wife or child, could (Mr. Thorold Rogers informs us) earn 1*l*. 7*s*. 8*d*. a-year; but after the Black Death, which, by enormously reducing the supply of labour, increased proportionately the remunerations of industry, he could earn 1*l*. 18*s*. When assisted by a wife and boy, the same working-man, before the Black Death, earned 2*l*. 7*s*. 10*d*.; after that pestilence, 3*l*. 15*s*. But, as the poor curates must be regarded as unmarried men, it is best to compare their stipends with the wages of the unmarried agricultural labourers. By this comparison we see that, before the pestilence, the unmarried farm-workmen received from a third to one-half the amount that a curate could earn; whilst after the Plague, the agricultural labourer could win nearly one-half the highest rate of payment for curates, who performed annualia as well as routine parish-duty, and 4*s*. 8*d*. per annum more than half the stipend of a clerical substitute, who was not required to perform private masses. At the present time, when such a labourer earns at the most thirty pounds per annum, the curate in full orders earns from ninety to two hundred pounds a-year, or from three to considerably more than six times as much as the working-man. It is true that, as the farm working-man of the thirteenth century was in a much higher degree of material prosperity than the farm-labourer of the present time, the stipendiary curate of Wycliffe's England could, with his narrow means, secure a much larger amount of material comfort than might be inferred from hasty reasoning upon the foregoing comparisons; but the fact remains, that in the fourteenth century the stipendiary curate's earnings were much nearer the earnings of an ordinary peasant than they are now.

That the stipendiary curate of the middle ages was not solaced in his lowly fortunes by the sympathy of his ecclesiastical superiors, we may learn from the treatment which he endured at their hands after the Black Death, which reduced the numbers of the inferior clergy, at least as much as it diminished the numbers of any other equally indigent class. The humbler priests suffered terribly from the pestilence. It is the fashion with writers of a certain kind to extol those miserable clergy, who fell in the plague, for the courage which they displayed in the face of death; and to glorify them as martyrs, who laid down their lives in heroic endeavour to succour the perishing multitude. That many of them did really display the nobility and devotion for which they are thus applauded, I make no doubt; but still I am inclined to attribute their wholesale destruction by the disease to other causes than those to which romance gives most prominence. The epidemic was of the nature of typhus fever; and after the wont of low fever, its havoc was most awful amongst the over-worked and comparatively ill-fed classes,—amongst the poor, who had neither the stamina to resist the action of the malady, nor the means wherewith to purchase the best remedies for its cure. Being those classes, the stipendiary clergy perished in vast numbers, —not so much because they disdained to desert the poor, as because they were themselves poor. Anyhow, they disappeared by hundreds upon hundreds: and when the pestilence had passed away, there was such a dearth of stipendiary curates, as well as of every other kind of humble workmen, that the absentee incumbents were at a loss how to find properly ordained substitutes. Unable to hire seculars at the old low rates to officiate in their impropriated parishes, the monasteries were compelled either to raise their stipends for such workers, or to appoint a larger number than usual of their own high order to discharge the humble functions of parochial ministers. Whilst their lordships of the monasteries were thus in doubt whether to lure the surviving clerks to their service by offers of more liberal payment, or to supply the vacant churches in their own persons, the pluralists at great men's courts and cathedral towns were in the same difficulty. Finding their services in greater demand than heretofore, the stipendiary seculars, like all other workmen, the value of whose labour had been enhanced by the diminution of their numbers by the Black Death, very naturally and rightly asked for higher payment.

But to affluent monks and pluralists, to well-placed deans and overbearing bishops, this reasonable conduct of the poor clergy seemed the language of earthly discontent and greed. In the superior ranks of ecclesiastical society, the sentiment prevailed that stipendiaries ought to be content with their grinding poverty, and that their petition for a larger share of the world's goods was impious rebellion against the Providence whose benevolence and wisdom had decided that they should be paid no more than from three to four pounds a-year. Giving utterance to this view of the crisis,—the view which the rich are apt to take of all attempts to diminish their riches,—Archbishop Simon Islip complained that 'priests nowadays, through covetousness or love of ease, not content with reasonable salaries, demanded and received excessive pay for their labour.' Growing yet more indignant against these poor priests, whose crime was that they had dared to ask for the full market-value of their labour, the archbishop maintained that 'they discharged their intemperance in vomit and lust; they grew bold, and drowned themselves in the abyss of vice, to the great scandal of ecclesiastics, and the evil example of laymen.' In the end, acting like the legislature, that, in dealing with difficulties arising from the same crisis, responded to the demands of labour by voting against a supreme political force, the chief of the National Church ordered that no stipendiary curate should demand or be paid a higher remuneration than the sums already mentioned for routine duties. But the angry primate, who lived in times when even an archbishop of Canterbury could not be reasonably expected to know much about political economy, is less worthy of ridicule for his edict against the poor stipendiaries, than those many clerical writers who, in times subsequent to Adam Smith's labours, and even to the publication of Mr. John Stuart Mill's work on political science, have expressed their abhorrence of the extortionate spirit that animated the inferior clergy after the Black Death.*

* '*The spirit of extortion* in the labouring classes, which required the interposition of the government, *extended to the inferior clergy*, and in 1362 provoked the rebuke of Archbishop Islip, who required 'that no rector should give, and that no curate should receive, more than one mark above what had been yearly

Just as two widely different accounts, supported by the statements of contemporary writers, may be given of clerical morals in the fourteenth century, so may two altogether opposite pictures be painted of the intellectual attainments of the parish-priests of that period. Whilst, on the one hand, Chaucer extols his poor parson as 'a learned man, a clerk,' and commemorates the zeal in study and thirst for learning which distinguished his clerk of Oxenforde — a character who, though 'he hadde geten him yet no benefice,' may be regarded as a representative of the erudition frequently found amongst the more cultivated seculars; Wycliffe, on the other hand, exclaims indignantly at the intellectual incompetence of the parish-priests, of whom, by the way, the Oxford Theological Professor was himself one.*

given for the same service before the plague.'—*Vide* 'The Life and Opinions of John De Wycliffe, D.D. Illustrated principally from his unpublished Manuscripts. By Robert Vaughan.

* ' For though they *know not one point of the gospel*, nor what they read, they will take a benefice, with cure of men's souls, and neither knowing how to rule their own soul nor other men's, nor will learn, nor suffer other men to teach their parishioners the gospel and God's commands truly and freely.'—WYCLIFFE's *Office of Curates.* This scornful language points to the existence of much ignorance in the clerical order; but against its ' know not one point of the gospel '— an expression which, of course, is not to be construed literally — must be set the Oxford clerk, of whom Chaucer says:—

'Ful thredbare was his overest courtepy,
For he hadde geten him yet no benefice.
Ne was nought worldly to have an office.
For him was lever han at his beddes hed
A twenty bookes, clothed in black or red,
Of Aristotle, and his philosophie,
Than robes riche, or fidel, or sautrie.
But all be that he was a philosophre,
Yet had he but litel gold in cofre,
But all that he might of his frendes hente,
On bokes and on lerning he it spente,
And besily gan for the soules praie
Of hem, that yave him wherwith to scolaie.
Of studie toke he moste cure and hede,
Not a word spake he more than was nede;
And that was saide in forme and reverence,
And short and quike, and ful of high sentence.
Souning in moral vertue was his speche,
And gladly wolde he lerne, and gladly teche.'

By the light of this piece of evidence, no impartial reader will construe literally the words of the Ploughman:—

' Such that cannot say her Crede,
    With praier shall be made prelates ;
Nother can the gospel rede,
    Such shall now welde high estates.'

Whatever may be its claims to respect on the score of enlightenment and learning, a profession, consisting of many thousands of persons, and requiring simultaneous service from the majority of its members, must necessarily comprise and employ a considerable number of individuals, whose natural capacities and attainments are of a very humble order. Notwithstanding its high repute for culture, which it owes to the mental characteristics of the generality of its less important members, even more than to the intellectual pre-eminence of exceptionally learned ecclesiastics, the clerical order of our existing Church numbers several hundreds, indeed some thousands, of highly useful and respectable gentlemen, whose information and natural ability to acquire information are universally allowed to be slight, and whose intellectual condition is sometimes mentioned with misdirected contempt by persons too apt to forget that zeal, sincerity, and sound common sense, are of more value than much scholarship to ministers, appointed to discharge routine duty in rural parishes, where they seldom come in contact with persons of any great knowledge apart from their special worldly avocations. And, since this is true of our own clergy in the nineteenth century, and is, moreover, no matter for regret, we can easily believe that the same state of things was even more noticeable, and less productive of occasional inconvenience, in the clergy of such a comparatively unenlightened period as the fourteenth century. That a considerable proportion of the parish-priests of Wycliffe's England could not say a Latin mass without making false quantities, which would provoke a smile of disdain from any Oxford graduate of our own time, is more than probable. That the learning of the most erudite amongst them was pedantic and narrow we cannot doubt, when we remember that it was chiefly acquired during a few years of youthful study, at universities, whose system, though very serviceable, was not distinguished by breadth, and under difficulties of which the university-men of the present epoch, abounding in books and various sources of instruction, can only form a faint and inadequate conception. If Chaucer's studious clerk, who spent on literature every farthing he could procure beyond his few material wants, possessed no more than some twenty manuscript volumes, we can imagine that the dwelling of an ordinary curate contained but few appliances for mental exercise. It would, however, be most unjust to regard the general body of the parochial clergy as intellectually lethargic, or despicably ignorant; for whilst participating, to a degree that appeared reprehensible to many observers, in the action of generations conspicuous for mental activity, they had, for the most part, been trained in the same seminaries as the few bishops who encouraged art and fostered letters.

Like many other of our remarks on the state of clerical society in Wycliffe's England, the foregoing observations, with respect to sacerdotal culture and ignorance, are applicable to the generations that intervened between the suppression of political Lollardy, and the successive struggles which resulted in the establishment of the Reformed Church—struggles prolific of controversies that so quickened the wits, expanded the intellect, and raised the condition of the clergy, that, in the earlier part of the seventeenth century, the learning and polemical skill of the English ecclesiastics became a proverb throughout the Latin Church.

This statement is made in no forgetfulness of the many stories that might be told of ludicrous blunders, in theology and history, perpetrated by conspicuous ecclesiastics of the fifteenth and sixteenth centuries. When Archbishop Chicheley, in the former of those centuries, taught that the Lord's day was the seventh of the week, and kept in commemoration of the Almighty's cessation from creative labour, he was not the only great ecclesiastic of the time and country who held the same scarcely accurate view. That a vast amount of utterly scandalous ignorance existed within the ranks of the clergy in the earlier stages of the Reform Epoch no one is likely to deny, after perusing Strype's pungent anecdotes of the clerical incapacity of that period, and the successive injunctions which Henry the Eighth and Edward the Sixth published for the better teaching of those priests whose lack of knowledge, in the language of one of King Edward's sets of injunctions, is described as causing them to be 'much disdained and evil spoken of by some of the laity.' Nor am I unmindful of the suggestive circumstance, that in Jewell's time the mere fact of studying Greek was regarded by the more bigoted Oxonians as a sign of heresy, or of the vivid and comically doleful accounts which such authorities as William Tyndale* and Bishop Bale have given us of clerical ignorance. But, just as Wycliffe was not the only learned priest amongst the parochial clergy, whose inefficiency he denounced, we must remember that Oxford—which was the nurse of Lollardy in the fourteenth century—at a subsequent period was the school from which Tyndale derived much of his enthusiasm for learning and many of his attainments. And, as the social ways of the world-loving clergy of Chaucer's England cannot be rightly estimated until it is compared with the general usages of the period, so also it is necessary to regard the clerical ignorance of that and the two following centuries side by side with the intellectual condition of the well-to-do and respectable laity, if we would ascertain its true significance.

* This learned and glorious martyr speaks of priests 'who have seen no more Latin than that only which they read in their portueses and missals (which yet many of them scarcely read), except it be "Albertus, De Secretis Mulierum;" in which yet, though they be never so sorrily learned, they pore day and night, and make notes therein, and all to teach the midwives, as they say; and also another, called "Lindwood," a book of constitutions to gather tithes, mortuaries, offerings, customs, and other pillage, which they call not theirs, but God's part, the duty of holy church, to discharge their consciences withal. For they are bound that they shall not diminish, but increase all things, unto the uttermost of their powers, which pertain to holy church.' Still, priests so unlearned as many persons imagine the old clergy to have been, could have found neither amusement in 'Albertus' nor instruction in 'Lindwood.' And it is of the most ignorant priests that Tyndale is speaking.

CHAPTER IX.

THE POOR AND THE RICH.

HOW to create and preserve from every kind of deterioration a clergy, which shall at the same time be so opulent and highly cultivated that it may possess due influence and respect in the higher sections of society, and yet be in perfect sympathy with the poor and illiterate, has been one of the difficult problems which the Church cannot be said to have perfectly solved, even in the most felicitous periods of her history. Unless it possesses, either in its corporate character or through the material endowments of its members, a liberal share of the riches of the community, a priesthood is without proper power amongst the aristocracy; and when deprived of the sympathy and cordial co-operation of the aristocratic classes, it is prone to experience opposition and contempt from those divisions of the community that occupy the space between the aristocracy and humblest order of citizens. Sydney Smith spoke a truth familiar to all social observers when he urged, that it was not in the nature of the average tradesman of an English town to cherish hearty respect for a rector who was distinctly his inferior in regard to worldly means. But it would be unfair to the lower middle classes to represent them as greatly differing in this particular from their social betters. The disesteem in which they hold a poverty-stricken priesthood corresponds to, if it be not altogether identical with, the disdainful indifference which aristocracy almost invariably exhibits to a clergy that is uniformly oppressed by indigence.

Wealth begets in every class, which enjoys it with security, the tone of thought, the refinement of person, the dignity of carriage, which, even more than the political influence and material advantages pertaining to opulence, command the respect of hereditary aristocracies. On the other hand, the classes that lack wealth are more or less distinguished by deficiency in those intellectual and moral endowments which the polite and proud inheritors of ancestral privilege value more highly than any other intrinsic qualities. To be in unison with the powerful of the earth, the sacerdotal order must, therefore, be invested with a degree of affluence that bears an appearance of incongruity with those professions of contempt for earthly distinctions, and lively abhorrence of the temptations engendered by riches, which are conspicuous features of the Christian theory.

That the clergy of the Christian churches became, at a very early date of their history, chargeable with pursuing worldly honours and material strength, from a passion for mere personal aggrandisement rather than for the furtherance of purely religious purposes, cannot be denied; but, even at the times when they displayed the keenest avidity for earthly distinctions and perishable riches, they could plead in behalf of their conduct that, by increasing their own wealth and dignity, they enhanced the importance of their order, and that the entire Church was affected beneficially by whatever tended to make the sacerdotal class paramount over all other social elements. That there was a fallacy in this argument, based on the assumption that the interests of an ecclesiastical organization are necessarily identical with the interests of religion, it is needless to observe. Nor are we required by the purposes of this work to inquire how far the fallacious argument was in harmony with the secret opinions and sincere convictions of the clergy, who used it to justify or palliate every kind of ecclesiastical encroachment. For the special ends of our undertaking it is enough to say, that this clerical mode of regarding clerical wealth was commended to ordinary minds by the rapid developments of ecclesiastical power, which, growing with the affluence and magnificence of the sacerdotal class, almost appeared to derive its vigour from that which was, in fact, nothing more than its outward garb. By their riches, and qualities proceeding from riches, the medieval priests, rising from an extreme point of social lowliness, became the companions of nobles, the counsellors of kings, and, finally, the supreme tribunal to which earthly monarchs combined to render obeisance.

But priests of the very best and noblest sort are no more than very good men; and however eminent may be its services, and however splendid the virtues of a considerable proportion of its members, a numerous priesthood must be expected to share in the frailties and actively evil qualities of human nature. This expectation was certainly not disappointed by the medieval clergy, in whom prosperity begot the tendencies which good fortune invariably produces in every kind of men, and in whose hearts the possession of exorbitant wealth and political supremacy engendered the insolence, and luxurious disposition, and appetency of rule, which will always characterise in a high degree every class that is excessively opulent and dangerously powerful. And in proportion as wealth wrought its universal results in the natures and lives of ecclesiastical persons, those results in their turn brought forth fruit,—first, in a diminution of the love and reverence with which the poor had previously regarded the clergy, and then in the partial substitution of sentiments of passionate hostility for the affection which, in the Church's nobler days, every devout person in the lowlier walks of life had cherished for his priest.

In justice to the medieval clergy it must be admitted, that the dissatisfaction and warmer antagonism, which animated a considerable proportion of the humbler people against their spiritual teachers, were less due to causes for which any individuals of the ecclesiastical order can be held blameworthy, than to the forces which, in every state of society, work severance between the rich and the poor, even when the rich are not disposed to tyranny, and the poor cannot be accused of an inclination to rebellious discontent.

The most widely received theory respecting society in the middle ages insists that, notwithstanding the sharpness of the lines which divided class from class, and notwithstanding the regulations which invested 'class' with some of the odious qualities of 'caste,' the members of the various social grades were animated by such an universal sense of common fellowship, and were so firmly united, and so agreeably influenced by the mutual obligations and courtesies of social intercourse,

Part I.—Wycliffe's England.

that every one was thoroughly content with the situation to which, as the Catechism runs, it had pleased God to call him. According to this pleasant picture, our forefathers of the feudal epoch were one vast happy family, and spent their days in reasonable toil and a continual exchange of spoken or unspoken compliments. Whilst the earl seized every occasion to exhibit his high personal esteem for the merchant, the yeoman, and the peasant, no humble member of society experienced even the faintest annoyance at the incidents of his obscure estate, or strove to exchange it for one of greater privileges and fewer inconveniences. Whereas a wide gulf separates the rich and the poor in these hard times, which have built a city for the opulent in Belgravia, and another city for the indigent in Bethnal Green, and will not permit the wanderers of the town to occupy the seats, for which capitalists pay rent, in fashionable chapels: in the golden age of feudalism the humble toiler and the gilded child of affluence lived within a stone's throw of each other, and were equals so soon as they had crossed the threshold of a church. As a protest against many unjust things, written by intemperate denouncers of feudalism, this fantastic theory may perhaps be credited with having done transient good; if, indeed, a falsehood ever does good that might not be more thoroughly achieved by a declaration of the exact truth. Some persons are of opinion that, whilst daily experience shows the difficulty of killing a falsehood by truthful refutation, it is comparatively easy to annihilate a lie by a counter-lie; and such persons may esteem highly the past services of this particular historic fiction. Anyhow, the time has come when it must be withdrawn from the current cant permissible to persons who like to throw a veil of specious words over the more repulsive aspects of our past story. Not only in society at large, but in every social grade, the rich and the poor of feudal life were more widely and harshly divided than the affluent and needy of the present day. Fierce as every chapter of feudal narrative is with passions evolved by the contentions of classes—the insolence which the rich as a class exhibited for the poor as a class, and the bitter resentments which the poor as a class nursed against the rich as a class throughout the middle ages, animate our ancient domestic chronicles more consistently than any other kinds of hostile emotion. That the rich of our own time neither know the poor so intimately, nor sympathise with them so cordially, as they ought, there is abundant reason to deplore; but it is a mistake to suppose that the incidents of opulence, more especially of opulence neither newly attained nor insecurely held, did not in former ages segregrate the rich from the poor, and that the incidents of poverty had no corresponding effect in making the poor regard themselves as distinct from the rich.

As they grew in opulence, the English clergy, like the ecclesiastics of other western countries, became more and more the confederates of the rich, less and less the trusted counsellors of the poor; and though this change was greatly due to the insolence, pride, luxury, and other positive faults which wealth generated in the clerical order, it was also to a great extent consequent on the direct influence which the mere fact of the sacerdotal prosperity had on the minds of the poor, who, even if the clergy had retained all their primitive zeal and piety, would have conceived something of envy, antagonism, and distrust for a priesthood appertaining, by reason of its affluence, to the division of society, to which, by reason of their poverty, indigent folk did not belong.

The difficulty and weakness of the medieval churches in this respect will be best demonstrated to the ordinary reader by drawing his attention to the clergy of our Established Church, whose position and acknowledged merits afford something that resembles a practical solution to the problem stated at the commencement of this chapter. Drawn chiefly from the aristocracy and higher middle class; educated at public schools and universities, where, as the companions of the youth of our best families, they acquire the views and tone of the rulers of the country; possessing, in very many instances, large private means; permitted by the wise liberality of our Ecclesiastical Polity to improve their domestic fortunes, whilst they gratify their natural affection by marriage with the opulent families of the grades to which they belong; allowed to speak with potential voice on all public affairs in the Upper House, whilst they are encouraged to apply their great influence to all political movement outside the walls of Parliament; and endowed with so liberal a share of the national wealth, that whilst it is deemed excessive by their opponents, no one within the ecclesiastical pale ventures to call it an inadequate provision for a national priesthood,—the ecclesiastics of the Anglican Establishment are universally allowed to be, upon the whole, the best descended, most learned, and most powerful clergy that can be found in any Protestant nation. Though a contrary opinion prevails almost universally, I believe that they are richer and not less politically influential than the strictly national clergy of times prior to the Reformation. But, however much critics may differ from this view, no one is likely to deny that the social status of our clergy is enviably fortunate in comparison with the priesthoods of other Protestant countries, and even of countries where the Papal authority remains paramount over religious interests. That this clergy is not without lukewarm friends, and an enormous army of resolute enemies, no one needs to be told; but though I have made it my business to ascertain the opinions of those adversaries of the National Church, I have failed to discover within their ranks any widely prevalent feeling that the members of our ecclesiastical order are generally chargeable with remissness, or sloth, or any of the more flagrant of those faults which wealth is too apt to generate in a hierarchy. On the contrary, the most clear-sighted and resolute Nonconformists of my acquaintance are never loth to express admiration for the enlightenment, zeal, and social virtues that usually render our clergy objects of respect to those who envy their privileges, and cherish no particle of reverence for their apostolic authority.

What is the weakness of this powerful and noble clergy? The answer is best given by stating that they do not, as a class, possess the confidence of the poor. So far as a clergy possessing a strictly-defined theology can be in perfect harmony with a very numerous and highly-cultivated class of persons, in a country whose liberality is so extreme that it regards with proud complacency the number of the conflicting elements which constitute its intellectual life, our clergy may be said to be in singular accord with the aristocracy of the land. The higher middle classes are no less in unison with the established priesthood; for, notwithstanding the importance of the actual number of Nonconformists amongst our untitled gentry, they are very few in comparison with the middle-class supporters of our ecclesiastical system. But as soon as we look at the social grades below the superior middle class, we find the opponents of the National Church become more and more numerous—the prevalence of dissent increasing in proportion as the observer approaches those sections of the community that are commonly called the working classes, in which the influence of the State clergy is noticeably slighter than that of religious ministers who receive no support from the nation. Of course, opinions differ widely as to the degree in which the clergy are powerful or powerless in these humblest of our social grades, and upon a matter so manifestly beyond the reach of all methods of precise measurement it would be ridiculous to speak confidently, and with an air of exact knowledge. It is, however, universally conceded, that the working classes of our cities may be described as living almost entirely outside the pale of the Established Church. Here and there a clergyman of unusual energy, and extraordinarily endowed with the qualities that win the affections of humble people, may be seen to draw a few of their adults to his church, and a considerable number of their children to his schools; but such instances of clerical success amongst the poor of our large towns cannot be produced in disproof of the general assertion, that the humble toilers of our urban populations—the members of what may be termed the artisan class—live, from early manhood to death, without any kind of habitual communion with the national clergy. Whilst working men are either conspicuous by their total absence, or seen only in very small numbers, in the public congregations of the churches of those brighter districts of London which are familiarly termed 'residential quarters,' the churches in those parts of the metropolis where the poor principally reside are either devoid of worshippers, or are so few that, even when they succeed in gathering average congregations, the entire number of their customary attendants is trifling in comparison with the multitudes who, dwelling in the same localities, never enter or think of entering a church. The most popular and attractive services of our London clergy—the 'Special Services' of the Cathedral and Abbey—draw dense throngs of well-dressed and outwardly prosperous persons, but the slight show made by people of the operative class at those gatherings is significant of the unanimity with which the members of that class have withdrawn themselves from the National Church—significant, that is to say, of the completeness of the severance between our ecclesiastical system and the workpeople of the metropolis. Nor is this state of things peculiar to London; or even more noticeable in London than in our other large centres of commerce and industry. Even of our small cathedral towns, where clerical influence is paramount in all social matters apart from religion, it may be asserted that the majority of their humbler inhabitants are not regular church-people.

To account for this painful fact excellent clergymen have been driven to the still more painful conclusion, that the absence of the poor from the ecclesiastical services of our urban churches is mainly referable to infidelity and irreligion, presumed to be largely prevalent amongst the working classes. That a zealous and exemplary churchman, holding high position in the clerical order, should have ventured to assert publicly his concurrence in this very erroneous view, is a fact strongly illustrative of the severance which he deplored, and also of the speaker's ignorance of the intellectual and moral condition of the persons against whom he inveighed. The real cause of this withdrawal of the working classes from the Establishment is frankly stated by the Journeyman Engineer, in his capital volume of essays on 'The Great Unwashed;'* where, after repudiating the charges of irreligion and infidelity, he declares roundly that the thoughtful and pious of his class are seldom church-people, because they have very generally come to the opinion, that the Church of England does not respond to the religious requirements of the period; that, whilst professing to be the church of the poor, it is in fact the church of the rich. To charge the very mistaken holders of these sentiments with a spirit of unbelief and a morbid taste for infidel literature is not more the act of injustice than of sheer ignorance; for, whilst the members of our

---

* Prosperous persons who wish to know more about their less fortunate brethren of the working classes, their faults and virtues, their views and desires should peruse this excellent contribution to the literature of Social Science.

working classes are great readers of strictly religious publications, which have not even the faintest savour of sceptical thought, but are, on the contrary, remarkable for dogged adherence to the dogmas of orthodox theology, they take hardly any notice of the writings of free-thinkers. That neology is popular in the higher classes of society the ledgers of our publishers afford conclusive testimony; but the infidel literature, which is supposed by some persons to be the chief intellectual food of our artizans, exists nowhere except in the imaginations of simple people, who are more clever at creating 'bogies' for their own alarm than at discovering facts that are irreconcilable with their favourite misconceptions. Nor is it less unjust and unreasonable to attribute irreligion to the multitudes who throng Roman Catholic churches, swell the growing congregations of Nonconformity, and frequent all places of Christian worship except the temples, which the upholders of church-rates used to designate pathetically the homes of the poor.

In the country circumstances are far more conducive to clerical influence than in the towns. What may be called the parson-power of an average agricultural parish is so much stronger than the clerical force of a city parish, that all the residents of the former locality can be, and usually are, known individually by their ministers of the established religion; whereas the incumbent and curates of an ordinary city living, however zealous they may be, are seldom able to establish personal relations with a twentieth of the individuals nominally committed to their care. Knowing his humbler parishioners by sight and name, acquainted also with their pursuits and domestic interests, the country parson is a parochial magnate, whose favourable opinion is an affair of special concern to those who may need his good word or pecuniary aid under the continually recurring exigencies of sickness and poverty. As the distributor of some portion of his wealthier parishioners' bounties to the poor, as the official trustee of funds for the relief of local indigence, as a comparatively affluent person, both able and willing to alleviate distress by his private means, he possesses sources of influence that seldom pertain to non-conforming ministers. His recommendation is continually found of sufficient power to secure eligible employment for the children of humble attendants at his church. Usually he is keeper of the squire's conscience, and directs at pleasure the streams of munificence that flow from the Hall to the cottages of a patient peasantry. His means for making himself beloved are scarcely greater than his opportunities of making himself feared by the most dependent class of his flock. And yet, notwithstanding all these facts, the Church is seldom able to do more than 'barely hold its own' against the conventicle in a rural parish. Village artizans, ready enough to cap the parson and fawn to the squire, for a weekly loaf or a Christmas shilling, show signs of independence and manly spirit when they are reproved for attending a dissenters' meeting-house; and, even amongst those of them who appear punctually at the squire's church, and exhibit every external sign of religious conformity, not a few are regular attendants of the prayer-meetings of Baptist teachers. A rector may pass five-and-twenty years of his life in a Suffolk parish, working sedulously in his schools, and exhibiting all the qualities of a model parish-priest, and yet, after all his toil, and charity, and sympathetic benevolence, he will know less of its farm-labourers than the Wesleyan minister who has come to the district only the other day, and will move from it in three years. The gulf between humble folk and gentry is so deep and wide that, though a gentle and opulent clergy may throw a bridge over it, they can never fill it up.

CHAPTER X.

THE BEGGAR PRIESTS.

HAVING their origin in one of those religious agitations—which, common in every age of the Church, have in these later times acquired the name of revivals—the mendicant orders arose in the last years of the twelfth, and the opening decades of the thirteenth, century, to renew the enthusiasm of believers; to protest against the luxury and pride largely prevalent amongst ordained persons; to combat the heresies which had sprung from the growing discontent with ecclesiastical authority; and to recall mankind to the ascetic ways and hardy virtues of the early Christians. Composed of enthusiasts, burning with indignation at sacerdotal corruptions, and ardent, with a passionate desire, to bring the usages of priestly men into harmony with their professions, these orders made poverty the first rule of their existence. Neither the individuals of their class, nor the brotherhoods into which they gathered themselves, should be capable of possessing any property, beyond the barest sufficiency of bodily clothing, and the few articles necessary for the pursuit of the apostle's vocation and the discharge of the priest's functions. Like their Divine Master, and His immediate servants, they would be no less conspicuous for penury than holiness. As paupers they would go forth to the world—to the castles of the rich and the cabins of the poor; to cities bright with splendour and villages built by the rudest art for the accommodation of despised rustics—and from those who accepted their ministrations they would take no material payment, save a bed of straw, a draught of water, and a meal of coarse bread.

It speaks pathetically of the goodness and devotion, which must have qualified the selfishness and cruelty of medieval society, that these zealots—meanly clad, and possessing no single title to human respect apart from their spiritual gifts and aims—were instantly recognised by a considerable proportion of their contemporaries as fit objects for confidence and homage; and that, even before the official controllers of social opinion had expressly sanctioned their proceedings, or deigned to notice their existence, they received from the rich, whose riches they disdained, and from the poor, whose poverty they affected, abundant demonstrations of approval and love. Drawing to themselves a large amount of the pious sympathy and romantic admiration which, in previous generations, had been lavished on the soldiers of the Cross, and were being fast withdrawn from the adventurers of the later crusades, these pious beggars became the heroes of a new warfare against the powers of Satan; and whilst the abject and forlorn, and all who either envied the wealth or resented the corruptions of the higher clergy, applauded their virtues and besought their benedictions, even the coldest and most cynical spectators of the novel movement were disposed to think that it would have beneficial results in promoting true religion in the lowest, and correcting sacerdotal insolence and apathy in the higher, ranks of the Christian church.

The first pontiff to accord favour to the beggar-priests was Innocent the Third, who occupied the papal throne from 1198 to 1216, and is memorable in English story for his excommunication of King John; but in little more than half-a-century these wandering brothers had become so numerous and insubordinate, that Gregory the Tenth found it advisable, in 1272, to suppress all the mendicant brotherhoods which had sprung into existence since Innocent's council of 1215. By this repressive measure Gregory reduced the entire army of friars, or mendicant monks—whom he most uncivilly designated an 'unbridled throng'—into four regiments,—the Carmelites, Augustinian Eremites, Dominicans, and Franciscans.

The Carmelites originated in Palestine in the twelfth century, and after migrating to Europe, were recognised as an order of the Western Church by Honorius the Third, A.D. 1226; and the Augustinian Eremites—constituted by the fusion of several societies of Eremites, obeying the regulations of William the Eremite, and of Augustinians living under the rules of Augustine—owed their institution to Alexander the Fourth, who united them in the bonds of brotherhood just thirty-six years after Dominic of Calahorra, the parent of the Inquisition, and the merciless persecutor of the Albigensian heretics, had enjoined on his disciples, convened at Bologna, a strict observance of their vows of poverty ; and thirty years after the death of Francis Assisi, whose fraternity of pious zealots surpassed even the early Dominicans in manifestations of humility and disdain of worldly riches. In their first years these two last-mentioned orders,—destined soon to contend with ferocious bitterness in disputes about questions of precedence, and in struggles for earthly superiority,—found occasions for difference in their modes of demonstrating the austerities of the mendicant system. Whilst the early Dominicans boastfully proclaimed their appointment to confute heresy and overthrow ignorance, terming themselves *Fratres Prædicatores*—Preaching Brothers, Francis of Assisi forbade his monks to assume a designation so lofty and arrogant as even the modest title of brethren. The Franciscans were commanded to exhibit modesty within the lines of the priesthood, as well as towards the laity, and announce their inferiority to other friars by styling themselves Little Friars, *Fraterculi*, or *Fratres Minores*, from which latter term of distinction proceeded the word Minorites, which became their ordinary designation in this country. In contrast to the excessive humility of these Minorites, the Dominicans, or *Fratres Prædicatores*, were well pleased to hear themselves spoken of as *Fratres Majores*. Nor were these the only names given to Dominic's followers, who in France were called Jacobins, or Jacobites, from their earliest Parisian college in the Rue St. Jaques, and Black Friars from the colour of their costume, which is still commemorated by the name which continues to distinguish the locality where they first established themselves in the English metropolis. In like manner the Franciscans, or Minorites, were commonly called Grey Friars, and the Carmelites White Friars, from the colours of their dress. But notwithstanding their diversities of appellation, and the number of hostile sects into which they were divided and subdivided in the course of a very few generations, the friars were restrained within the bounds of the four orders* to which Gregory the Tenth had reduced their unbridled throng.

From what has been said in a former chapter of the poverty of the inferior grades of our parochial clergy, it might be supposed that, whatever discontent the laity might harbour towards the sacerdotal order, their disaffection was not of a kind that could be remedied by a fresh creation of pauper-priests. To many a contemporary observer it must have seemed improbable that the religious disquiet and irritations of the humbler people could be assuaged by increasing the number of their unendowed clergy, since their disease had originated and progressed in times when village curates were little richer than superior artizans. But the indigence of the lowest sort of our secular priests had not exercised on the popular mind an influence similar to that which proceeded from the voluntary pauperism and ostentatious humility of the earlier mendicants. Indeed, it had tended to increase rather than diminish the growing hostility to the ecclesiastical system. The presence of thou-

---

* Writing at a time when the friars were cordially detested by the majority of our National Church Party, the author of 'The Song Against the Friars,' published in Mr. Thomas Wright's 'Political Poems and Songs, accession Edward III. to accession Richard III.,' plays with characteristic asperity on the initial letters of the four societies,—Carmelites, Augustinians, Jacobites, and Minorites:—

'Thai say that thai distroye synne,
And thai mayntene men moste therinne;
    For had a man slayn al his kynne,
Go shryve him at a frere,
And for less than a payre of shone,
He wyl assoil him clene and sone,
And say the synne that he has done,
    His saule shal never dere.
It semes sothe that men sayne of hayme
in many dyvers londe,
That that catyfe cursed Cayme
first this order fonde.

Nou se the sothe whedre it be swa,
That frer Carmes com of a *k*,
That frer Austynes come of *a*,
    Frer Jacobynes of *i*,
Of *m* comen the frer Menours;
Thus grounded Caym these four ordours,

That fillen the world ful of errours
    And of ypocrisy.
Alle wyckednes that men can telle,
    regnes ham among;
Ther shal no saule have rowme in helle,
    Of frers there is suche throng.

Thai travele yerne and bysily,
To brynge doun the clergye,
Thai speken thereof ay vilany,
    And thereof thai done wrong.
Whoso lyves oght many yers,
Shal se that it shall falle of frers,
As it dyd of the templers,
    That wonned here us among.
For thai held no religioun,
    bot lyved after lykyng:
Thai were distroyed, and broght adown,
    thurgh ordynance of the kyng.'

sands of stipendiary curates, barely sustaining an appearance of outward respectability on the beggarly stipends doled out to them by pluralist rectors, instead of conciliating our medieval radicals to the policy of the national church, only stimulated their antagonism to a system that permitted the idle and worldly priests to live in luxury, whilst it diminished the remunerations of its servants in proportion as they were more zealous and useful. On the other hand, in spite of their poverty, the majority of the stipendiary seculars exhibited qualities of tone and temper which demonstrated their participation in the failings which wealth had generated in their order. Arrogant, dictatorial, and covetously grasping every petty fee or privilege to which they had the shadow of claim, they too often differed, from the least worthy kind of beneficed priests, in no respect save wealth and power. And whilst this was the case with the greater number, the minority of them comprised many able and clever men, in whom the humiliations and hardships of obscure need had engendered such animosities against their ecclesiastical superiors, and the whole scheme of ecclesiastical government, that they were more ready to foment than to allay the strifes and passions which menaced the Church with serious embarrassment. Hence it arose, that the most dangerous and vindictive of medieval demagogues were members of the clerical vocation.

From this condition of affairs it followed, that on entering England, the pauper-priests found an extensive field for their special activity, and were received with open arms—by the populace whose notions of religious consistency and sincerity disposed them to applaud the peculiar characteristics of the mendicant brotherhoods; and by the chiefs of the National Church party, who, delighted by the zeal with which the itinerant brothers denounced priestly sloth and luxury, were guilty of the prodigious error of supposing that the influence of the new orders, coming, though they did, straight from Rome, and deriving all their exceptional privileges from the patronage of pontiffs, would, upon the whole, strengthen the conscientious seculars, and proportionately weaken the Papal party. Amongst the prelates and dignified churchmen who erred thus egregiously was Robert Grosthead, who, from the first settlement of the Dominicans in Oxford, until he had for several years governed the diocese of Lincoln, gave his valuable support to the itinerants, and was sanguine enough to hope that the rivalry which sprung up between the pauper-priests and the parochial clergy would stimulate the latter to an uniformly efficient discharge of their duties, without producing any kind of scandalous commotion within the bounds of the hierarchy. But, ere long, Bishop Grosthead saw reason to repent of his generous patronage of a class of ordained agitators, who, not content with railing at the indolence of the wealthy monks, and exaggerating the merits of Papal government, aggravated every popular discontent against the seculars, and were lamentably successful in their endeavours to render the parochial clergy odious and contemptible to the humbler people.

To show the character of the injuries and insults which the friars heaped upon our parochial clergy notice must be taken of the special privileges which the mendicants derived from the pontiffs, and of the insufferable insolence and treacherous meanness with which they exercised those privileges for their own aggrandisement, and for the degradation of the secular priesthood. Of these peculiar prerogatives, alike humiliating to the curates and prejudicial to episcopal authority, the most offensive and intolerable was the right which every friar possessed of discharging every function of the priestly office, wheresoever he might be, without any respect or liability to the bishop within whose diocese he preached, or administered the sacraments. He might enter any parish-church, and, without the incumbent's permission, disarrange the procedure of Divine service, and harangue the congregation upon their rector's ignorance, sloth, and total incompetence to minister to their spiritual wants. And this power, as we shall soon see, the mendicant revivalists and mendicant agitators exercised always with aggravating arrogance, and often with contumacious insolence.

Their power to vex and injure the parochial clergy was farther enlarged by the pontifical grants, that empowered them to sell indulgences and pardons, and thereby extort from the superstitious money which would otherwise have passed to the hands of the ordinary curates, for the relief of the sick and poor, or other pious uses. It is, of course, needless to say that they did not enjoy a monopoly of this lucrative traffic; but they became the chief traders in these spiritual wares through the munificence of the pontiffs, who rewarded their prosecution of papal interests by constituting them agents for the sale of relics and remissions of penance. And in this respect, no one of the other three orders was more fortunate than the Franciscans, who derived from this singular commerce a large proportion of the wealth, which accumulated so rapidly in their hands, that even the more liberal of grey-habited ecclesiastics were at a loss how to reconcile their retention of prodigious wealth with the vows of utter poverty, until Innocent the Fourth—so early as the year 1245, the twentieth year after St. Francis's death—decided that pauper-priests might, with easy consciences, enjoy the usufruct of lands, houses, chattels, and every sort of material possession, provided that the property and actual ownership of the things so enjoyed were vested in St. Peter.* This pleasant distinction, which none but a lawyer can fully appreciate, was by no means satisfactory to the more earnest and sincere paupers; who were slow to discern honesty in a feat of mere verbal jugglery, by which it was pretended that a college of clergymen could at the same time be penniless beggars and great capitalists. To set forth minutely the dissensions which, originating from the delicate question, whether men can be indigent whilst in practical possession of great riches, broke up the Franciscans into virulently antagonistic sects, and occasioned the other orders continual perplexity, is no purpose of this work; but for several reasons, it is desirable that the reader should remember at how early a date those priests—whose dis-

---

* That the beggar-priests not only availed themselves of this decision as a justification of their wealth, but used it as argument in support of their mendicant entreaties, may be inferred from the following words of Jacke Upland:—' Whose been all your riche courtes that ye han, and all your riche juells? sithe ye seyne that ye have nought ne in proper ne in common? If ye sayne they bene the popes? why gether ye then of poore men and lords so much out of the kinges hand to make your pope riche? And sithe ye sayne that it is great perfection to have nought in proper ne in common? why be ye so fast about to make the pope that is your father rich, and put on him imperfection?' Whence it appears that the verbal fiction, which vested the ecclesiastical property of their estates in the Pope, or rather the saint whom the Pope specially represented on earth, furnished the friars with an apt defence of their extortions, since it enabled them to say that they begged and accumulated, not *for* themselves, but *for* the holy Father of the Church.

tinctive profession was poverty, whose original title to popular affection was their voluntary indigence, and whose distinguishing personal characteristic continued to be an outward affectation of the garb and mien of penury—had entered on that race for wealth and worldly power, in which the medieval ecclesiastics were seldom equalied, and never surpassed, by their contemporaries of the laity.

The material prosperity of the beggar-priests was in exact proportion to the influence which they gained amongst all classes of the laity, and was not the only demonstration of the esteem in which they were held. Wherever they built churches it was found that the congregations deserted the older places of worship, in order that they might hear the sermons, and profit by the ministrations, of the mendicant divines. Such was the enthusiasm for the Four Orders that many European cities were divided into four districts; of which the first was appropriated to the Dominicans, the second to the Franciscans, the third to the Carmelites, the fourth to the Augustinians. In the universities they gained possession of the theological chairs; and disputes arose between them and the scholastic authorities, on whose prescriptive ground they intruded—disputes fruitful of tumults in the seats of learning, and of anxiety to successive pontiffs. Content with no such secondary parts in the ecclesiastical drama, as would have accorded with their original professions of lowliness, they arrogated to themselves the right to dominate in every department of the Church; and so completely did the Dominicans and Franciscans achieve their ambitious purposes, that they became as powerful in the pre-Lutheran Church as the Jesuits became after the Reformation. The credulity of the middle ages is not more forcibly illustrated than the overwhelming influence of the friars, by the general acceptance of the ridiculous fable, which attributed special sanctity to the scapular, or short mantle, which the Carmelites wore upon their shoulders. At the commencement of the thirteenth century it was asserted, that the Virgin Mary had honoured Simon Stock, the general of the Carmelites, with a private interview, and a gratifying assurance that no human being should be damned eternally who should wear a Carmelitan scapular at the moment of his last breath. The dissemination of this blasphemous fancy had so beneficial an effect on the fortunes of the White Friars, that the other orders of pauper-priests were not slow to discover the same marketable virtue in their respective costumes. The old coat of a Franciscan friar was found to be endowed with a mystic property that afforded security from the pains of hell and purgatory, to every human soul whose mortal body should be interred in its folds; and, in order that they might profit by this miraculous efficacy of cast-off clothing, rich laymen were glad to buy worn-out Franciscan habits at preposterous prices.*

But, though riches and success produced an abundant crop of arrogance in the ranks of the mendicants, the pauper-priests of Wycliffe's England were certainly commendable for personal activity, and the zeal which they evinced in promoting the interests of their respective orders. Overflowing with insolence to the monks, whom they reproved for their luxurious sloth, and with disdain for the secular clergy, whose real or imputed ignorance and incompetence they held up to popular derision, they were affable to the laity, whose goodwill it was their especial policy to cultivate. Itinerating the country with

* In his 'Exposition upon the Sermon on the Mount,' Tyndale says, 'And those friars that teach men to believe in St. Francis's coat, how that they shall never come in hell or purgatory, if they be buried therein, may not be passed over in silence.' Latimer has recorded that in his earlier life he believed that ' he should never be damned, if he were once a professed friar.' During the prevalence of this superstition, rich men in declining health often bought their admission into the ranks of the mendicants, in order that they might be saints in heaven; just as affluent laymen became monks, in order that they might be gentlemen on earth. With respect to these matters, Jacke Upland asks the friars, 'Why make ye men beleue that he that is buryed in your habite shall neuer come in hell, and ye wyte not of yourselfe whether ye shall to hell or no? and if this were sothe, ye shuld sell your hye houses to make many habites for to saue many men's soules. . . . . Frere, what charitie is this, to prease upon a riche man, to entice him to be buryed among you from hys parish church, and to such riche men giue letters of fraternitie confirmed by your generale seale, and thereby to beare him in hand that he sh ll haue part of all your masses, mattens, preachinges, fastinges, wakinges, and all other good dedes done by your brethren of your order (both while he liueth and after that he is dead), and yet wytten neuer whether your dedes be acceptable to God, ne whether that man that hath that letter be able by good liuing to receiue any part of your deedes, and yet a poore man (that ye wyte well or supposen in certain to have no good of) ye ne geuen to such letters, though he may be a better man to God than such a riche man.'

packs and bags,—containing indulgences, relics, pardons, nicknacks, and articles of haberdashery,—they were merchants, whose pursuit of gain appeared peculiarly honourable, since its acquisitions were devoted to pious uses; priests, who heard confessions and gave absolution in every village they entered; and news-carriers, whose gossip made them acceptable at the tables of gentle and simple. As regular clergy they shared in the respect socially accorded to monastic priests; but unlike the monks, their superiors in extraction and culture, they never wounded the self-love of non-clerical persons by an air of patrician disdainfulness.* Long after they had laid aside the downcast mien and severe discipline of the primitive brothers, they retained much of their old humble air towards the laity, together with their unassuming dress and practice of mendicancy. The clever, cheery talkers of the fourteenth century, no less pleasant in manner than glib of tongue, they tickled their feminine hearers with sly flatteries, and made the men roar with droll tales. Many of them were comely fellows, and contrived to impart a foppish set to their semicopes of double worsted; and there are good grounds for believing that, in their intercourse with women, they seldom failed to achieve their lawful purposes through disinclination to humour the innocent weaknesses of the gentler sex. But, notwithstanding the grave charges made against their morals by popular satirists, I am disposed to think that their general demeanour to women was far less reprehensible than the author of the 'Song against the Friars' would have us believe; for had they been such licentious and impure creatures as their bitterest enemies represent, it is not probable that, like Chaucer's friar, they would have been 'well beloved and familiar' with the freeholders of the whole country, and would have encountered alike, from nobles and commonalty,

---

* As regular clergy, the friars might have asserted a right to the honourable prefix of 'Don;' and 'Dons' they were at an early date in the universities and seats of learning. But in their familiar and sociable intercourse with the laity, they do not appear to have affected a title which would have tended to put a gulf betwixt themselves and ordinary folk. The itinerant beggar-priest was content to be addressed as 'sire,' 'dear sire,' 'master,' 'good master;' but he preferred to be accosted by his peculiar designation—'Holy Frere,' or Holy Brother.'

those cordial welcomings and lavish hospitalities which were affairs of daily occurrence to the itinerants of the Four Orders.*

As an ecclesiastical reformer, sympathising warmly with the National Church Party, and never omitting an opportunity to speak a good word for the Lollard clergy, Chaucer was in no degree favourable to the itinerant brothers; but whilst abound-

* Chaucer's friar—loquacious, plausible, equipped to play alternately the pedlar and the priest—is thus seen in the prologue of the ' Canterbury Tales :'—

'A Frere there was, a wanton and a mery,
A limitour, a full solempne man.
In all the ordres foure is non that can
So moche of daliance and fayre langage.
He had le ymade ful many a mariage
Of yonge wimmen, at his owen cost.
Until his order he was a noble post.
Ful wel beloved, and familier was he
With frankeleins over all in his contree,
And eke with worthy wimmen of the toun:
For he had power of confession,
As saide himselfe, more than a curat,
For of his ordre he was licenciat.
Ful swetely herde he confession,
And plesant was his absolution,
He was an esy man to give penance,
Ther as he wiste to han a good pitance:
For unto a poure ordre for to give
Is signe that a man is wel yshrive.
For if he gave, he dorste make avant,
He wiste that a man was repentant.
For many a man so hard is of his herte,
He may not wepe although him sore smerte.
Therfore in stele of weping and praieres,
Men mote give silver to the poure freres.
His tippet was ay farsed ful of knives,
And pinnes, for to given fayre wives.
And certainly he had a mery note.
Wel coude he singe and plaien on a rote.
Of yeddinges he bare utterly the pris.
His nekke was white as is the flour de lis.
Thereto he strong was as a champioun,
And knew wel the tavernes in every toun,
And every hosteler and gay tapstere,
Better than a lazer or a beggere,

For unto swiche a worthy man as he
Accordeth nought, as by his faculte,
To haven with sike lazars acquaintance.
It is not honest, it may not advance,
As for to delen with no swiche pouraille,
But all with riche, and sellers of vitaille.
And over all, ther as profit shuld arise,
Curteis he was, and lowly of servise.
Ther n'as no man no wher so vertuous.
He was the beste begger in all his hous:
And gave a certaine ferme for the grant,
Non of his bretheren came in his haunt.
For though a widewe hadde but a shoo,
(So plesant was his *In principio*)
Yet wold he have a ferthing or he went.
His pourchas was wel better than his rent.
And rage he coude as it hadde ben a whelp,
In lovedayes, ther coude he mochel help.
For ther was he nat like a cloisterere,
With thredbare cope, as is a poure scolere,
But he was like a maister or a pope.
Of double worsted was his semicope,
That round was as a belle out of the presse.
Somewhat he lisped for his wantonnesse,
To make his English swete upon his tonge;
And in his harping, whan that he hadde songe,
His eyen twinkeled in his hed aright,
As don the sterres in a frosty night.
This worthy limitour was cleped Huberd.'

Part I.—Wycliffe's England.

ing with reflections on their meanness and dishonesty, the poet's writings are no less rich in illustrations of the good terms on which they lived with the laity, and of the vexations which they occasioned the parochial clergy. Of the variety and sharpness of those irritations, no reader of the 'Canterbury Tales' is ignorant; for those valuable memorials of English life in the fourteenth century contain no more vivid social portraitures than those which demonstrate the mutual animosities of the mendicants and secular priests. And if the Wycliffian curates were unjust to these wandering interlopers, it cannot be said that they erred in this respect without provocation; for it is difficult to imagine anything more calculated to rouse resentment in the breast of a zealous parish-priest than the systematic action of the strolling friars. Attended by a single comrade,*— and sometimes by an additional servant, equipped with a sack, in which to put bulky contributions,—the begging limitor, *i.e.* a friar invested with the right to beg within the limits of a certain district, was constantly passing to and fro through the parishes of his assigned field† for mendicancy. One night he slept at a baron's castle; the next he spent in the manor-house of an hospitable knight; the third would see him under the roof of a wealthy yeoman; and as he travelled from point to point in his rounds, the pious circuiteer called at every wayside house where he was likely to get a penny in gift, or make a penny by merchandize, or acquire any such contribution to his sack as a loaf of bread, a piece of cheese, or a roll of woollen cloth.‡ At one homestead he would hear a housewife's con-

---

* Jacke Upland says, 'What betokeneth that ye go tweyne and tweyne together? If ye be out of charitie, ye accord not in soule.'

† Jacke Upland asks, 'Why hyre ye to ferme your limitors, geuing therefore ech yeare a certayne rent, and will not suffer one in an othere's limitation, right as ye were your selfes lordes of countreys ?'

‡ 'And whan this frere had said all his entent,
With *qui cum patre* forth his way he went.
Whan folk in chirche had yeve him what hem lest,
He went his way, no lenger wold he rest,
With scrippe and tipped staf, ytucked hie:
In every hous he gan to pore and prie,
And begged mele and chese, or elles corn.
His felaw had a staf tipped with horn,
A pair of tables all of ivory,
And a pointel ypolished fetisly,

fession, and give her absolution for a few farthings; at another he would make arrangements to marry a couple of lovers at the nearest parish-church, and so draw to his pocket the fee that would otherwise go to a secular curate; at a third he would shrive some superstitious but impenitent landowner, who, out of pure avarice, had withheld tithe from a pious rector. And wherever he went about, draining a rural district of superfluous money that had previously accrued to the secular clergy of the district, the wary and malignant limitor sowed the seeds of hatred and scorn for the ordinary parochial ministers in the breasts of simple people, whom he ought rather to have confirmed in their past habits of affectionate dutifulness to the priests of their local churches.

Their enemies in the ranks of the secular priesthood were wont to declare that the friars won the hearts and cash of the laity by underselling the parochial curates,—that is to say, by performing the special offices of the Church for smaller fees than the customary charges sanctioned by the bishops. But this assertion is scarcely consistent with the imputations of greed and extortionate knavery which the same accusers preferred against the same invaders of secular privilege; and the constant reiterations of the charge are attended by circumstances which incline us to regard the statement as an unfair attempt to fix dishonour upon the popularity of the mendicants. Nor is this the only point on which the opponents of the four orders are at the same time so inconsistent amongst themselves, and so contradictory to ascertained facts, that the impartial reader declines to put implicit reliance on their representations, which, ev.―

And wrote alway the names, as he stood,
Of alle folk that yave hem any good,
Askaunce that he wolde for hem praye,
"Yeve us a bushel whete, or malt, or reye,
A Goddes kichel, or a trippe of chese,
Or elles what you list, we may not chese;
A Goddes halfpeny, or a masse peny;
Or yeve us of your braun, if ye have any,
A dagon of your blanket, leve dame,
Our suster dere, (lo here I write your name)
Bacon or beef, or swiche thing as ye find."
A sturdy harlot went hem ay behind,
That was hir hostes man, and bare a sakke,
And what men yave hem, laid on his bakke.
And whan that he was out at dore, anon
He planed away the names everich on,
That he before had written in his tables:
He served hem with nifles and with fables.'—*Sompnoure's Tale.*

when they are marked by honesty of intention, very often err through onesidedness or excessive vehemence.

Of the charges ordinarily preferred against the friars, a complete summary is found in Jacke Upland's famous arraignment of the four orders, from which it appears, that whilst the beggar-priests were supplanting the old clergy in the confidence and affections of the people, the most odious rumours against the intruders were circulated by their antagonists. Indeed, every fault, except sloth and neglect of the interests of their class, was imputed to them. It was affirmed that, notwithstanding their professions of asceticism, they surpassed the world-loving seculars in the pursuit of carnal pleasures;* that whilst pilling the poor of pence and farthings, they were obsequious time-servers and servile adulators of the rich lords and ladies, who selected them as spiritual directors in preference to parochial curates; that departing from the rules of their founders, who, in imitation of their Saviour, were houseless wanderers, they built magnificent residences, in which they stored jewels and gold, and emulated the splendid luxury of the old monasteries; that they were habitual stealers of young children,† taking them craftily from their parents, and educating them to be friars; that they occasioned public scandal by the noisy wranglings and disputations which arose from the internal dissensions and rivalries of the four orders; and that,

---

* 'Frere,' inquires Jacke Upland, 'what charitie is this to the people, to lye and say that ye follow Christ in poverty more than other men done, and yet in curious and costly howsing, and fine and precious clothing, and delicious and liking feeding, and in treasures and jewels, and rich ornamentes, freres passen lordes and other riche worldly men . . . . Frere, what charitie is this, to be confessoures of lordes and ladies, and to other mighty men, and not amend hem in hir liuing, or rather as it seemeth, to be the bolder to kill poore tenauntes, and to liue in lechery, and there to dwell in your office of confessour for wynning of worldly goodes, and to be holde great by colour of suche ghostly offices: this seemith rather pride of freres than charitie of God.'

† This odious accusation is preferred by Jacke Upland on hearsay evidence. 'Why shall some sect of your freres pay eche a yeare a certayne to her generall provinciall or minister, or els to her souereignes? but if he steale a certayne number of children (*as some men sayne*), and certes if this be sothe, then we be constreined upon a certayne payne to do theft agaynst God's commandments, "*Non furtum facies.*" . . . . Frere, what charitie is this to beguile children or they commen to discretion, and bynde hym to your orders that byn not grounded in Gods law against her frendes will ?"

not content with curtailing the proper influence, and encroaching upon the ancient privileges, of the parish-priests, they sought occasions for offering unmannerly insults to the curates, whom they systematically harassed and injured.

That this last accusation was literally true, there is no room for question; for whilst all their opponents concur in supporting it, the attitude of the friars to the older kinds of clergy could not have been maintained by courteous action, and must have been fruitful of continual and scandalous altercations. When the friar of the sompnoure's tale approached the couch of bedridden Thomas, almost the first words uttered by the holy man were expressive of disdain for the negligence and inefficacy of common curates:—

> ' I wol with Thomas speke a litel throw;
> Thise curates ben so negligent and slow
> To gropen tendrely a conscience.
> In shrift, in preching is my diligence
> And study, in Peters wordes and in Poules,
> I walke and fishe Cristen mennes soules,
> To yeld our Lord Jesu his propre rent;
> To sprede his word is sette all min entent.'

And on ascertaining that Thomas was content with his parish-priest, had indeed on that very morning been shriven by the curate, and was resolved upon dismissing his mendicant visitor without giving him a single farthing, the zealous itinerant went off in a consuming rage, which was in no degree pacified by the laughter that followed the announcement of his discomfiture at the hospitable table of ' the lord of that village.'

It is easy to imagine how, smarting under the recent indignity put upon himself and his class, this angry itinerant avenged himself at the earliest opportunity by exhibiting unusual arrogance to the curates in his ' limit;' how, on the following Sunday, or Saint's day, he entered the chief church of the district, just as the congregation were preparing to listen to their rector's postillizing exposition of a chapter of sacred writ; and how, after insolently waving aside the officiating secular with a movement of his hand, or an elevation of his staff, he ascended the pulpit, and preluded his sermon with some galling remarks on the superiority of the four orders to all other kinds of clergy, and on the worthlessness of the best secular curate in all Christendom in comparison with the stupidest and laziest monk of the whole country.

If he possessed a license* to sell pardons and relics, this angry friar would pass from his criminatory exordium to an enumeration of the various indulgences, relics, and charms, which the terms of his commission empowered him to vend from the pulpit to the crowd of gaping rustics, whom he induced to buy his costly wares by poignant anecdotes of their power to

---

* The Pardoner's statement (in the 'Canterbury Tales') of his method and manner in the pulpit, is an excellent illustration of the insults which the parochial clergymen of Chaucer's England were required to endure meekly whenever they came into collision with the itinerant priests:—

'Lordings, quod he, in chirche whan I preche,
I peine me to have an hautein speche,
And ring it out, as round as goth a bell,
For I can all by rote that I tell.
My teme is alway on, and ever was;
Radix malorum est cupiditas.
  First I pronounce whennes that I come,
And than my bulles shew I all and some:
Our liege lordes sele on my patent',
That shew I first my body to warrente,
That no man be so bold, ne preest ne clerk,
Me to disturbe of Cristes holy werk.
And after that than tell I forth my tales.
Bulles of popes, and of cardinales,
Of patriarkes, and bishoppes I shewe,
And in Latin I speke a wordes fewe,
To saffron with my predication,
And for to stere men to devotion.
Than shew I forth my longe cristal stones,
Ycrammed ful of cloutes and of bones,
Relikes they ben, as wenen they echon.'

Whilst the pardoner reads his bulls, and in the fashion of a cheap-jack at a country fair announces the articles which he has for sale—bones of saints, charms for the prevention and cure of disease in cattle, mystic mittens for hands of farmers whilst sowing corn, and other like products of religious imposture—the auditors keep upon their legs; but no sooner does the itinerant begin his sermon on the evils of avarice, than the congregation resume their three-legged stools. The pardoner, with delicious pungency and droll impudence continues:—

'By this gaude have I wonnen yere by yere
An hundred mark, sin I was pardonere.
I stonde like a clerk in my pulpet,
And whan the lewed peple is doun yset,
I preche so as ye han herd before,
And tell an hundred false japes more.
Than peine I me to stretchen forth my necke,
And est and west upon the peple I becke,
As doth a dove, sitting upon a berne:
Myn hondes and my tonge gon so yerne,
That it is joye to see my besinesse.
Of avarice and of swiche cursednesse
Is all my preching, for to make hem free
To yeve hir pens, and namely unto me.

*   *   *   *

Than I tell hem ensamples many on
Of olde stories longe time agon.
For lewed peple loven tales olde;
Swiche thinges can they wel report and holde.

abate the annoyances, or completely stay the progress of adverse fortune. Such appeals to popular credulity were never made in vain; and when the pious huckster descended from his stage, on quitting the church he seldom omitted to heighten the vexation of its secular priests by a parting taunt at their incapacity, or an ironical prayer for their spiritual and temporal welfare.

What? trowen ye, that whiles I may preche
And winnen gold and silver for I teche,
That I wol live in poverte wilfully?
Nay, nay, I thought it never trewely,
For I wol preche and beg in sondry londes,
I wol not do no labour with min hondes,
Ne make baskettes for to live therby,
Because I wol not beggen idelly.
I wol non of the apostles contrefete;
I wol have money, wolle, chese, and whete,
Al were it yeven of the pourest page,
Or of the pourest widewe in a village:
Al shulde hire children sterven for famine.
Nay, I wol drinke the licour of the vine.'

Of course this satiric picture of the mendicant priest of the fourteenth century is surcharged with animosity against his class; but however unjust it may be, to the general conditions of the four orders, there is a superabundance of testimony that the portraiture was not wanting in fairness to unfavourable specimens of the migratory brothers. But in palliation of the dissolute friars, no less than of the world-loving curates, reference may be made to the prevailing tastes and morality of a period in which habits, that are nowadays a proof of utter depravity, were held to be nothing worse than trivial misdemeanours.

CHAPTER XI.

LOLLARDY: MANNERS AND SOCIAL ASPECTS.

IT still remains for us to pay more particular attention than we have hitherto done to the politico-religious agitators of the fourteenth century, who are very generally termed, and may fairly be regarded as, the originators of the movement which resulted in our great ecclesiastical reformation. But though it is the custom to call them the Fathers of the British Reformation, and though their title to high rank amongst restorers of the national faith is indisputable, the reader must never forget that in matters of religious opinion they differed widely from the orthodox members of the Reformed Church, and that their social characteristics and political principles— apart from the dangerous communistic opinions which they cherished to their great obloquy, and the hindrance of what was excellent in their religious sentiments and views on ecclesiastical government—give them greater resemblance to the non-conforming Puritans of the seventeenth century, and the Methodists of the Wesleyan Revival, than to the original framers and supporters of the Anglican Establishment.

A consideration of the insulting name affixed to them by their contemptuous and bitter adversaries will lead us conveniently to the ground from which we may gain a fair, though necessarily imperfect, view of their most noteworthy peculiarities of thought and demeanour.

Just as the Waldensian heretics of an earlier period were

erroneously supposed to have derived their name from Peter Waldus,* who has been demonstrated to have been born at a time subsequent to the rise of the sect from which he in fact gained his surname, it has been represented on no stronger evidence, and in opposition to the strong presumptive testimony of monastic writings, that the Lollards were indebted for their appellation to Walter Lollardus, who was burnt for heresy at Cologne in 1322, and who doubtless acquired his designation *from* the party of which he was a conspicuous member. Another derivation of 'Lollard' from a German source, is the supposition that it sprung from 'lollen,' to sing with a low voice ; but though this way of accounting for the term has the countenance of so learned and critical a writer as Mosheim, who seems on this point to have been guided by patriotic predilection rather than the light of his exact and deep erudition, it is far more probable that the name came from the Latin 'Lolium,' which presents us with the sense in which the odious nickname was consistently used by the monkish utterers, who may be justly credited with its manufacture. It is thus that 'Lollardi' is used in the 'Song against the Lollards'† by a pungent master of clerical vituperation, who calls the religious agitators, the tares, brambles, and darnels that have sprung up

---

* Foxe the Martyrologist observes, ' In the time of this Alexander sprang up the doctrine and name of those who were then called, ' pauperes de Lugduno,' who, from one Waldus, a chief senator in Lyons, were named "Waldenses,"' but Foxe's learned editor, the Rev. George Townsend, M.A. remarks on this point, ' Our author has fallen into the very common error of confounding the Waldenses with the "Pauperes de Lugduno," or "Poor men of Lyons," and of deriving their origin from Waldus, or Peter Waldo, of Lyons. The earliest period assigned to Peter Waldo is the year 1160, but there is a document of the year 1100, " La Nobla Leycson," which speaks of the Waldenses, or Vaudois, under the term Vandés. It is therefore much more probable that Peter Waldo was named after the community called Vandés than that the Waldenses should take their name from his.'

† This most instructive of political ballads says,

3. Sed hostis tui populi,
   Auctor omnis periculi,
     Gravi spumans invidia,
   In humo hujus hortuli
   De fundo sui sacculi
     Modo jecit zizania ;

Quæ suffocant virentia,
   Velut frumentum *lollia*,
     Ac spinæ, vepres, tribuli ;
Sic florida marcentia,
Fragrantia, fœtentia,
     Sicci sunt fontis rivuli.

in the garden of Christ's Church, to choke the fruitful and flowering plants of faith and devotion. The same writer covers the detested reformers with charges of hypocrisy, malice, disloyalty, and extortionate dishonesty,—charges which the spokesmen of majorities in the wrong have never been slow to hurl at minorities in the right. By their warmest denouncers, Wycliffe's pious, and for the most part humble followers, were accounted wolves in sheep's clothing, sanctimonious breeders of sedition, spawners of atrocious doctrine vomited upon the earth's surface from Satan's jaws, sowers of dissension, pestilent fire-brands, thieves bent on plundering the rich in the name of religion, shameless demagogues ready to trample on the poor in the name of justice. In a single word, they were 'Lollards;' and the epithet thus hurled at them in wrath, and scorn, and hatred—even as 'Tory,' 'Whig,' 'Radical,' sprang from the political animosities of later generations—clung to them, took permanent place in the popular tongue, passed into royal injunctions and Acts of Parliament, and was used by the Reformers themselves, who, converting a stigma of shame into a badge of honour, adopted the opprobrious designation as their rightful appellation.

The persons to whom evil was thus imputed, were for the most part of humble birth and mean estate. Whilst the gentry of the realm were upon the whole zealous supporters or tolerant defenders of an ecclesiastical system, whose vestments and dignities were borne by themselves or their nearest kindred, and whose abuses could not be remedied without detriment to

4. Lollardi sunt zizania,
 Spinæ, vepres, ac lolia,
  Quæ vastant hortum vineæ;
Nam pejor pestilentia
Non fuit in ecclesia,
 Incedens tam erronee,
Quorum linguæ vipereæ,
Et dentes sunt et frameæ,
 Omni pleni fallacia.
Hi telæ sunt araneæ,
Parvis et magnis foveæ,
 Cunctis occultant retia.

5. Sub sanctitatis specie
 Virus vomant malitiæ
  Cunctis qui ipsos audiunt.
Zelatores ecclesiæ,
Sectatores justitiæ,
 Seipsos esse garriunt.
Sic simplices decipiunt,
Et mobiles inficiunt
 Sub simulata facie,
Vulpes incautos rapiunt,
Lupi in agnos sæviunt.
 Hostes omnis ecclesiæ.

Thomas Wright's ' Political Poems and Songs.'

their pecuniary interests, or violence to their political prejudices, the people who clamoured or murmured against sacerdotal luxury and clerical worldliness were of the kind that is nowadays designated by the term 'lower classes.' So notoriously were they, as a class, wanting in the respectability which accrues from the possession of ample means, that the author[*] of 'The Complaint of the Ploughman' uses 'loller' and 'londlese' almost as convertible terms. But notwithstanding their general humility, they gained the support of several important personages—such as Sir Thomas Latimer, Sir Lewis Clifford, the unpopular but powerful Duke of Lancaster, Lord Henry Percy, Sir John Montague, the Earl of Salisbury, and Lord Cobham the martyr, who, either from political motives, or concurrence in their religious sentiments, extended protection to the despised Reformers.

It is impossible to state with precision the numbers of these new malcontents; but it is certain that under Wycliffe's influence they became sufficiently numerous and intelligent to alarm the party of resistance in every quarter of the kingdom. Wycliffe's contemporary, Knighton, the Leicester canon, estimated their force at about one-half of the population. 'The number of those,' this authority assures us, 'who believed in Wycliffe's doctrine very much increased, and were multiplied, like suckers growing from the root of a tree. They everywhere filled the kingdom, so that a man could scarcely meet two people in the road but one of them was a disciple of Wycliffe.'

---

[*] The luxury of the higher clergy and the poverty of early reformers are put in sharp contrast by the caustic satirist. Of the splendid and sumptuous monk he says,—

'He is proud as prince in hall,
  In meats, and drinke, and all thing.
Some wearen mitre and ring,
With double worsted well ydight,
With royal meat and riche drinke,
And rideth on a courser as a knight.'

  Subsequently he says,—
'That one side is that I of tell,
  Popes, cardinals, and prelates,

Parsons, monkes, and freres fell,
Priours, abbots, of great estates.

*   *   *   *

The other side ben poore and pale,
  And people put out of prease,
And seeme caitiffs sore-a-cale,
  And ever is one without encrease,
Ycleped loller and londlese.'
    The Complaint of the Ploughman.

And he adds, 'They so prevailed by their laborious urging of their doctrines, that they gained over the half of the people, or a still greater proportion, to their sect. Some embraced their doctrines heartily, others they compelled to join them from fear or shame.' Knighton, however, like most of his contemporaries on both sides of the battle-field of Lollardy, doubtless regarded as Lollards all persons who exhibited any signs of tolerance for Wycliffian sentiments.

The most efficient instruments of the directors of this memorable agitation, were Wycliffe's 'poor priests,' a new sort of clergy, who, resembling primitive friars in their poverty and itinerant habits, perambulated the country in every direction, instructing the populace in the words of the sacred Scriptures, and encouraging them to put their trust in the book that saves, instead of relying on the merely human authority of priests. Bound by vows to hold no ecclesiastical preferment, lest the possession of wealth should lure them to the sloth and pride prevalent amongst the beneficed curates, these indigent and zealous ministers acquired much of the popular favour that had rewarded the self-denial and labours of the earlier mendicant brothers; and whilst thus diminishing the influence and repute of the friars, they concurred with the four orders in weaning the simpler folk from their ancient servility to ecclesiastical control.

Like the Elizabethan Puritans; like the primitive Baptists of James the First's reign; like the Quakers, who maintained almost to the present day the most conspicuous peculiarities of the early Baptists, of whom they were the immediate offspring; and like most of our other sects of nonconforming religionists, the Lollards of the fourteenth and fifteenth centuries were noticeable for their simplicity and soberness of attire; for their scrupulous avoidance of language that had even the slightest taint of profanity; for their disapprobation of frivolous amusements; and for a distinctive severity of aspect and demeanour, which procured for them an exaggerated reputation of sadness. Belonging to a generation that delighted in external display, and living in times when wealthy monks and seculars vied with the affluent laity in gorgeousness of costume, the Lollard preachers were known at sight by the dinginess of their russet or dull-blue gowns, and by their bare feet.* And just as the Quakers of the other day were charged by their enemies with bearing hearts full of insolence and uncharitableness, from which the homeliness of their drab clothes was designed to divert attention, the Lollards of old time were derided as hypocrites, who hoped to gain a reputation of humility by affecting a mean dress. Amongst the many coarse insults which Archbishop Arundel heaped on pious William Thorpe, was the disdainful and profane exclamation, 'Thou judgest every priest proud that will not go arrayed as thou dost. By ———! I deem him to be more meek that goeth every day in a scarlet gown, than thou in thy threadbare blue gown.' Nor were the Lollard men more noticeable for avoidance of personal decoration than their women, whose spiritual teachers—from the rector of Lutterworth down to the humblest of the rector's itinerant clergy—never omitted an opportunity of urging them to abstain from the use of trinkets and gauds for the enhancements of their natural charms, which, however disguised, were deplorably apt to fire men's hearts with sinful passions.†

* Their monkish satirists, gentlemen who prided themselves not a little on the cut and material of their own fashionable boots, maliciously asserted that Wycliffe's 'poor priests' were well supplied with stout shoes which they used when no one saw them, and concealed in the ample pockets of their sanctimonious gowns when they prepared to enter a town or village or solitary homestead to the admiration of their dupes. On this point the singer of the ballad, 'Against the Lollards' says,—

' 8. Villarum in exitibus,   Poenas foris amplificant,
    Se nudant solitaribus,   Intus tamen lætificant,
       Cum populo ludificant.   Se multis voluptatibus.
    Nudis incedunt pedibus,   Seipsos sic magnificant,
    Cum appropinquant foribus,   Quod alios parvificant
       Locorum quibus prædicant.   Multis pravis sermonibus.'

† In 'The Poor Caitiff' the rector of Lutterworth says, 'And women that array themselves nicely, to be seen of fools, sin grievously, for by their nice array and countenance they cause the loss of many souls . . . . And also let each woman beware that neither by countenancy, nor by array of body, nor of head, she stir any to wed her to sin. Not crooking her hair, neither laying it up on high, nor the head arrayed about with gold and precious stones, not seeking curious clothing, nor of nice shape, showing herself to be seemly to fools. For all such array of

Part 1.—Wycliffe's England.

Even more than by their plain attire the Lollards were distinguishable from other persons by mildness of tone, moderation of speech, and studious abstinence from words of imprecation: and many a person who would have found no offence in their prim and homely attire, had it not been united with other peculiarities implying disapproval of earthly vanities, could not tolerate the conscientious preciseness of speakers whom no irritation or surprise ever betrayed into the utterance of an oath. Few characteristics of medieval manners differ more widely from prevailing usages than the freedom with which the members of both sexes, of every rank and every degree of culture, of every age and pursuit, used to season their language with vows by the saints, familiar appeals to the sacred persons of the Holy Trinity, or impious allusions to the mysteries and incidents of the Saviour's story. Every vocation, every disease, every calamity, every class of desires, every appetite, had its special saint; and at every moment of trivial agitation the Englishman of this period would display a critical appreciation of the exact nature of his position by selecting out of a score or hundred different spiritual agents the power whose peculiar efficacy was most applicable to his case. A clever swearer would in a few brief sentences call to his assistance half-a-dozen angelic beings, —the guardian of his trade, the angel whose function it was to heal his particular malady, the saint after whom he was named, the tutelary saint of his family, the saint of the parish in which

women St. Peter and St. Paul by the Holy Ghost's teaching openly forbid. But let them be in clothing of shame-facedness and soberness; being subject to their husbands, after the rule of reason, as St. Peter and St. Paul teach: that they who believe not God's Word be won to health, beholding in awe the holy and chaste conversation of women. Thus in old time good women and holy, believing in God, adorned themselves as St. Peter saith. In the same strain the anonymous author of 'The Lantern of Light' (*circa* 1400) inveighs against the vain attire of frivolous men and women. ' Those are the men that loose out their breath, pinch in their bodies, part their hose, crakowin their shoes, and all disguisers of their garments. These are those that nicely dress their faces, that bridle their heads with head-bands, that set above honeycombs, with much other attiring, to make themselves keen to sin, and expose themselves to catch men with their lime-twigs. For God saith by the prophet Isaiah, " Because the daughters of Zion are become so proud, and come with stretched forth necks, and with vain, wanton eyes, seeing they come in tripping so nicely with their feet, I will make bald and smite the daughters of Zion." '

he was residing or travelling, the saint to whose shrine he made an annual pilgrimage. Chaucer's exemplary prioress was so dainty a lady, and so moderate a swearer that 'hire gretest othe n'as but by Seint Eloy;' but with one exception the other characters of the Canterbury Tales were bold and vehement swearers. The miller's wife swears by Saint Thomas of Kent: the carpenter by St. Frideswide: handy Nicholas by 'Goddes corpus:' Gerveis by 'Christes foot,' 'Christes sweet tree,' Saint Neot; the sumpner by 'Goddes armes two;' the host, 'as he were wood,' by Saint Thomas of India, 'nailes and bloode,' Saint Marie, Saint Ronion, 'Goddes dignitee,' and 'Goddes bones.' Amongst the other oaths of the merry talkers are 'Christes pain,' 'Goddes sowle,' 'Christes sowle,' 'Christes passion.' Against this excess of ingenious and anatomical blasphemy no one of the pilgrims makes any protest or sign of disapprobation, with the solitary exception of the poor and pious parson who has scarcely evinced his disgust at the host's ribald language, when he finds himself an object of suspicion and contempt to his companions who regard his squeamishness as an indication of Lollardy.

Nor were the conscientious scruples of the Lollards about the use of oaths confined to matters of colloquial swearing.

* On this point 'The Shipmannes Prologue' deserves special attention:—

'Our Hoste upon his stirrops stode anon,
And saide, "Good men, herkeneth eve-rich on,
This was a thrifty tale for the nones.
Sire parish preest," quod he, " for God-des bones,
Tell us a tale, as was thy forward yore.
I see wel that ye lerned men in lore
Can mochel good, by Goddes digni-tee."
The Person him answerd, "Bene-dicite!
What eileth the man, so sinfully to swere?"
Our Hoste answerd, "O Jankin, be ye there?

Now good men," quod our Hoste, "herk-neth to me.
I smell a Loller in the wind," quod he.
Abideth for Goddes digne passion,
For we shul han a predication:
This Loller here wol prechen us somwhat."
" Nay, by my fathers soule, that shal he nat,"
Sayde the Shipman, "here shal he nat preche,
He shal no gospel glosen here ne teche.
We leven all in the gret God," quod he.
" *He wolde sowen som difficultee,*
Or springen cockle in our clene corne.
And therfore, Hoste, I warne thee be-forne,
My joly body shal a tale telle."'

The last of the lines printed in Italics, which charges the Lollards with sowing

Making their yea yea, and their nay nay, and refraining from imprecations to saints in their ordinary conversation, they also maintained, with respect to judicial oaths, the doctrines which, still insisted on by the followers of George Foxe, are very generally, and no less erroneously, supposed to have originated amongst the Quakers, or their immediate progenitors, the primitive Baptists. The views of the early Lollards on this important subject may be gathered from the 'Examinations' of William Thorpe, who, on his appearance before Archbishop Arundel, argued that judicial oaths were sinful, and expressly prohibited by the scripture which declares 'that it is not lawful in any case to swear by any creature.' The book of the gospel was a creature, or rather 'nothing else but divers creatures of which it is made;' and, therefore, to swear by it was to swear by a creature, and hence a sin. The Christian citizen therefore, on being pressed by human authority to swear, should solicit permission to make his statements on solemn affirmation, instead of oath; 'but if a man may not excuse himself, without oath, to them that have power to compel him to swear, then he ought to swear only by God, taking Him only that is Truth for to witness the truth.' On finding, however, that his judge would not be satisfied with a solemn affirmation, or an oath by the Almighty, Master William Thorpe consented to lay his hand upon a copy of the Gospel, and swear in the usual form; solacing himself, however, in the pains of submission to a profane practice, by reminding his hearers that, though he swore by a creature, he could not be said to swear by the Gospel, because he touched the literary creature which represented the words of the Gospel,

cockle (*i. e.* weeds) in the clean corn-field, shows that the populace accorded to the word 'Lollard' the sense of its Latin derivation. Elsewhere we shall notice more fully the great number of the saints honoured by our forefathers in Catholic times, and the way in which the labour of guarding pious mortals was divided and subdivided amongst them,—a matter at which the author of the 'Dialogue of Familiar Talk' (1554), only glances when he says, 'Twenty years ago, who could say the Lord's Prayer in English? Who could tell any article of his faith? Who had once heard of any of the Ten Commandments? Who knew what Catechism meant? Who understood any point of holy baptism? If we were sick of the pestilence, we ran to St. Rook; if of the ague, to St. Pernel, or Master John Thorne. If men were in prison, they prayed to St. Leonard. If the Welshman would have a purse, he prayed to Davel Gathorne. If a wife were weary of her husband, she offered oats at St. Paul's in London to St. Uncumber.'

since, according to his understanding, 'the holy gospel of God may not be touched with man's hand.'*

Like the Friends and other non-conforming precisians of later times, the Lollards of Wycliffe's England disapproved of instrumental music as an element of Divine service, and even carried their disapprobation of the melodious art to the length of inveighing against the artificial melody of 'musitioners' as an influence prejudicial to the religious life of mankind, even when it was used for the diversion of human beings in periods of recreation. The doings of organists and choristers † beneath the roofs of the cathedrals they abhorred as Satanic devices to convert God's worship to man's amusement; and they cherished almost as lively a detestation for the fifers, bagpipers, clarion-blowers, and other minstrels, who used to accompany the parties of pilgrims to and fro, from their starting-places to their destined shrines, and back again. In estimating the relative forces of the many causes of the odium in which the Lollards were held by their social superiors and the great body of their world-loving contemporaries, it would be difficult to rate too highly the unpopularity which they incurred from their denunciations of the musical services that afforded a continual current of pure and elevating delight to the majority of their fellow-countrymen, and from their aspersions of an art that contributes more largely than any other to the social enjoyment of our

---

* 'I said, Sir, since I may not now otherwise be believed but by swearing, I perceive, as Augustine saith, that it is not speedful that ye, who should be my brethren, should not believe me: therefore I am ready by the word of God, as the Lord commanded by His word, to swear. Then the clerk said to me, Lay thine upon the book, touching the holy gospel of God, and take thy charge. And I said, Sir, I understand that the holy gospel of God may not be touched with man's hand.'—*Vide* William Thorpe's 'Examinations.'

† Concerning musical services Archbishop Arundel and William Thorpe exchanged some decided words. 'And the Archbishop said to me,' Master William Thorpe tells us, in the record of his 'Examinations,' 'Lewd lesel, is it not lawful for us to have organs in the church to worship therewithal God?' And I said, Yea, sir, by man's ordinance; but by the ordinance of God, a good sermon to the people's understanding were much more pleasant to God. The Archbishop said that organs and good delectable songs quickened and sharpened men's wits more than should any sermon. But I said, Sir, lusty men and worldly lovers delight, and court, and travail to have all their wits quickened and sharpened with divers sensible solaces.'

species. Had their condemnation of music only earned for them the antagonism and scorn of the numerous class who subsisted in feudal England by sacred or secular minstrelsy, it would have raised against their views a strong army of opponents in every quarter of the kingdom; but, by outraging the feelings of all persons who derived spiritual edification or innocent exhilaration from musical performances, it created for Lollardy a host of enemies, of whom the professional musicians and bigoted Churchmen were only a minority.*

Offending the lovers of personal display by the plainness of their apparel, offending swearers by their punctilious avoidance of oaths, offending intemperate livers by their abhorrence of carnal pleasures, offending people of taste by their dislike of music, offending the proud by their ostentatious humility, offending the rich by their pride of poverty and disdain of worldly wealth and honours, the Lollards caused still greater scandal to ordinary pleasure-seekers by their strict observance of the Sunday; which, in direct opposition to prevailing opinion, they regarded as a day whose sacred nature Christians were bound to mark, by abstinence from all worldly cares of business or enjoyment, by fasting, and by prayerful humiliation. There is not wanting evidence that this view of the Christian Sunday was adopted by many devout and orthodox Churchmen during the

* One of the earliest decrees concerning the musical services of the English Church was enacted by Archbishop Cuthbert's Synod (747 A.D.), which, amongst other injunctions to the clergy, directed ' That in a modest voice they should sing in the church.' Just ten years later, according to the 'Polychronicon,' ' was sent first into France the invention of organs out of Greece, by Constantine V., emperor of Constantinople.' The grounds on which the Lollards disapproved of choral services are thus set forth in 'The Ploughman's Prayer:' ' Lord, Ezechiel the prophet saith, that whan he spake to the people thy words, they turned thy words into songs and into tales: And so, Lord, men done now: they singin merilich thy words, and that singing they clepen thy service. But, Lord, I trow that the best singers no herieth thee not most. But he that fulfilleth thy words he heryeth thee ful wel, though he wepe more than sing. And I trow that weeping for breaking of thy commandements be more pleasing service to thee than the singing of thy words. And would God that men would serue him in sorrow for their sinnes, and that they shoulden afterward seruen thee in mirth. For Christ saith, yblessed ben they that maken sorrow, for they shoulden ben ycomforted. And wo to them that ben merry and have their comfort in this worlde. And Christ said that the world should joyen, and his seruants shulden be sory, but their sorrow should be turned into joy.'

fever of Lollardy, and in generations prior to the Wycliffian agitation. The author of 'Speculum Ecclesiæ' enjoined devout persons to maintain the holiness of Sabbaths by saying matins at church, by hearing mass with reverent silence, by listening to sermons, by doing works of charity to the poor and sick, by saying grace after dinner (a special direction which does not say much for the daily demeanour of pious Englishmen in the thirteenth century), by avoiding taverns and all such worldly amusements as wrestlings and dances, and by concluding the day with religious service. It should be borne in mind, that the Archbishop regarded Saints' days and other feasts as having equal claim with Sundays to be kept holy as Sabbaths. But though Sabbatarianism is of much older date than many writers are aware, and probably before the rise of Lollardy found considerable favour amongst sober English families, the Sunday—as will be more minutely demonstrated in a later section of this work—was a day which, according to modern notions, our ancestors profaned scandalously. It was the day of the whole week for marriages and marriage-feasts; for revels in the tavern and feasts at the squire's table; for pageants at princely courts, and dramatic interludes in sacred precincts; for fairs in country-towns, and sports on the village-green. The abstinence from secular industry on this holiest of days was only partial; and of those who abstained altogether from business on the first day of the week, the majority converted the time into an occasion for festive indulgence. Against this abuse of a holy institution the Lollards protested, to the disgust and derision[*] of most of their contemporaries, who upbraided

---

[*] A perusal of 'The Poor Caitiff' will inform readers how universal was the profanation of Sunday in the fourteenth century, and also show the frankness with which the great Chief of Lollardy denounced the 'Sunday amusements' of the period. 'Men,' urges the Reformer, in this fine manual of religion and vivid record of social manners, 'should busy themselves on the holy day to learn God's law, which might teach them to flee sin, and to rest in their God: and they should flee fleshly lusts, taverns, and chafferings, that hinder this end; and bewail their before-done sins, beseeching grace and might to withstand others to come.' That this doctrine must have been extremely unacceptable to a large number of people may be inferred from the Reformer's subsequent statement: 'But many men and women of this world travail busily all the week, and yet they will not rest on the Sunday. If there be either fair, or market, or any other place where they may win any money, then they, and their servant, and their work-beast, shall busily

them for their sadness, sourness, moroseness: just as the Cavaliers of the Caroline period, in the same spirit and under almost the same provocations, imputed malignity and gloom to the austere Puritans, who, in defiance of the 'Book of Sports' and the feelings of 'society,' declaimed against the stage and the maypole.

Another cause of the unpopularity of the Lollards was their disapproval of the domestic pilgrimages, which were important sources of social diversion to the inhabitants of feudal England, who were induced to take part in them quite as much by appetite for amusement and change as by a desire for religious edification. The pilgrimages to national shrines afforded our forefathers the same kind of recreation and excitement that English people of the present generation derive from a Swiss trip, a run to the Highlands, an autumnal sojourn at a seaside watering-place. Occasions for seeing the world and making pleasant acquaintances, they were excursions to which the young and old of both sexes looked forward as times of love, adventure, and glee; and it is not difficult to believe that, in spite of their predominating hurtfulness, they gave rise to a large amount of innocent pleasure. But, whatever might be said in behalf of their influence, no thoughtful observer can deny that they were also attended with many evils. By their costliness they tended to the impoverishment of the humbler people, whom they

labour therefore.' 'The Poor Caitiff' continues: 'In the second manner many men break this commandment, for many cease on the holy day from great bodily travails, but they occupy themselves in great spiritual sins. . . . . Nevertheless St. Augustine saith, that is less trespass to go to the plough, to dig, or delve, and for women to spin on the holy day, than to lead dances and frequent taverns. For such folk in a manner hallow the work-days, doing good and lawful works, and in the holy days spend their life in drunkenness and gluttony, lechery and pride, and such great deadly sins. . . . . In the third manner this command is broken by them that spend their time in idle and vain plays, and have great liking to behold and see vanities, and to hear and to tell idle tales, and to speak of filth and of sin, and to backbite their fellow-Christians when they sit together.' The 'Lantern of Light' speaks not only of fairs held on Sundays, which were common, but of fairs held on Sundays *in churches*, which were less common, though by no means infrequent. 'Against this (the fourth) commandment the fiend and his members give leave to chapmen to buy and sell, yea, within the sanctuary, on the holy Sunday; and victuallers of the country hold common markets. Yet see more against this command of God. The great fairs of the year, for the most part, are set on the Sabbath-day, by the fiend's counsel.'

caused to spend, on offerings to shrines and the various requirements of travel, money that could have been saved to advantage, or laid out to better account. The ordinary arrangements of a party of pilgrims were conducive to nearly every sort of carnal excess. Thrown together for many days, the fellow-pilgrims amused themselves on the road with light tales and frivolous conversation. On halting for food at the wayside hostelries, they too often ate and drank after the manner of revellers, instead of exhibiting the moderation of devout persons journeying to a scene of religious exercise; and under the excitements of liquor and feasting, music and merry talk, they not seldom gave the reins to violent passions and evil desires. In short, the pilgrimages of Wycliffe's England had become little else than secular merry-makings, and were attended by all the worst incidents of the village wake. So far as they influenced the life of devout people, they were promoters of superstition rather than nurses of genuine religious sentiment. Recognising these facts, many persons, to whom Lollardy was odious, regarded them as relics of ancient usage that had better be discontinued, and even denounced them with a fervour similar in kind and degree to the warmth with which our evangelical clergy express their disapproval of theatres. That the disapprobation of pilgrimages was not confined to Wycliffe's followers may be inferred from the fact, that Archbishop Sudbury—whose death is sometimes regarded as one of the outrages of Lollard fanaticism, and whose archiepiscopal seat derived so much benefit from the continual flow of pilgrims to St. Thomas's shrine—openly assured a party of Canterbury worshippers, that they wasted their zeal and substance in journeying from their homes to purchase unavailing indulgences.*

But the opinion of the more enlightened ecclesiastics, who saw and declared the evil consequences and futility of pilgrimages, availed nothing with the majority of people who upheld

* A generation later Archbishop Arundel enunciated a very different view respecting the efficacy of pilgrimages. 'What!' exclaimed his grace to William Thorpe, 'janglest thou against men's devotion? Whatsoever thou or such other say, I say that the pilgrimage that now is used is to them that do it a praisable and a good mean to come the rather to grace. But I hold thee unable to know this grace, for thou enforcest thee to hinder the devotion of the people.'

the old pilgrimages from the influence of habit, superstition, or antagonism to all changes that threatened to curtail their pleasures. And whilst the shrine-worshippers paid no heed to Archbishop Sudbury's counsel, they warmly resented the fervour with which Lollardy inveighed against their favourite practice, as prejudicial to morals and the social well-being of the multitude, and scandalously conducive amongst the most ignorant folk to the sin of idolatry. Since this life was a pilgrimage, and all human beings were nothing but pilgrims passing onwards to the realm of eternal bliss or the abode of everlasting pain,* the stout Lollards maintained that the travellers in so solemn a pilgrimage, instead of amusing themselves with jocund trips to the graves of pious men of olden time, had better give all their time and care to the conduct of the one great journey from the grave to the gates of eternity.

Conspicuous for their munificence to the sick and to persons poorer than themselves, the poor Lollards offended prevailing opinion by their manner of doing alms and their choice of objects for Christian benevolence. Whilst the wealthier people of Wycliffe's England, in compliance with the ostentatious spirit of feudal manners, gave liberally to mendicants who thronged their outer doors,† or cheered them with servile acclamations as they rode in splendour to the hunting-ground or the tournament, they were criminally negligent of the claims of such human misery as lay remote from their daily paths. Whilst stout beggars scrambled for the largesses insolently

---

* 'Moreover,' said Lord Cobham, 'in this I am fully persuaded, that every man dwelling on this earth is a pilgrim, either towards bliss or pain. And that he which knoweth not, nor will know, nor yet keep the holy commandments of God in his living here, albeit that he goeth on pilgrimage into all quarters of the world, if he departeth so, he shall surely be damned. Again, he that knoweth the holy commandments of God, and so performeth them to the end of his life to his power, shall without fail be saved in Christ, though he never in his life go on pilgrimage, as men use nowadays to Canterbury, Walsingham, Compostella, and Rome, or to other places.

† 'But alms-doers in the fiend's church feed many wretches, as stiff beggars, and strikers over the land, and groaners without cause, that need not their goods. Yea, to minstrels, to jugglers, and other vain japers, they deal largely their goods and call it alms. But these men say goods are thus dispended all amiss. And if they do anything as need is, presently they seek vain-glory, and lose all their reward.'

thrown to them by the lords of the soil, the miserable sufferers from extreme sickness and utter indigence too often died in hovels or ditches, without human sympathy. The deaths of these wretched creatures were stigmatised by Lollardy as 'murders'—done, perhaps, more through want of thought than want of heart, but still murders,* for which the rich would be held accountable at the final judgment: and to mitigate the pains of the forlorn outcasts, the new devotees denied themselves the comforts and necessaries of life, to the disgust of their opponents, who saw in such eccentric charity only another insidious attempt to promote discontent in the lowest classes of the populace.

* 'Also,' says Wycliffe in 'The Poor Caitiff,' 'there is manslaughter in other manner, in which man is said to slay his fellow-Christian; as he or she hath the goods of the world, and seeth man or woman in great default or mischief, and will not help them. I speak not of pardoners, nor of bold beggars, but of them that are poor, feeble, crooked, blind, and lame, or in some other mischief by the sufferance of God; and others who have pain and default, who are ashamed to ask and would rather suffer much mischief than beg; of whom it is said in Holy Writ, Thou hast seen a man dying for hunger, if thou hast not fed him thou hast slain him.'

CHAPTER XII.

LOLLARDY: TENETS AND POLITICS.

IT would be a great mistake to suppose that the difference between the Lollards and the conservative Churchmen of the fourteenth century, on matters of religious opinion, was so great as it has been represented by the many historians, who wrote under the very erroneous impression that the theology of the earlier Reformers was nearly identical with the theology of Edward the Sixth's prelates, and who would have us believe that the Marian martyrs died in support of views universally accepted by Wycliffe's 'poor priests.' At its outset, a protest against the corruptions of a clergy, rather than a revolt against the doctrines of a church, the Lollardy of Wycliffe's England, during the first stages of its career, directed its force against vicious practices much more than against erroneous dogmas; and it had made great advances to the fullness of its perilous power, and a perfect development of its dangerous political principles, before the leaders of the movement converted an agitation for social reform into a battle for new faith.

To state the precise time at which this change was effected in the operations and designs of the Reformers would be impossible, even if history had preserved the minutest particulars of a struggle, the greater part of which is involved in impenetrable obscurity; for it is not in the nature of things that the large number of persons concerned in the movement of attack can have acted with uniform harmony and exact concurrence of sentiment. Long after it had altered the nature of the conflict, and had distinctly repudiated some of the principal tenets of orthodox theology, the Wycliffian party was unanimous in nothing but a resolve to withstand Papal encroachments, a strong desire to render the clergy amenable to some sort of public opinion, and a general purpose to employ the enormous wealth of the ecclesiastical institutions for the relief of the poor and the promotion of true religion. Just as the Liberal party in the House of Commons, during Lord Palmerston's ascendancy, comprised politicians of several kinds—from cold patrician Whigs to ardent Radicals—the Lollards of the fourteenth century, together with a large proportion of persons far advanced in theological heresy, numbered many hundreds of supporters, whose faith was not at direct variance with any of the doctrines authorised two centuries later by the Council of Trent. On purgatory, penance, transubstantiation, baptism, the efficacy of priestly absolution, and all other principal topics of polemical warfare, Wycliffe and his more learned associates underwent successive changes of opinion during the various stages of the protracted contest, that brought them in the course of years to conclusions, from which they would have turned with abhorrence at the outset of their inquiries into the foundations and sources of religious opinion. And whilst the chiefs of the new party were continually modifying and reforming their articles of faith, so that it was impossible for the intelligent and impartial observer to state precisely what they continued to believe, and what they had rejected of old tenets, and how far they had marched beyond the outer boundaries of religious orthodoxy, the multitude of their comparatively unenlightened followers presented every conceivable shade of thought and diversity of sentiment between the darkness of Papal error and the light of evangelical truth.

The biographers who maintain that Wycliffe's theology agrees in every important particular with the doctrines of Latimer and Cranmer, either overlook, or make childish attempts to explain away, the numerous passages which demonstrate how largely the Father of the Reformation concurred to the last in opinions which the Protestants of the sixteenth century repudiated unanimously as superstitious and hurtful. On the doctrine of purgatorial punishment* the Rector of Lutterworth

---

* In that quaint chapter of 'The Poor Caitiff' entitled 'The Armour of Heaven,' Wycliffe says, ' Two spurs it is needful that thou have to thy horse, and that they be sharp to prick thy horse if needful, that he loiter not in the way: for many horses are slow if they are not spurred. These two spurs are love and

held views that no clergyman of Elizabeth's church could have taught without incurring censure and deprivation. His 'Poor Caitiff' contains a grateful recognition of the salutary uses of purgatorial terrors; and though a passage of the 'De Veritate Scripturæ' countenances faintly the opinion that the author in a more merciful mood excluded the punishment of fiery torture from his conception of an abode, where he describes the saints as passing their time in unconscious repose, there is no lack of evidence that his more enlightened disciples long continued to pray for the liberation of souls from the confinement and sharp discipline of purgatory. Of the mass of testimony affecting this point, one of the most characteristic items is the brief record of the expenditure of a certain deceased John Gamalin's estate on the purchase of a copy of 'The Poor Caitiff,' the successive holders of which manual of seasonable counsel were required, in consideration of the benefit derived from its pages, to pray for the soul of the poor Lollard with whose earthly substance it had been purchased. 'This book,' runs the record of this singular bequest, 'was made of the books of John Gamalin, for a common profit, that the person, that has this book committed to him of the person that hath power to commit it, have the use thereof for the time of his life, praying for the soul of the same John. And that he that hath this aforesaid use of commission, when he occupieth it not, leave he it for a time to some other person. Also that the person to whom it was committed for the term of life, under the aforesaid conditions, deliver it to another the term of his life. And so be it delivered and committed from person to person, man or

dread; which of all things must stir men to the way of heaven. The right spur is the love that God's dear children have for the lasting weal that shall never end. The left spur is dread of the pains of purgatory and of hell, which are without number, and never may be told out.' Other places where Wycliffe appeals to his disciples' dread of purgatorial torment are familiar to all readers of the Reformer's works. In the 'De Veritate Scripturæ' he speaks of 'the saints sleeping or resting in purgatory;' which gentle and tranquillising picture of purgatorial existence caused Dr. James, one of the Reformer's *un*historical biographers, to exclaim triumphantly, 'Surely by this division Popish purgatory is thrust clean out of doors. For there is little rest and less sleeping there, if we believe them that have (feigned to) come from thence, and have told us so. And by this reason, if this fire of purgatory be clean put out, the smoke of it, that is prayers for the dead, must needs in a very short time vanish away.'

woman, as long as the book endureth.' The book of Lollard Devotion thus purchased and bequeathed on trust for the benefit of John Gamalin's soul, together with other Harleian MSS., has passed into the possession of the trustees of the British Museum—a body of eminent gentlemen, whose Protestantism forbids them to fulfil the requirements of the trust in John Gamalin's spiritual behalf.

Long after the Lollards had arrived at something like uniformity of opinion upon several doctrinal questions, and had completely freed themselves from the doctrine of transubstantiation and belief in the mediation of saints, they clung to the theory of purgatorial discipline, and with affectionate concern for those who had been dear to them in this life, continued to purchase priestly prayers for their well-being in, and liberation from, the intermediate state of existence which was supposed to lie between this life and eternity. That the belief in purgatory prevailed amongst the multitude of devout gospellers down to the time of our final rupture with Rome, may be inferred from the significant fact that so learned and courageous an inquirer as William Tindal retained it amongst the articles of his creed after he had thrown in his lot with that of the Reformers. 'I promised him,' says Humphry Monmouth, the London draper, in the record of his intercourse with the pious scholar, when the latter was sedulously occupied with the work of translating the Scriptures, 'ten pounds sterling to pray for my father's and mother's souls. I paid it to him when he went to Hamburgh.'* That he overcame the influence of early instruction with respect to this article of the Catholic faith soon after his receipt of Humphry Monmouth's fee, his writings supply satisfactory testimony; but his continuance in the error, at a time when his heretical opinions and labours had rendered him an object of persecution, enables us to conceive what must have been the theological condition of the less learned members of his party,

---

* From what has been said concerning the countless diversities of religious opinion among the earlier Lollards, the reader will not be surprised to find some of them strongly disposed to reject the doctrine of Purgatory, more than a hundred years before Tindal's secession from the ranks of orthodoxy. 'The second sort,' says Lord Cobham, in the declaration of his Christian Belief, 'are in purgatory, '*if any such there be by the Scriptures*, abiding the mercy of God and a full deliverance of pain.'

Part I.—Wycliffe's England.

and is of itself sufficient to discredit the representations of historians, who would have us think that the Reformers of the earlier years of Henry the Eighth's reign were divines of the same texture and complexion as Cranmer and Ridley in their closing years.

Another delicate and dangerous subject on which the earlier Lollards differed greatly amongst themselves, and from their successors of the sixteenth century, was the use of images and pictures in divine worship; but though Wycliffe and his contemporary followers were not agreed as to the usefulness and hurtfulness of these instruments of religious education, and were by no means of one mind as to the measure of respect that might be shown to *simulacra* of the sacred persons of the Holy Trinity, they exhibited a degree of tolerance, in regard to images and pictorial representations of the Saviour's story, that would have greatly scandalised the gospellers of Henry the Eighth's later years, and is still more at variance with the spirit of those Elizabethan and Caroline Puritans, who could not see two sticks of straws lying cross-wise in a street without giving utterance to an expression of abhorrence.

Far from discerning profanity in the ecclesiastical decorations, which the prosecutors of Archbishop Laud regarded with an animosity more fanatical and scarcely less superstitious than the primate's fondness for hierarchical toys and gauds, Wycliffe was of opinion that the artistic devices of the roodloft and other such similitudes might be profitable to simple worshippers, who, unable to read the sacred word, might be taught to understand the characters wrought by the sculptor's chisel and the painter's brush.* In the following century, when bolder inquiry and fuller consideration of the perils inseparable from the use of images had induced the more advanced Lollards to cherish a cordial disapproval of the effigies and *simulacra*, that were incentives to the heinous sin of idolatry far oftener than

---

* 'All such similitudes or images,' says the author of 'The Poor Caitiff,' 'should be as kalendars to ignorant folk; and as clerks say in their books what they should do, so ignorant folks, when they lack teaching, should learn by images whom they should worship and follow in living. Each man is forbidden to do God's worship to images, but it is good to each man to learn by the sight of them to follow saints living.'

aids to pure devotion, William Thorpe had made considerable advances from the forbearance which characterised Wycliffe's sanction of artificial similitudes to the spirit which animated the iconoclasts of the sixteenth and seventeenth centuries. But notwithstanding his courageous firmness* in declaring against idolatrous reverence of images, William Thorpe displayed none of that fervour against the sinfulness of using images, which would have distinguished his declarations had he lived a century and half later, and been examined by Bonner or Gardiner, instead of Archbishop Arundel. This tolerance is the more noteworthy, as the Lollards had a lively abhorrence of the sin of idol-worship, their repugnance to which offence, and to all things likely to engender a disposition to it, was a chief cause of their disapproval of pilgrimages.

But though the earlier Lollards concurred to some extent with conservative Churchmen in recognising the usefulness and salutary influence of substantial similitudes, so long as the respect shown to them did not assume the nature of idolatrous

* When the circumstances of his trial are considered, William Thorpe may be commended for courage and firmness: but it cannot be denied that his answers with respect to image-worship have an air of disingenuousness, and abound with indications that he felt and thought much more than he ventured to say. Arguing very sophistically that, as all things may be worshipped in so far as they are worshipful, images ' are worshipful in their kind, and to the end that God made them for,' the Reformer says to Arundel, ' and therefore to the end that God made them to, they are all praiseable and worshipful, and especially man, that was made after the image and likeness of God, is full worshipful in his kind; yea, this holy image, that is man, God worshippeth. And therefore every man should worship other, in kind, and also for heavenly virtues that men use charitably. And also, I say, wood, tin, gold, silver, or any other matter that images are made of, all these creatures are worshipful in their kind, and to the end that God made them for. But the carving, casting, and painting of an imagery, made within man's hand, albeit this doing be accepted of men of highest state and dignity, and ordained of them to be a calendar to unlearned men, who neither can nor will be learned to know God in His word, neither by His creatures, nor by His wonderful and divers workings: yet this imagery ought not to be worshipped in form, nor in the likeness of man's craft. Nevertheless, that every matter the painters paint with, since it is God's creature, ought to be worshipped in the kind, and to that end that God made and ordained it to serve man.' On being pressed by his contemptuous examiner, Thorpe spoke more manfully, and declared against the use of images, as well as the idolatrous abuse of them, saying, ' They that come to the church to pray devoutly to the Lord God, may in their inward mind be the more fervent, that all their outward senses be closed from an outward seeing and hearing, and from all disturbance and lettings.'

Part I.—Wycliffe's England.

homage, they were in continual controversy with their opponents as to the degree and kind of respect which simple folk might render to the artistic symbols. Admitting that unlearned men might derive some assistance in devotional exercises from pictures and statues, provided they regarded such devices as nothing more than kalendars, from which their minds might gain the same sort of guidance that educated persons obtained from the letters of written gospel, Lollardy at a very early date exclaimed against the way in which the multitude was trained to bow the knee and address words of adoration to stocks and stones. The orthodox clergy, on the other hand, refused to detect any idolatrous quality in these expressions of reverence. Professing due abhorrence of idolatry, the defenders of old usage insisted that the ordinary demonstration of reverence, paid by Christians to the rood and the similitudes of blessed saints, were never paid to the materials of which the images were made, but to the divine or sacred persons, of whose existence and awful power the adorers were reminded by the works of human art. The worship of idols they upheld as decent and salutary; but on their lips, and also on the lips of their adversaries, 'worship' did not signify the adorative service of an intelligent creature to his Creator, but merely conveyed the idea of dutiful respect, just as it continues to do at the present time, when it is employed to mark the esteem in which civil magistrates of worshipful degree should be held by loyal citizens. Archbishop Arundel would have repudiated with horror, as a thing unscriptural and blasphemous, an assertion that images were fit objects of devotion; but he warmly contended that worship, *i.e.* respect, should be shown to 'images that move men to devotion.'

One of the favourite arguments with the defenders of this kind of idol-worship is so characteristic of the men who used it, and of the period in which it was fashionable, that we may not pass it by without a word of special notice. Throughout feudal Europe it was the custom for persons of inferior degree to recognise the authority of their superiors by honouring its *emblems* with acts of servile deference that in later times were only exacted when the superiors were personally present. The respect which Herman Gesler required the Swiss to show to his hat was nothing more than such homage as they would have willingly paid the emblem of his authority if they had recognised the lawfulness of his rule, and the validity of his claims on their allegiance. The movement of respect was in itself nothing more than what the patriots were doing daily, and without any sense of personal degradation, towards their rightful rulers. The same men who disdained to bow to the Austrian governor's hat, on the eve of an insurrection against the national oppressor, would have imputed lack of courtesy or patriotism to any of their countrymen who had omitted to pay a similar compliment to their liberator's cap. The same servile courtesy prevailed in every part of Western Europe. When a lord's banner was borne along a public way, all beholders who owed him fealty instantly uncovered, and remained with bare heads till the gaudy emblem of lawful power had passed from their sight. When a great man's messenger delivered a letter sealed with his master's signet to a person subject to the authority, of which the picture on the wax was an emblem, the receiver of the epistle removed his cap and rendered formal obeisance to the seal before he ventured to open the paper. Of course the obeisance was not rendered to the seal, but to the authority of which the seal was a sign; and in like manner it was maintained by the defenders of image-worship,* from the days of the early Lollards till

---

* Arundel stated the case to William Thorpe thus: 'I grant well that nobody ought to do worship to any such images for themselves. But a crucifix ought to be worshipped for the passion of Christ that is painted thereon, and so brought thereby to man's mind; and thus the images of the blessed Trinity, and of the Virgin Mary, Christ's mother, and other images of saints, ought to be worshipped. For lo, earthly kings and lords, who use to send their letters sealed with their arms, or with their privy signet, to them that are with them, are worshipped of those men. For when those men receive their lords' letters, in which they see and know the wills and biddings of the lords, in worship of their lords they do off their caps to those letters. Why not, then, since in images made with man's hand we may read and know many and divers things of God and His saints, shall we not worship their images?' About a century and a half later, Stephen Gardiner, bishop of Winchester, wrote to Captain Vaughan (May 3, 1547), 'For the destruction of images containeth an enterprise to subvert religion, and the state of the world with it, and especially the nobility, who, by images, set forth and spread abroad, to be read of the people, their lineage and parentage, with remembrance of their state and acts; and the poursuivant carrieth not on his breast the king's name, written with such letters as few can spell, but such as all can read be they never so rude, being great known letters in images of three lions and three fleur-de-lis, and other beasts holding those arms. And he that

Part I.—Wycliffe's England.

Mary's fires had ceased to burn, that the people who knelt and bowed to images and relics addressed their obeisance *through* visible creatures *to* unseen powers. To teach them to abstain from corporeal expressions of reverence to the visible creatures would wean them from their devout dutifulness to the Divine authority; just in the same way that, by teaching the multitude to refrain from similar tributes of respect to the ensigns of human power, disloyal innovators would diminish all the forces of secular government.

Another of the several significant facts, that are consistently overlooked by writers who delight to represent the earlier Lollards as reformers of sixteenth-century type, is the reluctance which Wycliffe's disciples evinced to disbelieve the miracles which appeared to be wrought at the numerous shrines frequented by the superstitious populace—a reluctance which

cannot read the scripture written about the king's great seal, yet he can read St. George on horseback on the one side, and the king sitting in his majesty on the other side; and readeth so much written in those images as, if he be an honest man, he will put off his cap. And although, if the seal were broken by chance, he would and might make a candle of it, yet he would not be noted to have broken the seal for that purpose, or to call it a piece of wax only, whilst it continueth whole. . . . . If this opinion should proceed, when the king's majesty would hereafter show his person, his lively image, the honour due by God's law amongst such might continue: but as for the king's standards, his banners, his arms, they should hardly continue in their due reverence for fear of Lollards' idolatry, which they gather upon scripture beastly—not only untruly.' In the same spirit it was averred that the interests of trade would be prejudicially affected by the destruction of images: for when they had destroyed all the roods and abolished all the coats-of-arms in the realm, the iconoclasts would break up all the shop-signs and trade-marks,—in which case, how would dealers and customers contrive to come together conveniently, or protect themselves against commercial impositions? In far other language does Cranmer denounce images. 'And here appears the abuse of our time,' says the Primate-Martyr, 'which, following rather the fancy of the carvers or painters than the word of God, have set up in the churches the images, as they call it, of the Trinity, where they portrayed God the Father like an old man, with a long hoary beard. And what can simple people learn hereby but error and ignorance? Have not many thought that God the Father is a bodily substance, and that He hath a face and beard, hands and feet, because they see Him so painted? And for this consideration, saith Augustine, it is a detestable thing for Christian men to have any such image of God in the church: whereby it appeareth that in Augustine's times there were no such images in Christian churches, but that it is an invention of the Papists, brought in of later years, which brings us not unto the true knowledge of God, but leads us into errors and ignorance of God.'

illustrates the slowness with which the scriptural inquirers freed themselves from the trammels of misleading teachers, and indicates the vast amount of Catholic error which they retained long after they had repudiated Papal authority. Rejecting with disdain the impudent fables of the pardoners and relic-mongers, setting their faces against the customary pilgrimages to the scenes of the apparently supernatural phenomena, and thoroughly convinced of the mendaciousness and foolishness of the priests through whose instrumentality the marvels were wrought, almost down to the very eve of the Reformation they scarcely appear to have suspected the mechanical nature of many, and the utter spuriousness of all, of the reputed miracles. That the wonders were true miracles, *i.e.* miracles wrought by Divine agency for the benefit of their spectators, they could not believe, for it was altogether contrary to their conception of the Divine Being to think that He would endow false priests with powers which, coming from Him, would have seemed conclusive evidence of His approval of a corrupt clergy. Yet the marvels were wrought before orthodox churchmen and sceptical inquirers in such a manner, that the latter, in the absence of sufficient grounds for proclaiming them mere impostures, could only account for the inexplicable results by referring them to Satanic agency. One after another, in their successive examinations before the authorities of the Church, the sagacious and fearless Lollards proffered statements which they knew would ensure their committal to the stake; but on being pressed for their opinions concerning the spurious miracles, they did not venture to call the strange sights mere illusions, or to stigmatize them as devices of charlatanry. A common charge against the heretical preachers was that in their sermons they had attributed the wonders to the influence of the fiend. When Archbishop Arundel demanded William Thorpe's estimate of the marvels wrought at Walsingham and the north door of St. Paul's, the reformer, acquitting the priests of jugglery, assigned the marvels to the devil.*

---

* ‘It is to be feared, that for the unfaithfulness of men and women, the fiend hath great power to work many of the miracles that now are done in such places. For both men and women delight now, more to hear and know miracles, than they do to know God's word and to hear it effectually.'—*William Thorpe's 'Examinations.'*

A hundred and twenty years later, the same view was taken of the spurious miracles by Bilney, the Norwich martyr, when amongst other accusations of heresy, it was charged against him that he had taught that the miracles, wrought at Walsingham, Canterbury, and Ipswich, ' were done by the devil, through the sufferance of God, to blind the poor people.' In his reply, instead of attributing the phenomena to human invention and craft, he expressly declared his belief in their supernatural character, assigning them to Satan's maleficent contrivance. ' These wonders,' he said, ' which they call miracles, be wrought daily in the church, not by the power of God, as many think, but by the illusion of Satan rather, who, as the Scripture witnesseth, hath been loose now abroad five hundred years, according as it is written in the book of the Apocalypse. After a thousand years Satan shall be let loose, &c. Neither are they to be called miracles of true Christian men, but illusions rather whereby to delude men's minds; to make them put faith in our lady and in other saints, and not in God alone, to whom be honour and glory.' Whence it appears that, notwithstanding the force of his sentiments against the actual workers of the tricks, and, notwithstanding the righteous pleasure which he would have taken in tracing the phenomena to the agency of wicked priests, the acute and learned Thomas Bilney was so completely imposed upon by the juggleries and marvels of the shrines that he believed them to be achievements out of the ordinary course of nature, brought about by the immediate operation of the Evil One. By a careful consideration of Bilney's mode of accounting for the spurious miracles, an insight may be gained into the intellectual condition of our ancestors with respect to the unseen world, who, even in the more enlightened sections of society, continued to believe in witchcraft almost to the dawn of the eighteenth century, and whose belief in the miraculous efficacy of the royal touch was so general in the later half of the seventeenth century that the learned Dr. Thomas Fuller—the keen critic and piquant derider of the pretended miracles of the Catholic Church—took occasion in his ' Church History ' to animadvert upon the froward and malapert persons who ventured to deny that Charles the Second possessed the supernatural power over human disease, which had been inherent in the sovereigns of England from the time of Edward the Confessor.*

If they had forborne to add the crime of political discontent to their numerous offences against popular taste and religious orthodoxy, the Lollards would have been cordially detested by the majority of their fellow-countrymen for their many dis-social peculiarities, their austere preciseness of speech and style, and their intellectual contumacy towards the official teachers of religion. But these affronts to the self-respect and pre-judices of their neighbours holding contrary views would have elicited from the laity no fiercer demonstration of resentment than the taunts and gibes of angry derision, had the reformers proved themselves peaceable and loyal citizens, submissive to established authorities and averse to the revolutionary projects which incessantly agitated the minds of our poorer ancestors throughout the fourteenth century. To the misfortune, how-ever, of those of the Lollards who aimed only at a regeneration of the religious life of the nation, and were content that the secular institutions should be preserved and employed to main-tain order and correct the social evils of the time, it came to pass through various causes that the religious reformers and political visionaries coalesced in such a manner as to render it very difficult for a conservative spectator of their doings to dis-tinguish between the Lollard who was merely bent on reforming the church, and the Ballite who longed for universal redistribu-tion of wealth, followed by a thorough reorganization of society on principles analogous to those of modern communism. In a vast number of cases these two characters were united in the same person. But whilst, on the one hand, it would be ridi-

---

* 'And yet,' says Fuller, 'this noisome disease is happily healed by the hands of the kings of England stroking the sore; and if any doubt of the truth thereof, they may be remitted to their own eyes for further confirmation. But there is a sort of men who, to avoid the censure of over-easy credulity, and purchase the repute of prudent austerity, justly incur the censure of affected frowardness. It being neither manners nor discretion in them, in matters notoriously known, to give daily experience the lie, by the backwardness of their belief.' In the space of fourteen years, Charles the Second exercised his miraculous powers on 92,107 persons — some 6579 cases per annum; and that nearly the whole of these nu-merous sufferers were cured by the royal manipulation we have the testimony of a court physician, Dr. Wiseman. What stronger evidence can be needed?

culous to suppose that the majority of Tyler's insurgents were incited to rebellion by religious enthusiasm, it would, on the other hand, be no less absurd and unjust to adopt the view of the Feudal conservatives who were convinced that, beneath an appearance of mildness and sobriety, and under plausible professions of devotion towards God and benevolence towards man, every Lollard cherished a malignant design of plunging the nation into revolutionary war, so that he might profit by the wholesale despoliation of the rich.*

It must always remain matter for conjecture in what proportions the entire Lollard army was composed of pious zealots, who desired only to promote their Creator's glory and man's ghostly welfare; of mere worldly agitators, who covered their political designs with religious professions; and of persons who, with various degrees of hypocrisy and genuine devotion, united in their zeal for change the fervour of spiritual revivalists with the passions and unscrupulous ambitions of revolutionary partisans. But, though it is impossible to state precisely their relative forces, enough is known of the most remarkable and inscrutable agitation of feudal time to satisfy the impartial inquirer that each of these three elements of Lollardy was an important ingredient in the party of revolution.

Wholesome repugnance to all popular movements that savour of revolution, or in any degree aim at rendering the intelligent and thoughtful subordinate to the untaught and violent sections of society, has induced many writers, more zealous for Wycliffe's honour then eager for historic truth, to deny that the reformer's influence can be justly credited with any share in the

---

* Concurring with the majority of his contemporaries, the author of the 'Song against the Lollards' takes this view of the early Reformers:—

' Vetant dari stipendia,	Hinc clades, homicidii,
Decimas ac novalia,	Venit et fax incendii
Curatis dum sunt miseri;	Servilis ac rebellio.
Nec dominis servitia,	
Redditus, vel homagia,	13. Johannes Balle hoc docuit,
Quamdiu se dant sceleri.	Quando morti succubuit,
* * *	Propter suam nequitiam,
' Hi sunt auctores odii	Quod quidem nidus tenuit
Cleri, vulgi dissidii,	Pullos pravos, et aluit
Et regni perturbatio.	In regni ignominiam.'

insurrectionary disturbances which alarmed and dishonoured England towards the close of the fourteenth century. Because Wycliffe was unquestionably a sincere and zealous Christian, ambitious above all things for the perfect triumph of the gospel of peace, these eulogists declare it an impious calumny to represent that he was either an originator or contributor to a rebellious ferment, which, had it been permitted to pursue its course to its natural and desired ends, would have placed religion and civilisation under the feet of an infuriated rabble. The facts of history, however, are at variance with this sentimental defence of the devout agitator. That Wycliffe ever designed to rouse the humbler classes to take carnal arms against existing authorities, or that he would have persisted in any course, after discovering that such persistence might possibly result in popular rebellion, no reader is likely to suggest after perusing the reformer's writings, and surveying the circumstances and conditions under which he endeavoured to rouse the intellect of the nation from a state of spiritual lethargy. But it is certain that his appeals were in the highest degree inflammatory, and that, with a more complete knowledge of their influence on the populace, and of the various conflicting forces which they must necessarily call into action, he could not have failed to see how eminently calculated his writings and spoken addresses were to fire the humbler folk with a consuming spirit of insubordination to their temporal rulers. It is ridiculous to extol him as a religious reformer, and at the same time to forget that, whereas in every state of society a religious reformer must necessarily be to some extent a political innovator, Wycliffe lived at a time when politics and religion were so intimately blended that to assail the latter was to create a deep commotion in the former. If at the present time, when 'Church and State' has become little more than a hustings cry, no change, however small, can be effected in the Church without a profound agitation of all the secular elements of the Commonwealth, it may be easily seen that in feudal England, with its complex government, no less theocratic than monarchical, no less hierarchical than aristocratic, an agitation for fundamental religious change was necessarily political in its nature, instruments, and ends.

On tithes and all kinds of ecclesiastical endowments

Wycliffe held and enunciated opinions which, to use a modern phrase of terror, may be fairly described as utterly subversive of social order, and opposed to the interests of property; and, though it may not be forgotten that his views with respect to church property appeared far less outrageous to the conservatives of his time than they would appear coming from the lips of a nineteenth-century reformer to conservatives of our own day, his proposals for dealing with the emoluments of the Church were of the nature of spoliation. And in this respect, the more ardent of his contemporary disciples and immediate successors went far beyond their teacher, whose sufficiently daring counsels soon came to appear timid and flagrantly inadequate by the side of their bolder suggestions. Lord Cobham —a typical lay Lollard, whom biographers extol for his religious zeal, whilst shutting their eyes to his seditious practices— was one of those leaders of reform who would have made a clean sweep of the Church, as corrupt and mischievous beyond all hope of cure. 'The Pope and you,' exclaimed the noble Lollard to one of his judicial questioners, 'together make complete the great Antichrist, of whom he is the great head; you bishops, priests, prelates, and monks are the body, and the begging-friars are the tail, for they cover the filthiness of you both with their filthy sophistry. Never will I in my conscience obey any of you at all, till I see you, with Peter, follow Christ in conversation.'

The student of history is apt to regard with mingled amazement and incredulity the pages which record the audacious projects which the commonalty of conservative England cherished for the spoliation of the ecclesiastical establishments of the fourteenth century, until he has taken into attentive consideration the various influences by which they had been trained to regard such proposals as reasonable and just. For generations the friars, alike in the first days of their humble mendicancy, and in their later stage of extortionate insolence, had been infusing them with hostility to the opulent monks, and with contempt for the ignorant seculars,—encouraging them to turn from the authority of ecclesiastical traditions to the authority of holy writ, and leading them to look upon the more ancient orders of clergy as nothing better than usurpers, whom they would do well to dispossess of wealth which they omitted to apply to the purposes for which it had been entrusted to their official precursors. Called into existence, partly by the teaching of the Mendicants, and partly by the animosities and antagonisms to which the Four Orders gave rise, the Wycliffian agitators, differing from the friars in every other respect, concurred with them in throwing contempt on the discipline and traditions of the priesthood, and in educating the populace for ecclesiastical revolution.

But the most cogent and effective of all teachers are events; and the opening of the fourteenth century was marked by an event that produced a deep and permanent impression on the national mind. By the authority and at the direct instigation of the Pope, the most splendid and powerful of all the ecclesiastical corporations of Christendom had been suppressed, to the mingled dismay and regret of the more intelligent people, who honoured the Knights Templars for their glorious deeds in the East, and admired them for their gorgeous pomp at home. In every land that recognised the Papal authority, these exemplars of Christian chivalry had been the objects of superstitious pride; but nowhere had they acquired more ample possessions or higher dignity than in England. Their estates lay in eighteen different counties; their palace in England's chief city, with its noble church looking upon the bright Thames, was one of the wonders of the country; their roll comprised the most heroic names of English story. And yet—notwithstanding the lustre of its history, the vastness of its possessions, the virtues and honours of its members—this corporation had been broken up, its estates divided for awhile amongst churchmen and laity, its surviving members driven forth to indigence or utter beggary.* By those who believed aught of the stupendous falsehoods, by which the persecutors of the Templars had pretended

---

* Of this wholesale despoliation Fuller observes,—'The chief cause of the ruin of the Templars was their extraordinary wealth. As Naboth's vineyard was the chiefest ground of his blasphemy, and as in England Sir John Conwall, Lord Fanhope, said merrily, not he, but his stately house at Amptbill, in Bedfordshire, was guilty of high treason, so certainly their wealth was the principal cause of their overthrow.' The anecdotical historian adds, that 'to get at the honey it was necessary to burn the bees.'

Part I.—Wycliffe's England.

to justify their atrocious action against the dangerously powerful but deserving order, it was averred that, whatever their faults, the injured knights were no worse than the hospitallers of St. John, or the members of any other religious college. By those who acquitted the Templars of all the heinous and all the trivial offences charged upon them, it was predicted that the spoliation of so superb a brotherhood would sooner or later prove a dangerous precedent, fraught with evil, to the Church. And this prediction was fulfilled to the letter. All the incidents of the suppression—the judicial inquiry, the tortures practised on the knights, the appropriation of their personal wealth, the division of their estates, the subsequent transference of the greater part of those estates to the brotherhood of St. John, the litigation and unpopular enactments which resulted in the transference—were matters of familiar talk in every household of the country. The lesson of the affair was not missed. Confiscations are seldom single. The appetite for strong measures of spoliation grows with its gratification; and as the popular hatred of the wealthy monks grew fiercer and more general, it was asked why the nation should not act on the precedent which Rome had given, and confiscate the monasteries?

This sentiment found memorable expression just a century after the suppression of the Templars, when the Commons of England—in that famous *parliamentum indoctum,* from which clever Cardinal Chancellor Beaufort had contrived illegally to exclude lawyers, under the very erroneous impression that a parliament devoid of lawyers would prove a submissive and manageable assembly—recommended Henry the Fourth to supply his pecuniary wants by appropriating to the uses of himself, nobles, and gentry, all the revenues of the Church, with the exception of just so much of them as would suffice for the support of a hundred hospitals, and the maintenance of an adequate staff of parish priests, paid in yearly salaries of seven marks a-piece. The unlearned Commons assured their sovereign, 'That without burthening his people, he might supply his occasions by seizing on the revenues of the clergy; that the clergy possessed a third part of the riches of the realm, which evidently made them negligent in their duty; and that the lessening of their excessive incomes would be a double advantage, both to the Church and State.'

It is needless to say that Archbishop Arundel's pathetic eloquence persuaded the king not to act upon the disinterested suggestions of his faithful Commons. That such advice was given by the Commons, and for a moment was taken into consideration by the monarch, is, however, one of the many facts which admonish us how widely the modern view of the rights of ecclesiastical proprietors differs from the light in which those rights were regarded by our ancestors of the Plantagenet period.

PART II.—PERSECUTION.

CHAPTER I.

THE ANIMUS OF PERSECUTION.

STUNG by shame for the ferocious cruelty of their ancestors, and dismayed by the horrors of the period of religious contention that opened with William Sawtre's fiery death and closed with the lurid flames and agonizing cries of the Marian persecution, Englishmen of the present generation are wont to seek relief, from the anguish of their pity for the victims and their disgust at the instigators of the futile barbarities, in the inadequate consolations of two somewhat contradictory theories. Whilst the one of these theories strives to soften the repulsive features of the ghastly retrospect by urging that human flesh was less sensitive of pain four centuries since than now, the other offers the comfort of a flattering assurance that the progressive civilization of these later generations has wrought such changes in the moral nature of our race as render it incapable of reviving the horrors of English martyrology.

By those who maintain the former of these comfortable theories it is urged that, in the absence of the luxury and enervating refinements which distinguish modern society from feudal life, our ancestors of the fifteenth century enjoyed a degree of physical hardihood and a comparative insensibility to inflictions of bodily suffering, which preserved them, whilst under the hands of their torturers, from such excruciating agonies as their more delicate and fragile descendants would endure from the punishments of the whip, the rack, and the stake. Flogging that would result in death to a Victorian Englishman was nothing worse than a rather disagreeable stimulant to the nervous system of a Marian yeoman. The Lollard of Henry the Fourth's reign experienced, no doubt, a transient discomfort from the discipline which stretched his body with cords and rollers till his principal joints were dislocated, and his consciousness of the temporary inconvenience terminated in a deathlike swoon; but it would be most absurd to suppose that men, who, from pure delight in giving and tasting pain, used to beat each other once a-week with thick quarter-staves, regarded the muscular disarrangements of the rack with more dread and repugnance than qualify the feelings with which a schoolboy of to-day anticipates a smart caning. Whilst they found familiar pastime in the infliction and endurance of such moderate degrees of pain as they were capable of causing and feeling, the men of the Feudal epoch are also said to have held human life as a thing of scarcely greater moment than human suffering. Shedding each other's blood in trivial quarrels, they would often exchange fatal blows in perfect good-fellowship — friend killing friend for the sake of the pure excitement of danger, and because they could find no more congenial occupation for their leisure time and surplus energy. Cruelty and tenderness are such variable and relative qualities that the cruelty of one state of society may differ little from the tenderness of another; and it is clear that a generation which found diversion in bloodshed must have had a standard of cruelty altogether different from any scale by which the moral sense of a gentler and softer age estimates the humanity of contemporary actors. It would therefore, urges the theory, be most unjust to attribute to the Feudal Churchmen who endeavoured to suppress Lollardy by the branding iron, the scourge, and the fire, the same degree of ferocious vindictiveness that it would be fair to impute to any rulers who should attempt to extirpate dangerous opinions by the same revolting means at the present time, when the general sentiment of mankind is so averse to penal inflictions of bodily torture that we have abolished the lash from the ordinary discipline of our army and are reluctant to use it for the correction of the most odious criminals,—and when our repugnance to capital punishments makes us slow to terminate by force the lives of the most heinous offenders against human and Divine law.

Part II.—Persecution. 173

It would be difficult to decide how far ascertained facts are in accordance with the hypothesis that the average Englishman of the feudal period was less sensible of bodily pain than the average Englishman of our more luxurious time; but against those who use the hypothesis to palliate the atrocities of the old religious persecutors, it may be fairly urged that an immediate object of those angry zealots was the infliction of intense agony on their wretched victims, and that nothing which is known of their temper justifies the opinion that they would have been less sparing in their exhibitions of physical torture, had the heretics been more susceptible of corporeal anguish. Nor is it by any means clear that pain and death were more lightly regarded in mediæval society than they are in the nineteenth century, when warfare, without being less fashionable, is far more productive of death and bodily suffering than it was in the days of the Plantagenets and Tudors, and when no kinds of inventive labour are more promptly and liberally rewarded than those exertions of human ingenuity from which we derive new contrivances for rendering martial conflict more destructive of life, and more fruitful of bodily torment.

That we have purged our penal system of the atrocious provisions which formerly disfigured our criminal code, is perhaps a fact more creditable to our intelligence than our clemency; for, though the merciful amendments of our criminal law may from one point of view be regarded as concessions to the humane instincts of our nature, and though the workers of those amendments were chiefly actuated by compassion for the victims of cruel legislation, it may be questioned whether the beneficent labours of Buxton and Romilly were more indebted for their success to the growing abhorrence for barbarous punishments, than to the discovery that mental torture was in fact a sharper punishment than bodily discomfort, however acute to the sufferer, and however revolting to spectators,—and that there were privations which malefactors regarded with stronger dread than deprivation of existence. Far from concurring with those who think that death and coporeal pain were less repugnant to human sensibility in the days of Lollardy than in our own time, I believe that recent philosophy, whilst mitigating the horrors of death, has inspired the majority of living Englishmen with such an indifference to mere physical torture as their ancestors never enjoyed, and that the present century—lavish of human life for the attainment of even trivial ends, and no less careless of whatever human pain seems requisite for the achievement of its purposes—is remarkable amongst the centuries of English story for the low price that it sets on mere existence, and the unconcernedness with which it purchases the objects of its desires with incalculable sums of bodily suffering and mental anguish. This statement is so directly opposed to current opinion, that it will probably be derided as fanciful; but to those who are disposed to accord respectful attention to paradoxical utterances, an assurance may be given that it is not propounded in thoughtless levity. Yet, further, I would venture to suggest, that inflictions of bodily pain and death are common and popular punishments in proportion as men are apt to regard death with the coward's horror, and to shrink from pain with servile fear; that human legislation does not have recourse to what are ordinarily termed milder punishments until human experience has ascertained that the dread of death and the prospect of corporeal anguish are comparatively inefficacious on the minds of persons disposed to do ill; and that a criminal code more surely reflects the fears of the persons whom it is designed to terrify, than the cruelty or the mercifulness of its framers. That the reformers of our criminal law were impelled by merciful motives, no one is likely to question; but it is no less certain that the milder punishments of our almost bloodless code indicate more precisely the corrections which we most strongly dread, than the penal system of our grandfathers represented the experiences most keenly feared by the generation that expunged its most repulsive provisions.

The other of the two theories is so flattering to our self-love, that it costs us a struggle to recognise its untruth; but in spite of the numerous facts which give it a specious appearance of justice, no candid inquirer can do otherwise than admit its fallaciousness, when he has considered separately and attentively each of the three kinds of malevolent passion that simultaneously inflamed the breasts of the persecutors of Lollardy, and has compared the actions of those intolerant zealots with the stern and vindictive measures to which Englishmen, of more than ordinary kindliness, and wanting none of the graces of civilization, sometimes have recourse at the instigation of only one of those three disturbing influences.

To estimate rightly the moral condition of the persecutors, who committed the fifteenth-century Lollards to agonizing deaths, and of the later enemies of religious reform, who exulted at the glare of the flames that reduced Latimer's aged body to a little pile of ashes, the reader must remember that the hatred, which animated the enemies of Lollardy against the objects of their implacable wrath, comprised the rancour of domestic feud, the blind vehemence of political contention, and the rage of fanaticism. To the disdainful antagonism which men of refinement and fairly amiable dispositions are wont to exhibit in this age of charity and forbearance to those who offend their taste by actions and sentiments that violate no higher laws than the conventional rules of civil behaviour and polite breeding, the reader must add the fierce anger which we are still capable of cherishing for political opponents, and the resentful abhorrence that pious natures cherish for the habitual contemners of the objects of their religious veneration; and when he has thus combined the consuming heats and poisonous agitations of these different animosities, he will still fail to realize all the sources of tempestuous emotion, and all the incitements to cruelty, that deprived the old persecutor of reason and pity— filling his brain with madness and his heart with fire.

How completely men of our time and race—men of gentle nurture and chivalrous generosity, reared from childhood under the softening influences of the Christian faith, and disposed no less by constitutional goodness than by noble training to shape their course with conscientious regard to sacred principles— can divest themselves of all the restraints which religion imposes on human passion, and through fatal misconceptions of their duty to their fellow-creatures can stifle pity in their breasts, and surrender themselves to the brutalising phrensy of Pagan vindictiveness, we have had in recent times several no less painful than instructive illustrations; and if we would understand how our forefathers—many of them, like Sir Thomas More, marvels of domestic gentleness and fireside amiability, so tender of heart, that they shrank from the thought of subjecting their children to the discipline of the rod, and so little prone to irritability, that they reproved their scolding wives with no sharper instruments than smiles and soothing words— could steel their hearts to perpetrate enormities that fill us with mingled horror and disgust, we must judge them by the light of our own doings under weaker provocation, and bear in mind the ruthlessness with which we trample under our feet and destroy those of human kind whom we have learnt to regard as miscreants, whose existence is incompatible with the paramount interests of our species, or the progress of our national welfare.

Recalling how,—from a sincere desire for the public good, and in a genuine belief that our conduct was necessary, justifiable, righteous,—we have used our strength in recent times against men of our own race and nationality, and against men of races inferior to our own victorious and unconquerable stock, whose extermination has appeared to be demanded by civilization ; recalling how, not many months since, when a momentary fear prevailed that a foolish and besotted treason would plunge our land in the horrors of a new kind of revolutionary conflict, our countrymen of all ranks took the first steps towards a condition of public feeling that would have put mercy in abeyance until military vigour had secured the safety of the State ; recalling how, in those brief hours of terrible excitement, the loudest cries for 'vigorous measures' against the imaginary foe came from men to whom even calumny would not venture to impute any lack of pitifulness and Christian charity ; and from these reminiscences, gathering how our humane and peace-loving citizens would feel and act towards an army of domestic traitors, who should throw fire into our homes, and menace our most sacred institutions with ruin,—let us arrive at the temper in which, and the ground from which, we may judge fairly the animus which impelled our conservative forefathers, whose nature we inherit, together with their blood and lineaments, to exhibit a repulsive and ferocious sternness to those disturbers of religion and social order, whom they no less sincerely than erroneously regarded as enemies of the Christian faith and the public weal, inspired by a diabolical antipathy to sacred things and wholesome government.

Part II.—Persecution.

In these days of free inquiry and latitudinarianism, to say that the persecutors of the fifteenth and sixteenth centuries put the Reformers to death for differing on matters of religious opinion from the majority of their contemporaries, is no sufficient or fair statement of the motives which actuated the opponents of change, since it omits to give due prominence to the awful results which the champions of orthodoxy imagined to be the inevitable consequences of the new heresies, and gives occasion for the very erroneous inference, that orthodox believers of our own time attribute to theological unsoundness the same horrible effects which the staunch Churchmen of Catholic England unhesitatingly assigned to Lollard misbelief. To do these Churchmen of old time bare justice we must remember that their sincerity and devoutness were in proportion to their zeal and intellectual narrowness, and that, whilst on the one hand they were fully persuaded that eternal salvation was eventually assured to every faithful and obedient member of the Pope's Church, they were, on the other hand, thoroughly convinced that no human creature could embrace the religious tenets of Lollardy, and, dying in his heretical sin, escape the doom of everlasting torture.

To persons holding this gloomy and terrifying view of the certain results of heresy, the Lollard was not merely a miscreant whose wickedness abundantly merited its sure reward of eternal agony. Had his sin against heaven and its consequences to himself comprised the whole enormity, and all the fruits of his spiritual rebellion, the faithful would, for the most part, have been content to leave him alone in his iniquity, or even have exhibited compassion for him, in consideration of the endless miseries he would endure after death. But, though its punishment was in a certain sense his own affair, his sin closely concerned every believer who came in contact with him, and was liable to receive from his accursed lips the poison of infidelity. Partaking of the perilous qualities of an infectious malady and a contagious disease, his spiritual leprosy communicated some of its baneful essence to everyone who touched him in Christian fellowship, or breathed the air which his corruption loaded with morbific seeds. Regarded in this light, he appeared to his superstitious contemporaries an unclean beast rather than one of their own species,—an unclean and pestiferous beast, who, having earned his own damnation, was bent on making the whole family of true believers the companions of his degradation, and dragging them with him into the bottomless pit. For the sake of simple creatures—the unwary men and foolish women, the impetuous boys and credulous maidens, the prattling children and lisping babes—who might become the sharers of his crime and doom, it was incumbent on all benevolent persons to put him and all his kind clean out of life, and in selecting a method for their destruction to think only of the interests of the innocent, without giving a moment's pitiful heed to the sufferings of the incurably wicked. What claim to human mercy had the wretches whose conduct was likely to result in the everlasting misery of members of their species? What were the transient torments of such abominable adversaries, that they should be put even for a moment in the balance against the well-being of all right-minded persons? What could it matter whether the culprits, doomed to eternal flames, experienced something more or something less of bodily anguish in this transitory life?

From the time when it was first possible for such a production as Pope's 'Universal Prayer' to become a widely popular poem amongst all ranks and parties of the English people, it has been very difficult for the historical inquirer to realise the spirit of religious fervour which animated our forefathers against the teachers of true religion, and to understand the mercifulness of the purpose for which they carried out those hideous and wholesale executions of pious men and women, for the atrocities of which proceedings we are asked to account by the hypothesis that the moral nature of our race has been modified and altogether changed since the Reformation by the softening influences of scientific discovery and material progress. That this hypothesis is pleasant to the self-esteem of the present century, no one can deny, and that it will long continue to hold its place amongst popular fallacies, no observer of human nature would hesitate to predict; but the impartial inquirer is disposed to discard it as less reasonable than flattering, in proportion as he succeeds in placing himself in the intellectual condition of the Plantagenet and Tudor persecutors,

Part II.—Persecution.

and in proportion as a dispassionate survey of the religious phenomena of existing society leads him to the conclusion that the disposition towards persecution depends less on moral than mental causes,—is the outgrowth of intellectual narrowness and blindness rather than of any constitutional pitilessness and inherent proneness to cruelty.

That we shall never renew on this island the horrors of the Marian persecution we have good grounds for hoping; but our reasonable sense of security from all risk of a similar outbreak of national fanaticism springs from a proper recognition of our real superiority in wisdom rather than our fancied superiority in goodness to the Englishmen of Bonner's time. It is not because we are gentler in heart, but because we are clearer and stronger in head, that we may congratulate ourselves on having altogether outlived the possibility of reproducing the religious errors of our not very remote ancestors. But should we ever be alarmed and inflamed to the extent that the old persecutors were terrified and incensed—should we ever find ourselves in conflict with intestine adversaries, who should seem to us the irreconcilable foes of our nation and our nature—it is certain that our measures of repression would neither fail through mercifulness, nor err in the direction of leniency. Under such circumstances it is not probable that we should torture our enemies with the rack, or burn them to ashes; but most unquestionably we should enforce our views by an unsparing use of the cat, the gun, and the gallows.

CHAPTER II.

THE LAW OF HERESY.

AT a very early period of our history the common law invested our sovereigns with power to issue writs for the execution of miscreants who, on trial before the Archbishop at a provincial synod, had been declared guilty of the crime of heresy: but, though the Crown was thus authorised to slay heretics whom the Primate had personally examined and found heretical, the sovereign was free to pursue his pleasure with respect to these proved enemies of the Christian faith. The writ *de hæretico comburendo* was no writ of course,* but a writ issuing on the special action of the monarch who might award a free pardon to misbelievers whom the Archbishop had declared worthy of death. How frequently this writ was issued in pre-Lollard times is unknown: but from the nature of the court, on whose judgment alone the sovereign had power to slay a person for religious error, it may be safely inferred that the execution of a misbeliever was a rare occurrence before the close of the fourteenth century.

On insufficient authority it has been asserted that the first heretics to appear in England after the coming of the Saxons were the Gerardites, who came to this country from Germany in the reign of Henry the Second, which monarch in acknowledg-

---

* 'And therefore we find among our ancient precedents a writ *de hæretico comburendo*, which is thought by some to be as ancient as the common law itself. However, it appears from thence, that the conviction of heresy by the common law was not in any petty ecclesiastical court, but before the archbishop himself in a provincial synod; and that the delinquent was delivered over to the king, to do as he should please with him: so that the crown had a control over the spiritual power, and might pardon the convict by issuing no process against him; the writ *de hæretico comburendo* being not a writ of course, but issuing only by the special direction of the king in council.'—*Vide* Blackstone's 'Commentaries.'

ment of their benevolent endeavours to tamper with the orthodoxy of his people, ordered that the pious adventurers should be marked on the forehead with branding irons, flagellated, and turned out into the streets to starve in the freezing atmosphere of an unusually severe winter. It is probable that the king forbore to commit them to the flames from an opinion that under the circumstances exposure in the open air would prove a more excruciating and no less sure means of death than exposure to a large bonfire. That the fiery execution was the ordinary fate of heretics is demonstrated by the writ already mentioned: and the monkish annalists notice cases in which that writ was executed to the letter, not very many years after the barbarous treatment of the poor Gerardites. During King John's reign, some Albigensian heretics were burnt to death in this country: and in 1222 the same punishment was awarded to a clerical delinquent whom a synod, held at Oxford, found guilty of having embraced Judaism in order that he might simultaneously embrace the person of a lovely Jewess.

The first legislative enactment against Lollardy was an irregular statute, for which the assent of the Commons was neither obtained nor asked, and which the Commons, in consideration of its illegality, exerted themselves successfully to set aside in the year following its unconstitutional authorization. The country was still in the first ferment of the agitation consequent on Tyler's insurrection, and the rector of Lutterworth's troublous life was drawing near its close, when in the parliament held at Westminster in the fifth year of Richard the Second, Archbishop Courtenay procured the passing of the informal measure which directed 'the sheriffs, and other ministers of our sovereign lord the king, or other sufficient persons learned, and according to the certifications of the prelates thereof to be made in the Chancery from time to time, to arrest all such preachers, and also their fautors, maintainers, and abettors, and to hold them in arrest and strong prison till they will justify themselves according to reason and the law of Holy Church.' Whence it appears that the framers of this informal act designed to empower the bishops to seize and hold in confinement all Lollard preachers and disciples, and all persons guilty of favouring the new views,—to apprehend them at will, to exercise their own discretion in taking measures to ascertain the nature and extent of their heterodoxy, and to retain them in strong prison until they had recanted their heretical opinions. In many cases this extraordinary measure, had it not been repealed, would have resulted in the imprisonment for life of a devout layman whose gravest fault was an imputed abhorrence of image-worship, and whose pious crime had only been ascertained to the satisfaction of a bishop or bishop's commissary,—instead of the satisfaction of twelve jurymen.

The preamble of this singular device of arbitrary power * gives us in a few words a vivid picture of the doings of Wycliffe's poor priests, and other teachers of Lollardy throughout the kingdom. 'Forasmuch,' says the drawer of the bill, 'as it is openly known that there be divers evil persons within the realm, going from county to county, and from town to town, in certain habits, and under dissimulation of great holiness, and without the license of the ordinaries of the places, or other sufficient authority, preaching daily, not only in churches and churchyards, but also in markets, fairs, and other open places where a great congregation of people is, divers sermons containing heresies and notorious errors.' The imagination is weak that cannot create scenes of strong excitement and picturesque interest out of this cold, official mention of the itinerant preachers at the markets and fairs of feudal England, surrounded by crowds of eager sympathisers and angry antagonists,—hinds and yeomen, priests and scholars, vagrant pedlars and burly squires, matrons in homely or rich costumes, and girls bright with maidenly blushes and gay apparel.

The number of Lollards rapidly increasing, in spite of the vexatious and illegal means which the bishops employed for their suppression, and the superstitious fear and abhorrence with which they inspired the majority of their fellow-countrymen growing more intense, it appeared politic to by far the

* Though the Commons procured the repeal of this illegal law on October 6 of the next year, its repeal was neither published to the country nor inscribed amongst the other statutes of the 6th of Richard II.; and the king's letters-patent to Archbishop Courtenay and to the Chancellor and Proctors of Oxford, dated respectively June 26 and July 13, sufficed to give the clergy a plausible pretext for disregarding the repeal, *i. e.* for continuing to act as though the statute were in force.

greatest part of the secular nobles, the clergy, the lay gentry, and the simple folk of the country, to accord to all diocesan bishops within their dioceses, and commissaries specially appointed by the bishops, the power over heretical offenders which had hitherto pertained solely to the archbishop presiding in provincial synod. The maintainers of heterodox opinions having become so numerous that the majority of them would necessarily escape the extreme penalty accorded by the common law to their crime, if their conviction and sentence to the stake could be procured only through trial in a provincial synod, it was determined to institute a new method of procedure for their examination and prompt correction. To meet the emergencies of the crisis, the Act *Ex Officio* was passed with every requisite formality in the second year of Henry the Fourth, by which statute persons accused of heresy, on anyone's information, might be seized and thrown into bishops' prisons, and after trial with conviction in the bishops' courts might be sentenced to various kinds of penance, in cases where they submitted and recanted, or might be made over to the secular authorities for execution by fire, in cases where they either persisted in their errors or were proved to have relapsed into heresy after recantation.*

To readers of the present time the hardships of this memorable act appear so numerous and flagrant, that it seems almost incredible that our forefathers, who had for generations displayed abundant courage in resisting the encroachments and

---

* The section of the act, which sets forth with no strict limitations the most terrible of the bishops' powers against heretics, runs thus:—'And further, if any person within the said realm and dominions shall be sententially convicted before the diocesan *or* his commissaries of the said wicked preachings, doctrines, opinions, schools, and heretical and erroneous informations, or any of them; and will refuse duly to abjure the said wicked sect, preachings, teachings, opinions, schools, and informations; or if, after abjuration once made by the said party, he be pronounced as relapsed by the diocesan of the place, *or* his commissaries in this behalf: that then the sheriff of the said county, and the mayor and sheriffs, or the sheriff, mayor, or bailiffs of the city, town, or borough of the same county, next to the said diocesan or his said commissaries, shall personally be present, as oft as they shall be required, to join with the said diocesan or his commissaries in giving sentence against the said persons, or any of them; and, after the said sentence so pronounced, shall receive them, and any of them, and cause the same to be burned in an eminent place before the people.'

despotic temper of the Church, can have concurred in sanctioning a measure which placed the lives and liberties of Englishmen at the mercy of fanatical priests. That they did thus surrender their dearest social privileges to an ecclesiastical order, of whose growing power they had uniformly displayed the strongest jealousy, demonstrates how thoroughly they sympathised with the clergy in detesting the Lollard doctrines, and how profoundly they were impressed with the necessity of suppressing the heresy and exterminating the heretics at any cost.

The most prominent hardship of this act was its refusal of the securities of trial by jury to the unfortunate objects of persecution. In the ordinary courts of the common law, whatever his offence, and however odious his crime, the prisoner at the bar derived from the institution of trial by jury an assurance that the verdict on his case would most probably be in accordance with justice,—that, at the worst, it would not directly contradict the evidence of facts. The jurymen might be dull men, and err on difficult points, through sheer stupidity, but as honest and true men, with a superstitious fear of the consequences of perjury, and wholesomely influenced by the reflection that the time might come when their own good fame and lives would depend on the integrity of jurors, they would do their best to ascertain the truth. Whatever prejudices and passions might dispose their minds against him, their social equal and personal comrade, were feelings of the general public of which he was himself an unit, not the sentiments and animosities of a single class to which he did not belong. Instead of being his prosecutors, they were in a certain sense his defenders, pledged indeed to state the truth of his case to the best of their ability, but encouraged to refrain from mentally pressing an uncertain point against him, and to give him the full benefit of every element of doubt that qualified their opinion of his guilt or innocence. But the Lollard on trial before his bishop had no such sources of security. His prosecutor was his judge, and it lay within the province of the prosecuting judge to state whether his witnesses established the charges of heresy,—whether his witnesses proved the alleged facts—whether the ascertained facts amounted to proofs of the alleged crime.

Part II.—Persecution.

Another grievance of this harsh enactment was its neglect to define the opinions and practices which it was designed to suppress. Lollardy was a vague and comprehensive term for a vast number of sentiments and acts which orthodox Churchmen regarded with disapprobation; and in the absence of an intelligible and authoritative rule deciding what were the precise tenets of the denounced heresy, and what deeds should be construed as declaratory of heretical guilt, it rested with each judge or bench of judges examining, on the authority of the statute, a person suspected of Lollardy, to decide what particulars of thought, speech, or action amounted to the crime to which the penalty of death was affixed.

In the opinion of liberal and lenient judges, no person was a Lollard who admitted all the fundamental doctrines of the Christian faith, abstained from expressly repudiating the doctrines of the Church, and rendered all customary signs of respect to clerical authority. Judges of a more intolerant and severe kind, not content with this general acquiescence in the opinions of the clergy, could detect Lollardy in persons who had been heard to speak disapprovingly of notorious clerical delinquents, who had avowed in bitter terms the difficulty which they experienced in satisfying the tithal or other pecuniary claims of their parochial curates, or had expressed in private conversation with religious neighbours an opinion that it would be for the spiritual benefit of simple folk if the services of the Church were performed in the vulgar tongue. To have eaten a meal in a house where a few Lollard books had been discovered by the emissaries of the Church, after the law had required that all such works should be surrendered to the diocesans, afforded, in the opinion of these stricter judges, presumptive evidence that the person who had thus broken bread under an ill-reputed roof was himself a student and admirer of the proscribed literature. Moreover, the act against heresy enjoined 'that no man hereafter do by any means *favour* any such (*i. e.* Lollard) preacher, or any maker of such (*i. e.* Lollard) conventicles, or any maker or writer of such (*i. e.* Lollard) books;' from which words many of the fiercer enemies of the abhorred teachers inferred that any person who had given a crust of bread and a cup of cold water to one of Wycliffe's poor priests was a 'maintainer' and 'fautor' of Lollardy, within the intention of the statute, and might properly be dragged on a charge of heresy into the bishop's court, from which no object of persecution, however manifest his orthodoxy, could hope to escape without humiliation, cost, and loss of social repute.

The proceedings under the new law were alike simple and vexatious. On receiving information from some parochial busybody that John Styles was a Lollard, the diocesan of the said John Styles, or commissaries appointed by the diocesan to seek out and harrass heretical offenders, ordered that the said John should forthwith be arrested and put upon his trial. Sometimes the informer was poor Styles's private enemy who hoped to gratify his spite and obtain some social advancement by putting Styles out of the way or discrediting him amongst his neighbours. Sometimes the informer was Styles's parish-priest, who had been reproved by Styles for neglect of duty or tavern-haunting propensities. That private animosity dictated a large number of the informations against the milder and less dangerous Lollards, no historical inquirer is likely to question; but the original documents, quoted in Foxe's 'Acts and Monuments,' make it clear that the great majority of persons against whom the diocesans proceeded under the provisions of the statute *Ex Officio*, were decided and far-advanced Lollards,—and that it was a very unusual case where a person, put on his trial by that act, had not at least shown unquestionable symptoms of sympathy for and tendency towards Lollard misbelief. When John Styles, therefore, appeared before his judge or judges, it almost invariably happened that there was some good legal ground for the proceedings against him.

He had expressed doubt of the power of the Saints in Heaven to save human souls; by his fireside he had declared to a party of his friends his inability to see how the consecrated wafer could be a piece of his Saviour's body, in the sense in which it was asserted to be so by the priests; he had spoken confidently about the inutility and mischief of pilgrimages; he had admitted his conscientious objection to judicial oaths and image-worship; without uttering any desire for the profanation or destruction of Churches, he had spoken profanely of those sacred places by asserting that prayers uttered in them were of no greater avail than prayers uttered in the private houses of Christians; he had confessed himself unable to see the holiness of Thomas à Becket's life or the excellence of his death, and was a known questioner whether St. Thomas was a saint in heaven; he had been heard to declare that a medicinal and consecrated lotion, sold by a Pope's pardoner as a specific in all cases of cattle-disease, had failed to cure his sheep of the scab and the maggot; he had been heard to murmur that priests would do well to think less of their fees, and more of their duty; he had declared in open market that he was strongly disposed to question whether the bell-music of church steeples had any effect on thunder and lightning. These and a score other such charges could usually be established against John Styles.

But the mode by which his guilt was demonstrated by his judicial prosecutors was altogether at variance with rules observed by secular tribunals. Let us suppose the case of poor John Styles before a court of these commissaries. Having commenced their enquiry by reading the articles objected against him, *i. e.* particulars drawn up by the commissaries themselves on the information of irresponsible persons, whose names were frequently withheld from the prisoner and the public, the judges intimated that he must disprove the accusations or he would be deemed guilty in respect to them. It was no part of their duty to prove his guilt, it was for him to demonstrate his innocence by repudiation of the doctrines attributed to him, and denial of the acts charged against him. Still, for convenience's sake and the satisfaction of public opinion, they were not neglectful of any measures that might render his crime manifest and deprive him of human sympathy. Sometimes they confronted him with witnesses who spoke to the facts alleged in the articles of arraignment, and whom he was permitted to cross-examine with the deference due to witnesses for the prosecution; but his chances of acquittal and his danger of extreme punishment depended far less on what the witnesses urged against him and what he could urge against the witnesses, than on his own admissions to the three commissaries whose searching interrogatories he was required to answer as he valued his life. Whatever of his answers were in denial of the articles of arraignment the judges passed over as statements unworthy of credence; whatever of his replies were acknowledgements of heresy or heretical sympathies, the same judicial enquirers pounced upon as admissions swelling the bulk of evidence against him; when he held his tongue in doubt, or confusion, or despair, his silence was construed as conclusive testimony of his guilt.

By this process it was seldom difficult for the judges to satisfy themselves that John Styles was guilty on one or more of the numerous articles charged against him; and to have thus ascertained his guilt on any one of the charges was enough to justify them in deciding that his heretical condition was demonstrated, and that he must either abjure or suffer death. By abjuring he might avoid the fiery execution, and escape with a sentence affecting his person, liberty, or estate, to a degree according with the supposed enormity of his misdemeanour. When thus fortunate in escaping with a minor sentence, the poor fellow, for a time at least, took good heed to clothe his life with an appearance of conformity to his abjuration of Lollardy. But men naturally deficient in prudence often find it especially difficult to be circumspect when exceptional penalties are attached to their indiscretions: and pardoned heretics were exposed to peculiar social annoyances, arising from the coldness of old friends, and the prying vigilance of censorious neighbours, that co-operated with a secret sense of shame and remorse for their insincere recantations, to goad them into a course of action which rendered them liable to the fate of relapsed heretics. Hence, a considerable number of the misbelievers, who received mild sentences at a first inquisition, eventually surrendered their lives at the stake.

When a spiritual court had sentenced a heretic to death, the judgment was executed by the arm of civil authority; and the assistance which the civil thus rendered to the ecclesiastical power is deserving of special consideration, both because it demonstrates the unanimity with which laity and clergy combined to persecute heretics, and because it has been an occasion for misrepresentation with writers less zealous for truth than for the obloquy of the Catholic Church. Even Blackstone lays aside his customary moderation so far as to speak with contemptuous disdain of 'the Romish ecclesiastics determining,

Part II.—Persecution.

without appeal, whatever they pleased to be heresy, and shifting off to the secular arm the odium and drudgery of executions with which they themselves were too tender and too delicate to intermeddle.' When a lawyer of Blackstone's learning and general freedom from illiberal animosities is found speaking thus vindictively and unfairly of the clerical persecutors, who, in leaving the execution of their capital sentences to the secular magistrates, were only acting in submission to the ancient precedents of the common law, there is no need to express surprise at the warmth with which Protestant partizans, alike unlearned in law and devoid of the judicial temper, have, on the same grounds, censured the clergy for thus keeping within the limits assigned by the custom of the land, from remote antiquity, to their power over the lives of heretics.

It does not seem to have occurred to these denouncers of clerical craft and cruelty to ask themselves what they would have said about the insolence and odious barbarity of priests, had the ecclesiastics, who procured the enactment of the statute *Ex Officio*, inserted in that measure a clause which would have empowered them to execute their capital sentences. Had the clerical framers of the statute enriched it with such a clause, and, availing themselves of their new privilege, put to death with their own hands the persons whom they adjudged heretics, the same writers, who are indignant at their policy in 'shifting off to the secular arm the odium and drudgery of executions,' would have recorded in language of passionate loathing how Henry the Fourth's bishops availed themselves of the popular alarm and abhorrence to usurp the ancient functions of the secular power; how, under the guise of zeal for the preservation of the Christian faith, they obtained the enactment of a law that gave them arbitrary power over the lives of all persons, both lay and clerical; and how, in their abominable lust for the delights of cruelty, they violated an important principle of the old common law, merely that they might have the pleasure of personally executing their barbarous judgments upon the bodies of pious Christians.

In bare justice to the clerical persecutors it must be admitted that they never manifested any disposition to avoid the responsibility and odium of the measures by which they endeavoured to exterminate the heresies of Wycliffe and Luther. To argue, as Blackstone does, that they were guilty of diabolical hypocrisy because they uttered expressions of concern and words of prayer for the convicted heretic, ' well knowing at the same time that they were delivering the unhappy victim to certain death,' is no less unjust than it would be for any writer of the present day to impute the same atrocious spirit to Mr. Justice Blackstone himself, because in passing sentence on a convicted sheep-stealer or murderer he used to pray for divine mercy on the offender's soul, ' well knowing at the same time that he was delivering the unhappy victim to certain death.' Nor does this charge of clerical hypocrisy derive any substantial support, or aught more than a faint and superficial colour of justification, from the fact that the canonists and ecclesiastical judges used to account for their inability to carry out the capital sentences of the spiritual courts by pompous and formal professions that it would be derogatory to their sacred character to discharge the functions of lay sheriffs. The terms used by such specious apologists for an ecclesiastical disability were not intended to imply that the speakers either deprecated the cruelty of the law, or would have shrunk from the responsibility of fulfilling its behests, had it required them personally to consign the condemned heretics to the flames.

The assertion that the ecclesiastics endeavoured to avoid the odium of executioners arises from the vulgar mistake of supposing that the executions were no less odious and repugnant to the moral sense and refinement of orthodox Catholics of the fifteenth century than they are in the retrospect to delicate readers of the present epoch. At the date when Blackstone describes the clerical persecutors as shrinking from a particular obloquy, there was no such odium for them to shrink from. The horror consequent on Tyler's insurrection, in which the Lollards were largely implicated, and for which they were generally deemed altogether accountable, deprived Lollardy of nearly all its reputable favourers amongst the rich and noble, and in the course of a few years reduced the ranks of its adherents to a tithe of their number before the rebellion. The Wycliffian agitators were thoroughly discredited, and the measures against Lollardy were so popular that politicians noisily proclaimed their approval of the statute *Ex Officio*. At a time when the spectacle of a heretic's execution by fire was a sight to which pleasure-seekers of every degree and both sexes flocked by hundreds and thousands; when the victims of fanaticism were put to death amidst all the usual signs of popular festivity; and when the delighted spectators of the executions adjourned from the scenes of suffering to joyful entertainments of food, wine, and music, it is absurd to suppose that the laws against Lollardy occasioned a general feeling of disapprobation of which the clergy were anxious not to be principal objects.

Numerous facts testify that the priests, well pleased, no doubt, with the cordial co-operation of the laity, took all possible steps to be regarded as the chief promoters and most active instruments of the persecution. No class of the community was more openly busy in laying information and gathering evidence against suspected heretics. When the laity evinced signs of flagging zeal in the labour of extermination, the pulpits roused them to fresh and fiercer exertions against the enemies of Catholic dogma; and, on the approach of every execution, the clergy admonished their congregations to witness and rejoice over the torments of the martyrs. To stimulate the popular fury against the reformers it was the custom of the priests*

---

* In his record of Thomas Harding, a Buckinghamshire martyr, who was burnt at Chesham in 1532, Foxe notices the characteristic zeal of Rowland Messenger, the Vicar of Great Wycombe:—'Thus at last they sent him to the bishop's prison, called Little Ease, where he did lie with hunger and pain enough for a certain space, till at length the bishop, sitting in his tribunal-seat like a potentate, condemned him for a relapse to be burned to ashes, committing the charge and oversight of his martyrdom to Rowland Messenger, vicar of Great Wycombe. This Rowland, at the day appointed, with a rabble of others like to himself, brought Father Harding to Chesham again; where, the next day after his return, the said Rowland made a sermon in Chesham Church, causing Thomas Harding to stand before him all the preaching time . . . . When they had set fire on him, there was one that threw a billet at him, and dashed out his brains: for what purpose he did so it is not known, but, as it was supposed, that he might have forty days' pardon, as the proclamation was made at the burning of William Tylsworth above mentioned: where proclamation was made the same time, that whosoever did bring a fagot or a stake to the burning of a heretic should have forty days of pardon: whereby many ignorant people caused many of their children to bear billets and fagots to their burning. In fine, when the sacrifice and burnt-offering of this godly martyr was finished, and he burnt to ashes, in the dell going to Botley, at the north end of the town of Chesham,

to promise exceptional indulgence to those of the faithful laity who should distinguish themselves at burnings by throwing opprobrious words and blazing brands on the dying wretches; and, in the crowds that surrounded the penal flames, the clergy of all orders — monks, friars, seculars — were always conspicuous by their numbers, and their zeal in furthering the ghastly proceedings. Nor was there any affectation of 'tenderness and delicacy' in the clergy with respect to those departments of persecution in which they were the personal inflictors of bodily pain. With their own hands they flogged suspected Lollards by way of torture, to elicit from them confessions that might be used as evidence to justify their committal to the flames. With their own hands, also, they discharged the functions of common beadles, and fustigated the penitent heretics in the presence of their congregations; and, though in submission to the requirements of the law they surrendered the convicted heretics after judgment to the secular power, they took pains to show that no sense of mercifulness or decorum restrained them from longing to be the executioners of their hideous sentences. When the

Rowland, their ruler of the roast, commanding silence, and thinking to send the people away with an "*Ite, missa est,*" with a loud voice said to the people these words, not advising belike what his tongue did speak, "Good people! when ye come home, do not say that you have been at the burning of a heretic, but of a good, true, Christian man." And so they departed to dinner; Rowland, with the rabble of other priests, much rejoicing at the burning of this good man. After dinner they went to church to evensong, because it was Corpus Christi even; where they fell to singing and chanting, with ringing, and piping of the organs. Well was he that could reach to the highest note, so much did they rejoice at this good man's burning.' Foxe's narrative of Harding's martyrdom may be taken as a picture of the general character of the proceedings immediately before, at, and directly after the burning of a heretic, in a soundly conservative and orthodox rural district. At such scenes the popular leaders were the priests, whose conduct was certainly marked by no assumption of tenderness and delicacy.

Another characteristic case of clerical and popular zeal occurs in Foxe's narrative of Dr. Redyng's conduct at the execution of Peke, who was burnt at Ipswich, temp. Hen. VIII. When Peke, advised at the stake and whilst the fagots were crackling to recant, had refused to comply, Dr. Redyng exclaimed to the bystanders, 'To as many as shall cast a stick to the burning of this heretic is granted forty days of pardon by my lord Bishop of Norwich. Then Baron Curzon, Sir John Audley, knight, with many others of estimation, being there present, did rise from their seats, and with their swords did cut down boughs, and throw them into the fire, and so did the multitude of the people.'

popular taste for executions by fire was on the wane; and yet later, when the atrocities of the Marian persecution roused a general sentiment of pity for the martyrs, and disgust at the promoters and immediate workers of their sufferings, the clergy were more remarkable for officious zeal at public burnings than for any assumption of coy reluctance to compromise their reputation for Christian tenderness by taking part in the revolting ceremonials of the stake.

That the laity were not less zealous than the clergy in the field of persecution, that they would have resisted any attempt of the spiritual authorities to exclude them from so honourable a sphere of pious exertion, and that, not satisfied with their ancient executory rights, they were jealous of the privileges of the bishops' courts, and from no merciful motive would gladly have diminished the ecclesiastical power over heretics, may be inferred from the stat. 2 Henry V. c. 7, which, rendering heresy indictable in the King's courts, accorded to those tribunals in matters of heresy concurrent jurisdiction with the consistories. Another chief object of this act of A.D. 1415, which was at the same time an enlargement and amendment of the statute *Ex Officio*, that had been in operation barely fifteen years, was to enrich the sovereign by the forfeiture* to the crown of all property pertaining absolutely to persons convicted of heresy with capital sentence.

The next important alterations in our law of heresy were effected by the stat. 25 Henry VIII. c. 14, and the stat. 31 Henry VIII. c. 14. The former of these measures declared that offences against the Papal authority should not be deemed heretical, and that the bishops should not prosecute persons for heresy, unless the charges of heresy were preferred by two

---

* 'And moreover, that all the goods and chattels of such convicted be forfeit to our sovereign lord the king, so that no person convict of heresy, and left unto the secular power (according to the laws of holy church), do forfeit his lands before that he be dead. And if any person so convicted be enfeoffed, whether it be by fine or by deed, or without deed, in lands and tenements, rents or services, in fee or otherwise, in whatsoever manner, or have any other possessions or chattels by gift or grant of any person or persons, to the use of any other than only to the use of such convicts; that the same lands, tenements, rents or services, or other such possessions or chattels, shall not be forfeit unto our sovereign lord the king in any manner wise.'—*Vide* Stat. 2 Hen. V. c. 7.

reliable witnesses, or had been declared in a common law court sufficient to sustain an indictment for criminal misbelief. The provisions of this act greatly limited the power of the clergy, and to an equal extent enlarged the authority of the laity in matters of religious opinion; but it was a slight instalment of reform in comparison with the later statute of 31 Henry VIII., which, notwithstanding the cruelty of its declarations, and the atrocities perpetrated under its authority, in one most important respect was highly beneficial to religious inquirers, who, without relinquishing the doctrine of transubstantiation or desiring to oppose the sovereign's decisions on the last five of the memorable Six Articles, sympathised with the Reformers. Attaching the penalty of the fiery death to repudiation of transubstantiation, and rendering the transgression of any one of the five last articles a felony punishable, for a first offence, with forfeiture and imprisonment, and, in case of a second offence, with death, the statute enjoined that offenders should be proceeded against by two reputable witnesses, and should be tried by a jury of twelve men in an open court presided over by a mixed bench of clerical and lay assessors.* Enacted at a time long prior to the introduction of the 'cat with nine tails' into our penal system, but when the populace were familiar with a six-tailed instrument of flagellation, this measure — barbarous in some, though merciful in other respects — was promptly christened the Whip with Six Strings by the pungent wit of the rapidly growing party, whose leaders were not without personal reasons for trembling at the six incisive articles, which to their terrified imaginations bore a strong similitude to six bloody thongs. Of the atrocities done by the wielders

* With respect to disbelievers of transubstantiation the statute enacted, that 'every such person so offending, their aiders, comforters, counsellors, consenters, and abettors therein (being thereof convicted in form underwritten, by the authority abovesaid), should be deemed and adjudged heretics, and every such offence should be adjudged manifest heresy; and that every such offender and offenders should therefore have and suffer judgment, execution, pain and pains of death by way of burning, without abjuration, benefit of clergy, or sanctuary, to be therefore permitted.' With respect to punishments against the other five articles — having reference to communion in one kind, celibacy of clergy, monastic vows, sacrifice of mass, and auricular confession — it was enacted 'that every such person or persons, who, after the day aforesaid, by word, writing, printing, ciphering, or otherwise, did publish, declare, or hold opinion contrary to the five

Part II.—Persecution.

of this legislative scourge there is no need to speak at length; but to the credit of Henry and his advisers it must be remembered that it was deprived of much of its terrors and capability for working injustice by the measure A.D. 1544, which provided that presentments of heretical offence should not be brought before any court of Heresy Commissioners, 'otherwise than by the oaths of twelve men, or more, of honesty and credit.'

One of the first steps taken by Edward the Sixth's advisers with the authority of parliament, in the first year of his reign, was the repeal of the entire group of statutes against heresy; but in 1555,—whilst all loyal subjects of Mary Queen of England were offering up prayers that her majesty might be safely delivered of 'a male-child, well favoured, and witty'— the English parliament revived Richard the Second's unconstitutional act against Lollardy, and the statutes to suppress heresy, of 2 Henry IV. and 2 Henry V., so that all the obsolete and atrocious system of consistorial prosecutions, without trial by jury and the other safeguards of common-law procedure, was re-established. But though Mary's parliament abstained from affording to suspected heretics the securities of trial by jury, it should be observed that to the Royal Heresy Commissioners, appointed in 1556, the miserable woman and ill-reputed queen intrusted the power of impanelling juries according to the pleasure of the commissioners, who were directed to act with or without the help of jurymen, and were authorised to use 'all other means and politic ways that they could devise' for the extirpation of Lollardy and Lutheranism.

articles above expressed, being for any such offence duly convicted and attainted: for the first time, besides the forfeit of all his goods and chattels, and possessions whatsoever, should suffer imprisonment of his body at the king's pleasure; and for the second time, being accused, presented, and thereof convicted, should suffer as in case of felony aforesaid.' With respect to modes of procedure and trial of offenders, the statute provided 'that full authority of inquisition of all such heresies, felonies, and contempts, should be committed and directed down into every shire, to certain persons specially thereunto appointed: of which persons, three at least (provided always the archbishop, or bishop, or his chancellor, or his commissary, be one) should sit four times at least in the year; having full power to take information and accusation, by the depositions of any two lawful persons at least, as well as by the oaths of twelve men, to examine and inquire of all and singular the heresies, felonies, and contempts above remembered.'

Immediately upon Mary's fortunate death, all her legislative machinery for persecuting Protestants was swept away by stat. 1 Eliz. c. 1, which repealed all statutes in restraint of religious freedom, and restored the jurisdiction of heresy to the state in which Richard the Second's churchmen found it. Though permitted to exercise their ancient powers of examining heretics, and punishing them with censures and inflictions of penance, *pro salute animæ*, the ecclesiastical courts thereby lost their dangerous privilege of sentencing heterodox persons to the fiery death,—which fearful punishment it still remained in the power of the Crown to inflict, through the operation of the writ, *de hæretico comburendo*, on persons adjudged in a provincial synod. But Elizabeth's statute rendered religion a still greater service than the repeal of the odious enactments against Lollardy by defining for the first time in our history the crime of heresy, which was thereby stated to consist in the maintenance of any tenet or tenets which have been expressly declared heretical ' by the words of the canonical Scriptures ; or by the first four general councils, or such others as have only used the words of the Holy Scriptures ; or which shall hereafter be so declared by the parliament, with the assent of the clergy in convocation.'

But though the writ *de hæretico comburendo* remained in force throughout the reigns of Elizabeth, and her two nearest successors on the English throne, and till the latter part of Charles the Second's time, it was rarely put in execution after the final expulsion of Papal authority from Great Britain. Elizabeth issued the writ against five holders of doctrines condemned by the first four general councils, who consequently perished at the stake in accordance with the cruel provisions of the old common law; and in the ninth year of his reign, James the First put the writ in force against Bartholomew Legate, who was burnt in the last of the Smithfield fires, and Edward Wightman, who was executed in like manner at Lichfield ; but on seeing that these two last-mentioned burnings roused in spectators far more of compassionate admiration than of abhorrence for the sufferers, the king arrived at the sound opinion that the time had come for relinquishing so ineffectual a method

Part II.—Persecution.

of maintaining religious uniformity amongst his people.* Neither Charles the First nor Charles the Second entertained our ancestors with what Thomas Fuller politely designated the amusing solemnity of a public execution for heresy; and in the twenty-ninth year of the latter monarch, the barbarous writ, which had in past time consigned so many pious persons to a revolting death, was abolished by a statute, which restricted the punishment of religious heterodoxy to the milder forms of ecclesiastical correction, *pro salute animœ*. Noticing which amelioration of our national law, Blackstone observes with grateful exultation, 'For, in one and the same reign, our lands were delivered from the slavery of military tenures; our bodies from arbitrary imprisonment by the Habeas Corpus Act; and our minds from the tyranny of superstitious bigotry by demolishing this last badge of persecution in English law.'

* 'God may seem,' says Fuller, 'well pleased with this seasonable severity, for the fire thus kindled quickly went out for want of fuel: I mean, there was none ever after that openly avowed these heretical doctrines, only a Spanish Arian, who, condemned to die, was notwithstanding suffered to linger out his life in Newgate, where he ended the same. Indeed, such burning of heretics much startled common people, pitying all in pain, and prone to asperse justice itself with cruelty, because of the novelty and hideousness of the punishment; and the purblind eyes of vulgar judgments looked only on what was next to them, the suffering itself, which they beheld with compassion, not minding the demerit of the guilt which deserved the same. Besides, such being unable to distinguish between constancy and obstinacy, were ready to entertain good thoughts even of the opinions of those heretics who sealed them so manfully with their blood. Wherefore King James politicly preferred that heretics hereafter, though condemned, should silently and privately waste themselves away in the prison, rather than grace them and amuse others with the solemnity of a public execution, which in popular judgments usurped the honour of a persecution.'— *Vide* 'Church History of Britain.'

CHAPTER III.

FIRE AND SHRINE.

OF the various revolting modes * of inflicting pain and death by which the Pagan persecutors of Christianity endeavoured to exterminate the teachers and suppress the doctrines of the true faith, the originators of the canonical provisions against heresy selected the punishment of fire as the most appropriate and politic way of destroying the enemies of the Church. Some of the considerations which guided them to this choice are obvious. Typical of the doom awaiting sinners beyond the grave, the spectacle of the blazing pile, which slowly reduced a heretic's body to ashes, was especially qualified to strike beholders with abhorrence and terror,—abhorrence of the impious sentiments which had brought the sufferer to so ghastly an

* 'Wherein,' says Foxe, 'marvellous it is to see and read the numbers incredible of Christian innocents that were slain and tormented, some one way and some another, as Rabanus saith, and saith truly: "Some slain with sword; some burnt with fire; some with whips scourged; some stabbed with forks of iron; some fastened to the cross or gibbet; some drowned in the sea; some their skins plucked off; some their tongues cut off; some stoned to death; some killed with cold; some starved with hunger; some their hands cut off alive, or otherwise dismembered, have been so left naked to the open shame of the world." Whereof Augustine also thus saith: "Ligabantur, includebantur, cædebantur, torquebantur, urebantur, laniabantur, trucidabantur, multiplicabantur, non pugnantes pro salute, sed salutem contemnentes pro servatore." Often the unhappy victims were not permitted to taste death until they had endured each or several of those various kinds of maltreatment. Famous amongst the female sufferers of the Eighth Persecution are the three virgins, Maxima, Donatilla, and Secunda, who endured martyrdom at Tuburba in Africa, after undergoing a series of outrages of which the martyrologist writes: "They first had given them for their drink vinegar and gall; then with scourges were tried; after that upon the rack were tormented, and rubbed with lime; then were scorched upon the fiery gridiron;

Part II.—Persecution.

ending; and terror lest Satan's abominable subtleties should lure them to the same fate which, horrifying to witness and fraught with indescribable agonies though it was, might be deemed a passage of pleasurable sensations, in comparison with the eternal tortures which it prefigured. There seemed also a peculiar propriety in purifying the Church of its pollutions and poisonous diseases by the element which was a familiar instrument with men of every pursuit for the destruction of evil qualities in the material world, and for the separation of hurtful or worthless from beneficial and precious things.

That the ancient canonical persecutors were also induced to adopt this revolting punishment by a high and extravagant estimate of its painfulness, is more than probable; but whilst rendering proper recognition to their ferocious instincts and cruel purpose, I do not doubt that in selecting this particular kind of capital execution—a mode of inflicting death employed by our ancestors from the most ancient times against secular offenders—they were influenced by considerations of sound policy even more than by resentful fury or any other passions of barbarous fanaticism. And amongst these more respectable motives, place may be unquestionably assigned to a cold and judicial preference for a penal process, which, besides putting an end to the offender's life, destroyed and dissipated the parts and elements of his body, so that no single bone or hair of it remained after his execution to rekindle the enthusiasm of

at last were cast to the wild beasts; who, being not touched of them, finally with the sword were beheaded." The red-hot gridiron is the method of applying fire, with which St. Laurence's death is universally associated. "Away with him!" exclaimed St. Laurence's judge; "away with him! whip him with scourges, jerk him with rods, buffet him with fists, brain him with clubs! Jesteth the traitor with the Emperor? Pinch him with fiery tongs, gird him with burning plates, bring out the strongest chains, and the fire-forks, and the grated bed of iron. On the fire with him; bind the rebel hand and foot; and when the bed is firehot, on with him: roast him, broil him, toss him, turn him. On pain of our high displeasure do every man his office, O ye tormentors!" The commands were obeyed as closely as circumstances permitted; and, says Foxe, 'after many cruel handlings, this meek lamb was laid, I will not say on his fiery bed of iron, but on his soft bed of down.' The severest tortures inflicted by the Church on her heretical children were mild in comparison with the atrocities perpetrated by Pagan rage on the early Christians; and to supplicators for mercy towards heretics the Church could answer, that the culprits for their error suffered nothing worse than St. Mark endured for preaching the truth.'

his admirers, or to aid in preserving his memory from total extinction.*

In ages when the relics of the dead were cherished with a fervent and superstitious affection, to which our cold and philosophic regard for such memorials bears only a faint resemblance, the eradicators of condemned philosophies were justified in taking every precaution against such a perpetuation of a teacher's dangerous influence as was likely to result from reverence for his tomb, or possession of any portion of his relinquished body. Had the ancient guardians of Christian orthodoxy destroyed heretics by the rope or the knife, and after execution of sentence openly awarded some kind of decent or contumelious interment to their corpses, every heretic's grave would have become a shrine, whither the approvers of his errors would have flocked to meditate with pious emotion on his consecrated story, and to fortify themselves in satanic infidelities by services of prayer and praise. Or if, after thus executing the offenders by some process that did not involve corporeal dissipation, the champions of ecclesiastical authority had contented themselves with secretly consigning the corpses to unknown and undiscoverable places of interment, popular imagination would have created a score of tombs for the body of every martyr thus mysteriously put away from human sight; and ere long a new brood of heretical relic-vendors, emulating the commercial zeal and romantic inventiveness of the orthodox speculators on pious credulity, would have discovered ten times as many bones of his body as that ill-used tenement could by any possibility have contained. It was therefore in the highest degree desirable that the execution of heretics should be effected in such a manner as to render it notorious that their bodies had been utterly destroyed, and put as far beyond the relic-seeker's touch, or the shrine-worshipper's gaze, as their lives had been placed beyond the reach of human mercy.

* The contents of ancient receptacles of human ashes show that funereal incremation did not necessarily destroy every particle of the burnt bones; but the evidence is abundant that the mode in which the English Lollards were burnt, and the subsequent precautions taken to destroy utterly their bodily remains, must have resulted in the practical annihilation of every recognisable substance that could have been used as a corporeal relic of the pious victims of fanaticism.

To effect this end no known mode of inflicting capital punishment was more precisely calculated than the public execution by fire, which, whilst enhancing to superstitious minds the dreadfulness of the criminal's death by ostentatiously cutting him off from all part in the benefits of Christian burial, consumed his body in the presence of a dense assembly of spectators, in such a manner that on the accomplishment of the awful sentence, no process at that time known to human ingenuity could separate the ashes of his body from the ashes of the fagots which had been instruments of his death,—could separate the dust of his bones from the dust of the burnt fuel, that were usually thrown together into the teeth of a strong wind, or cast upon a convenient dung-hill, or hurled in the rapid water of the nearest stream.

That the Lollards would gladly have exhibited for the tombs of martyrs, whose dust had been interred in known places after incremation, the same reverential love and superstitious fondness which, in the case of orthodox believers, resulted in the idolatrous practices of the shrine-worshippers and preservers of saintly relics; and that, had the remains of their executed teachers been consigned to the grave without having undergone destruction of form and substance, the more zealous and ignorant of the early reformers, having gained possession of the undestroyed bones, would have worn them as amulets, may be seen from the pious awe with which they regarded the sites of martyrdoms, and from the affectionate devotion with which they cherished little handfuls of wood-ashes gathered from the pyres of the victims of persecution.

One of the most characteristic instances of this sentimental tendency occurred during Henry the Sixth's reign, when the simple disciples of William Wiche, a priest burnt for heresy on Tower Hill, went the perilous length of raising a small heap of stones surmounted by a cross on the spot where his soul, escaping from a tortured body, had ascended from a scene of human rage to the abode of everlasting and divine love. A rumour had become current that shortly before the termination of his mortal agonies the miserable man had declared that soon after his death the postern of the Tower would sink, and that his friends should receive this subsidence of massive masonry as a conclusive proof of his acceptance amongst the noble army of martyrs who glorify their Father in heaven. The rumour stated further that the promised sign had been given, and that this miraculous sinking of a portion of his majesty's tower several inches beneath its former level was sure evidence that Wiche had been executed unjustly, and had been rewarded for fidelity to his priestly office with immediate admission to paradise. The first result of this singular report was the erection of the rude memorial on the exact place where he had expired, to which there forthwith flocked such crowds of credulous enthusiasts eager to pray before the cross and implore this martyr's saintly intercession, that the king deemed it worth his while to disperse the assembled pilgrims with an indignant proclamation* which pledged the royal word that the deceased Richard Wiche

* The latter part of the royal writ, enjoining his magistrates for London and Middlesex to take instantaneous steps for the suppression of the new and irregular pilgrimages to Tower Hill, runs thus:—' Nay rather they' (*i.e.* Wiche's credulous worshippers) 'do most shamefully, with their vain devices, and wickedly conceived imaginations, blaze abroad that he' (*i.e.* Wiche) ' was, and died a good, a just, and a holy man, and that he doth many miracles; whereas, indeed, no such miracles be done by him. Which disordinate persons we may well, and upon probable causes, repute and deem culpable, not only of heretical pravity, but also of high treason, and as rebels to our person, majesty, and violators of the peace and dignity of our realm, as withal breakers and trespassers against the sacred canons of the Church, who dare so presumptuously adventure to worship the said Richard as a saint, whereas it is not lawful to worship any manner of person, be he ever so holy, before he is canonised by the authority of the Bishop of Rome: We, therefore, being very careful for the good preservation of our peace, and desirous to abolish from out of all the coasts of the same all manner of idolatry, do charge and command you, that, in certain places within your liberties, where you shall think most convenient, you cause, forthwith, proclamations to be made on our behalf, straitly charging that no person from henceforth presume to resort to the place where the said Richard was executed, under colour of a pilgrim, or for any other cause of devotion whatsoever; nor send any offering thither, nor worship hereafter openly or secretly, or adjudge, esteem, repute, name, or talk of him as otherwise justified or innocent, than such as the said reverend father, by his definitive sentence, hath pronounced him to be: upon pain and penalty to be taken and reputed for a heretic or a favourer of heretics, and to receive condign punishment provided *for* heretics. And that you arrest all and every person whom you shall find to do anything contrary to this our proclamation, and the same, so arrested, commit to our prison; there to remain until we shall think good to send countermand for their deliverance.—Witness the King, at his manor of Easthampstead, the fifteenth day of July, in the eighteenth year of his reign. *Per ipsum Regem.*'—*Vide* Foxe's ' Acts and Monuments.'

was no saint, but an abominable heretic, and, peremptorily ordering instant discontinuance of the insane demonstrations of respect to the heretic's memory, enjoined that all persons failing in obedience to the princely command should be forthwith committed to prison. This characteristic manifesto of the royal opinion and purpose even went so far as to declare it to be heresy for any person to 'esteem' Richard Wiche otherwise than as a heretic, and to attach to every person venturing to differ from his majesty's estimate of the said Richard Wiche all the penalties and liabilities incurred by entertainers of heretical notions.

Of the reverence manifested for the victims of the stake by the Lollards of the fifteenth century, another characteristic instance is found in the records of what occurred with respect to the ashes of the venerable Joan Boughton, who was burnt in Smithfield for her Wycliffian heresies in the ninth year of Henry the Seventh. A lady of honourable degree who was believed to have impregnated her daughter, Lady Young, with her detestable opinions on matters pertaining to religion, Joan Boughton had completed her eightieth year when the official guardians of Christian orthodoxy, unable to vanquish her in argument or subdue her sublime courage, caused her feeble body to be chained to a stake and burned to ashes, to the delight and edification of London sight-seers. 'And when,' says Foxe, ' it was told her that she should be burnt for her obstinacy and false belief, she set nothing by their menacing words, but defied them: for she said she was so beloved of God and His holy angels that she passed not for the fires: and in the midst thereof she cried to God to take her soul with His holy hands. *The night following that she was burnt, the most part of her ashes were had away by such as had a love unto the doctrine she died for.*'

After his death on the 31st day of December, 1384, John Wycliffe was interred at Lutterworth in accordance with the rites of the Church which he had vainly endeavoured to reform; and, after his bones had remained without disturbance for forty-four years, they were exhumed, burnt, and thrown into an adjacent rivulet, in compliance with an ecclesiastical order for the execution of the sentence uttered against the reformer at the Synod of Constance, thirteen years before. The Council of

Constance had not directed the incremation of the rector's bodily remains, but had only ordered with respect to them 'that his body and bones, if they might be discerned from the bodies of other faithful people, should be taken out of the ground, and thrown away far from the burial of any church, according as the canons and laws enjoin.' When, however, this order of the Council of Constance was carried out, the ecclesiastical authorities reduced the skeleton to ashes, which were cast into the river Swift,—a procedure that enabled Fuller to remark with mingled quaintness and sublimity, 'This brook hath conveyed his ashes into Avon, Avon into Severn, Severn into the narrow seas, they into the main ocean; and thus the ashes of Wickliffe are the emblem of his doctrine, which is now dispersed all the world over.'*

Many of our Protestant writers of ecclesiastic history and religious biography have concurred in the opinion that this profanation of Wycliffe's grave was an outrage dictated by sheer clerical malignity and spite against the reformer whose life had passed beyond the reach of human malevolence; but though it may have occasioned vindictive exultation to the more passionate enemies of his doctrines, and may have resulted in some measure

* In a like strain of fanciful tenderness Foxe the Martyrologist observes:— 'What Heraclitus would not laugh, or what Democritus would not weep, to see these so sage and reverend Catos occupying their heads to take up a poor man's body, so long dead and buried before, by the space of forty-*one* years; and yet, peradventure, they were not able to find his right bones, but took up some other body, and so of a Catholic made a heretic! Albeit, herein Wickliff had some cause to give them thanks, that they would at least spare him so long till he was dead, and also give him so long respite after his death, forty-*one* years to rest in his sepulchre, before they ungraved him and turned him from earth to ashes: which ashes they also took and threw into the river; and so was he resolved into three elements, earth, fire, and water, thinking thereby utterly to extinguish and abolish both the name and doctrine of Wickliff for ever. Not much unlike the example of the old Pharisees and sepulchre-knights, who, when they had brought the Lord unto the grave, thought to make Him sure never to rise again. But these and all others must know, that as there is no counsel against the Lord, so there is no keeping down of verity, but it will spring up and come out of dust as ashes, as appeared right well in this man: for though they digged up his body, burnt his bones, and drowned his ashes, yet the word of God and the truth of His doctrine, with the fruit and success thereof, they could not burn; which yet to this day, for the most part of his articles, doth remain, notwithstanding the transitory body and bones of the man were dispersed, as by this picture here set forth to thine eyes (gentle reader) may appear.'

from fanatical fury, I am disposed to take a less painful and less humiliating view of these proceedings against the insensate bones of a man who had been dead for nearly half a century, and to think that the violators of the tomb were actuated less by futile hatred of the individual than by a politic purpose to lessen the influence of the teacher's reputation, and do away with the substantial memorials which unquestionably tended to quicken and perpetuate the popular affection for the father of Lollardy.

Disapproving excursions to the shrines of saints, on account of their tendency to promote superstition and encourage idolatry, the Lollards might resist, but could not altogether free themselves from, the social influence of the ancient usages which had made the pilgrimage a source of wholesome diversion; and when they had very generally, though without any approach to unanimity, decided to take no part in the customary journeyings to the more famous sepulchres and cathedrals, they were drawn by the force of habit, no less than by their human sympathies and religious affections, to substitute new recreations for discarded amusements. Though conscientious scruples forbade them to travel, for change of air and scene, with the parties of itinerant holiday-makers who yearly wended their festive ways to Canterbury or Walsingham, they found innocent and edifying pastime in trips to village-churches, where Wycliffian preachers enunciated doctrines agreeable to the favourers of Lollardy, or to rural churchyards, that were peculiarly sacred to Lollard sentiment because they contained the graves of departed gospellers. Hence, amongst the new seekers after truth, the tranquil journey to a Lollard's tomb replaced the riotous pilgrimage to a saint's shrine; and, in the forty years immediately following Wycliffe's death, the continual stream of visitors to Lutterworth Church proclaimed the pious reverence in which his memory was held by a considerable, though relatively small, minority of his countrymen. The feelings with which narrow churchmen regarded this steadily maintained show of attachment to the reformer were none the less acrimonious and disdainful, because the pious strangers prudently abstained from conduct that might have resulted in their committal to prison on charges of Lollardy. The pilgrims came to the church, as they had every right to do; they knelt down on its pavement, and prayed silently with every visible sign of adorative fervour; they spent several minutes, looking pensively at the reformer's grave—conduct not yet rendered penal by the statute *Ex Officio;* perhaps they ate a frugal meal under the shadow of the great elm that stood in the corner of the churchyard; maybe, in the warm summertime, they rested there for an hour, listening to the music of the tree's melodious boughs; and then they passed onwards, full of burning thoughts about the idol of their pious imaginations.

Not only upon the Lollards of this country, but also on the minds of Continental reformers, the Lutterworth shrine was known to exercise an influence which orthodox believers necessarily regarded with sorrow and consternation. One of the many very singular pieces of evidence adduced against John Huss by his ecclesiastical persecutors, makes mention of a pious Bohemian, one of the numerous foreign pilgrims to Lutterworth, who 'brought out of England a certain small piece of the stone of Wycliffe's sepulchre;'* which small piece of stone was regarded by the Hussites, to whom it was exhibited by the fortunate possessor, with 'reverence and worship as a thing most holy.' When the tomb of a teacher was an object of such deep interest to his disciples of a distant land, that a fragment of its masonry could rouse within their breasts emotions of reverential love, it may be readily believed that the sepulchre and its contents were to people of his own nation an influence which the conscientious opponents of his doctrines, living in an epoch of

* 'Then the Englishmen exhibited the copy of a certain epistle, which they said was falsely conveyed into Prague, under the title of "The University of Oxford," and that John Huss did read the same out of the pulpit unto the people, that he might commend and praise John Wickliff unto the citizens of Prague. When they had read the same before the Council, the Englishmen demanded of John Huss whether he had read the same openly or no. Which when he had confessed, because it was brought thither by two scholars under the seal of the University, they also inquired of him what scholars they were. He answered: "This my friend" (meaning Stephen Paletz) "knoweth one of them as well as I: the other I know not what he was." Then they first inquired of John Huss, as touching the last man, where he was. John Huss answered: "I heard say, that on his return into England he died by the way." As touching the first, Paletz said that he was a Bohemian, and no Englishman, and that he brought out of England a certain small piece of the stone of Wickliff's sepulchre, which they that are the followers of his doctrine to this present do reverence and worship as a thing most holy.'—*Vide* 'Acts and Monuments,' Townsend's edition, vol. iii. pp. 483, 4.

pious credulity and superstitious imaginations, had good reasons for discrediting and putting out of sight. From those, therefore, who have brought themselves to attribute sincere devoutness and humane intentions to the persecutors of Lollardy, we require no more than consistency of judgment when we invite them to believe that the same creditable motives which impelled our blind and misguided ancestors to torture and kill living gospellers may also have caused them to violate the graves and offer indignity to the bones of dead heretics.

Nor is it to wander far from the subject under consideration, or make any exorbitant demand on Christian forbearance and charity, to suggest that the same generous judgment should be extended to those extreme offenders against tenderness and decency who, in more recent times, have desecrated the tombs and insulted the corpses of their enemies, at the instigation of political animosity, and for the attainment of political ends.

The influence of a religious teacher upon the affections of his disciples bears so close a resemblance to the power which a political chief, of the highest class of public actors, gains over the moral and intellectual life of his followers; and the passions, both of noble and ignoble kinds, elicited by political contention are so nearly allied to, where not actually identical with, the sentiments brought into play by polemical warfare, that no thoughtful person is likely to assign to an irreverent spirit this comparison of the ordinary circumstances of religious conflict with the usual features and results of political strife. Very often the interests of religion are so thoroughly and delicately interwoven with the concerns of secular politics, that it is impossible to unravel the social web, and separate its warp from its woof, so as to put the one material apart from the other. And whenever this is the case with any matter of vehement controversy, he must be a man of unusual self-command and singular clearness of perception who can throw himself into the struggle, and in the heat of the fight distinguish precisely between his political fervour and his religious zeal, between the ends which he pursues from mere public spirit, and objects for which he strives from devotion to his Creator. And even in fields of social welfare, that to disinterested spectators seem to lie distinctly apart from the domain of religious concerns, politicians of generous ardour and enthusiastic natures are so prone to magnify the consequences of their possible failures and successes, so quick to regard the interests of their party as identical with the highest interests of mankind, and consequently so disposed to glorify the chief whose gallantry and address have led them to victory, or whose courageous resoluteness has rallied them under defeat, that no feeling of surprise or of inability to account for the phenomena submitted to our notice disturbs our sympathetic admiration of the inextinguishable enthusiasm and pathetic devotedness which loyal followers cherish for the memory of a supreme and heroic statesman whom death has taken from their gaze.

Of the influence which the sight of such a chieftain's tomb or coffin may still exercise on the imaginations and hearts of such faithful soldiers, and, stranger to relate, may exercise on the natures of vast multitudes of men who were never bound to him by any tie of personal attachment, the world of our time had an example when the first Napoleon's bones were brought in tender triumph from St. Helena to Paris. Of all the unwise and suicidal acts of the later years of Louis Philippe's reign, it is universally admitted that none was more imprudent or more clearly fraught with ruin to his government than the welcome which he accorded, in blind generosity or presumptuous foolhardiness, to the relics which reminded every Napoleonian sympathizer of the heroic prowess and glorious achievements of the idolized emperor.

The memory of how France vibrated and heaved with patriotic emotion and romantic enthusiasm, when she gained possession of the handful of insensate dust to which the imperial form and presence of her unrivalled ruler had dwindled, may perhaps affect the reader's judgment of our ancestors' revolting outrage to the Protector's ashes. No words of apology or indignant regret can remove the blot which that hideous insult to the corpse of the glorious dictator has bitten into our national honour. But in behalf of the men who perpetrated the heinous offence against chivalry and decency; in behalf also of the people to whom the record of that enormity is an inalienable inheritance of shame, it may be urged that the Carolinian zealots, who exhumed Cromwell's body to cast it upon a dung-

Part II.—Persecution.

hill, were perhaps actuated by motives less infamous than satanic malignity and ape-like spite, when they determined that London should contain no shrine which should remind its citizens of the terrible leader of his people, who had raised his country from a condition of abasement, soothed her distractions, restored her shattered energies, and made her glorious, prosperous, and dreaded in every foreign country, and on every sea, in the days when she had no king.

CHAPTER IV.

THE STAKE.

FROM the brief and often contradictory statements of the martyrologists, it appears that the preparations for the burnings of heretics, and the proceedings at places of execution, presented numerous points of difference: and this absence of uniformity in the arrangements for accomplishing the mandates of the tribunals seems to imply that, so long as they obeyed the directions of the spiritual or other legally constituted courts, and the royal writs, with seasonable expedition, the secular authorities might consult their own convenience, or be guided by a regard for exceptional public interests, and the peculiar exigencies of the various cases, in giving effect to the sentences of the law. Acting in most instances under the voluntary supervision of powerful ecclesiastics, the civil magistrates exercised the discretionary powers, accorded to them by loosely-drawn instructions, in giving special effectiveness to the penal conflagrations, and rendering them no less acceptable to popular taste than conducive to the supposed welfare of religion.

Sometimes the execution followed immediately upon the utterance of the sentence; in other cases the condemned gospeller remained for days, weeks, months in the custody of the secular arm, before he was permitted to testify by a tranquil or openly jubilant demeanour at the stake his gratitude for the distinctions of martyrdom. For one convict the fagots would be stacked within sight of the court-house in which he had undergone examination and judgment; for another it would be decided that, instead of suffering near the place of his trial, he should be sent for execution to some remote quarter of the diocese or province—to the place of his nativity, or the scene of his heretical practices—where the flames, which consumed his body, would fill his kindred with terror and shame, and prove a salutary warning to the simple folk amongst whom he had sown the seeds of diabolical error. With respect to site, guards, time, fuel, accommodation of spectators, the executions varied greatly.

The law required that the burnings should be effected in 'eminent places before the people;' and it usually rested with the sheriffs to select the localities that were at the same time eminent and convenient for the consummation of the law's behests. The chosen place might be a market-square, a wide thoroughfare in a principal city, the court of a jail or castle, a parish-common, a paddock in the rear of a country-town, or a spot that, instead of being eminent itself, was remarkable chiefly for the boldness and abruptness of the eminences at whose feet it lay. In London, the most usual spots for execution by fire were Smithfield and Tower Hill,— the two places of the capital to which the Londoners of the fifteenth and sixteenth centuries resorted most regularly and numerously for amusement and business; but other less central districts of the town were occasionally stirred with the pageantry and excitements of a burning. Lord Cobham was burnt in St. Giles's Fields, a place were several of his Lordships associates paid the penalty of their piety and rashness. Sir Roger Acton was drawn through London to Tyburn where he was killed by the hangman; but whether the knight's body was burnt after its strangulation is a matter of uncertainty. In provincial capitals heretics were usually burnt in the market-square, where all the incidents of the fiery execution could be comfortably witnessed by spectators of local quality and influence from the windows and roofs of the surrounding houses. And whilst the provincial town thus imitated the metropolis in customary readiness to convert its chief place into an execution-yard, it also resembled the first city of the kingdom in occasionally sending its heretics beyond its walls to suffer death in the green fields.

The general appearance of Smithfield on the occasion of a public burning may be ascertained from several of the illustrations in Foxe's 'Acts and Monuments,' and more especially from the martyrologist's picture and account of the arrangements for Anne Askew's martyrdom. Together with this lady, whose heroic fortitude and Christian virtues are matters of familiar story in every English home that cherishes the truths of Protestantism, there perished three men,—Nicholas Belenian, the Shropshire priest; John Adams, a tailor; and John Lascelles, a gentleman formerly attached to Henry the Eighth's household. Instead of linking the victims together, the authorities erected three stakes for the four convicts. To one of the stakes Anne Askew was secured; to the second, one of the male prisoners (probably John Lascelles) was bound; and to the third, the other two condemned persons were fixed back to back by fastenings of iron. To restrain the crowd from pressing upon the ground near the stakes and thereby impeding the executioners, a ring was made of railings, which no one was permitted to enter with the exception of the four sufferers, the officials who conducted the prisoners to their doom or ministered to the flames, and Dr. Shaxton, the priest, whose duty it was to urge the necessity of repentance on the victims, and to harangue the crowd upon the heinous nature of the offences which the prisoners had perpetrated against religion. Amongst the doctor's auditors were—women and children who, notwithstanding the weakness of sex and the feebleness of tender years, struggled with violent men and noisy varlets to gain access to the railings; and persons of the highest quality and official eminence, such as Lord Chanceller Wriothesley, the Duke of Norfolk, the Earl of Bedford, and the Lord Mayor, for whose accommodation there had been raised a grand and richly ornamented stand, the occupants of which structure could sit at their ease and survey with critical calmness the agonies of the martyrs.* Besides the populace on the ground, and the patrician company thus furnished with seats suitable to their rank, Dr. Shaxton's discourse and the subsequent spectacle of the fiery punishment were applauded by the dense multitude of civic residents and country sight-seers who filled every

---

* 'The sermon being finished, the martyrs, standing there tied at three several stakes ready to their martyrdom, began their prayers. The multitude and concourse of the people was exceeding; the place where they stood being railed about to keep out the press. Upon the bench under St. Bartholomew's Church sat Wriothesley, Chancellor of England, the old Duke of Norfolk, the old Earl of Bedford, the Lord Mayor, with divers others.'—*Vide* Foxe's 'Acts and Monuments.'

Part II.—Persecution.

window, and covered every convenient roof that commanded a view of the painful scene.

In the previous year a similar scene was enacted in the market-place of Ipswich, before two thousand persons assembled to see the fiery sentence carried out against Kerby, who, together with Roger Clarke, of Mendlesham, in Suffolk, was convicted of heresy, in 1545, before Lord Wentworth and other commissioners for the discovery and punishment of heretics. For the proper accommodation of his lordship and his fellow-commissioners, and such superior personages as ' the justices of those quarters,' and other members of county families, a gallery had been built and tastefully decorated, from the front of which canopied platform Dr. Rougham, formerly a monk of Bury, after making characteristic apologies for his unpreparedness to officiate on so solemn an occasion, began his sermon on the sixth chapter of St. John,—a discourse that terminated in an unseemly altercation between the preacher and the condemned heretic, in which contention the heterodox disputant gained so manifest an advantage, that the doctor fell ' in his dumps, and spake not one word more to Kerby after.' In justice to the spectators of this martyrdom, it should, however, be remarked that their humanity and compassionateness were so profoundly and sharply stirred by the gospeller's demeanour, that, whilst the noble president (Lord Wentworth) ' did shroud himself behind one of the posts of the gallery,' so that his tears might not be seen by the people, other demonstrations of sympathy for the burning martyr occasioned lively offence to the more fanatical witnesses of his destruction, of which display of feeling the martyrologist briefly says, ' Then fire was set to the wood, and with a loud voice he called unto God, knocking on his breast, and holding up his hands, so long as his remembrance would serve, and so ended his life: the people giving shouts, and praising God with great admiration of his constancy, being so simple and unlettered.'

Kerby's associate in martyrdom, instead of being burnt at Ipswich, was sent from the scene of his trial to suffer death at the other chief town of Suffolk; but though their spacious and picturesque square offered them a most artistic and convenient site for the execution of an offender against the religion which had given them their historic abbey, the inhabitants of Bury St. Edmunds preferred that Roger Clarke should die beyond the bounds of their charming town. On his way to the stake, which had been prepared for him beyond the South Gate, Roger encountered the procession of the host at a point where the ecclesiastics of the old monastic town had doubtless designed to meet him for the sake of a piece of theatrical effect. Enjoined by his armed conductors to render due obeisance to the sacred presence, and its attendant pageantry, the martyr refused to bow with cap or bend with knee, and exclaimed against the idolatrous usages of his priestly persecutors with a zeal which appears to have highly incensed the officers who had charge of him, without rousing any feelings in his favour amongst the fanatical bystanders.

Ten years later the authorities charged with the execution of Rowland Taylor—who was conveyed from London, after his condemnation, to Suffolk, in order that he might die in the presence of the congregation whom he had impregnated with the seeds of heresy—conducted the most famous and exemplary of the Suffolk martyrs beyond the boundaries of the town of Hadleigh to Oldham Common,* where he was burnt, to the dismay and affectionate agitation of several hundreds of spectators, who, weeping for the downfall of their beloved teacher, cheered him in his last moments by exclaiming, ' God save thee, good Dr. Taylor ! Jesus Christ strengthen thee, and help thee : the Holy Ghost comfort thee.'

Another of the Eastern Counties' martyrs who, like Roger Clarke and Rowland Taylor, suffered death outside the walls of the towns to which they were sent for execution, was the famous

---

* John Kirby, in ' The Suffolk Traveller ' (1764), says that the common within the parish of Hadleigh, on which Rowland Taylor died, is ' commonly, but improperly, called Oldham Common ;' but the error of the designation, if error there be, has the sanction of ancient usage, for Foxe the Martyrologist knew of the place by that name. ' At last,' says the author of the ' Acts and Monuments,' ' coming to Oldham Common, the place assigned where he should suffer, and seeing a great multitude of people gathered thither, he asked, " What place is this ? and what meaneth it that so many people are gathered hither?" It was answered, " It is Oldham Common, the place where you must suffer; and the people are come to look upon you." Then said he, " Thanked be God, I am even at home !" and so alighted from his horse, and with both his hands rent the hood from his head.'

Part II.—Persecution.

reformer Thomas Bilney, for whose burning at Norwich was selected a site that met with the cordial approval of connoisseurs in executions by fire. The directors of these hideous proceedings were at great pains to invest them with theatrical impressiveness, and many of the fanatical champions of orthodox opinion concurred in thinking that no spot was more suitable to the nature and chief purposes of a penal conflagration for heresy than the bottom of a deep dell, whose abrupt sides presented in some degree the conformation of a natural amphitheatre, and afforded the multitude of spectators far better means of observation than such as could be had when burnings were solemnised in civic squares, or on level commons. The selection of such a situation for the stake was no doubt in literal disobedience to the statute, *Ex Officio*, which directed that the fiery execution should be solemnised on ' eminent ' ground; but the deviation from the exact letter of the act was defended by artistic persecutors with representations—that the typical force of the penal flames was heightened to the imaginations of beholders by a site which could not fail to remind them of the bottomless pit; and that, besides the convenience of a locality which enabled every person present to be an eye-witness of the actual accomplishment of the sentence, the sight of the flames, regarded from higher ground, and of the smoke, curling upwards between the natural walls of the place of conflagration, was inexpressively tragic and horrifying. In accordance with these views Thomas Bilney was taken from his prison in Norwich and led " to the place of execution without the city gate, called Bishops' Gate, in a low valley, commonly called The Lollards' Pit, under St. Leonard's Hill, environed about with great hills (which place was chosen for the people's quiet, sitting to see the executions.' Amongst the people thus quietly entertained, were earnest inquirers and anxious students who had hastened over from Cambridge to see the final trouble of a man whose learning they had proved, and whose virtues they had reverenced throughout the course of their long and familiar friendship. One can imagine the emotions of pity and admiration for the sufferer, mingled with selfish apprehensions for their own fate in coming years, that agitated these mournful witnesses of the tedious and revolting scene of which the historian of our English martyrs says with graphic simplicity, 'Then the officers put reeds and fagots about his body, and set fire to the reeds, which made a very great flame, that sparkled and deformed the visor of his face; he holding up his hands, and knocking upon his breast, crying sometimes, 'Jesus!' sometimes 'Credo!' which flame was blown away from him by the violence of the wind, which was that day, and two or three days before, notably great; in which it was said, that the fields were marvellously plagued by the loss of corn; and so, for a little pause, he stood without flame, the flame departing and recoursing thrice ere the wood took strength to be the sharper to consume him: and then he gave up the ghost, and his body, being withered, bowed downward upon the chain. Then one of the officers, with his halberd, smote out the staple in the stake behind him, and suffered his body to fall into the bottom of the fire, laying wood upon it; and so he was consumed.'

In the earlier days of the Lollard persecution, heretics in England were sometimes hung as well as burnt,—the double punishment being inflicted either because the secular authorities were pleased to regard heresy as savouring of treason, or because the offenders against ecclesiastical opinion had been guilty of treasonable acts against the king whilst in the performance of their heretical misdeeds. Considerable obscurity attaches to the circumstances under which persons are said to have been thus simultaneously punished for offences against religion and offences against secular law: and it has even been questioned whether the writers, who speak of these twofold executions, were not mistaken with respect to the law's manner of dealing with the cases under consideration. Neither the Common Law, nor any statute against heresy empowered the secular arm to hang heretics. The capital punishment for such offenders was burning: but whilst it would have seemed reasonable enough to the sheriffs and lawyers of the feudal period to combine the two penal processes in the cases of heretical traitors, *i. e.* heretics found guilty of treasonable conduct apart from their religious offences, it is quite credible that some of the fiercer enemies of Lollardy, amongst the sheriffs and other functionaries appointed to carry out the ecclesiastical sentences against heretics, may have been induced by legal pedantry to regard heresy as

Part II.—Persecution.

treasonable in itself, and therefore punishable with a simultaneous or nearly concurrent use of cord and fire. It is, however, certain that between the commencement of the fifteenth century and the close of the Marian persecution the notion was generally prevalent amongst our countrymen that heresy was a political as well as a religious offence, and was punishable in the first character with hanging, in the second with fire.*

There are several well-attested cases in which heretical traitors, whilst being burnt for heresy, were also reminded of their treasons by suspension in chains. That Lord Cobham was a heretic, according to the Catholic use of the term, no one is likely to question; that he was also a traitor to his sovereign even the admirers of his religious sentiments and courageous impetuosity are constrained to admit; and at his death, his claims to double punishment were recognised by his executioners, who slung him in chains over the fire that suffocated and roasted him to death. The well-known illustration in the 'Acts and Monuments' exhibits his lordship hanging over the

---

* With respect to the thirty-six Lollards who are often represented as having been hung *and* burnt in St. Giles's Field before Lord Cobham's death, Foxe says, 'But to conclude: whatsoever this Sir Roger Acton was, this is the truth, which I may boldly record, as one writing the acts and things done in the Church, that he was at length apprehended, condemned, and put to death or martyrdom, three years and more before the Lord Cobham died. Likewise Master John Brown, and John Beverley the preacher, suffered with him the same kind of death, as some say, in the field of St. Giles, with others more, to the number of thirty-six, if the story be true; which was in the month of January, anno 1413, after the computation of our English stories, counting from the Annunciation: but after the Latin writers, counting from Christ's nativity, anno 1414. These men, as is said, suffered before the Lord Cobham about three years, of whose death divers do write diversely. Some say they were hanged and burnt in St. Giles's Field: of whom is Fabian, with such as follow him. Other there be who say, that some of them were hanged and burned. Polydore, speaking only of their burning, maketh no mention of hanging. A certain other English Chronicle I have in my hands, borrowed of one Master Bowyer, which, somewhat differing from the rest, recordeth thus of Sir John Acton, that his judgment before the justice was this,—to be drawn through London to Tyburn, and there to be hanged; and so he was, naked, save certain parts of him covered with a cloth, &c. "And when certain days were past," saith the author, "a trumpeter of the king's, called Thomas Cliff, got grant of the king to take him down and bury him; and so he did," &c. And thus have you the story of Sir Roger Acton and his fellow-brethren. As touching the cause, whether it were true, or else by error mistaken of the king, or by the fetch of the bishops surmised, I refer it to the judgment of Him who shall judge both the quick and the dead.'

flames, much after the fashion of a caldron over a kitchen-fire.* He had been drawn to the place of execution 'upon a hurdle, as though he had been a most heinous traitor to the crown.' William Tyndale was strangled by the hangman before his body was committed to the flames; but consummated in a foreign country, in obedience to the imperial decree at the assembly of Augsburgh, his martyrdom affords no evidence with respect to English usages against heretics. Like Lord Cobham, more than a century earlier, Friar Forest was slung ' in chains, upon a gallows quick, by the middle and arm-holes;' and thus hung over the fire which slowly consumed his body. Sometimes, to prolong the actual or apparent sufferings of the burning martyrs, the fuel was withdrawn from their scorched bodies, and after a brief interval, restored to its former position round the charred stake; but I am not aware that the secular arm of English law ever had recourse to the barbarous contrivance which was employed by the Portuguese executioners of William Gardiner† (A.D. 1552); who, instead of being secured closely to a stake, was slung over the flames by means of a rope adjusted to a pulley, so that he could be raised and lowered from time to time in accordance with the wishes of his torturers.

* Foxe says, 'And, upon the day appointed, he was brought out of the Tower, with his arms bound behind, having a very cheerful countenance. Then he was laid upon a hurdle, as though he had been a most heinous traitor to the crown, and so drawn forth into St. Giles's Field, where they had set up a new pair of gallows. As he was coming to the place of execution, and was taken from the hurdle, he fell down devoutly upon his knees, desiring Almighty God to forgive his enemies .... Then was he hanged up there by the middle in chains of iron, and so consumed alive in the fire, praising the name of God so long as his life lasted .... This terrible kind of death, with gallows, chains, and fire, appeareth not very precious in the eyes of men that be carnal, no more than did the death of Christ when He was hanged up among thieves.' Of course the picture in Foxe's work is evidence of nothing but of his belief concerning the mode in which this martyr was exposed to the flames.

† ' There was in that place a certain engine, from which a great rope coming down by a pulley was fastened about the middle of this Christian martyr, which first pulled him up. Then was there a great pile of wood set on fire underneath him, into which he was, by little and little, let down; not with the whole body, but so that his feet only felt the fire. Then was he hoisted up, and so let down again into the fire; and thus oftentimes pulled up and down. In this great torment, for all that, he continued with a constant spirit; and the more terribly he burned, the more vehemently he prayed.'—FOXE's *Acts and Monuments.*

To the last it was our ancestors' custom to use chains, fitted with iron staples and bolts, for the purpose of confining the martyrs to their places of torture; the victim being usually secured by the single iron fastening of a chain passing round the middle of his body. Sometimes a second iron band with staple and bolt brought his neck into contact with the stake against which he was made to stand. When several martyrs were to be burnt together, so many stakes were fixed in the ground as were deemed necessary for preventing their escape, but the posts were seldom of equal number with the victims; and, when the condemned persons had been put in position, the fagots and reeds were piled round and between them, so that they were consumed in a single fire. Occasionally, however, martyrs entered heaven by the fiery path without having been bound to any stake whatever. For instance, when the thirteen martyrs were simultaneously consumed by fire at Stratford-le-Bow, on June 27, 1556, 'The eleven men were tied to three stakes, and the two women loose in the midst without any stake; and so they were all burnt in one fire, with much love to each other, and constancy in our Saviour Christ, that it made all the lookers-on to marvel.' In 1410, John Badby, instead of being fastened to a stake, was exposed to the flames, standing in a barrel.

An illustration of the variations of the treatment accorded to persons condemned to death for heresy or ecclesiastical contumacy occurred in 1540, when Barnes, Jerome, and Garret, were executed in company with three Catholics, Powel, Featherstone, and Abel, whose offence was the denial of King Henry's supremacy. 'Which six,' says Foxe, 'being condemned and drawn to the place of execution, two upon a hurdle, one being a Papist, the other a Protestant; thus, after a strange manner, were brought into Smithfield, where all the said six together, for contrary doctrine, suffered death: three, by fire, for the gospel; the other three, by hanging, drawing, and quartering, for popery.' It was the spectacle of this execution of six that caused a beholder, strange to the existing agitations of the English people, to exclaim, '*Deus bone! quomodo hic vivunt gentes! hic suspenduntur papistæ, illic comburuntur antipapistæ.*'

In removing heretical convicts from their places of trial or confinement to the spots where they were appointed to die, the secular arm exhibited different degrees of caution and carelessness, clemency and harshness. On his way from his last prison to the stake, the martyr was always surrounded by an escort of halberdiers, mounted or on foot, who were near enough to the prisoner to prevent him from running away, and strong enough to render any attempt at a rescue ineffectual; but it was usual for the sheriff's javelin-men and other armed officers to discharge their functions with mercifulness, and to give their charge the means of conversing with the crowd who attended him to death. Sometimes the martyr paused to bid farewell to wife and children, an old friend, or an attached servant; he was even permitted sometimes to give presents of money or clothes to individuals who bade him adieu as he neared the end of his troubles; and often, whilst he thus exchanged greetings with kindred and comrades, his guards were moved to tears by the humanity and sweetness of his discourse. Usually he approached the scene of execution on foot; but sometimes, as we have seen, he was drawn thither on a hurdle; and, in some few cases, he rode up to the stake on horseback.

Rowland Taylor's journey from London, where he was tried, to Suffolk, where he was executed, is, perhaps, the most pictorial and pathetic, as well as the most familiar, of the many terrible stories recorded with admirable tenderness and simplicity by John Foxe. In the gloomy darkness of a raw February morning, when the church clocks had scarcely struck the second hour after midnight, he was passing 'St. Botolph's church-porch beside Aldgate,' when he was accosted by his wife, his daughter Mary, and the thirteen-year-old Elizabeth, whom he had adopted on the death of her parents. Over the scenes that ensued before the church and the Woolsack Inn, without Aldgate,—scenes which the labours of the painter, the diction of successive poets, and the perpetual tears of the martyr's posterity, have combined to glorify,—there is no need to linger on the present occasion. * When the sheriff of Essex

---

* Let the incidents, however, be mentioned in Foxe's exquisite words :—' On the next morrow after that Dr. Taylor had supped with his wife in the Compter, as is before expressed, which was the 5th day of February, the sheriff of London

Part II.—Persecution.

was ready to receive the prisoner, Rowland Taylor was placed on a horse, and, surrounded by an adequate cavalcade, he rode out of the Woolsack Yard upon his journey, through Essex, to

with his officers came to the Compter by two o'clock in the morning, and so brought forth Dr. Taylor; and without any light led him to the Woolsack, an inn without Aldgate. Dr. Taylor's wife, suspecting that her husband should that night be carried away, watching all night in St. Botolph's church-porch beside Aldgate, having with her two children, the one named Elizabeth, of thirteen years of age (whom, being left without father or mother, Dr. Taylor had brought up of alms from three years old), the other named Mary, Dr. Taylor's own daughter. Now when the sheriff and his company came against St. Botolph's Church, Elizabeth cried, saying, " O my dear father ! Mother, mother, here is my father led away!" Then cried his wife, " Rowland, Rowland, where art thou ?"— for it was a very dark morning, that the one could not see the other. Dr. Taylor answered, " Dear wife, I am here;" and staid. The sheriff's men would have led him forth, but the sheriff said, " Stay a little, masters, I pray you, and let him speak to his wife:" and so they staid. Then came she to him, and he took his daughter Mary in his arms; and he, his wife, and Elizabeth, kneeled down and said the Lord's Prayer. At which sight the sheriff wept apace, and so did divers others of the company. After they had prayed, he rose up and kissed his wife : " Be of good comfort, for I am quiet in my conscience. God shall stir up a father for my children." And then he kissed his daughter Mary, and said, " God bless thee. I pray you all stand strong and stedfast unto Christ and His word, and keep you from idolatry." Then said his wife, " God be with thee, dear Rowland : I will, with God's grace, meet thee at Hadleigh." And so was he led forth to the Woolsack, and his wife followed him. As soon as they came to the Woolsack he was put into a chamber, wherein he was kept with four yeomen of the guard, and the sheriff's men. Dr. Taylor, as soon as he was come into the chamber, fell down on his knees, and gave himself wholly to prayer. The sheriff then, seeing Dr. Taylor's wife there, would in no case grant her to speak any more with her husband, but gently desired her to go to his house and take it as her own, and promised her she should lack nothing; and sent two officers to conduct her thither. Notwithstanding she desired to go to her mother's, whither the officers led her, and charged her mother to keep her there till they came again. Then remained Dr. Taylor in the Woolsack, kept by the sheriff and his company, till eleven o'clock; at which time the sheriff of Essex was ready to receive him : and so they set him on horseback within the inn, the gates being shut. At the coming out of the gates, John Hull, before spoken of, stood at the rails with Thomas, Dr. Taylor's son. When Dr. Taylor saw them, he called them, saying, " Come hither, my son Thomas." And John Hull lifted the child up, and set him upon the horse before his father; and Dr. Taylor put off his hat, and said to the people that stood there looking on him, " Good people, this is mine own son, begotten of my body in lawful matrimony; and God be blessed for lawful matrimony." Then he lifted up his eyes to heaven and prayed for his son; laid his hat upon the child's head and blessed him; and so delivered the child to John Hull, whom he took by the hand and said, " Farewell, John Hull, the faithfullest servant that ever man had." And so they rode forth, the sheriff of Essex with the four yeomen of the guard, and the sheriff's men leading him.'

Suffolk ; but ere he could get well clear of the gates, his horse was stopped, and his little son Thomas was raised to his saddle for a last paternal valediction.

On nearing Brentwood the cavalcade was met by Arthur Faysie, in past time one of Rowland Taylor's servants, who, seeing his former master riding with every appearance of freedom, accosted him with a congratulation, uttered under the erroneous impression that the martyr had recovered his freedom, ' Master John, I am glad to see you again at liberty!' exclaimed the servant, shaking the clergyman's hand with pleasant familiarity. ' Soft, sir,' quoth the sheriff, irritated and alarmed by the incident, ' he is my prisoner; what hast thou to do with him?' To which Arthur Faysie answered, ' I cry you mercy, I knew not so much, and I thought it no offence to talk to a true man.' Whereat the sheriff was very wrath, and packed Arthur Faysie off with a flea in his ear. To prevent more mistakes of the same kind, which might occasion turmoil and riot in districts where Rowland Taylor was well-known and beloved, the sheriff's officers, on arriving at Brentwood, ' caused to be made for Dr. Taylor a close hood, with two holes for his eyes to look out at, and a slit for his mouth to breathe at. This they did, that no man should know him, nor he speak to any man; which practice they used also with others.' Foxe's words seem to imply that this head-covering was a new contrivance, and leave us free to conjecture that it may have been the origin of the ghastly white cap which was put over convicts' heads at a later date, to disguise them from spectators watching them on their way from prison to Tyburn Field, or to any other place of execution remote from their places of previous detention. Thus used in the eighteenth century, when the authorities had reason to apprehend an attempt of the mob to rescue a culprit on his way to death, this ' condemned cap' became part of the costume of prisoners at the gallows, and was retained amongst the paraphernalia of our capital executions long after there was any need of it. Even at the present time the white cap is usually drawn over the countenance of a prisoner about to be hung, just before the hangman takes his life.

But though the custodians took careful charge of their prisoner, they treated him with consideration and kindness.

One of the four yeomen of the guard (Homes by name) exhibited moroseness to the captive, but the other three yeomen, the successive sheriffs, and their javelin-men, displayed much tender courtesy to the heretic, treating him rather as familiar comrade than as culprit under capital sentence.

Either to aggravate the pains of the victims, or more probably to hasten their destruction, the sheriffs sometimes placed immediately under the feet of martyrs at the stake materials more inflammable than the reeds and fagots with which they were built up. In 1532 Bainham was placed on a pitch-barrel, before fire was put to the fuel of his funereal pile. Gunpowder was often placed upon or near the stake-bound heretics for the merciful purpose of shortening their torments. At Anne Askew's execution, there was a momentary panic amongst the more timid of the august personages, who had seats on the grand stand, lest the gunpowder, with which one at least of the four martyrs was known to be provided, should put the spectators in jeopardy; but the fears of the gentleman who raised the alarm were removed by 'the Earl of Bedford declaring unto him how the gunpowder was not laid under the fagots, but only about their bodies, to rid them out of their pain, which, having vent, there was no danger to them of the fagots.' Bishop Hooper was provided with bladders of gunpowder when he stripped and arranged himself for death; but the explosive material did little or nothing to diminish his pains or quicken the course of his destruction, which was unusually prolonged by the high wind, that blew the flames from the martyr, and caused the dry reeds to be consumed before the fagots had been thoroughly kindled. Gunpowder also was exhibited with imperfect success at the execution of Bishop Ridley, who received from his brother's hand a bag of gunpowder, after the chain, with its staple and bolt, had girded him to the stake. 'Then his brother,' says the chronicler, 'did bring him gunpowder, and would have tied the same about his neck. Master Ridley asked what it was. His brother said, "Gunpowder." "Then," said he, "I take it to be sent of God; therefore I will receive it as sent of Him. And have you any," said he, "for my brother?" meaning Master Latimer. "Yea, sir, that I have," quoth his brother. "Then give it to him," said he, " betime; lest ye come too late." So his brother went, and carried some of the same gunpowder unto Master Latimer.'

No general survey of our ancestors' modes of dealing with heretics would be otherwise than culpably deficient which omitted to notice some of the irregular and exceptional incidents that occasionally intensified the horrors and repulsiveness of the fiery death. Of such peculiarly revolting exhibitions of fanatical zeal, a characteristic specimen may be found in Foxe's narrative of William Tylsworth's martyrdom (*circ.* 1506), at Amersham, Buckinghamshire, whose only daughter, Joan Clark, ' was compelled with her own hands to set fire to her dear father,' whilst her husband, John Clark, was required to do penance for heresy by bearing a fagot at his father-in-law's burning. Another execution, that was in like manner rendered exceptionally atrocious by a barbarous violation of the most sacred of human affections, occurred in 1521, when John Scrivener's children were constrained to put fire to the pile by which he was consumed. At other burnings the exceptional incidents were less atrocious, but more barbarously grotesque. For instance, when the mad lawyer Collins—mad through mental anguish occasioned by the infidelity of a lovely wife— was executed at the stake in London, the same little dog, which he had held up in derision of the host, was burnt with him.

Notwithstanding the universal belief in the extreme painfulness of the fiery death, I am disposed to think that it was much more terrible to the imaginations of sympathetic beholders, than excruciating to the sufferers themselves. When the piles were badly arranged, so that the reeds burnt with a clear, crackling fire for some minutes before they ignited the wood; or when the fagots were so green that it was difficult to make them burn at once, and quickly cause enough smoke to effect the martyr's suffocation; or when a high wind bore away the flames from the sufferers' bodies, and the smoke from their mouths and nostrils,—the victims of the hideous punishment suffered acutely, and for a considerable length of time. But it is no less consolatory than reasonable for us to believe that under ordinary circumstances the steady ascent of such black smoke, as necessarily results from the quick combustion of a huge pile of wood-fuel, stifled the martyrs, and reduced them to unconsciousness long before their bodies were so far consumed, that the executioners deemed it fit time to knock down the stakes with their halberds, and conclude the burning with measures that ensured the perfect destruction of the corporeal fragments. When the martyr had walked to the stake, had stript himself to his shirt, had endured the harsh counsels of the officiating chaplains, and having distributed his cast-off raiment amongst friendly bystanders had been placed against the fatal post, the worst of his pains were, in most cases, at an end. Usually the actual punishment, I am happy in thinking, was neither longer nor more painful than death by strangulation — effected at the old gallows-tree before the use of the ladder, or, in yet more remote days, before the merciful invention of the drop.

This view of the case is sustained by the calmness which the martyrs invariably exhibited during the execution,—a calmness which is too generally attributed altogether to religious fortitude, whereas much of it was doubtless due to physical insensibility. That many of the martyrs made it an affair of honour and conscience to assume an air of sublime indifference to the tortures which, in their estimation, were the brief passage to everlasting bliss, no reader requires to be told; and that of these patient and courageous sufferers of indignity, a considerable proportion would have refrained from uttering a single cry of pain under any kind of corporeal anguish, there is no room for question. But known facts do not permit us to think that such fortitude was the universal characteristic of the sufferers, some of whom were feeble women, whilst others were raw youths or tottering octogenarians, and not a few were persons to whom bodily torment was so horrible that dread of it had induced them in former time to recant. That many of the persons who expired without a cry for pity at the stake would have screamed with heart-rending shrillness under the fiery cuttings of the knotted cat I hold to be a matter of physical certainty; and that they were enabled to pass from their last scene of earthly trouble with all their purposed quietude, there is a sweet relief in assigning to their preservation from the sharpest degrees of physical agony.

In recalling the horrors of the old executions at the stake, the reader is likely to be guilty of injustice to the church, and the persons who rendered themselves most conspicuous as persecutors of religious opinion, if he fails to remember that, instead of being used only for the punishment and repression of heresy, the fiery death was the penalty awarded by our ancient usages and statutes to several crimes outside the domain of Lollardy, and that long after it had ceased to be employed against misbelief it was awarded to female offenders against the civil laws of this realm. So far as England is concerned, the penalty was of Druidical origin; and in using it for the correction of women, in cases where male culprits were liable to the less frightful though probably not more agonising punishment of being drawn and hanged, our ancestors were probably actuated by notions of decency rather than by especial severity to the weaker sex.* The same king who discontinued the ancient practice of burning heretics made the law against witchcraft more stringent and cruel. The mild and conscientious chief justice Hale sentenced witches to death by burning; and so late as the thirtieth year of George the Third, women found guilty of coining false money, wives convicted of murdering their husbands, and female servants proved to have killed their actual masters or any master whom they had at any time served, were punishable with death by fire. The relinquishment of fire, as a means of death for secular delinquents, was doubtless in some degree a result of the abhorrence and disgust with which the nation reflected upon its inordinate use during the Marian persecution.

* 'In the case of coining, which was a treason of a different complexion from the rest, the punishment was always milder for male offenders, being only to be drawn, and hanged by the neck till dead. But in treasons of every kind the punishment of women is the same, and different from that of men. For as the decency due to the sex forbids the exposing and mangling their bodies, their sentence (which was to the full as terrible to sensation as the other) was, until recently, to be drawn to the gallows, and there to be burned alive: but now to be drawn to the place of execution, and to be there hanged until dead.'—BLACKSTONE'S *Commentaries:* Stewart's edition.

CHAPTER V.

SECONDARY PUNISHMENTS AND DEGRADATION.

THE secondary punishments, which the bishops in accordance with their lawful powers inflicted on penitent heretics, varied greatly in harshness and length of term,—from impositions that required the offenders to perform certain ceremonial acts of penance which brought upon them nothing worse than transient humiliation before their neighbours, to sentences that involved servitude for a long term of years, or even for the rest of their lives. The penalty of the submissive Lollard, who humbly promised never again to sin against Mother Church, might be a nominal fine, a few blows with a white wand laid publicly upon his head by a priestly corrector, or the degradation and discomfort of walking with bare feet and no adequate supply of clothing in an ecclesiastic procession to a saint's image; but sometimes it exceeded in severity the punishments which are now-a-days awarded to malefactors whose misdeeds have only just fallen short of the offences still punishable with death. The bishop might inflict a fine the payment of which would reduce the culprit to beggary: he might order the remorseful heretic to be flogged in open markets and crowded churches: he might with hot branding irons, applied to the poor wretch's face, disfigure him for life: or he might send the miserable creature to a distant monastery, to pass the rest of his days in the hardest slavery.

The treatment of the earlier Lollards was merciful in comparison with the handling of the later reformers. In 1387, when William Smith, Roger Dexter, Alice Dexter, (Roger's wife) were constrained to do penance in Leicester, Archbishop Courtenay exhibited a degree of consideration for the offenders, that would be looked for in vain in the records of Bonner's judgments against married clergymen and ignorant peasants. It was ordered ' that the Sunday next after their returning to their own place, they holding in their right hands, William an image of St. Katherine, and Roger and Alice each a crucifix, and in their left hands every one of them a taper of wax, weighing half a pound weight, in their shirts and breeches, and Alice in her chemise alone, do walk before the procession of the collegiate church of St. Mary in the Newarks at Leicester; and thrice, that is to say, in the beginning of the procession, in the middle of the procession, and in the latter end of the procession, to the honour of Him that was crucified, in memorial of His passion, and to the honour of the aforesaid virgin, devoutly bowing their knees and kneeling, shall kiss the said images so held in their hands: and so, with the same procession they, entering the church again, shall stand during all the time of holy mass before the image of the cross, with their tapers and crosses in their hands: and when the mass is ended, the said William, Roger, and Alice, shall offer to him that celebrated the mass. Then, upon the Saturday, next ensuing, the said William, Roger, and Alice, shall in the full and public market, within the town of Leicester, stand in like manner in their shirts, without any more clothes upon their bodies, holding the aforesaid images in their right hands; which images three times they shall devoutly kiss, reverently kneeling upon their knees; that is, at the entrance, in the middle, and at the end of the market-place. And the said William, for that he is somewhat more learned, shall repeat an antiphone with the collect of St. Catherine, and the aforesaid Roger and Alice, being unlearned, shall say devoutly a ' Pater Noster' and an ' Ave Maria.' And thirdly, the Sunday next immediately after the same, the said William, Roger, and Alice, in their parish church of the said town of Leicester shall stand and do, as upon the Sunday before they stood and did in the collegiate church of St. Mary Newarks aforesaid in all things: which done the aforesaid William Roger and Alice after mass shall offer to the priest or chaplain that celebrated the mass, with all humility and reverence, the wax tapers which they shall carry in their hands. And because of the cold weather that now is, lest the aforesaid penitents might peradventure take some bodily hurt, standing so long naked; being mindful to moderate partly the said our

Part II.—Persecution.

rigour, we give leave, that after their entrance into the churches above-said, while they shall be hearing the aforesaid masses, they may put on necessary garments to keep them from the cold, so that their heads and feet notwithstanding be bare and uncovered.' The humiliations involved in this sentence were considerable to the penitents who were thus required to practically recant their previous sentiments respecting image-worship, to make themselves the laughing-stock of two congregations, and to endure the derision of their fellow-townsmen of the market. To offer obeisance to the priests must have afflicted them not a little: and doubtless the actual cost of their oblations to the officiating clergy tended sensibly to their impoverishment. But the care shown for their bodily comfort and safety by the clause which permitted them to put on warm clothing after they had entered the church is a display of clemency which would not have marked their punishment had the rage of persecution been at full heat.

Some forty years later, punishment of a much severer kind was inflicted on Thomas Pie and John Mendham, two penitent heretics of Suffolk, in the presence of the parishioners of Aldeburgh Church and the attendants at Harleston market. Themselves inhabitants of Aldeburgh, the little borough and fishing-town on the Eastern Coast chiefly famous as the birthplace of the poet Crabbe, Thomas Pie and John Mendham were made to walk in front of the ordinary solemn procession, which every Sunday made the circuit of their parish church, and after so exhibiting themselves to receive three whippings. This exposure and corporeal discipline they were sentenced to endure on six several Sundays. They were also corrected with three whippings in the market-place of Harleston on three principal market days. Alike at Aldeburgh, whilst going before the Sunday procession, and at Harleston, whilst presenting themselves for punishment in the open market, they wore nothing but their shirts and breeches, and each of them carried in his right hand a taper of a pound-weight. On the completion of their punishment the penitents presented their tapers at the high altar of Aldeburgh Church at the time of the offertory of the high mass on 'the last Sunday after the penance finished.' How many blows were given to each culprit on each of the successive Sundays does not appear from their sentence; but on each of three days of punishment at Harleston the chastisement allotted to each was twelve stripes. Making the round of the market-place in the presence of chaffering yeomen and talkative dames they paused four separate times, and at each pause the Dean of Rodenhall laid three strokes on the head of each culprit. At Aldeburgh the whippings were administered by the parish priest. This kind of flogging was a very common punishment for submissive heretics whose offences against religion were of a comparatively venial nature. It was usually called 'fustigation,' and the instrument with which it was administered by the officiating priest was a white wand. The learned editor of the 'Acts and Monuments,' the Rev. George Townsend, observes 'The manner of this disciplining was with a white rod thrice laid upon the head of the penitentiary;' but he omits to remark that a single fustigation often numbered several successive sets of three blows—as in the case of Pie and Mendham, who received between them seventy-two blows on the head before the assembled marketers at Harleston. If we assume, as we fairly may, that the fustigations at Aldeburgh were not less severe than the disciplinings administered in the neighbouring town, each of the men received in the course of six weeks one hundred and eight raps on the head with a piece of wood which, though it may be pleasantly designated a wand, was in point of fact a good stout stick. The violence which marked such sacerdotal administrations of the stick varied with the physical strength and the temper of the fustigators; but sometimes the blows were laid on with a force that broke the skin of the penitent's head and brought him senseless to the ground.

Not less painful than an ordinary fustigation, and far more dreaded than the stick because of the life-long ignominy resulting from it, was the punishment of branding, which was inflicted on penitents in considerable numbers. In 1506 thirty Lollards were branded at the same time by the orders of the Bishop of Lincoln. 'The manner,' says Foxe, 'of their burning in the cheek was this:—their necks were tied fast to a post or stay with towels, and their hands holden fast that they might not stir, and so the iron, being hot, was put to their cheeks; and thus bare they the prints and marks of the Lord Jesus about

Part II.—Persecution.

them.' This odious punishment was all the more afflicting to the disfigured persons, because branding was very generally applied to felons whose crimes had just fallen short of bringing them to gallows. To hide the marks that made them objects of suspicion and aversion to orthodox believers, that is to say, to the great majority of their countrymen, the scarred penitents used to wear their head-dresses or grow their beards so as to protect their cheeks from observation; but no sooner had the victims of fanaticism employed these means to avoid the worst consequences of their maltreatment, than the bishops forbade them to seek an escape from the scorn of their fellows by any such devices. In 1521, Longland, bishop of Lincoln, enjoined a numerous company of branded penitents, under pain of the fiery death should they disobey the order, to shave their beards at least once in every fourteen days, and to refrain from hiding the marks on their cheeks with 'hat, cap, hood, kerchief, or napkin.'

The commonest of all the various penances imposed on heretics after recantation was the necessity of bearing fagots in ecclesiastical processions, or at the burnings of unyielding Lollards. It was seldom that a martyr went from prison to the stake without some of these penitential fagot-bearers preceding or following him to the scene of execution. It was seldom that a pile was heated for a burning, to which no addition of fuel was made by some of these faint-hearted misbelievers. When the recanters had, in compliance with their sentences, thrown their fagots on the penal heap, they were required to stand and watch the ensuing conflagration, and see in the martyr's agonies the doom that awaited them in case they relapsed into heresy. And having duly borne their bundles of wood, the unbranded[*] penitents were usually required to wear on their coats badges of cloth, or pieces of silk embroidery, fashioned to resemble fagots. Sometimes the badge was borne

---

[*] As the indelible scars on the branded heretic told the story of his misbehaviour to every observer, no purpose could have been attained by requiring him to wear the badge-fagot, which was used as a merciful substitute for the marks of the branding-iron; as a temporary stigma, which should mark his dangerous character until he had given such proofs of his orthodoxy as would justify his ecclesiastical rulers in removing it.

on the left, in other cases it was worn on the right sleeve: frequently the penitent was required to wear two badge-fagots, one in the front and the other at the back of one of his arms. The terms during which the recanters bore these marks of disgrace were various, being for months, for a definite number of years, or until ecclesiastical permission was accorded for the relinquishment of the signs of disgrace. Thus William Sweeting, in an early year of the sixteenth century, after his recantation 'was constrained to bear a fagot at Paul's Cross and at Colchester; and afterwards to wear a fagot upon his coat all his life, which he did two years together upon his left sleeve, till at length the parson of Colchester required him to help him in the service of the Church, and plucked the badge from his sleeve, and there he remained two years, being holy water clerk.' Foxe's 'Acts and Monuments' contains several cases of martyrs who were in like manner 'discharged of their badges or signs of their fagots.' After obtaining this particular discharge Thomas Harding of Chesham, the Buckinghamshire Lollard, who eventually suffered death as a relapsed heretic, was required to give evidence against certain of his acquaintance who were suspected of heresy, and 'because he, contrary to his oath, dissembled, and did not disclose them, was therefore enjoined, in penance for his perjury, to bear upon his right sleeve, both before and behind, a badge or patch of green cloth or silk, embroidered like a fagot, during the whole of his life, unless he should be otherwise dispensed withal.' After he had abjured his heterodox opinions, John Tewkesbury, (A. D. 1529), was ordered, amongst other penances enjoined upon him by the Bishop of London, to wear 'two signs of fagots embroidered, one on his left sleeve and the other on his right sleeve, which he should wear all his life-time, unless he were otherwise dispensed withal.'

Next to death at the stake the severest punishment used by the bishops for the suppression of heresy was the penalty of perpetual penance, which must be stigmatized as inordinately cruel, when it is remembered that it implied slavery for life, and was awarded to Lollards who had abjured their heterodox opinions. Amongst the multitude of heretical persons corrected with divers sentences by John Longland, Bishop of Lincoln, were some fifty individuals, men and women, whom that prelate distributed amongst several religious houses of his diocese, with orders that they should undergo life-long penance; *i.e.* be the hard-worked and harshly-treated slaves of the ecclesiastical corporations to whose possession they were committed. The great offence charged against these miserable people was the declaration of heterodox views concerning the real presence. It was proved, or asserted, that they had avowed that they had 'never believed in the sacrament of the altar, nor ever would; and that it was not as men did take it.' Their other crimes were disrespectful conduct to parish priests, rejection of the sacramental character of matrimony, derisive speeches against images, flippant words tending to the dishonour of church-bells, contumacious language in the presence of the consistorial officers who had arrested their kindred. Some of them were indicted 'for saying that worshipping of images was mawmetry; some for calling images carpenter's chips; some for calling them stocks and stones; some for calling them dead things.' Isabel Bartlet, out of wifely affection for her husband, had ventured to weep openly at his arrest on a charge of heresy, and 'was brought before the bishop and abjured, for lamenting her husband, when the bishop's man came for him; and saying that he was an undone man, and she a dead woman.' Robert Rowe, on 'hearing a certain bell in an uplandish steeple,' had impiously remarked, 'Lo, yonder is a fair bell; an it were to hang about any cow's neck in this town.'

After due inquiry into the abominable doings of these atrocious sinners, the bishop adjudged them to suffer penance for the rest of their lives, or until they should receive from his lordship pardon or commutation of sentence. 'My loving brother,' wrote the Bishop to the Abbot of Ensham, 'I recommend one heartily unto you; and whereas I have, according to the law, put this bearer, R. T., to perpetual penance within the monastery of Ensham, there to live as a penitent, and not otherwise, I pray you, and, nevertheless, according to the law command you, to receive him, and see ye order him according to his injunctions, which he will show you, if you require the same. As for his lodging, he will bring it with him; and for his meat and drink, he may have such as you give him of your alms. And if he can so order himself by his labour within your house in your business, whereby he may deserve his meat and drink; so may you order him as ye see convenient to his deserts, so that he pass not the precinct of your monastery. And thus fare you heartily well.' From this letter readers may infer the treatment generally accorded to prisoners under sentence of perpetual penance.

When a person in holy orders had been convicted of heresy and sentenced to the fiery death, the Church rendered him meet for the profane touch of the secular arm by degrading him from his religious rank, stripping him of his ecclesiastical vestments, and depriving him of every sign of his spiritual character. This ceremony of degradation was no less impressive to superstitious spectators than ingeniously insulting to the culprit. The priest, about to be thus stripped of the robes and ensigns of his office, was prepared for his formal expulsion from the sacerdotal body by hands that arrayed him in every ecclesiastical dress which he had ever worn in his ascent from the initiatory orders of the church to the rank of a priest. Thus attired he was brought before his bishop or archbishop, who forthwith degraded him step by step—from the priesthood, the diaconate, the subdiaconate, the acolyteship, the order of an exorcist, the order of a reader, the honour of a sexton. Finally, to complete his severance from the hierarchical estate, his judge or judges caused his 'clerical tonsure to be rased away and utterly abolished,' and the 'coloured cap of a secular layman to be put upon his head.' Thus deprived of the surplice and keys of sextonship, the lections and habit of readership, the book and habit of an exorcist, the candlestick, taper, and dress of acolyteship, the albe of the subdiaconate, the gospels and stole of the deacon, the paten, and chalice, and cazule of the priesthood, and the tonsure of his clerical degree,* he was handed over in the garb of a layman to the lay executioners.

The degradation of Richard Bayfield, priest and heretic, was performed under circumstances of unusual pomp, and with extraordinary personal violence by the Bishop of London, A.D. 1531, in the choir of St. Paul's Cathedral, and in the presence

* The exact words with which the Archbishop of Canterbury pronounced William Sawtre's degradation (A.D. 1401) may be found in Townsend's edition of Foxe's 'Acts and Monuments,' vol. iii. pp. 227, 228.

of a splendid array of ecclesiastical dignitaries and exalted laymen. The Abbot of Westminster, the Abbot of Waltham, the Prior of Christ's Church, the Primate's Auditor and Vicar-general, were amongst the clerical witnesses of the ceremony, which was also beheld by the Earl of Essex, Richard Gray, brother of the Marquis of Somerset, the mayor and sheriffs of London. Having stripped the offender successively of all the various vestments and ensigns of his clerical orders, from the highest to the lowest, and pronounced with impressive solemnity the successive sentences of degradation, the bishop concluded the work of expulsion from the hierarchy by striking the martyr a heavy blow with his crozier-staff. During the tedious process of his degradation William Bayfield knelt on the highest step before the high altar; and he was still kneeling there when the blow from the prelate's crozier, delivered upon his breast, ' threw him down backwards' with such force that his head was broken, and he was deprived of consciousness. After recovering his senses he was 'led forth,' says Foxe, 'through the choir to Newgate, and there rested about an hour in prayer, and so went to the fire in his apparel manfully and joyfully; and there, for lack of a speedy fire, was two quarters of an hour alive. And when the left arm was on fire and burned, he rubbed it with his right hand, and it fell from his body, and he continued in prayer to the end without moving.'

In the case of a bishop or an archbishop, degradation was accomplished in the same gradual manner, the ensigns of episcopal or archiepiscopal rank being taken from the condemned ecclesiastic, who was then lowered step by step downwards to the profane condition of a layman. When the bishops, who were appointed to degrade Cranmer, laid their hands on the archbishop's pall,* his grace asked, ' Which of you hath a pall, to

---

* Fuller, in his 'Church History,' says, ' By the way, this pall is a pontifical vestment, considerable for the matter, making, and mysteries thereof. For the matter, it is made of lamb's wool and superstition. I say of lamb's " wool, as it comes from the sheep's back, without any artificial colour;" spun, some say, by a peculiar order of nuns; "first cast into the tomb of St. Peter;" taken from his body, say others; surely most sacred if from both : and superstitiously " adorned with little black crosses." For the form thereof: " in breadth not exceeding three fingers " (one of our bachelor's lambskin hoods at Cambridge would make three of them), having " two labels hanging down before and behind," which the

take off my pall,' thereby implying that his ecclesiastical inferiors could not lawfully deprive him of the mark of his archiepiscopal dignity; but, relying on the powers which they possessed as delegates of the Pope, Bonner and Thirleby took away the lamb's-wool vestment, and completed the ceremony of their primate's degradation. After the bishops had deprived their victim of all his orders, clipped his hair, and 'scraped the tips of his fingers where he had been anointed,' Cranmer, alluding to the pile of vestments that had been taken from his body, observed, 'All this I needed not; I had myself done with this gear long ago.' In place of the gear thus contemptuously mentioned, the dispalled primate received 'a poor yeoman-beadle's gown, full bare and nearly worn, and as evil favouredly made, as one might lightly see, and a townsman's cap on his head.' Regarding his disfigured and broken foe with malicious exultation Bonner exclaimed,—' Now you are no lord any more.' And Bonner spoke the truth. Cranmer was no longer a lord. Henceforth his highest honour was to be one of the Lord's martyrs.

archbishops only, when going into the altar, put about their necks, above their pontifical ornaments. Three mysteries were couched therein. First, humility, which beautifies the clergy above all their costly copes. Secondly, innocency, to imitate lamblike simplicity. And thirdly, industry, to follow Him who fetched His wandering sheep home on His shoulders. But to speak plainly, archbishops receiving it showed therein their dependence on Rome; and a mote in this manner, ceremoniously taken, was a sufficient acknowledgment of their subjection. And, as it owned Rome's power, so in after ages it increased their profit. For though now such palls were freely given to archbishops, whose places in Britain for the present were rather cumbersome than commodious, having little more than their pains for their labour, yet in after ages the Archbishop of Canterbury's pall was sold for five thousand florins: so that the Pope might well have the golden fleece, if he could sell all his lamb's wool at that rate.'

CHAPTER VI.

THE DEATH OF PERSECUTION.

TO enumerate all the benefits which accrued to our nation and race from the religious persecutions of the fifteenth and sixteenth centuries would be a task beyond the province of these volumes; but on closing a superficial survey of repulsive occurrences, which are too apt to rouse in generous and impetuous natures emotions of unreasonable hostility against the church which was mainly responsible for the barbarous outrages, it is desirable that the reader should soothe his agitated feelings by reflecting that the hideous maltreatment of the Lollards and reformers was in various ways fruitful of good to the intellectual and moral life of our forefathers, and that some of its advantageous consequences were of a kind that would justify Protestant Englishmen of the nineteenth century in regarding the malignant persecutors of Lollardy as national benefactors.

The persecutions were fitful and partial,—never raging with unabated fury for any long series of years, and never covering at the same time the entire length and breadth of the land. Even in the dark interval between Edward the Sixth's death and Elizabeth's accession, the agents of Mary's superstitious madness and Pole's fanatical cruelty were chiefly active within two dioceses, and the number of their victims,[*] great though it was, falls far

---

[*] Historians differ as to the number of the Marian martyrs. Strype puts the number of persons executed in all the years of Mary's reign, for religious misbelief, at 284; Speed estimates them at 277; Weaver, in the 'Monuments,' says, 'In the heat of whose' (*i. e.* Mary's) 'flames were burnt to ashes five bishops, one-and-twenty divines, eight gentlemen, eighty-four artificers, an hundred husbandmen, servants, and labourers, twenty-six wives, twenty widows, nine virgins,

short of the number of persons whom, in several more recent agitations, English rule has put to death with questionable legality, in far briefer spaces of time and within much narrower limits of country, for the maintenance of public order or the attainment of inferior political ends. But though the persecutions burnt most fiercely in special localities, the struggle between new opinion and old dogma was the affair of the whole nation, and every fresh outbreak of fanatical zeal in a particular diocese intensified the national interest in the discussion of the matters at issue, and quickened the intelligence of the whole people. When the fires were lit in Buckinghamshire, the men of Northumberland or Hampshire, Cornwall or Yorkshire, felt that ere a few months had passed similar conflagrations might warm their own market-towns. When Gardyner and Bonner let loose their fury in the sees of Winchester and London, every household in the kingdom was roused with a vivid sense of imminent danger. To fortify themselves in the rules of orthodoxy, and to satisfy themselves that the law was right in putting heretics to death, ordinary folk according to their various degrees of learning had recourse to their manuals of devotion and their priests, and reconsidered every point of the proscribed doctrines. On the other side, to render it clear to their own minds that they could not relinquish the Protestant tenets at the instigation of fear and prudence, without sinning against the Divine Giver of the Gospel light, the reformers read their Bibles in secret more heedfully than ever, raised subtle questions for debate with fellow-companions in heresy, and, in anticipation of the time when their English Scriptures might be taken from them, learnt daily by heart whole chapters of the sacred writings.

And whilst each of the two parties was thus stimulated to intellectual exertion, the persecution was working, in every social circle and single family, moral results no less important to the national life than the ordinary mental consequences of the

---

two boys, and two infants; one of them whipped to death by Bonner, and the other, springing out of the mother's womb from the stake as she burned, was thrown again into the fire. Sixty-four more were persecuted for their profession of faith; whereof seven were whipped, sixteen perished in prison, twelve were buried in dunghills. Many lay in captivity, condemned, but were released and saved by the auspicious entrance of peaceable Elizabeth.'

universal ferment. Wherever martyrs perished under the fiery death, domestic dramas were enacted to the illustration of the sublimest and sweetest, the darkest and the meanest, qualities of human nature: and the spectacle of such dramas was an awful education to beholders of quick brain and fine sensibility. Throughout the special districts of persecution, every home that harboured religious inquirers had reason to dread the approach of that most despicable of all domestic traitors, the fireside spy — who, availing himself of the opportunities and powers accorded by hospitality, would wheedle himself into the confidence of simple enthusiasts, and then hand them over to the law, so that they should be burnt for words whispered in their private chambers. Nor were the effects of the pathetic scenes of human malignity and heroism confined to the actual witnesses of their dramatic occurrences. Every story of the persecution was carried from homestead to homestead, and, growing in poetic loveliness and force as it passed from roof to roof, spread in all directions the seeds of romantic excitement and spiritual sympathy.

The average Englishman of the present time is ever ready to extol Shakespeare as the greatest creator of our literature; but he too often needs to be told that Shakespeare's mind was in perfect proportion and harmony with the intellectual life of his period, and that, instead of being a giant amongst dwarfs, as popular adulation too frequently represents him, the poet was a giant amongst giants. We compare him to the Alpine monarch of mountains, but are prone to forget the mountains that surrounded him. He is called a monarch of the forest by obsequious worshippers who forget that to estimate rightly the greatness of its height and the enormity of its girth, the sovereign tree of a primeval wood must be compared with the trees of vast, though smaller, growth, which it overtops, and not with the scrub and brushwood at its foot. No fair notions can be formed of Shakespeare's dignity, and power, and perfect naturalness, if he is considered apart from the times that produced him, and the times which he influenced through personal contact. Separated from his contemporaries, and transplanted as it were from his own grandly heroic period to the present generation, he loses much of his sublimity and the greater part of his significance. Whilst marvelling at his stature we have nothing at hand, greater than our own smallness, against which to contrast it; and so we must either abstain from critical examination of his parts and proportions, or must try to measure the universe with an inch-rule. Moreover one of the first uses of heroes, when they have passed away, is the light which they throw on their own particular periods. Important though it is that we should know Shakespeare, it is of even greater importance that we should know the generation in which he lived, the London in which he surrounded himself with companions. And this information Shakespeare affords us with a clearness and completeness, characteristic of all his intellectual services, if we regard his genius and career in relation to the social conditions under which he worked, and remember that in intellectual quickness, comprehensiveness, and force he bore to the foremost of his contemporaries just the same proportions as are now-a-days borne by the exceptionally great thinker and artist in letters to the brightest and strongest of his contemporaries. His age was emphatically the heroic age of English story,— an age prolific of great statesmen, gallant explorers, subtle thinkers, and fearless seekers after truth. Besides a new drama, which can never be surpassed, it gave us new lands the fullness of whose natural capabilities is still amongst matters of conjecture, new philosophy by whose conclusions we direct our labours of inquiry, a new faith within whose limits the great majority of educated Englishmen are still happy to remain. It was the epoch of Frobisher, and Hawkins, and brave Sir Humphrey Gilbert; of daring Raleigh, and high-souled Sydney; of Francis Bacon and Sir Edward Coke; of Jewell and Hooker, Browne and Cartwright. It was a time when courtiers were men of letters, and soldiers could tell in fitting verse the victories which they won. More than any other age in our story it distinguished itself by sweeping away the rubbish of old errors and setting up the lights and lessons of new discovery, and was remarkable for its abundance of fervour and force in every department of intellectual activity. To account for this excess of mental vigour and enterprise, historians refer to the invention of printing and the revival of letters; and, without doubt, the discovery of the printer's art and the stimulus which it imparted

Part II.—Persecution.

to learning were great agents in giving birth to this heroic time, but, though great, they were only contributory influences to the manifold causes which resulted in the Reformation which was at the same time the immediate cause and the immediate product of the finest intellectual qualities of Elizabethan England. In an early year of the seventeenth century it was remarked by a competent observer that the religious struggle for ecclesiastical reforms found our priesthood the most ignorant and left it the most learned clergy in all Europe. And what the struggle, betwixt keen-witted innovators on the one hand and subtle champions of tradition on the other, effected for our clergy, it also accomplished for the entire body of the laity,—changing every market-town to a seat of learning, and raising clerks and warehousemen to be students and disputants.

In so far as the present generation is benefitted by the extraordinary intellectual activity of the Elizabethan period, it must number amongst its benefactors all those promoters of the heats and animosities of the persecution to which that activity is largely attributable. Nor do its numerous results on the mental and moral life of the present time comprise all the reasons why we should regard with thankfulness a long social contention which, to those who study it thoughtfully, is fraught with valuable lessons for our guidance at those constantly recurring periods of strife which are apt to put reason and charity under the feet of prejudice and passion.

Elizabeth's accession is the event which divides the era of religious persecution in England from the period of religious toleration. That persons were still punishable for heterodox opinions, and that a few individuals were actually put to death for misbelief under the old common law by the virgin queen and her immediate successor on the English throne we have elsewhere observed; but the fact remains, that her assumption of the supreme power gave, so far as England is concerned, the death-blow to religious persecution, which, notwithstanding the tenacity with which it clung to existence, ultimately perished from the effects of the policy which she inaugurated. In saying this we only offer to the facts of history a bare recognition that commits us to no extravagant and romantic views respecting the sweetness and generosity of her disposition. A Tudor in brain and heart, the despotic queen was by no means devoid of the mental and moral qualities of a persecutor; and though her larger intelligence would under any circumstances have saved her from the perpetration of such ghastly blunders as marked her sister's deplorable rule, it is more than probable that she would have been much less disposed towards practical toleration of religious differences, had she possessed adequate power to enforce conformity in matters of opinion. But fortunately for her own reputation and the welfare of her people, she was compelled to adopt a policy of forbearance as the only policy that offered her, as a Protestant sovereign, a chance of preserving the allegiance of such a proportion of her Catholic subjects as would avail, in conjunction with the Protestant minority of the nation, to keep in subjection the strong and opulent body of English Catholics whom no concessions and conciliations could wean from their implacable and rancorous hostility to what they conscientiously regarded as her usurpation of authority.

To argue, as successive Protestant historians have argued, that the promptitude with which she repealed the statutes against heresy demonstrates her natural benignity and averseness to cruel measures, must appear idle in the extreme, when it is remembered that those enactments were specially directed against her own religious tenets. In expunging the bloody acts from the code of English law she showed proper care for herself and her fellow-believers, and a true perception of the interests of her people; but it is ridiculous to extol her for clemency and compassionateness because she lost no time in burning the rods that had been prepared for her own back. Nor is it more reasonable to credit her with higher qualities than prudence and sagacity, because, instead of retaliating on her Catholic subjects for the cruelties which Cardinal Pole and Bishop Bonner had inflicted on her companions in belief, she proclaimed her readiness to extend towards adherents of the old faith the same toleration which she required them to exhibit towards Protestantism. That this line of action towards the two great parties of her people, for which she has been extravagantly commended by indiscreet admirers, was the only policy open to her, when she had finally resolved to defy the Pope and adhere to the cause of Protestantism, is manifest when we remember that at the commencement of her reign the English Catholics bore to the English Protestants the proportion of two to one, and that, though the Protestant minority had a decided advantage over the Catholic majority in respect of intelligence, the Catholic party enjoyed an even greater preponderance over their opponents in respect of wealth and the social influence that attaches to hereditary distinctions. In fact, the Queen was the queen of a minority; a minority, moreover, deficient in property and aristocratic prestige, and labouring under the disadvantages which always weigh heavily on a party of progress, before it has achieved permanent successes and won the suffrages of the multitude. Her only chance of governmental success lay in the difficult game which she played with equal subtlety and coolness between the Protestant minority at her back and the Catholic majority in her front. By effecting a compromise between the hopes of her supporters and the fears of her opponents; by adopting an ecclesiastical policy that conciliated the lukewarm Catholics, at the cost of embarrassing discontent on the part of the more zealous Protestants; by restraining the zeal of her friends and at the same time conceding to the prejudices of her enemies,—she effected the desired combination of the more moderate members of both parties, and achieved the ends for which she strove with firmness and moderation throughout the vicissitudes of her long and perilous reign. Of the difficulties, which she encountered in playing this delicate and hazardous game, the most serious and irritating arose from the dissensions of the Protestant party and the divisions of the Anglican clergy.

In accordance with the policy of tolerance, by which she eventually won the devotion of the majority of her subjects, Elizabeth's conduct justified her profession, that she would punish no man's religion by taking his life. With the exception of the five persons, burnt for heresy under the provisions of the old common law, she can be charged with no act that can be justly stigmatized as an act of religious persecution, in the first and strictest sense of the term. For political ends she required her subjects, under various penalties in case of disobedience, to exhibit an outward conformity to the established religion; and, during the earlier years of her reign, these penalties were very light, so that persons, whose consciences might not permit them to render the required submission to the new church, should not be grievously afflicted by the legal consequences of nonconformity. Though restrictions were put upon the Catholic's inclination to make converts, and to promulgate the doctrines of his church, he was at liberty to cherish his belief in private. No spies caught up the words that fell from his lips over his own hearth, and made them the foundation of proceedings against him in consistorial courts. With pardonable unfairness Catholic writers are accustomed to claim the honours of martyrdom for the numerous Catholic priests who suffered death in Elizabeth's reign by the operation of the laws against Papists. The sufferers, however, were executed, not for their belief in the doctrines of the Catholic Church, but for their participation in practices which were contrary to law, and which had been declared illegal because it was judged that they were opposed to the welfare of the Queen and her realm. They died for political offences, not for religious misbelief; and, however much sympathy he may feel for some of the luckless enthusiasts, however ready he may be to credit them with conscientious motives, no candid student of English history, bearing in mind all the facts of Elizabeth's conflict with the Papacy, can question that the laws by which they perished were enacted as measures of national self-defence, and not with a view to punish Catholics for being Catholics.

The same view must be taken of the hardships which conscientious Protestant Dissenters endured at the hands of English Churchmen in the seventeenth and eighteenth centuries, and even till the other day, when an alteration of the law of church rates relieved Nonconformists from the obligation to contribute towards the maintenance of parish churches. That the old laws against Nonconformity were to a great extent dictated by the animosities and prejudices of religious contention, that they were cruel in design and sometimes absolutely barbarous in their results, that the persons who put them in force against offenders were too often inspired by the malignant spirit of the worst kind of religious persecutors, I wish that I could deny. It must also be conceded, that the sufferers from these miserable devices of polemical rancour and ecclesiastical narrowness

—these wretched blunders of foolish governments—were for the most part sufferers for conscience sake, and in consequence of their religious convictions; and that, therefore, their hard experiences had a strong savour of veritable martyrdom. But still the law dealt with them, in respect to religious matters, on political rather than on religious grounds; and they must, therefore, be regarded as the victims of political enmity rather than of religious persecution.

It is our custom nowadays to congratulate ourselves that England has come to the end of her religious persecutions; that men are free in this country of liberty to worship the Almighty according to their consciences, so long as they abstain from gross violations of social sentiment with respect to sacred things; and that, in spite of the warmth and bitterness frequently manifested in theological disputations, no Englishman has reason to fear the judgments of sectarian narrowness, or to tremble at the rage of bigotry. And on all these points our congratulations are justified by daily experience. But though religious persecution, in the sense which this work applies to the term, is (so far as England is concerned) the affair of those not very remote centuries when religion and politics, if not identical, were so intimately blended that every great ecclesiastical commotion involved disturbance to the secular interests of the entire commonwealth, it is a great, though by no means rare, error, to suppose that the passions which generated the storms of fanatical violence have passed from our nature, or ceased to be dangerous forces in our commonwealth. The vicious tendencies of man's mental and moral faculties, which must be held accountable for the most revolting characteristics of the politico-religious disturbances of feudal England, may be seen in full operation by every observer of the political contentions of our fellow-countrymen of the nineteenth century. The men are no more who condemned the reformers' doctrines without having first ascertained precisely what those doctrines were; who foresaw abominable results from a movement which resulted in the revival of Christianity; and who, under the impression that the disciples of Wycliffe and Luther were the spawn of Satan, and the destroyers of mankind, hastened to silence and kill them. But in every political battle that has been fought on English soil since the death of Mary, honest, impetuous, wrongheaded Englishmen have repeated the blunders and sins of the old persecutors. Every political party in the state still has its blind and furious partisans who call truth falsehood whenever it comes from an adversary's lips; who honestly believe every baseless calumny that has been levelled at an opponent's character or doctrine; and who, mistaking prejudice for knowledge, and private passion for public spirit, credit themselves with philanthropy and patriotism, when they are doing their utmost to make the world worse, or hinder it from growing better.

PART III.—CLERICAL WOMEN.

CHAPTER I.

CLERICAL WIVES IN PRE-ELIZABETHAN TIMES.

THE limits prescribed for this survey of ecclesiastical persons and usages preclude us from taking into consideration the nature and functions of the deaconesses of the early Christian churches; but I avail myself of this opportunity to refer general readers, who wish for information concerning the female diaconate of ancient times, to a learned and thoughtful little book which came from Mr. John Malcolm Ludlow's pen some four or five years since.*

So much also has already been said in this volume about the services rendered by the medieval nuns, as instructors of children and ministrants of Christian benevolence, and as promoters of religious enthusiasm, that I may be excused for not lingering longer over the fascinating story of their modes of life, which, I have been at pains to show, bore a greater similitude to the social usages of the secular women of their times, and were less marked by romantic eccentricity, than their poetical admirers in the present century are disposed to fancy.

Nor is there any need for me to repeat my former remarks

---

* 'Woman's Work in the Church. Historical Notes on Deaconesses and Sisterhoods.' By John Malcolm Ludlow. Strahan.

on the peculiar, and in many respects painful experiences of the Englishwomen who, wives in the opinion of the old common law, but dishonoured women according to the canons of the Church, were bound in wedlock, that endowed their offspring with legitimacy, to priests whose domestic condition was deemed abominable by the regular clergy, and, though enjoying an indefinite and indescribable social sanction, was regarded with considerable disapprobation by the majority of the laity. Of the proportion which these concubinary priests bore to the celibate clergy it is impossible at the present date to form an estimate, or even to make a conjecture; but though a minority, a decidedly small minority, throughout the interval betwixt Anselm's death and the later years of Chaucer's England, they were unquestionably numerous enough to form a distinct and conspicuous feature of clerical life. Their numbers doubtless varied, and were subject to sudden fluctuations in the various parts of the kingdom, in accordance with the variations of episcopal opinion, and the irregularities of episcopal zeal. A bishop, whose private history disposed him to think lightly of the canons prohibiting priests from marriage, would refrain from harrassing his concubinaries so long as they were quiet and in all other respects inoffensive men. The sentiments and temper of such a prelate would, of course, give a stimulus to sacerdotal marriage in his diocese, and would also draw within its boundaries numerous concubinary priests from other dioceses where stringent and vexatious measures were taken to enforce the requirements of Papal authority by divorcing the concubinaries from their wives. But the constant recurrences of synodal decrees against the married clergy, the repeated (and *vainly* reiterated) orders for their discovery, and the disturbances that were continually arising from futile attempts to render celibacy universal throughout the clerical order, show that the canons were, in this particular, disobeyed by an important percentage of the secular priests.

Of the almost countless incidents, alternately pathetic and laughable, which attended the long conflict between the celibates and the concubinaries from the tenth to the fourteenth century, none were more dramatic and affecting than those which distinguished Anselm's futile warfare* against the priests whose domestic affections found a harsh and extortionate patron in Henry the First who, whilst Anselm was pursuing his ambitious designs at the Papal court, permitted the priests, whom the primate had separated from their wives, to resume their old domestic consolations on paying a sum of money into the royal exchequer. The more affluent of the married curates availed themselves of his majesty's prudent concession with thankfulness; but there were many of the divorced clergy who, wishing to recover their wives, were unable to indulge themselves in so costly a luxury. Wereupon two hundred of these needy and affectionate creatures, clothed in their albes and priestly vestments, walked barefoot in procession to the king's palace, and forcing their way into the queen's presence implored her, with an abundance of tears and lamentations, by her womanly tenderness and wifely love, to intercede for them with her husband, and procure his permission that they might regain possession of their dames without payment. But though the queen was grievously afflicted by their miserable plight, she could give them nothing more efficacious than compassionate words, and durst not attempt to move the king in their behalf. From an early year to the close of his reign Henry appears to have pursued this policy to his married ecclesiastics, save during times when he was not strong enough to oppose the authorities of the church with respect to so delicate a department of priestly discipline. Under the primacy of William de Curbellio, having summoned a council in London, Henry obtained from the spirituality jurisdiction over the offences of ordained offenders against the canonical laws relating to celibacy; and no sooner

---

* The conflict elicited the following verses, together with other like satirical effusions:—

> ' O, male viventes, versus audite sequentes,
> Uxores vestras, quas odit summa potestas,
> Linquite propter eum, tenuit qui morte trophæum,
> Quod si non facitis, inferna claustra petitis.
> Christi sponsa jubet, ne Presbyter ille ministret,
> Qui tenet uxorem, Domini quia perdit amorem!
> Contradicentem fore dicimus insipientem ;
> Hæc non ex rancore loquor, potius sed amore.'

had he obtained this power, than he invited the divorced priests to buy back their wives. It is probable that his course of action in this particular originated the ancient notion that Englishmen might sell their wives. Since buyers cannot exist without sellers, and the thing bought by one person must be sold by another, when the rumour ran through Christendom, that clerical wives could be bought in London, it followed as a corollary that clerical wives were sold there; and if clerical wives, the rarest of all wives, were articles of commerce in the English capital, it also followed that a brisk trade was done on the banks of the Thames in wives of the commoner sorts.

The persecution of Lollardy tended in various ways to diminish the number of the married clergy, almost to the point of extinction. By combining the great majority of lay persons in every section of society to crush the misbelievers, the excitements of that movement brought almost the entire mass of the people into cordial cooperation with the church, and resulted in an uprecedented extension of the papal power in every part of the country. The married clergy were consequently deprived of that large measure of social toleration and sanction which their domestic relations had hitherto enjoyed. But a matter of still greater effect upon the position of the married priesthood was the comparative union amongst the clergy,—a union, qualified with servile obsequiousness to the Bishop of Rome, which resulted from the operations against heretics. In the confusion of the moment, and in the absence of a legal or theological definition of Lollardy, any kind of resistance to the canons was liable to be construed as the crime for which offenders might be burnt under the statute *Ex Officio*. The Wycliffian reformers were for the most part opposed to the celibacy of the priesthood. Indeed Wycliffe's heterodoxy with respect to marriage had not stopt short of asserting the lawfulness of wedlock between brothers and sisters. A married priest was in imminent peril of being regarded as a Lollard priest; and in their detestation of Lollardy and its miscreants, the populace conceived a violent abhorrence of concubinary priests,—an abhorrence which maintained its place in popular sentiment long after the politico-religious agitators had been utterly exterminated, and which, surviving the Reformation, was cherished by a large number of Protestants throughout the reign of Elizabeth, who amongst other of her father's prejudices, is well known to have retained much of his strong aversion to married clergy.

Between the enactment of the statute *Ex Officio* and the repeal of the 'Six Articles,' a priest disposed towards matrimony seldom gratified the natural inclination unless he could ensure his archdeacon's connivance, and contrive means to guard his estate from discovery. Usually, before marriage, he relinquished his priestly garb and functions, and sought subsistence in a secular vocation. The Wycliffian martyr and priest, William White, who suffered at Norwich in 1428, 'gave over his priesthood and benefice' before he 'took unto him a godly young woman to his wife, named Joan.' When John Lambert, who suffered martyrdom in 1538, determined on the felonious course of matrimony, 'forasmuch as priests, in those days, could not be permitted to have wives, he left his priesthood, and applied himself to the functions of teaching, intending shortly after also to be free of the Grocers, and to be married. But God, who disposeth all men's purposes after His secret pleasure, did both intercept his marriage and also his freedom, and married him to His Son Christ Jesus, and brought him into the freedom of His spiritual kingdom, to reign with Him.' In like manner, before he married, Richard Spencer, priest and martyr (who suffered in 1541), separated himself as far as possible from his spiritual vocation, 'and became a player in interludes, with one Ramsay and Hewet, which three were all condemned and burned.' Bishop Bale married Dorothy in the Catholic time of Henry the Eighth's reign, although he had taken priest's orders; and when he went to his Irish see, his wife accompanied him.*
But by far the most famous of the illegally married priests of Henry the Eighth's reign, was Cranmer, who, having married and lost his first wife before entering holy orders, took his

* 'On the 19th day of December,' says Bale, ' I took my journey from Bishop's Stoke, with my books and stuff, towards Bristol, where I tarried twenty-six days for passage, and divers times preached in that worshipful city, at the instant desire of the citizens. Upon the 21st day of January we entered into the ship; I, my wife, and one servant; and being but two nights and two days upon the sea, so merciful was the Lord unto us, we arrived most prosperously at Waterford, in the coldest time of the year .... At supper the parish-priest' (of Knocktower), 'called Sir Philip, was very serviceable, and in familiar talk described

second wife—'a Dutchwoman, kin to the wife of Osiander'— prior to the formal abolition of the Papal authority from England, and shortly before his elevation to the primacy. During Henry's life he kept his wife secretly, so as to avoid the penalty he had incurred; but in the time of Edward the Sixth, priests' marriages having been expressly legalised, he 'brought out the said wife openly.'

In Edward the Sixth's time, a considerable number of the English clergy availed themselves of their newly-acquired privilege to take wives, without subjecting themselves to punishment; and those of them who, like Cranmer, had possessed wives secretly before Henry's death, lost no time in imitating the primate, and introducing their conjugal partners to the world. Of Edward's clergy, who thus openly entered the matrimonial estate, one of the most celebrated was John Knox, who, in the interval between his preferment to be one of the king's chaplains in ordinary, and his flight to France shortly after Mary's accession, married a young gentlewoman named Bowes, to whose mother he justified his sudden departure, saying, 'Some will ask, Why did I flee? Assuredly I cannot tell. But of one thing I am sure—the fear of death was not the chief cause of my fleeing.' Ten years later, having been a widower for four years, Knox took for his second wife a daughter of Lord Ochiltree.

The Marian persecutors displayed especial malignity and ferociousness against the married clergy, several of whom suffered at the stake quite as much on account of their domestic virtues as in consequence of their doctrinal heresies. John Rogers, Laurence Saunders, Rowland Taylor, William Flower, John Cardmaker, Robert Samuel, Bishop Ferrars, were some of the ordained martyrs who thus glorified sacerdotal wedlock in the reign immediately preceding that in which Bishop Hall's voice

---

unto me the house of the White Friars, which sometime was in that town; concluding in the end that the last prior thereof, called William, was his natural father. I asked him, if that were in marriage? He made me answer, "No. For that was," he said, "against his profession." Then counselled I him, that he should never boast of it more. "Why," saith he, "it is an honour in this land to have a spiritual man, as a bishop, an abbot, a monk, a friar, or a priest, to father."'

and pen demonstrated the honour of the married clergy. From the love which most of these men bore their mates and children, and the exquisite sweetness of their pathetic words of farewell to their wedded partners, one is justified in forming a high estimate of the women who became wives of the clergy in times when the position of a clerical wife was full of perils and inconveniences, and was attended by few of the circumstances which nowadays render it especially attractive to Englishwomen. 'For this,' wrote John Rogers, from his prison at Newgate, 'I most heartily, and, at this present, with weeping tears, most instantly and earnestly desire and beseech you all to pray; and also, if I die, to be good to my poor and honest wife, being a poor stranger, and all my little souls, hers and my children, whom, with all the whole faithful and true Catholic congregation of Christ, the Lord of life and death, save, keep, and defend, in all the troubles and assaults of this vain world, and bring at the last to everlasting salvation.' Of Rowland Taylor's final separation from the gentle parent of his nine children, notice has already been taken by this volume; and readers, searching for biographical illustrations of the virtues of the Anglican clergy in past time, will find an abundance of testimony suited to their purpose in Laurence Saunders's pathetic letters to, and in behalf of, his loving wife.

But of all the anecdotes of martyrology which exemplify the domestic kindliness and parental affectionateness of the married clergy of Edward the Sixth's time, none have a stronger vein of comedy running through their deep tragic interests than the records of Bishop Ferrar's (of St. David's) tenderness towards his little boy, whom the prelate used to amuse by whistling him tunes whilst the child lay in his nurse's arms. In proof of the primate's criminal folly, it was gravely urged against him at his trial, that to the scandal of religion he thus amused, or endeavoured to amuse, his helpless infant.*

---

* Here is a specimen of the ludicrous charges, on proof of which this Welsh prelate was committed to the flames:—

'FOLLY.

'XLVIII. Item. To declare his folly in riding, he useth a bridle with white studs and snaffle, white Scottish stirrups, white spurs, a Scottish pad with a little staff of three quarters long, which he hath not only used *superstitiously* these four

In reply to the charges respecting this labial music, and the circumstances of his child's baptism, the bishop replied in writing: 'To the LIst. he saith, that, after lawful prayer, it pleased God to give him a son begotten and born in honest marriage, whom he therefore caused to be named Samuel, presenting him to the minister to be received into Christ's Church as a poor member of Christ. By the holy sacrament of baptism was this done openly in the cathedral church, with earnest gravity, and without offending any man; and also two wives, being before at variance, desired both to be godmothers, which they both received to make unity between them, not knowing any law to the contrary, nor any offence conceived of the people. —To the LIId. he said, that he doth use with gravity all honest-loving entertainment of his child, to encourage him hereafter willingly, at his father's mouth, to receive wholesome doctrine of the true fear and love of God; and saith, that he hath whistled to his child, but said not that the child understood it; and that he hath answered to one that found fault with it, as is contained in the article.' But the brave old prelate—who, born under Henry the Seventh, had been a loyal servant to that king's son and grandson, and was bent on serving Queen Mary 'truly, with his poor heart and word'—

or five years, but in communication oftentimes boasted what countries he hath compassed and measured with the same staff.

'XLIX. Item. He hath made a vow that he will never wear a cap; for he saith, it is comely wearing of a hat, and so cometh in his long gown and hat, both into the cathedral-church and to the best town of his diocese, sitting in that sort in the king's great sessions and in his consistory; making himself a mock to the people.

'L. Item. He said he would go to the parliament on foot; and to his friends that dissuaded him, alleging that it is not meet for a man in his place, he answered, "I care not for that, it is no sin."

'LI. Item. Having a son, he went before the midwife to the church, presenting the child to the priest, and giving his name Samuel, with a solemn interpretation of the name; appointing two godfathers and two godmothers, contrary to the ordinance; making his son a monster, and himself a laughing-stock throughout all the country.

'LII. Item. He daily useth whistling of his child, and saith that he understood his whistle when he was but three days old. And being advertised of his friends that men laughed at his folly, he answered, "They whistle their horses and dogs, and I am contented; they might also be contented that I whistle my child." And so whistled him daily, all friendly admonition neglected.'

Part III.—Clerical Women.

had committed the heinous offence of marriage, and would not conform to Catholic requirements to the extent of putting away his wife, though most of the married clergy preserved their lives by timely submission on this point to the Church's order. To the Bishop of Winchester's exclamation, 'You made a profession to live without a wife,' the prelate on trial replied in words, which show the evasion by which married priests in Catholic times justified to their consciences their breach of canonical law, 'No, my lord, if it like your honour; that did I never, I made profession to live chaste — not without a wife.' This answer was enough to secure the condemnation of the prisoner, who, in due course, was burnt in the market-place of Caermarthen.

CHAPTER II.

CLERICAL WIVES IN ELIZABETH'S REIGN.

IN his famous ' third chapter '—that graphic medley of historic truths, ingeniously falsified facts, and reckless fictions,—speaking of the social condition of Charles the Second's clergy, Lord Macaulay says, ' A waiting-woman was generally considered as the most suitable helpmate for a parson. Queen Elizabeth, as head of the Church, had given what seemed to be a formal sanction to this prejudice, by issuing special orders that no clergyman should presume to marry a servant-girl without the consent of the master or mistress.' In support of this extraordinary statement the historian adds in a note, ' See the Injunctions of 1559, in Bishop Sparrow's Collection. Jeremy Collier, in his " Essay on Pride," speaks of this injunction with a bitterness which proves that his own pride had not been effectually tamed.' It would have been better for Lord Macaulay's literary reputation, had he acted upon the prudent counsel given to his readers, and looked into the Injunctions, which he can never have perused carefully, though his disingenuous words imply that he had studied them.

In the ' Essay on Pride,' committing the blunder which his lordship repeats, Jeremy Collier says, ' Because by those Injunctions a clergyman could not lawfully marry till he had gone and made his complaint against celibacy before two justices of the peace; and gained their consent, and the goodwill of the master or mistress whom the damsel served.' The special orders put no such universal obligation on clergymen wishing to marry servants. On the contrary, they distinctly empowered clergymen, enamoured of waiting-women, to marry their ' damsels ' without the consent, and in spite of the

Part III.—Clerical Women.

opposition, of their employers, save in cases where the damsels had no parents or known kindred,—in which rare cases the employers would stand towards the girls in the place of parents.

Of the Injunctions which Elizabeth published, for the guidance of her clergy and laity in religious matters, in the first year of her reign, the twenty-ninth runs thus:—' Item, although there be no prohibition by the word of God, nor any example of the Primitive Church, but that the Priests and Ministers of the Church may lawfully, for the avoiding of fornication, have an honest and sober wife, and that for the same purpose the same was by Act of Parliament in the time of our dear brother King Edward the Sixth made lawful; whereupon a great number of the clergy of this Realm were then married, and so continue. Yet because there hath grown offence, and some slander to the Church by lack of discreet and sober behaviour in many ministers of the Church, both in choosing of their wives and indiscreet living with them, the remedy whereof is necessary to be sought, it is thought therefore very necessary, that no manner of priest or deacon shall hereafter take to his wife any manner of woman without the advice and allowance first had upon good examination by the bishop of the same diocese, and two justices of the peace of the same shire, dwelling next to the place where the same woman hath most made her abode before her marriage, nor without the good will of the parents of the said woman, *if she have any living, or two of the next of her kinsfolks, or for lack of knowledge of such,* of her master or mistress where she serveth. And before she shall be contracted in any place, she shall make a good and certain proof thereof to the minister, or to the congregation assembled for that purpose, which shall be upon some holyday where divers may be present. And if any shall do otherwise, that then they shall not be permitted to minister either the word or the sacraments of the Church, nor shall be capable of any ecclesiastical benefice: and for the manner of marriages of any bishops, the same shall be allowed and approved by the metropolitan of the province, and also by such commissioners as the Queen's Majesty thereunto shall appoint. And if any master or dean or any head of any college shall purpose to marry, the same shall not be allowed but by such to whom the visitation of the same doth properly belong, who shall in any wise provide that the same tend not to the hindrance of their house.' These are the words of the ' special orders,' referred to by Lord Macaulay; and it may be satisfactory to his admirers as well as his enemies to know that they have been transcribed from the Sparrow's Collection, which he cites in support of his ridiculous assertion. Whereas Collier and his copyist imply that the injunction was inspired by the queen's disdain of her clergy, and aimed at depressing the ecclesiastical order; it is clear that it was dictated by no such spirit, and that its provisions were designed to heighten the general respect for married priests and prelates by preserving ordained servants of the Church from scandalous or palpably injudicious marriages.

The order contemplates the probability of clergymen wishing to marry domestic servants; but to argue from this fact, that it sanctioned their union with women whom members of the other liberal vocations, and men moving in the humbler grades of the landed gentry, or in the ways of superior commercial life, would have disdained to lead to the altar, is to display an unusual ignorance of feudal manners. So long as feudal society endured in England, the condition of the menial servant differed widely from domestic service in the nineteenth century. Whilst the sons of knights and affluent gentlemen of ancient lineage were proud to wear the livery of a great peer or officer of state, and serve him at table, bending their knees whenever they handed him a dish, the sisters of these well-born pages experienced no sense of degradation in serving with like service ladies, to whose degree they might reasonably hope to rise in due course by means of honourable marriage. The same state of things was observable in every social grade, from the nobles who surrounded the king to the rural squires who paid court to the lord of a shire, and even to the small territorial personages who were content with the means and style of opulent yeomen. Every lord's castle, every knight's hall, every squire's manorial residence, contained female servants, whose manners and birth were alike gentle, and who were never confounded with the daughters of ploughmen and hinds. They held the position of gentlewomen; and, when they were orphans, their masters and mistresses stood to them in the place of parents—to the extent of guarding them from the disadvantages of matrimonial misalliance, of preserving them from dangerous companions, and of helping them with counsel and bounties to desirable settlements in wedlock. Throughout Elizabeth's reign and the times of her two nearest successors on the English throne, domestic service retained these honourable qualities and characteristics with only slight impairment; and it had not altogether lost them in the later half of the eighteenth century, when ladies' personal and peculiar maids were often as well-born and well-taught as their mistresses. The gentlewoman's gentlewoman of Fielding's period was frequently the near kinswoman of her employer. Indeed, it was not until the demand for female teachers of young gentlewomen had created a new field of domestic usefulness for the daughters of poor gentlemen, that ladies finally relinquished the duties of family service, and felt that they could not for payment discharge menial offices without altogether surrendering their gentility. So far as social status and esteem are concerned, the superior female domestic servants of Elizabethan England were quite as well placed as the governesses of the Victorian period; and, though our clergy is at the present time more powerful and aristocratic than any priesthood in the world, no sane person would venture to suggest that a political paper, drawn upon the supposition that a percentage of English rectors would annually marry governesses, indicated a design to lower the ecclesiastical order in the opinion of society, or was conclusive evidence that clergymen and footmen were very nearly of the same social degree.

Various circumstances, however, combined to preclude the Elizabethan clergy from forming such advantageous matrimonial alliances as their official successors were generally able to contract in the seventeenth century. In the first place, the social status of the priesthood had been decidedly lowered by the Reformation. That the inferior members of the monastic orders contributed but little to the repute and prestige of the ecclesiastical class every reader is aware. The suppression of monasteries had, however, extinguished what may be termed the aristocratic section of the English clergy; and the rupture with Rome had still further lowered the status of the priesthood by depriving them of the sympathy and co-operation of that large majority of the aristocracy and gentry who secretly cherished their old attachment to the Papal see, and who, with mingled disdain and superstition, regarded the Reformed Church with scorn and abhorrence, as a new and impious device, revolutionary in origin and blasphemous in practice, which could not survive many years. And, whilst the Catholic families would have indignantly repudiated any of their women who inclined towards marriage with the heretical priesthood, the Protestant parents of the country discouraged their daughters from becoming the wives of Reformed priests. The feeling in favour of clerical celibacy was very prevalent throughout Protestant society, even during the later years of Elizabeth's government; and, in the earlier decades of her long reign, the Protestant laity were of opinion that, though it was prudent in the State to sanction clerical matrimony as the only practical way of avoiding the evils of clerical celibacy, married clergymen could not claim the same measure of respect to which the virtuous celibates of the ecclesiastical order were justly entitled. By the bare fact of marriage the Elizabethan rector surrendered a considerable amount of social respect. The young lady, therefore, who accepted the matrimonial overtures of a parson, knew, in the first place, that she was taking a suitor whose social degree was exceptionable; and, in the second place, was aware that, in consequence of his marriage, he would fail to enjoy the cordial respect of her acquaintance.

Another class of considerations tended to make clergymen ineligible suitors for the girls of prosperous families. So long as the stability of the Protestant state church was a matter about which even its warmest advocates were by no means confident, the material conditions of a beneficed parson lacked that element of security which, upon the firm establishment and success of the new ecclesiastical policy, contributed to make him a 'good match.' In case of another national relapse to the papal sway, it was more than probable that the married priest would atone for his matrimonial 'condescension' by the loss of his benefice. It was certain that he would be required to put away his wife or die at the stake, under the former of which alternatives she would at best receive from his income a mere pittance for her maintenance, whilst under the latter contingency she would be left a widow without any adequate provision for herself and her children. Bearing in mind what had, in Mary's time, befallen the clerical wives* who took their husbands in King Edward's reign, it was only natural that parents, in the early part of Elizabeth's rule, should show disfavour to clerical suitors for their daughters' affections.

Still, in spite of the many disadvantages under which they sought the consolations of wedlock, a large number of Elizabeth's priests became possessed of wives. In accordance with the terms on which the right of marriage had been conceded to them, they wooed and led their brides to the altar with the sobriety and sedateness of demeanour appropriate to men who were spoken of as 'condescending to matrimony,' who knew themselves to be objects of social contempt rather than social sympathy, and who professed to surrender their dignity of celibacy merely that they might preserve themselves from sin and increase their usefulness in the Church. It was understood that a conscientious parson was not to select his wife for beauty, or wealth, or social condition, or out of respect to any of those worldly considerations which are now-a-days permitted to influence a young rector in choosing a conjugal partner. He was not even allowed to be fastidious about her mental endowments, or particular in ascertaining her temper. So long as his most discreet neighbours were of opinion that a lady possessed the requisite qualifications for a minister's wife, the matrimonially-disposed priest was wont to take her to his parsonage on their recommendation rather than his own judgment. Very often he selected and wooed his wife by deputy, and never saw her till a

* Even during the Marian persecution married clergymen sometimes contrived to keep their wives without incurring the penalties attached to such disobedience of the canons. 'However strictly the married priests,' says Strype, 'were looked after and punished by divorce and loss of their livings, yet some escaped this inquisition; being the less suspected when they complied and conformed themselves to the religion of the State. Such an one was Fairbank, a curate of Warbelton in Sussex. He had not put away his wife, notwithstanding the queen's injunctions, but kept her secretly. This man had preached in his parish in King Edward's time, that none of them should believe any other doctrine than he did preach and teach them, according to the doctrine set forth in that king's days. But, in the beginning of Queen Mary, he preached doctrine clean contrary.' — *Vide* Strype's 'Ec. Mem.'

few days before their marriage or till the very morning of their union. The vicarious suitor might be his churchwarden, or a staid matron of his acquaintance, or some other decorous person whose recommendation of the affair would have the desired effect on the two neighbouring justices and the bishop of the diocese.

The story of Hooker's love affairs and matrimonial experiences affords some humorous illustrations of the spirit in which Elizabeth's clergy set about the grave business of marriage, and the meekness with which they endured the consequences of their 'condescension.'

A timid and thoughtful recluse, Richard Hooker, the famous champion of the Anglican Ecclesiastical Polity, combined Parson Primrose's simplicity and goodness with all the awkwardness and nervous shyness of the vicar's delineator. 'God and Nature,' says Isaac Walton, 'blessed him with so blessed a bashfulness, that as in his younger days his pupils might easily look him out of countenance; so neither then, nor in his age, did he ever willingly look any man in the face; and was of so mild and humble a nature, that his poor parish-clerk and he did never talk but with both their hats on, or both off at the same time; and to this may be added, that though he was not purblind, yet he was short or weak-sighted; and where he fixed his eyes at the beginning of his sermon, there they continued till it was ended.' When about thirty years of age, this gentle creature, whom a frown would confuse, and a harsh word put to silence, was summoned from his books and pupils at Oxford to preach at Paul's Cross. Clergymen, so called from the country to deliver sermons from the most important of the metropolitan pulpits, were in those days supplied with free entertainment at the Shunammite's House,* in addition to the fees paid for their services. At the time of Hooker's first appearance in the Paul's

---

* 'In order to which sermon,' says Isaak Walton, ' to London he came, and immediately to the Shunammite's House: which is a house so called, for that, besides the stipend paid to the preacher, there is a provision made also for his lodging and diet for two days before, and one day after his sermon. This house was then kept by John Churchman, sometime a draper of good note in Watling Street, upon whom poverty had at last come like an armed man, and brought him to a necessitous condition . . . . But to this house Mr. Hooker came so wet, so weary, and weather-beaten, that he was never known to express more

Cross pulpit, the Shunammite's House was kept by a Mr. Churchman—a decayed draper, formerly in good business in Watling Street; and it was through the affectionate assiduity with which Mrs. Churchman discharged the functions of hostess, that she contrived to plant her daughter, as a wife, on the confiding scholar. The journey from the university to the capital proved only a few degrees less perilous than grievous to Hooker, who made it on horseback, having been over-persuaded to give up his original design of walking from his college to the metropolis. Having received some general instruction in the theory of equitation, the college-tutor started on his way; but either because he thought his steed cantered when it trotted, and trotted when it cantered, or because, through misapprehension and confusion, he failed to accommodate himself to the animal's movements in accordance with the prescribed rules, he suffered cruelly in the process of locomotion. To make bad worse, it rained violently, so that on arriving in London the unfortunate gentleman was wet to whatever skin was left on his sore limbs and aching body. Very likely he would have expired of fatigue and inflammation, just about the time when he delivered his text to the gaping Londoners, had not clever Mrs. Churchman taken him in hand, and cured his cold before it had run into pleuritis. The woman was equal to the occasion. Putting her priest into a hot bed, she doctored him with warm drinks and possets, so that he was enabled to preach his sermon to the satisfaction of a critical audience.

Nor did Mrs. Churchman's solicitude for his welfare cease when she had brought him triumphantly through his cold, and aches, and cutaneous abrasions. On the contrary, she admonished him to be heedful of his delicate constitution, to wean himself from the perilous solitariness of a fellow's life, and to provide himself with an affectionate and competent wife, who

passion than against the friend that dissuaded him from footing it to London, and for finding him no easier an horse,—supposing the horse trotted when he did not; and at this time also, such a faintness and fear possessed him, that he could not be persuaded two days' rest and quietness, or any other means could be used to make him able to preach his Sunday's sermon: but a warm bed, and rest, and drink proper for a cold given him by Mrs. Churchman, and her diligent attendance added unto it, enabled him to perform the office of the day, which was in or about the year 1581.'

should know how to nurse him through future colds and rheumatisms. A zealous student, Richard Hooker loved his college; an enthusiastic churchman, he entertained the churchman's notion, that marriage was an inferior condition to celibacy; but the sweet modesty and blessed bashfulness of his nature put him in the power of his sympathetic assailant, who gained from him a commission to choose him a suitable helpmate.* Having thus yielded to her importunities, Hooker returned to

---

* 'But,' records Hooker's admiring biographer, 'the justifying of this doctrine did not prove of so bad consequence as the kindness of Mrs. Churchman, curing him of his late distemper and cold; for that was so gratefully apprehended by Mr. Hooker, that he thought himself bound in conscience to believe all that she said, so that the good man came to be persuaded by her "that he was a man of tender constitution," and that it was best for him to have a wife, that might prove a nurse to him: such a one as might both prolong his life and make it comfortable; and such a one she could and would provide for him, if he thought to marry. And he, not considering that the "children of this world are wiser in their generation than the children of light," but, like a true Nathaniel, fearing no guile because he meant none, did give her such power as Eliezer was trusted with,—you may read it in the Book of Genesis,—when he was sent to choose a wife for Isaac: for even so he trusted her to choose for him, promising upon a fair summons to return to London, and accept of her choice. And he did so in that, or about the following year. Now the wife provided for him was her daughter Joan, who brought him neither beauty nor portion; and for her conditions, they were too like that wife's which is by Solomon compared to a dripping house . . . . And by this marriage the good man was drawn from the tranquillity of his college—from that garden of piety, of pleasure, of peace, and a sweet conversation, into the thorny wilderness of a busy world; into those corroding cares that attend a married priest and a country parsonage; which was Drayton Beauchamp, in Buckinghamshire, not far from Aylesbury, and in the diocese of Lincoln, to which he was presented by John Cheney, Esq., then patron of it, the 9th of December, 1584 . . . . And in this condition he continued about a year; in which time his two pupils, Edwin Sandys and George Cranmer, took a journey to see their tutor; when they found him with a book in his hand,—it was the Odes of Horace,—he being then like humble and innocent Abel, tending his small allotment of sheep in a common field: which he told his pupils he was forced then to do, for that his servant was gone home to dine, and assist his wife to do some necessary household business. But when his servant returned and released him, then his two pupils attended him unto his house, where their best entertainment was his quiet company, which was presently denied them, for that Richard was called to rock the cradle: and the rest of this welcome was so like this, that they staid but till next morning, they having in that time rejoiced in the remembrance, and then paraphrased on many of the innocent recreations of their younger days, and other like diversions, and thereby given him as much present comfort as they were able, they were forced to leave him to the company of his wife Joan, and seek them a quieter lodging for next night.'

Corpus Christi College, where he must have arrived a far sadder man than when he departed from its tranquil walls a few days earlier.

Her husband being yet alive, Mrs. Churchman could not recommend herself for the vacant place; but with maternal considerateness, deserving more respect than Isaak Walton extends to it, she made choice of her own daughter. And true to his word, Richard Hooker adopted her selection, relinquished his fellowship, became Joan Churchman's true husband, and went to live at Drayton Beauchamp, Buckinghamshire,— the rectory of which parish he resigned on obtaining the mastership of the Temple, from which preferment he was fain to retire, before Walter Travers's thunderous assaults, to Boscomb, in Wiltshire, where he remained till he migrated to his last living and home, Bishop's-Bourne, Kent. It was at Drayton-Beauchamp that his old pupils, George Cranmer and Edwin Sandys, found him tending sheep during his farm-servant's absence, and formed an unfavourable opinion of his wife who interrupted their interview with their former tutor by calling him away from them to rock the baby's cradle. Commiserating his condition the young men did not protract their stay in his comfortless parsonage, and on bidding him farewell Cranmer found courage to allude sympathetically to the straits and pains of the good man's worldly circumstances. 'My dear George,' the uncomplaining pastor answered mildly, 'if saints have usually a double share in the miseries of this life, I, that am none, ought not to repine at what my wise Creator hath appointed for me, but labour—as indeed I do daily—to submit mine to His will, and possess my soul in patience and peace.'

There is no need to narrate the various circumstances which on the one hand afford justification to all the harsh and contemptuous speeches uttered against Mrs. Hooker, and on the other hand countenance the growing opinion that she has been judged more severely than her shortcomings warrant. Those who are curious upon such points may seek information from the numerous biographers, from Walton to Keble, who have maliciously exaggerated or generously palliated the poor lady's defects. But one fact which says much in her behalf should be omitted from no page that draws attention to the unhappiness which is believed to have marked her husband's domestic experiences. Hooker appointed her sole executor of the will by which he bequeathed 100*l.* to each of his four daughters and more than 600*l.* to his widow. This appointment certainly implies that Hooker had confidence in her intelligence and maternal dutifulness. That it also implies the testator's perfect forgiveness of whatever neglect and offences may have marked her behaviour to him, it is almost needless to observe; for men of Hooker's fine and almost sinless nature, incapable of exhibiting or harbouring resentments against their enemies, are not likely to be deficient in leniency to their wives. After examining all the evidence for and against her, I am disposed to think that poor Mrs. Hooker encountered less than bare justice from her husband's friends, some of whom, as high churchmen, were predisposed against the woman and her mother who between them had caused the passionless priest, and luminous defender of our Ecclesiastical Polity, to descend into matrimony.

Reverence for the author of 'The Laws of Ecclesiastical Polity' disposed Keble to regard Walton's account of Hooker's marriage as mere idle gossip; and another of the ecclesiastical apologist's more recent biographers speaks of the same record as 'one-sided and unreal,' and 'inconsistent with what Hooker discloses of his own character in his writings.' As to the narrative's inconsistency with the strength and resoluteness, and thorough good sense, of Hooker's literary reasonings, the same objection may be as fairly urged against the credibility of some of the most definitely ascertained facts of his life. No one would ever infer from the texture and *nerve* of the treatise on 'Ecclesiastical Polity,' that its writer was a diffident, bashful man, likely to be routed and driven out of high preferment by the acrimonious language of a noisy disputant. And yet that Hooker was a man of this mild and yielding kind, we know from his discomfiture in his controversy with Walter Travers, and from the very words of the beautiful letter in which he solicits the archbishop to release him from his duties at the Temple,—'My lord, when I lost,' the epistle begins, 'the freedom of my cell, which was my college, yet I found some degree of it in my quiet country parsonage. But I am weary of the noise and oppositions of this place; and, indeed, God and nature did not intend me for

Part III.—Clerical Women.

contentions, but for study and quietness. For, my lord, my particular contests here with Mr. Travers have proved the more unpleasant to me, because I believe him to be a good man.' Again, Walton's story of Hooker's submissiveness to Mrs. Churchman is in perfect consistency with the rest of the biographer's uniformly harmonious portraiture of the champion of the Anglican polity—a portraiture, be it observed, the general truthfulness and naturalness of which are not even called in question by the critics, who would discredit the portions of it that relate to the divine's love affairs. The whole of Walton's picture, moreover, is in thorough harmony with whatever can be learnt from other sources about its interesting subject.* Lastly, the particular story is countenanced by the known opinions and usages of Elizabethan pastors with respect to sacerdotal marriage. Surely, then, it is absurd to stigmatise the story as the outgrowth of gossip and invention because it shows that a pious and learned young clergyman of Elizabeth's time set about the work of condescending to matrimony in a spirit altogether different from that in which clergymen of the present day enter upon what they rightly think the higher estate of marriage.

Born some twenty years later than Hooker, Joseph Hall, (Bishop of Norwich) married just upon the close of the sixteenth

---

* Another incident, which demonstrates how Hooker's timidity put him at the mercy of designing women, is recorded by Walton, where he tells how a profligate creature succeeded in extorting sums of money from the gentle and bashful pastor by abominable threats, 'until at last Providence was pleased to concern itself for the righting wronged innocence. It so fell out, that this woman came to him when his two dear friends, Mr. Sandys and Mr. Cranmer, were with him. Wondering to see such a person come with so much confidence, they inquired of their tutor the occasion of it, who in a little time tells them the truth of the whole story.' With respect to this painful and characteristic affair, Prince, in the 'Worthies of Devon,' remarks: 'Which explains the obscurely told story of a scandal against Hooker's moral character, which occurs in Walton's Life. But this is certain, that he lay under the great charge, and the anxiety of this accusation, and kept it a secret unto himself for many months; and being a helpless man, had lain longer under this heavy burthen, but that the Protector of the innocent gave such an accidental occasion as forced him to make it known to his two dearest friends, Edwin Sandys and George Cranmer, who were so sensible of their tutor's sufferings, that they gave themselves no rest till, by their disquisitions and diligence, they had found out the fraud, and brought him the welcome news that his accusers did confess they had wronged him, and begged his pardon.'

century, at a time when much of the popular prejudice against sacerdotal matrimony had died out, and when clergymen were daily finding it less difficult to ally themselves in marriage with families of the substantial gentry. And of the facts which throw light on the clerical marriages of this period, one of the most important is Bishop Hall's assurance that, before ever he had looked upon his future wife, she had been selected to be his helpmate, and overtures made in his behalf for her hand by a grave and decorous friend. 'Being now, therefore,' says Hall, in his autobiographic sketch, referring to a period when he was between twenty-five and thirty years of age, ' settled in that sweet and civil country of Suffolk, near to St. Edmund's Bury, my first work was to build up my house, which was then extremely ruinous. Which done, the uncouth solitariness of my life, and the extreme incommodity of that single housekeeping, drew my thoughts, after two years, *to condescend to the necessity of a married estate*, which God no less strangely provided for me; for, walking from the church in the Whitsun-week with a grave and reverend minister, Mr. Grandridge, I saw a comely and modest gentlewoman standing at the door of that house where we were invited to a wedding-dinner; and inquiring of that worthy friend whether he knew her. "Yes," quoth he; "I know her well, and have bespoken her for your wife." When I further demanded an account of that answer, he told me she was the daughter of a gentleman whom he much respected, Mr. George Winniff, of Bretenham; *that, out of an opinion had of the fitness of that match for me, he had already treated with her father about it*, whom he found very apt to entertain it; advising me not to neglect the opportunity, and not concealing the just praises of the modesty, piety, good disposition, and other virtues that were lodged in that seemly presence. I listened to the motion as sent from God; and at last, upon due prosecution, happily prevailed, enjoying the comfortable society of that meet-help for the space of forty-nine years.' Had this statement, instead of coming to us from Bishop Hall himself, been the work of one of his contemporaries, it would have been discredited as mere gossip and amusing fiction by such writers as those who, on no evidence whatever, repudiate as incredible Walton's account of Hooker's love affairs.

Part III.—Clerical Women.

The good sense and moral rectitude of the Elizabethan clergy did more, I doubt not, than the provisions of the queen's twenty-ninth injunction, to preserve them from marriage with specimens of the inferior of the two sorts of women, about which two kinds of feminine nature an Elizabethan prelate (Aylmer, Bishop of London), observed in a court-sermon, delivered in the queen's presence,—' Women are of two sorts; some of them are wiser, better learned, discreeter, and more constant, than a number of men; but another and a worse sort of them, and the most part, are fond, foolish, wanton flibbergibs, tattlers, triflers, wavering, witless, without counsel, feeble, careless, rash, proud, dainty, nice, talebearers, eavesdroppers, rumour-raisers, evil-tongued, worse-minded, and in every sense doltified with the dregs of the devil's dunghill.' But that not a few of the clerical wives justified, by their frivolous demeanour and petulance, Bishop Aylmer's contemptuous account of the prevailing qualities of their sex, there is an abundance of evidence in memoirs, printed annals, and official documents. The Elizabethan complainants against the Dean and Chapter of Worcester charged the clerical ladies of the Cathedral Close with arrogance, insolence, idleness, and inordinate love of dress; and the splendour of their attire was all the more offensive to many of their censors because the gentlewomen of the Church were indebted for much of it to the despoliation of the Cathedral vestiaries, from which store-rooms large quantities of silk gowns, embroidered vestments, fine linen robes, and other paraphernalia of Catholic Ritualism had been taken in the course of the ordinary operations of ecclesiastical purification, and had been converted into millinery for canons' wives and daughters.

Long after social opinion had recognised the advisability of clerical marriages, and laid aside much of its prejudices against wife-encumbered parish-priests, it regarded the presence of clerical wives in cathedral closes and colleges with strong disapprobation. In the second year of her reign, Elizabeth's counsellor, Cecil, prepared a proclamation, ordering the expulsion of the wives of deans and canons from colleges and cathedral closes. Such dignitaries might marry; but having condescended from the higher estate of celibacy, they were required in the name of decency to throw a veil over their weakness, and keep their wives with all possible privacy. But it was beyond the power of royal proclamations and episcopal censures to keep the ladies in lowly subordination when they had once been allowed to put their dainty feet within the lines of the ecclesiastical order. The cathedral close yearly lost more and more of its old conventual character, replacing its ancient ways with usages in accordance with the needs and wishes of a married priesthood. The collegiate dinner in the common hall was relinquished when the majority of the canons and other cathedral ecclesiastics preferred to dine in private with their wives and children, instead of regaling themselves at the tables of their ancient refectories. The dean's chamber grew to be a stately mansion; the prebendary's rooms became a commodious house; the minor canon exchanged his narrow lodgings for a compact dwelling, provided with a drawing-room and nursery.

But even to the end of Elizabeth's reign, Protestant conservatives—the timid and reactionary reformers, who held that enough of a good thing was better than too much, and that of reform a little was enough—used to deplore the changes and innovations wrought in the cathedral colleges by feminine influence. And whilst the cautious lovers of old ways were of opinion that clerical ladies should be chiefly remarkable for unobtrusiveness and willingness to keep out of sight, the Catholic gentry averred that it would never again be well for England until every petticoat had been banished from every bishop's house and every college in the country. In his 'Memorial of the Reformation of England' (1596)—a crafty collection of proposals for a resettlement of the commonwealth on Catholic principles, drawn up with a view to conciliate Protestant adversaries, and soothe popular anti-Papal prejudices—Parsons, the Jesuit, urged that no time should be lost in banishing women from prelates' houses. 'All kinds of access and ordinary residence,' says the proposer, 'or traffick of women within a Prelate's house, for any occasion whatsoever, whether they be kindred or not, is indecent, suspicious, and full of disedification, except it were only upon some known cause, suit, or particular business without story, which yet ought to be avoided the most that it may.' Again, with respect to female residents in or near colleges, and their influence on students, the Jesuit says, 'And first of all for settling of Common Discipline, most evident it is, that all habitation, concourse, and negociation of women, which heretical Dissolution hath brought in, is utterly to be removed from all colleges and communities of students— and herewith all junkets, all lascivious banquetting, excess of apparel, dancing, fencing-schools, and the like; that no man leave hath to go forth, but by knowledge and license of his superior, and this to known honest parts and persons, at houses lawful, accompanied with his fellow, or more if need be, in decent apparel.'

CHAPTER III.

CLERICAL WIVES IN THE TIMES OF JAMES THE FIRST, CHARLES THE FIRST, AND THE COMMONWEALTH.

THAT Archbishop Williams, like many of the eminent Anglican ecclesiastics of the earlier decades of the seventeenth century, was not disposed to look with favour on married clergymen, appears from the reluctance which his *protégé* and biographer (Hackett) manifested to communicate the fact of his marriage to the dignitary through whose patronage he had made the first steps towards episcopal exaltation. It was during his tenure of the seals that Francis Bacon's successor on the woolsack presented the livings of St. Andrew's, Holborn, and Cheam, in Surrey, to his favourite courtier and future historian, who, upon Charles the Second's restoration, was preferred to the bishopric of Lichfield and Coventry. The London living was presented to the fortunate chaplain for the sake of his 'wealth,' the country preferment for the sake of his 'health;' and scarcely had he obtained the two rectorates in the same year, than he resolved to increase his clerical usefulness by taking a conjugal partner. 'And now,' says Bishop Hackett's biographer, Thomas Plume, D.D., 'having spent some time in his country solitariness at Cheam, where he had no company but his books (though formerly he never meant to have entered into a married state), he cast his affections upon a religious and virtuous gentlewoman, whom he made his wife. With this secret he had never acquainted his master the keeper, and, therefore, doubted how he would take it; but upon his lordship's first hearing thereof by another hand, he instantly took coach and made him a visit, and enjoyned him onely, as ever he had deserved well of him, to requite it unto her. By her God blessed him with several hopeful children, but she died anno 1637.' Only by a few degrees less noteworthy than Hackett's timorous reticence about his marriage to his munificent patron, is the care which Dr. Plume, writing so late as 1675, took to assure his readers that Bishop Hackett had not designed, at the outset of his career, to adopt the somewhat degrading course of matrimony, but was brought into wedlock by a kind of surprise when the influences of rural solitariness put him at the mercy of fond imaginations.*

In accordance with notions prevalent amongst the clergy of his time, the gentle George Herbert, in his 'Priest to the Temple,' depicts the model 'country parson' as a minister who 'considering that virginity is a higher estate than matrimony, and that the ministry requires the best and highest things, is rather unmarryed than marryed.' To avoid every occasion for

---

* The ecclesiastical biography of the seventeenth century abounds in illustrations of the disfavour with which married clergymen were regarded by clerical celibates. Every unmarried bishop or priest, celebrated by High-church writers, is strongly commended for what was quaintly termed his 'spotless virginity:' on the other hand, the domestic relations of the married clergy are invariably mentioned by the same scribes with terms of regret and apology. Writing so late as 1660, when the prejudices against sacerdotal matrimony were fast dying out, the biographer of Bishop Morton—successively Bishop of Chester, Lichfield, and Durham, to whose bad counsel and pernicious pen our ancestors owed James the First's disastrous 'Book of Sports'—remarks upon the domestic solitariness of that prelate, 'He lived a chaste and unblemished life, in a celibate and single condition; and albeit that cœlibatus and ἀζυγια (simply considered) is only to be reckoned inter ἀδιαφορα, or things indifferent; yet ἐγκρατεια, or the gift of continence, is to be esteemed a special privilege, or favour extraordinary, indulged by God to some choice and especial favourites, especially where it is improved (as it was in this prelate) to the highest pitch of elevation: for he was not onely free (all his life long, and long life) from any open crime, but even from the least secret malitious suspition. And indeed (excepting only those *primi motus*, as I think the schools call them), from the which no flesh living, or that ever did live (save that onely One), was totally exempted (and therefore onely He); but for any carnall knowledge of that female sex, or act of uncleanness with any woman living, or dead, I dare and must be thus far his compurgator, that he went as pure a virgin to the wombe of the earth as erst he came from the wombe of his mother. I could wish that all the votaries of the Romish Church, or at least some of them, who doe so proudly and presumptuously (to say no worse) condemne and decry that state in clergymen, which yet the great Apostle judged honourable amongst all men; I wish, I say, many of them would say as much, and withal so truly, for the honour of their Church before men, and for their own justification.'

scandalous gossip the country parson of Herbert's imagination, whilst in celibacy, employed no female servant in his house, and refused to speak with any woman in absence of witnesses to their conversation. Even before auditors he was very careful to address the fair sex with consistent seriousness, and with a precise avoidance of light and sportive language.* And when he found it his manifest duty to take a wife—a step which he, of course, took less for his own delight than the advantage of his parishioners—'the choyce of his wife was made rather by his ear than his eye; his judgment, not his affection, found out a fit wife for him, whose humble and liberall disposition he preferred before beauty, riches, or honour.'

After determining to withdraw himself from court-life and adopt the clerical vocation, as the sphere of life in which he could most profitably display his gratitude for Divine mercies, George Herbert appears for a time to have retained more of the style and garb of a layman than we should be prepared to find in an ecclesiastic of the humblest order. It is certain that whilst a deacon he continued to wear the sword and silk clothes of a modish gentleman, and that he did not don the canonical habit until he had been induced to accept the living of Bemerton, Wiltshire, and was on the point of applying to Dr. Davenant, Bishop of Salisbury, for priest's orders and institution in his recently acquired preferment.† Born of a high patrician

---

* 'The country parson considering that virginity is a higher state than matrimony, and that the ministry requires the best and highest things, is rather unmarryed than marryed . . . . If he be unmarried, and keepe house, he hathe not a woman in his house, but findes opportunities of having his meat dress'd and other services done by men-servants at home, and his linnen washed abroad. If he be unmarryed and sojourne, he never talkes with any woman alone, but in the audience of others, and that seldom; and then also in a serious manner, never jestfully or sportfully . . . . But yet as the temper of his body may be, or as the temper of his parish may be, where he may have occasion to converse with women, and that among suspicious men, and other like circumstances considered, he is rather married than unmarried.'—*Vide* George Herbert's 'A Priest to the Temple, or The Country Parson.'

† 'And at this time,' says Isaak Walton, 'Mr. Herbert presented his thanks to the Earl (of Pembroke) for his presentation to Bemerton, but had not yet resolved to accept it, and told him the reason why; but that night the Earl acquainted Dr. Laud, then Bishop of London, and after Archbishop of Canterbury, with his kinsman's irresolution. And the bishop did the next day so convince Mr. Herbert that the refusal of it was a sin, that a tailor was sent for to come

family, in 1593, George Herbert, younger brother of the famous Lord Herbert of Cherbury, was thirty-seven years of age when he took priest's orders, and two years had not elapsed since his priestly ordination, when he died, in February, 1630. But in that brief period of ministerial labour, he sedulously discharged the duties of his cure, and at his death left behind him a memory, the record of which will ever remain one of the brightest and most charming chapters of Anglican story.

He married shortly before his preferment to Bemerton; but though still wearing the sword and silks of a layman, the aristocratic deacon selected his bride in accordance with the spirit and considerations which—he lays down in his book about the Country Parson—should animate and guide a minister in choosing a wife. The daughter of an ancient Wiltshire family, the lady of his choice was of his own social status; but he selected her out of regard to the excellence of her repute, rather than in consequence of his personal observation of her character; at the instigation of their mutual friends, rather than at the prompting of his own desires. Miss Jane Danvers, we are told, had fallen in love with him ere ever she had seen him, the praises which she had heard of his piety and goodness having planted in her breast a hope that she might become his wife; and Herbert, whose imagination had been excited in her favour by the representations of his friends, formed her acquaintance under a corresponding predisposition to become her husband.

speedily from Salisbury to Wilton, to take measure and make him a suit of canonical clothes against next day; which the tailor did: and Mr. Herbert, being so habited, went with his presentation to the learned Dr. Davenant, who was then Bishop of Salisbury, and he gave him institution immediately—for Mr. Herbert had been made deacon some years before; and he was also the same day —which was April 26th, 1630—inducted into the good, and more pleasant than healthful, parsonage of Bemerton.'

In anticipation of this change of costume Herbert sings, in 'The Temple,' of the honour and power of the priesthood,—

> 'Blest order, which in power doth so excel,
> That with the one hand thou liftest to the sky,
> And with the other throwest down to hell
> In thy just censures; fain would I draw nigh,
> Fain put thee on, exchanging my lay-sword
> For that of the holy word.'

They met; and on the third day after their first interview they were united in wedlock.*

Jane was a bride of less than four months standing when her husband, on his return to Bainton from Bemerton,† to which latter place he had gone to take formal possession of his living, impressed upon her that now that she was a minister's wife, it was incumbent on her to think more meekly of herself than ever, and on all occasions to exhibit herself a model of Christian humility. 'You are,' he observed seriously, after kissing the gentle girl who had been trained, like other girls of ancient lineage and honourable condition, to know her place and take it in every procession and familiar ceremony, 'now a minister's wife, and must now so far forget your father's house, as not to claim a precedence of any of your parishioners; for you are to know, that a Priest's wife can challenge no precedence or place, but that which she purchases by her obliging humility; and I am sure, places so purchased do best become them, and let me tell you, that I am so good a Herald, as to assure you

---

* 'These, and his other visible virtues,' says Isaak Walton, 'begat him much love from a gentleman of noble fortune, and a near kinsman to his friend the Earl of Danby; namely, from Mr. Charles Danvers of Bainton, in the county of Wiltshire, Esq. This Mr. Danvers, having known him long and familiarly, did so much affect him, that he often and publicly declared a desire that Mr. Herbert would marry any of his nine daughters—for he had so many—but rather his daughter Jane than any other, because Jane was his beloved daughter. And he had often said the same to Mr. Herbert himself; and that if he could like her for a wife, and she him for a husband, Jane should have a double blessing. And Mr. Danvers had so often said the like to Jane, and so much commended Mr. Herbert to her, that Jane became so much a Platonic as to fall in love with Mr. Herbert unseen. This was a fair preparation for a marriage; but, alas! her father died before Mr. Herbert's retirement to Dauntsey; and yet some friends to both parties procured their meeting: at which time a mutual affection entered into both their hearts, as a conqueror enters into a surprised city, and love having got the possession, governed, and made them such laws and resolutions as neither party was able to resist: insomuch that she changed her name into Herbert the third day after the first interview.'— WALTON's *Herbert.*

† With respect to Herbert's induction Walton says,—' When at his induction he was shut into Bemerton Church, being left there alone to toll the bell—as the law requires him—he staid much longer than an ordinary time before he returned to those friends that staid expecting him at the church door, that his friend Mr. Woodnot looked in at the church window, and saw him lay prostrate on the ground before the altar; at which time and place, as he after told Mr. Woodnot, he set some rules to himself for the management of his life, and then thus made a vow to labour to keep them.'

that this is the truth.' Of the tone in which Jane replied to this announcement, at which many a clerical dame of the seventeenth century would have fired with indignation, the biographer records, ' And she was so meek a wife, as to assure him, " it was no vexing news to her, and that he should see her observe it with a cheerful willingness!" And, indeed, her unforced humility, that humility that was in her so original, as to be born with her, made her happy to do so.'

Herbert's doctrine respecting the social status of clerical wives, be it observed, was no mere whimsy hatched in the brain of a sentimental high churchman, but stated with exact truthfulness the view which 'society' in Elizabethan England and throughout the seventeenth century took or professed to take of priests' conjugal partners. The doctrine is not likely to be acceptable to their feelings, but it should not be overlooked by the numerous clerical wives of our time, who, descended from aristocratic ancestors, are wont to value themselves on their patrician descent, and by those not less numerous ecclesiastical ladies, who imagine themselves entitled to social precedence in respect of their husband's various degrees of ecclesiastical dignity. When it had reluctantly accorded right of marriage to clergyman, 'society' in old time attached to clerical brides a full share of the discredit which was supposed to belong to sacerdotal wedlock. Other married women partook of their husbands' social distinctions,—the peer's wife attaining the rank of a peeress by reason of her lord's honour; and the ladies of baronets and knights being furnished by courteous usage with titles declaratory of their participation in the dignity of their husbands. But the wives of bishops and deans were accounted of no greater importance than the wives of vicars and curates, who were placed by sticklers for rules of precedence beneath the wives of their humblest parishioners, having any claims to rank within the lines of local gentility. The bishop was a lord of parliament, but his wife was plain 'Mistress,' and to this day is styled less honourably than the dame of any tradesman who has been knighted. In the eye of social law and etiquette, a primate's wife was no higher personage than the wife of a country attorney. Married to a layman of inferior degree, a woman was permitted to retain the rank of a spinster of her father's house. After marriage with a commoner, the earl's daughter retained the title and privileges to which, as an earl's daughter, she had enjoyed a right in courtesy before marriage. But on uniting herself to an ordained husband, an English lady lost her right to 'challenge precedence or place.' As a minister's wife, she had no rank but that which she could 'purchase by her obliging humility.'

It is almost needless to say that the practice of society at no time accorded with the view which it professed to take of the clerical wives of the Reformed Church. No social theory, directly at variance with the facts of daily experience, can be maintained rigidly or even with an approach to consistency; and the world from the first year of Elizabeth's reign could not do otherwise than recognise a social difference between the wives of dignified ecclesiastics and the wives of poor vicars. It was beyond the power of the framers of rules of precedence to demonstrate the equality of ladies, who were the mistresses of castles and were peeresses in almost everything but title, and the wives of needy curates whose children were clothed and fed like the children of mechanics. In spite of all that might be urged against the propriety of recognizing grades in clerical wives, a bishop's dignity gave palpable importance to his wife, and the dean's lady became, in the general esteem of a cathedral town, a far more important personage than the helpmates of ordinary rectors or perpetual curates.

In like manner people defied the heralds and put to the credit of an ecclesiastic's wife whatever prestige had attached to her, before her marriage, as a woman of gentle lineage and aristocratic connections. Jeremy Taylor's first wife, Phœbe Langdale, was to the future bishop's associates a very humble person in comparison with his second spouse,* Joanna Bridges, who possessed the equivocal distinction of being Charles the First's natural child. Nor were clerical husbands slow to assert

---

* 'This second wife was a Mrs. Joanna Bridges, who was possessed of a competent estate at Mandinam, in the parish of Llangendor, and county of Carmarthen. Her mother's family is unknown, but she was generally believed to be a natural daughter of Charles the First when Prince of Wales, and under the guidance of the dissipated and licentious Duke of Buckingham. That the Martyr's habits of life at that time were extremely different from those which

with spirit and pride whatever claims their wives could prefer to the world's respect, apart from the honour due to them as ministers' helpmates. An instance of this marital spirit occurred when Peter Heylin—'lying Peter,' as Mr. Carlyle designates him with more justice than courtesy—was reproved 'for maintaining his wife so highly, like a lady,' in the presence of the Major-General before whom the loyalist clergyman vainly argued for the preservation of his estate from decimation. Biography informs us that Heylin's censor, 'one Captain Allen, formerly a tinker,' had wooed and wedded 'a poor tripe-wife.' The captain, therefore, felt the force of the clergyman's retort, when the latter replied impetuously, 'that he had married a gentlewoman, and did maintain her according to her quality, and so might he' (*i. e.* censorious Allen) 'his tripe-wife; adding withal this rule he always observed, "for his wife to go above his estate, his children according to his estate, and himself below his estate," so that at the year's end he could make all even.'

That Heylin was not the only affluent clergyman of the seventeenth century, to treat his wife and children thus liberally, may be inferred from the frequency with which the reader of the personal memoirs and social annals of the period encounters complaints against the prodigality and ostentatious vanity of the women of clerical families. From these records of past manners, it appears that the prosperous rector's wife was notable for the richness of her silk dresses and other apparel, that she often had a coach drawn by fine horses, that she seldom entered church on holy days without a smart page to walk before her, and that she was prone to interfere with a masterful air in the ecclesiastical affairs of her husband's parish. Receiving far less liberal salaries than curates of the present day, the stipendiary priests of England in the seventeenth century were generally allowed to keep whatever fees were paid

enabled him after a twenty years' marriage to exult, while approaching the scaffold, that during all that time he had never, even in thought, swerved from the fidelity which he owed to his beloved Henrietta Maria, there is abundant reason to believe; nor are the facts by any means incompatible.'—*Vide* 'The Whole Works of the Right Rev. Jeremy Taylor, D.D., Lord Bishop of Down, Connor, and Dromore. By the Rev. Reginald Heber, D.D.'

them for the performance of exceptional duties: and it was alleged to the discredit of rectors' wives that they often made extortionate terms with their husbands' professional subordinates, insisting on having the half of all sums paid to the curates for service at burials, churchings, weddings, christenings.*

It is a matter of certainty that the social status of the clergy steadily improved from the commencement to the end of Elizabeth's reign; that ecclesiastical persons grew in general esteem throughout the seventeenth century; that, notwithstanding the scandals which they brought to light and the suppression of the episcopal system, the parliamentary proceedings for the reformation of religion, during the civil disturbances and the interregnum, resulted in a decided elevation of the entire clerical class; and that in Charles the Second's time—which Lord Macaulay most erroneously depicts as remarkable for the general ignorance and degradation of the national priesthood—the average clergyman enjoyed a larger measure of esteem than he had enjoyed at any previous period since the Reformation. And as the clerical order thus rose in public opinion, its members found a greater willingness on the part of families in the superior classes to form matrimonial alliances with them. During the abeyance of episcopacy the officiating ministers of our churches were in a state of almost unprecedented unison with the sentiments of the laity, and found no difficulty in acquiring wives amongst the gentry and in the higher commercial circles. Nor does it appear that the clerical ladies of the Commonwealth period differed materially in their fashions and diversions from

---

* Some excellent illustrations of clerical life in Charles the First's time may be found in 'The Curates' Conference; or, A Discourse betwixt Two Scholars, both of them relating their Hard Condition, and consulting which Way to Mend it' (1641). The speakers in this satiric dialogue are Master Needham, curate of a poor little parish 'hard by Pinchback in Lincolnshire,' and Master Poorest, curate 'hard by Hungerford in Wiltshire.' With respect to the officious, extortionate, dress-loving, clerical wife of the period, the author of this pungent tract makes Master Needham say,—' Nay, since we have fallen upon it, I will tell you, our parson hath a living in London, as well as here, and his wife is so miserably proud, that both livings will scarce suffice to maintain her: insomuch that she takes out of the curate's wages, as, half of every funeral sermon; and out of all burials, churchings, weddings, christenings, &c., she hath half-duties, to buy lace, pins, gloves, fans, black-bags, sattin petticoats, &c., and towards the maintenance of a puny servitor to go before her: nay, she pays half towards the maintenance

the more decorous clerical ladies of the previous half-century.

The satiric literature of the Restoration period has greatly misled us with respect to the social life of England under Cromwell's rule, and caused us to magnify absurdly the sad and severely puritanical characteristics of the period. Because the party in power closed the public theatres, and insisted on a strict observance of sabbaths and fast days, we are disposed to accept without inquiry or doubt all the extravagant caricatures which cavalier wits and jesters produced of the gloom and grotesque dolour of the Cromwellian Puritans. But there is abundant testimony that the very measures, which diminished outward festivity at taverns and on village greens, gave a strong stimulus to domestic hilarity in those circles where the regime of the saints was regarded with disfavour. The authorities could pull down the Maypoles and forbid Sunday dances beneath the churchyard yews; but within their own walls the cavalier gentry might carouse to satiety, and dance to merry tunes till their limbs ached. That the Royalists availed themselves for festive purposes of the Englishman's right to do his will in his own castle, there is no lack of evidence: and of the many facts, which commemorate their gay doings at a political crisis when fanciful scribes would have us think that all social mirth had fled from merry England, by no means the least significant is the publication of 'The English Dancing-Master' (1651), which shows that so many as one hundred and four varieties of the country (contre) dance were taught and danced under the roofs of the knights

---

of a coach, which she either gets from her husband, or else from the curate, by subtracting his allowance at the quarter's day; and what is more, she made her curate in London to enter into bond privately to her husband, to leave the place at half-a-year's warning, or else her husband, the parson of the place, would not have granted him a license of the place.' Whereto Master Poorest rejoins,— 'Oh! strange! Is it possible that this old remainder of Popery should be yet upheld by our clergy, to have such Pope Joans to rule the Church? I have heard say, there are three places in which a woman never should bear any sway —the buttery, the kitchen, and the church: for women are too covetous by nature to keep a good house, and too foolish to rule a church . . . . And yet our she-regent is not unlike her: for she frets fearfully to hear a worthy gentleman, who lives in the parish, loves me so much: it galls her to the quick if the parishioners, out of their loves, give me anything to mend my salary. Oh! she thinks that all is lost that goes beside her hands.'

and esquires who desired nothing more earnestly than Cromwell's destruction and the re-establishment of monarchy.

Nor was mirth confined to the enemies of the government. Presbyterians and Independents warmed their houses and brewed good ale like their ancestors in episcopal times; and, just as the wives and daughters of Charles the First's rectors were reproved by satire for their levity and love of fine clothes, the wives and daughters of reverend Assembly-men were accused of being more zealous in pursuing pleasure than in seeking the Lord. When that notable Assembly-man and popular preacher, the Reverend Stephen Marshall, had preached himself into the affections of the rich gentlewoman who became his wife, he allowed her as much license, in respect to diversions and pecuniary expenditure, as ever Mrs. Heylin had enjoyed in the days before the Great Rebellion; and biography informs us, that though his more precise neighbours disapproved the fineness and fashion of his daughters' clothes, no one ventured openly to denounce the indulgent way in which the parson of Finchingfield brought up his children.*

During the conflict between Charles the First and the Parliament, the wives of the loyal clergy advanced themselves greatly in the general esteem of the cavalier aristocracy and gentry by the fervour with which they went with their husbands in the struggle, and by the enthusiasm of their devotion to his majesty's sacred cause. Whilst Oxford was a royal garrison

* The author of 'The Godly Man's Legacy to the Saints upon Earth' (1680) —a malicious and scurrilous narrative of the career of Stephen Marshall, sometime 'Minister of the Gospel at Finchingfield in Essex'—remarks: 'To his children he was (to give him his due) a very indulgent father, and perhaps more indulgent than was allowable. The most of their education was going from one good house to another, to eat cheese-cakes and custards. They were like gentlewomen in nothing besides their habits, and therein exceeded persons of good degree and quality. They followed the height of fashions with changeable taffatas and Naked Necks, insomuch that the godly party were sorely scandalized at it, but durst not complain, because it was Mr. Marshall who was concerned. He gave them great portions; and (as the History of Independency saith) married one of them with the Book of Common Prayer and a ring; and gave this for a reason, that the statute establishing that liturgy was not yet repealed; and he was loth to have his daughter . . . . turn'd back upon him for want of a legal marriage. Nevertheless he could declare against the use of it by others. And so the jugler plaid at fast-and-loose with the Service-book, as he had before with the people at Weathersfield.'

and the seat of a court of arms, it was crowded with ladies— gentlewomen who had entered the university in attendance upon Henrietta Maria; ladies whose husbands had come to vote at Charles's mock parliament; and ladies of inferior degree, who, on the Parliamentary forces taking possession of their husbands' parsonages, had fled with their families to the seat of learning where their reverend masters had received their education. Before the commencement of the war ladies had been barely tolerated at Oxford, where social opinion persisted in regarding the married clergy with the eyes of Catholic Churchmen, and where the old preference for a celibate priesthood cannot even at the present day be said to be utterly extinguished. But the civil troubles enabled them to get a firm and permanent footing in the university, from which no attempt, of more importance than the churlish protests of a few bookish misogynists, has since been made to expel them. Every college, every hall, every dwelling within the fortifications, afforded shelter to women in those stirring times, which were scarcely less fruitful of social *eclat* to the university than of perplexity and hurt to the country; and, when the king's garrison capitulated on highly honourable terms to the parliamentary besiegers, it was stipulated in behalf of the ladies, by the eighteenth of the Articles of Surrender, 'That all ladies, gentlewomen, and other women now in Oxford, whose husbands or friends are absent from thence, may have passes and protections for themselves, servants, and goods, to go on and remain at the houses of their husbands, or at their friends, as they shall desire; and to go or send to London, or elsewhere, to obtain the allowances out of their husbands' or parents' estates, allotted to them by ordinance of parliament.'

Many of the clerical ladies, however, loth to retire from the fair city into which it had cost them infinite trouble to win their way, declined to exercise this right of departure; and amongst them was Dean Fell's courageous wife, who stayed doggedly at her husband's official lodgings for just a year and ten months after the departure of the king's troops, when she was forcibly ejected from the deanery of Christ Church, to the keen delight of a multitude of parliamentary citizens. Rich though it is in quaint stories aptly told, Anthony à Wood's

' History and Antiquities of the University of Oxford' contains no more comical picture than the scene of Mrs. Fell's eviction from her academic home by a party of grinning soldiers. On Monday, March 27th, 1648, in anticipation of the arrival of the Earl of Pembroke, the restored chancellor of the university, the parliamentarian visitors, in consideration of Dr. Fell's ejectment from his place of dean, issued an order, 'requiring all that had the oversight or possession of the lodgings, or custody of the goods of the said doctor in Christ Church, to remove them forthwith, that Mr. Reynolds might presently take possession, to execute the place and office both of Dean and Vice-chancellor.' But the visitors little knew the stuff of which Mrs. Fell was made, when they imagined that she would pack her traps and move at the sight of their order. The lady budged not a single inch. On April 3rd, Monday, the visitors (Sir Nath. Brent, Mr. Henry Wilkinson, Mr. Cheynell, Mr Harrys, and some others), imagining that their appearance in the deanery would reduce the contumacious dame to submissiveness, 'went to Christ Church with an intent to enter the Dean's lodgings, to receive the members of that house according to order. But they finding them shut, and no one within who would open them, sent for Andrew Burrough, Provost Marshall of the garrison of Oxford, and a guard of musqueteers and others, who, being come with hammers and sledges, break open the said doors; wherein finding Mrs. Fell and her children, said, 'that they had come in a fair way to her, and desired her to quit her house.' But she refusing, they set a guard of soldiers in the rooms into which they had entered, where remaining for some time, endeavoured (as it is said) to weary her out with noise, rudeness, smell of tobacco.' But tobacco-smoke proving ineffectual upon the lady, who was resolved on clinging to her quarters so long as it was in her power to remain in them, the soldiers were at a difficulty, and must have had a notion that their employment was rather below the dignity of arms. For eight more days Mrs. Fell held her ground, when the soldiers, taking her and her women and children in their arms, carried them out of the deanery in sedan-chairs, or on stretchers. The finish of the fight is thus recorded by Anthony à Wood :—' *April 12th, Wednesday.* In the morning, the Chancellor (*i.e.* Earl of Pembroke), visitors, certain soldiers, and a great rabble of people, went to Christ Church; where, forthwith entering Dr. Fell's lodgings (he being yet in safe custody at London), the Chancellor desired Mrs. Fell to quit her quarters, telling her that "in so doing she would do God and her country good service;" but she refusing that kind proposal, had very ill language first given to her by him, and then she was carried into the quadrangle in a chair by soldiers. Her children also were carried out upon boards, as 'twas reported, and certain gentle-women that were then in the lodgings to the chairs; of which one, without the least sign of discontent, said that, 'though she was then carried away in a chair, she doubted not to come thither hereafter upon her own legs again,' which accordingly fell out. They being thus left in the quadrangle, they were conducted by Drs. Morley, Payne, Hammond, &c., out of the great gates to Quatervois, and thence to an apothecary's house against All Souls' College, where for some time they remained.'

And yet the son of this spirited lady, after acquiring possession of the official residence which she had defended so persistently, could write of marriage as an inferior state to celibacy; and, echoing the almost obsolete prejudices against sacerdotal matrimony, could represent that Dr. Hammond was peculiarly fortunate in having been preserved from the comparative degradation of wedlock. In his memoir of 'the most learned, reverend, and pious Dr. H. Hammond,' who, like his biographer and his biographer's father, was punished for his fidelity to the crown with ejection from university preferment, Dean (John) Fell remarked, 'In his first remove to Penshurst, he was persuaded by his friends that the matrimonial state was needful to the bearing of those household cares and other intercurrent troubles which his condition then brought with it, and on this ground he gave some care to their advices; which he did then more readily, for that there was a person represented to him, of whose virtue as well as other more usually desired accomplishments he had been long before well satisfied. But, being hindered several times by little unexpected accidents, he finally layed down all his pretensions upon a ground of perfect self-denial; being informed that one of a fairer fortune and higher quality than his was, or else was like to be, and consequently one who, in common account, would prove the better match, had kindness for her.' After a lapse of years Dr. Hammond again entertained an intention to condescend towards matrimony; but, on the first signs of the near troubles of the State, he laid aside the imperfectly conceived purpose. 'Upon which prospect,' says the dean, 'the good doctor casting a serious eye, and with prophetic sorrows and misgivings, fearing a parallel in this our nation, the second time deposited his conjugal intendments, and thenceforth courted and espoused (what he preserved inviolate) unto his death the more eminent perfection of spotless virgin chastity.'

CHAPTER IV.

CLERICAL WIVES, TEMP. CHARLES II. AND JAMES II.

THE story of the learned and pious Richard Baxter's love-affairs is of considerable value to the social historian, from the light which it throws on the social status of clergymen in the middle of the seventeenth century, and also from the evidence which it affords that evangelical ministers, averse to the distinctive principles and sentiments of high-churchmen, participated in the feeling that marriage, though blameless and permissible in all men, was more likely to diminish than increase a clergyman's usefulness.

An episcopally ordained clergyman, Baxter commenced his professional life in 1638; but though he preserved his loyalty to the king and his devotion to the house of Stuart, he discharged with equal zeal and efficiency the duties of the clerical office at Kidderminster, in times when episcopacy was in abeyance and the prayer-book of the established church was a proscribed work. On Charles the Second's restoration, the royalist statesmen and divines, who were bent on re-establishing Elizabeth's church, even whilst they feigned a willingness to act in harmony with the Presbyterians and Independents in bringing about a broad-bottomed church settlement, had the prudence to seek the support of the most learned and eloquent and exemplary member of the clergy, whom the king had found in his dominions on his return from exile. Richard Baxter was offered a bishopric, but he declined to accept so honourable a position in a church to whose doctrines and ritual he could not conscientiously conform. Ejected from his preferment, the preacher of Kidderminster became a Dissenter; and the learned divine and loyal citizen, who might have been an Anglican prelate at the price of certain concessions which it is too much the humour of the present day to call unimportant, was stigmatized by the pungent language of his adversaries a schismatical malcontent. In due course he was hunted from town to village by his persecutors, was denounced by 'society' as a pestilent fire-brand and sower of sedition, was prosecuted as a malefactor, and was deemed by persons of fashion to have escaped with less than his deserts when the truly pious and orthodox Judge Jeffreys refrained from causing the sweetest-tempered controversialist of his time to be whipped through the streets of London by the hangman.

Baxter was still in his forty-fifth year when, on September 10, 1660, he married at the church of Bennet Fink, in London, Margaret Charlton, who was for many years the loving sharer of his troubles, and to whose virtues he rendered an appropriate tribute of affection in his 'Breviate of the Life of Margaret, the Daughter of Francis Charlton, of Apply in Shropshire, Esq. And Wife of Richard Baxter, for the use of all. But especially of their Kindred.' That Margaret was her husband's superior by birth we have the assurance of Baxter himself, who says, 'we were born in the same county within three miles and an half of each other; but she of one of the chief families in the county, and I but of a mean Freeholder (called a gentleman for his ancestors' sake, but of a small estate, though sufficient); Her father, Francis Charlton, Esq., was one of the best justices of the peace in the county, a grave, worthy, sober man; but did not marry till he was aged and gray, and dyed while his children were very young.' To rate Mr. Charlton's position at its full worth, the reader must remember, that a justice of the peace was a much more important personage in Charles the First's than he is in Victoria's England; and that the owner of a fine county estate in the seventeenth enjoyed a higher degree of social homage than a squire of corresponding wealth in the nineteenth century. Thus born, Margaret Charlton had a fortune of 2000*l*, a sum which constituted a far more considerable estate two hundred years since than it does now, when money is cheap in proportion to its abundance. In Charles the Second's time a gentleman of landed estate was expected to settle on his wife an interest in his real property amounting to one hundred pounds per annum, for every thousand pounds which she brought him.

Part III.—Clerical Women.

Notwithstanding the eminence of his talents and the brightness of his virtues, Margaret Charlton was regarded by her kindred as having lost caste by becoming the wife of an undignified clergyman who had decided to take a course with respect to espiscopal government, which, it was already foreseen, would shut him out from all chances of professional advancement under the restored king's advisers. 'After the marriage was over,' says one of his biographers,* 'several of his wife's relations did look upon Mr. Baxter as inferior to the lady whom he had married; therefore the Lord Chancellor Clarendon (who had before proffered him a bishoprick, so he would conform), with all flourishes of oratory, did again perswade him to acquiesce to his requests, and accept of a rich benefice, as the Church government was then established.' Doubtless the Lord Chancellor imagined that his arguments against the clergyman's scruples would be supported by the lady's influence with her husband; but he would scarcely have entertained such a hope had he been acquainted with Margaret's character, and known the terms on which she had induced Mr. Baxter to accept her proffered hand.

For Margaret had herself made the offer which resulted in her marriage; and when she had demonstrated her innocence of womanly pride by suing for the companionship of her beloved minister, she barely escaped the pain and ignominy of a decided repulse. 'For,' says the historian of this singular courtship, which nothing short of the privilege enjoyed by ladies in leap-years could have invested with decorum, 'she, being a pious and devout young lady, fell in love with him, upon account of his holy life and fervency of preaching; and therefore sent a friend to acquaint him with her respects, in his chamber. His answer was, that since he had passed his youth in celibacy, it would be reputed madness in him to marry a woman, whilst he could not discharge the part of a husband in all respects. She at the door, overhearing, entered the chamber and told him, "Dear Mr. Baxter, I protest, with a sincere and real heart, I do not make a tender of myself to you, upon any worldly or carnal

---

* 'The Life and Death of that Pious, Reverend, Learned, and Laborious Minister of the Gospel, Mr. Richard Baxter, who departed this Life, December 1691, and of his Age 77.' (1692.)

account; but to have a more perfect converse with so holy and prudent a yoke-fellow, to assist me in the way to Heaven, and to keep me stedfast in my perseverance; which I design for God's glory, and my own soul's good." At this Mr. Baxter was at a stand, and convinced that, with a good conscience, he could not despise so zealous a proffer, springing from so pure a fountain.' The suitor triumphed. After due consideration, the reluctant minister yielded to his fair admirer's solicitations; but before finally surrendering the freedom of solitariness, he stipulated that he should never be called upon to put the claims of marital above the claims of pastoral duty. 'But,' says the biographer previously quoted, 'before the marriage, these were concluded upon: First, That Mr. Baxter should have nothing which before marriage was hers, that so he (who wanted no outward supplies) might not so much as seem to marry her for covetousness. Secondly, That she should so order her affairs, that he might not be entangled in any law-suits about the same. Thirdly, That she should expect none of his time, which his ministerial employment should call him for.'

Of the many clerical weddings solemnized during the abeyance of episcopacy, one of the most characteristic was the marriage of the Reverend George Bull, subsequently Bishop of St. David's, with Bridget Gregory, daughter of the Reverend Alexander Gregory, incumbent of Cirencester. An Oxford undergraduate, in residence at the beginning of 1649, when the Parliamentarian Visitors required every member of the university to swear, 'That he would be true and faithful to the Commonwealth of England, as it was then established,' George Bull was one of the many Oxonians who refused to take the prescribed oath; and retiring from the university with his loyalist tutor, Mr. Ackland, to North Cadbury, in Somersetshire, he there pursued his studies, together with a company of royalist fellow-collegians, who formed what is nowadays termed 'a reading party,' under Mr. Ackland's control and tuition. Eager to begin a course of ministerial labour, young Bull complied with existing regulations so far as to take Presbyterian orders, or, in the language of his biographer, Robert Nelson, to furnish himself 'with those sacerdotal powers which are the characteristic of a presbyter;' but dissatisfied with the presbyterian mode of ordination, he also sought and obtained episcopal ordination from Dr. Skinner, the ejected Bishop of Oxford, 'by whom he was ordained deacon and priest in one day,' when he had not yet completed his twenty-second year. 'This suffering prelate,' Robert Nelson observes of Bishop Skinner, 'had the courage, even in these times of usurpation, to send many labourers into the Lord's vineyard according to the liturgy of the Church of England, when the exercising this his power was made penal.'*

Thus armed with presbyterian orders, conferred on him openly, and with a bishop's ordination, obtained secretly and in defiance of the law, the priest-presbyter obtained the small living of St. George's, near Bristol, of which humble piece of preferment the annual emoluments did not exceed thirty pounds. Acting consistently with his principles, and with the mode in which he had qualified himself for the clerical office, the young clergyman, whilst feigning to lead his congregation in extempore prayer, used to repeat the words of the Prayer-book, and so lure his ignorant and unsuspicious flock into uttering the language of the proscribed services. In this subtle and scarcely honest practice he merely followed the example of Dr. Sanderson, and other leaders of the royalist clergy, who deemed themselves justified in using every kind of artifice and trickery against a government which they sincerely regarded as an impious usurpation. Robert Nelson tells exultingly that the young presbyter, who had learnt the forms of the Prayer-book by heart, was wont to use the words in his familiar

---

* But though his lordship 'was willing to ordain Mr. Bull, yet refused to give him or any other letters of orders, under his own hand and seal, for this prudential reason,—because he was apprehensive some ill use might be made of them, if they fell into the hands of those unjust powers which then prevailed, who had made it criminal for a bishop to confer holy orders.' With respect to the bishop's disregard of canonical rule in ordaining Mr. Bull a priest whilst still in his twenty-second year, Robert Nelson says,— ' By this account it appeareth, that Mr. Bull was but one-and-twenty when he was made priest, which is much short of that age which is required by the Canons of the Church from the candidates of the priesthood; but upon his examination he acquitted himself so perfectly well, that though the bishop was rightly informed as to that circumstance, yet he was pleased to say that the Church wanted such persons qualified as he was, and that he could not make too much haste when his pains and labour might be of such importance.'

administrations no less freely than in the presence of his parishioners assembled for Divine service; and the biographer narrates with especial triumph how the pastor of St. George's, on a more than usually felicitous occasion, baptized the sick child of one of his parishioners in exact accordance with the prohibited ceremony of the Church Prayer-book, and in doing so won the enthusiastic gratitude of the infant's father, who, little suspecting that he had been listening to the Popish Prayer-book, 'returned him a great many thanks, intimating at the same time with how much greater edification they prayed, who entirely depended upon the Spirit of God for his assistance in their extempore effusions, than those who tied themselves up to premeditated forms.' The scene thus described by Nelson is easily realised; but the biographer asks somewhat too much of our credulity, when he assures us that, on ascertaining the manner in which they had been played with, the dissenting father and his puritanical family forthwith became orthodox members of the persecuted Anglican Church.

That his marriage might be celebrated with due solemnity, Mr. Bull induced the Rev. William Masters, vicar of Preston, to use the prohibited service in the Book of Common Prayer when joining him in holy wedlock with Miss Gregory; and to impart extraordinary sacredness to this violation of the law, the bridegroom selected Ascension Day for the solemnization of his wedding, which was fruitful of all the happiness that he had presumed to hope, and of rather more children than he would perhaps have deliberately asked, from it. The wedding-ring, which he put on his bride's finger, in defiance of tyrannical enactments, had for its motto this Latin supplication, engraved on the inner surface, *Bene parere, parêre, parare det mihi Deus*. Bridget had her prayer,—she was a prolific mother, an obedient spouse, and an excellent housekeeper. She bore her husband eleven children, five sons and six daughters, lived happily with him for fifty years, and was regarded by her acquaintance as a model worthy to be imitated by all clerical wives of superior degree.

Another sign of the larger favour which the clergy of the Reformed Church accorded to matrimony towards the close of the seventeenth century, is the frequency with which they commended marriage from the pulpit. In Charles the Second's reign marriage-sermons were less common than funeral-sermons; but I am disposed to think that they were scarcely less frequent then than funereal discourses are at the present time. In many rural districts clergymen are still accustomed and required to deliver orations, of consolatory adulation, on the virtues of their deceased parishioners, who have recently departed this life after running careers of commonplace usefulness and respectability; but so far as my experience and inquiries justify me in speaking positively on the matter, marriage-sermons are affairs of the past. They were, however, things of ordinary occurrence in the later decades of the seventeenth century, and were usually delivered on the Sundays immediately preceding the marriages to which they drew especial attention. The last sermon preached by Dr. Fuller, the ecclesiastical historian, was a discourse on the marriage of one of his kinsmen, whose wedding was fixed to take place on the following day.*

But though the clergy and laity, in the later decades of the seventeenth century, had generally learnt to appreciate the advantages accruing to society from sacerdotal marriage, and had almost universally ceased to speak of celibacy as a holier condition than virtuous wedlock, the old prejudices against married priests lingered at the universities and in the coteries

* 'For,' says Fuller's biographer, 'being desired to preach a marriage-sermon on Sunday the twelfth of August to a kinsman of his, who was about to be wedded the day after, the good doctor lovingly undertook it: but on that Sunday at dinner felt himself very much indisposed, complaining of dizziness in the head . . . . Being in the pulpit he found himself very ill . . . . He proceeded in his sermon and prayer very perfectly, till in the middle (never using himself to notes other than at the beginning word of each head or division) he began to falter, but not so much out but he quickly recollected himself, and very pertinently concluded.'

That marriage-sermons came into greater vogue during the Civil disturbances and the Commonwealth period, and were by some persons esteemed amongst the religious innovations effected by the Parliamentarian clergy, may be inferred from a passage in Sir John Birkenhead's prose-satire, 'The Assembly-man,' written in 1647. Speaking of the ordained Assembly-man, Sir John says, 'He has a rare simpering way of expression; he calls a married couple "saints that enjoy the mystery," and a man drunk is a "brother full of the creature;" yet at wedding-sermons he is very familiar, and . . . . And hence it is he calls his preachment manna, fitted not to his hearers' necessity but their palate: for it is to feed himself, not them. If he chance to tire, he refreshes himself with the

of high churchmen. At Oxford and Cambridge conservative fellows still expressed resentment at the domestic privileges accorded to Heads of Houses; and it is not unfair to suggest that the disapprobation, which some of these grumblers cherished towards the feminine inmates of masters' lodges, would have been less bitter and obstinate had a more liberal relaxation of their collegiate statutes permitted them to retain their fellowships, and at the same time participate in the enjoyments of the estate which they professed to disdain.

The arrangements, which were made from time to time to afford better accommodation to the academic ladies, occasioned keen annoyance to the stubborn misogynists who poured forth querulous lamentations over the sin and profligate folly of spending on the dwellings of married principals funds which were designed for the promotion of learning and the support of poor students. The pride and wastefulness, the vanity and sickening arrogance of the fair settlers upon collegiate foundations were topics on which Anthony à Wood seized every opportunity to speak with comical asperity. When Dr. Bathurst became vice-chancellor of Oxford, Oct. 3, 1673, Anthony was constrained to admit that the doctor was 'a man of good parts, and able to do good things,' but the annalist qualified this reluctant commendation by adding, ' he has a wife that scorns he

people's hum, as a collar of bells cheers up a pack-horse.' But though the Parliamentarian clergy were frequent preachers of marriage-sermons, the clergy of earlier Protestant times often spoke from the pulpit of the sacredness of matrimony, and the honour of the married clergy. Moreover, it was agreeable to the spirit of the Catholic Church, which elevated marriage to a sacrament, that its divines should make the privileges and blessings of wedlock matter for commendation from the pulpit. The British Museum possesses a marriage-sermon preached in Elizabeth's time at Trafford, in Lancashire, on the marriage of a daughter of Sir Edmund Trafford (1586). That marriage-sermons were occasionally delivered in the middle of the eighteenth century, is shown by a passage in Fosbrooke's 'Gloucestershire.' In the account of the parish of Driffield, Fosbrooke says, ' One John Humphries, M.A., in February 1742, published a sermon preached at a wedding here. The Marriage Psalm, on the first Sunday of the couple's appearance at church, still continues.' For other particulars respecting obsolete matrimonial usages in churches, *vide* Brand's ' Antiquities,' vol. ii.

The oldest marriage-sermon of Protestant times with which I am acquainted is Queen Elizabeth's ' Homily on the State of Matrimony,'—a discourse which demonstrates that wedlock was a frequent topic with pulpit orators during the reign of the virgin-queen.

should be in print: a scornful woman—scorns that he was dean of Wells: no need of marrying such a woman, who is so conceited that she thinks herself fit to govern a college or university.'

When Sir Thomas Clayton, in spite of Anthony à Wood's opposition, succeeded in getting himself elected to the wardenship of Merton, Anthony feared that great evils would ensue to the college from the election of so unfit a person for so high an office. Sir Thomas was not that most atrocious of academic monsters, a married priest empowered to rule a college, for he was a layman and physician. But he had a wife to share his collegiate lodgings with him, and the rustle of a petticoat in monastic cloisters was so discordant a sound to the annalist's sensitive hearing, that if Sir Thomas, 'the stranger' from another and inferior college, had entered Merton with a deliberate purpose to exasperate Anthony into mortal phrenzy, he could have adopted no likelier means to effect his purpose than the steps which he took to make his lady comfortable in her new quarters. 'First, therefore,' records the infuriated Anthony, 'he' (*i.e.* Sir Thomas Clayton) 'and his family, most of them women-kind, (which before was looked upon, if resident in the college, a scandal and abomination thereunto), being no sooner settled, but a great dislike was taken by the Lady Clayton to the warden's standing goods, namely, chaires, stooles, tables, chimney-furniture, the furniture belonging to the kitchen, scullery, &c. all which was well liked by Dr. Goddard, Brent, Savile, &c. These, I say, being despised by that proud woman, because, forsooth, the said goods were out of fashion, must all be changed and altered to the great expense of the college. Secondly, the warden's garden must be altered, new trees planted, arbours made, roots of choice flowers bought, &c., all which unnecessary, yet the poor college must pay for them; and all this to please a woman. Not content with these matters, there must be a new summerhouse built at the south end of the woman's garden, wherein her ladyship and her gossips may take their pleasure, and any eavesdropper of the family may hearken what any of the fellows should say accidentally.'

Of the cost of these alterations Anthony speaks with equal

minuteness and resentment. The summer-house was to have cost the college only 20*l.*, but in the end it absorbed nearly 100*l.* from the Merton Exchequer. Nor did Lady Clayton's extortions cease with the attainment of her new summer-house. She required the college to furnish her with a private and peculiar 'key to the lock of the ladies' seat in St. Marie's Church, to which she would most commonly resort,' and with 'shoes and other things for her foot-boy.' Utterly regardless of the bursar's expostulations, the devouring and insatiable creature 'burnt in one year three-score pounds worth of the choicest billet,' and this choice fuel she consumed in her kitchen as well as in her sitting-rooms, 'without any regard to coal; which usually' (to save charges), the annalist explains, 'is burnt in kitchens and sometimes in parlours.' Then the lady, by her husband's egregious flatteries and her own odious arts, gained possession of the best set of rooms in the college—the same rooms which the fair Frances Stuart (afterwards Duchess of Richmond) had recently occupied—and annexed it to the Warden's already too large quarters.* Enumerating other costs to which she put the college, Wood says, 'Nothwithstanding all these things, yet the warden, by motion of his lady, did put the college to unnecessary charges and very frivolous expenses, among which were a very long looking-glass, for her to see her ugly face and body to the middle, ... which was bought in Hilary Terme, 1674, and cost, as the bursar told me, about 10^{li}. A bedstead and bedding worth 40^{li} must also be bought, because the former

* 'Sixthly,' runs Anthony's arraignment of this unscrupulous daughter of Eve, 'by increasing upon, and taking away the rooms belonging to the fellows. One instance take for all. Mr. Fisher quitted his lodgings (viz. an upper chamber with three studies, and a lower chamber with as many, in the great quadrangle) in July, an. 1665, upon notice that the king and queen should shortly come to Oxon, there to take up their winter quarters till towards the spring. When the king and queen came, which was about Michaelmas following, Mris. Franc-Stuart, one of the maids of honour (afterwards Duchess of Richmond), took possession of those lodgings, and there continued till February following; at which time the queen, who lodged in the warden's lodgings, went to Westminster, and Mris. Stuart with her, and then Mr. Fisher's lodgings laid empty for some time. At length the warden, finding that the lower chambers of the said lodgings were convenient for him, because they joyned on the south side to his parlour, and therefore they would make a dainty retiring-room, or at least an inner parlour, he did, by egregious flattery with some of the fellows, particularly with Mr. Sterry, by inviting him and them often to his lodgings, get their consent so farr,

bed-stede and bedding were too short for him (he being a tall man); so perhaps, when a short warden comes, a short bed must be bought. As his bed was too short, so the wicket of the common gate entering into the college was too low, therefore that was made higher in 1676, in the month of August. The said bursar, G. Roberts, hath several times told me, that either he the warden, or his lady, do invent, and sit thinking how to put the college to charge, to place themselves, and no end there is to their unlimited desire. He told me also, that there was no terrier taken of the goods he had, which were bought at the college charge; and, therefore, they did carry many of them, especially the looking-glass, to their country-seat, called The Vach, in Chalfont parish, near Wycomb in Bucks.'

But when Sir Thomas Clayton had passed away, and another principal reigned in his stead, Anthony Wood was scarcely at all better pleased; for, if Dr. Lydall was acceptable as a senior who had previously belonged to the college, he was also a married man, whose wife and numerous family would 'be fed with the bread belonging to piety and learning.' Writing of the new warden's encumbrances in 1693, Wood says, 'What they eat and drink will serve for exhibition of seven or eight poor scholars. *December 27th.*—The first thing that Dr. Lydall caused to be done after he was admitted warden, and before he settled in his lodgings, was to take down the old windows in the warden's dining-room, and hall under it, containing rebusses, fantastick devices in nearly all the panes, and set up square glass, yet

as when it was proposed at a meeting of the society to have the said rooms granted for his use, it was done conditionally, that the lower chamber, joining the bay-tree, in the first quadrangle, which did belong to the warden, may henceforth be allowed to that fellow which should hereafter come into that chamber over those lower rooms that were allowed for the warden's use. This being granted, the warden broke a dore through the wall that parts his parlour from the said lower rooms, and makes them fit for use, at his owne, and not at the College charge: and they yet remain for the warden's use; whereby the best lodgings in the College, which usually belonged to the senior fellow, were severed and spoyled: and all this to please a proud silly woman. But afterwards, when Mr. Sterry saw that he was made a shoeing-horn to serve the warden's turn (for afterwards he disused his company, and never invited him to his lodgings as formerly, only at Christmas, when the whole society used to dine there), he became his enemy, repented of what he had done before the society, and blamed his owne weakness much to be so much imposed upon, as he had been, by the most false and perfidious warden.'

caused the armes to be set up againe, the majestic light was lost. Had he been a single man, and not had a nice wife with six or seven daughters, this would not have been done; the next was to set up a coach, having had none before; yet had he been a single man, as Dr. Goddard was, he would have kept none.' But poor Anthony grumbled without effect. What would he have said had he lived to hear social reformers urge that ladies ought to be admitted as students to the university, and encouraged to compete in the schools with scholars of the stronger sex?

CHAPTER V.

LIFE INSURANCE.

MANY readers of these volumes will learn with surprise that Life Insurance is distinctly traceable to the abolition of clerical celibacy.

To get a perfect view of all the circumstances which resulted in this device for mitigating the evils of premature death, the reader must first of all bear in mind that the parochial clergy in the first centuries of our Reformed Church were a much poorer class of persons than the clergy of our own time, who, notwithstanding their general affluence, comprise within their ranks a large minority of indigent families. Whilst agriculture was in its infancy, the tithal dues of ecclesiastical incumbents were small in proportion to the low productiveness of the soil; and so long as the clergy were compelled to take their tithes in kind, when they could not arrange with the tillers of the soil for payment in money, an incumbent scarcely ever received from his parishioners all the emolument to which he was entitled. If he received his tithes in kind, he rarely drew to his barn a tenth of all the tithable produce of his parish; and in converting the produce, thus paid in kind, into money for the satisfaction of his creditors, no less than in bartering it with dealers for the commodities of which he stood in need, he was liable to loss from his ignorance of commercial business, from his inability to contend against extortionate usages, and from his unwillingness to offend his neighbours by rigid insistence on his pecuniary rights. Consequently, in times when from the general unproductiveness of the land they were entitled to only modest revenues, the clergy did not actually receive two-thirds of the little which they ought to have acquired. Compared with the gentry, the yeomanry, and the prosperous traders amongst whom they lived and laboured, the ordinary parochial incumbents of the seventeenth century were a needy class.

But if the resident incumbents of superior livings were poor, their material condition was affluence when put in contrast against the pecuniary state of the stipendiary curates,—a very numerous and ill-paid class throughout the Stuart period of our history. Whilst livings yielded bare pittances for the support of priests and the maintenance of religion, pluralism was very general; a single clergyman sometimes holding four, five, or even six incumbencies at the same time. And it was usual for these pluralists of old time to absent themselves for years together from their cures, which were left entirely to the ministrations of stipendiary curates who received a few pounds, 20*l.* or 30*l.* in yearly salaries, and the whole or part of whatever fees they could get for exceptional services from their flocks.*
Bishop Ken states that there were in his day four thousand one hundred and sixty-five parishes, in England and Wales, the incumbents of which were habitual absentees,—their duties being performed by miserably over-worked and under-paid stipendiaries, whose material condition, however, was scarcely, if at all, worse than that of many hundreds of occupants of poor benefices.

It must further be taken into consideration that most of these poor parsons and curates were men with wives and children. From the earliest years of Elizabeth's reign the social

---

* In the 'Expostulatoria, or the Complaints of the Church of England Againe,' the reader may gather many notable facts respecting Anglican pluralism in Charles the Second's time from an author zealous for the Church's honour, Bishop Ken—the pious prelate who fearlessly reproved Charles the Second's immoralities; the masterly preacher, whose eloquence drew crowds to every church in which he was announced to preach; the devout poet, the badness of whose more ambitious metrical effusions is forgotten in the excellence of his Doxology and the three hymns—' Morning Hymn,' ' Evening Hymn,' and ' Midnight Hymns,' specially written for the Winchester boys. Bishop Ken gives a summary of the parishes whose incumbents were in his time habitually non-resident, numbering in all 4165 cures, or rather sinecures. ' So that,' says the prelate, ' of the 12000 church livings, or thereabouts, 3000 or more being impropriate, and 4165 sinecures, or non-resident livings, what a poor remainder is there left for a painful and honest ministry, for the glory of God, and the salvation of souls!' Addressing the non-residents indignantly the bishop exclaims.—' Will

prejudice against married priests had been much weaker in the humbler than in the higher grades of society. The clergy of the humbler ecclesiastical degrees experienced much less difficulty in winning brides suitable to their modest estates, than the dignified priests who, valuing themselves on the eminence and grandeur of their preferments, were seldom in a position to make matrimonial overtures to the daughters of their social equals. Long after a country rector was looked upon as a fit mate for the daughter of a gentle yeoman or small squire, his bishop would have been thought guilty of presumption in aspiring to the hand of a baron's or even a baronet's daughter. In practice, marriage was a more honourable estate amongst ordinary parochial clergy than amongst bishops and deans. Moreover its consolations were more precious to priests whose lots were cast in private and obscure stations, than to ecclesiastics of higher status whose minds were withdrawn from dreams of domestic felicity by the various duties and pompous diversions of exalted rank. Hence it came to pass that clerical wives and children were most numerous in those sections of ecclesiastical society where the means for their maintenance were the least abundant.

Again, the social disturbances of the seventeenth century were cruelly productive of domestic impoverishment in clerical circles. By the action of the Parliamentary Committees, for the ejection of scandalous ministers and the advancement of religion, many hundreds of married clergymen during the Civil

---

you receive the tythes of God, and not do the work? Will you live by the gospel, and not preach the gospel? .... How will you look your ancestors in the face when you have taken their gifts and neglected their desires? What, take the tythe they gave and leave their posterity destitute? You will say, We have curates, and they perform our duties. Curates! What new generation of men are these curates? We have indeed some prophets, some apostles, some evangelists, some pastors, some doctors, but no curates .... Oh, sirs, you know not what to do when the three estates of the nation observe how much tythe goes to maintain your pride, vanity, and folly, and how little to maintain the service of God! They may say, What need this waste? Why do we throw away so much of the public revenues as amounts to two millions and a half; whereas half a million may maintain men to read prayers and do all the duties of ministers? A gentleman hath a parsonage of 200*l.* a-year in his gift. Why, saith he, shall I part with so much of my estate? Cannot I give 20*l.* or 30*l.* to a curate, as well as a clergyman?"

War were driven from their parsonages, and reduced to extreme indigence; and the fate of these unfortunate servants of the Church is all the more deserving of compassionate remembrance because, though many of them were dissolute creatures, whose crimes merited the severest punishment, it is certain that a far larger proportion of them were deprived of their livings on account of their contumacy to the Parliament, and for the attainment of political ends. Of the various causes which necessitated their deprivation, I shall take occasion to speak in a subsequent chapter; but for the present it is enough to notice the effect which the measures taken for their suppression had in swelling the vast amount of clerical distress in every part of the country. Unfortunately, there is no way of ascertaining the number of the preachers deprived of employment by the Parliamentary Committees; and the difficulty of making any fair computation of its probable amount is increased by the adverse scribes, who alternately exaggerated or diminished it in accordance with their political prejudices and animosities. Dr. Gauden —the royalist scribe, whose 'Icon Basilike,' notwithstanding the complete exposure of its purely fictitious nature, will permanently influence the popular estimate of Charles the First's character—reckons the pastors ejected by the Parliament as numbering between six and seven thousand. Dr. Pierce, on the strength of a boast, or threat, or minatory sentiment,* said to have been uttered by White the Centurist, but which probably never escaped from that politician's lips, would have us believe that they did not fall short of eight thousand. And 'in his ' Sufferings of the Clergy'—the most mendacious book ever written with a profession of statistical accuracy—Dr. Walker has the effrontery to urge that they were nearly ten thousand. The defenders of the Parliamentary Puritans on the other hand— such as Calamy and Neale—over anxious, perhaps, to show that the Royalist clergy were less hardly treated by the Rebel Parliament than the Commonwealth ministers by the resentful restorers of episcopacy, may probably somewhat underrate the victims, whom they put at one thousand seven hundred and

---

* White is said to have declared in the House of Commons that 'eight thousand *deserved* to be turned out.'

twenty-six. That the statements of the Royalist and Episcopal partisans on this matter are ludicrous exaggerations every historian is nowadays ready to admit. Walker's account contradicts itself; for after computing the ejected ministers as certainly eight thousand, and in all likelihood but slightly under ten thousand, it demonstrates by its supplementary index that they cannot have exceeded some two thousand four hundred. On the other hand, the computations by the friends of the Dissenters, ejected by the Act of Uniformity, in 1662, may perhaps err in placing the parliamentary ejectments during the Civil War somewhat too low. Still the Puritan calculations were made with honesty and on intelligible principles, and I am disposed to think them very near the truth. And if we accept the number at which Calamy puts the earlier ejectments, it is clear that the domestic suffering caused by them must have been very great.

To the honour of the Parliament we must remember that it did not omit to make some provision for the innocent victims of needful changes. In every case the provision was small, in no case can it have been otherwise than inadequate; still the measures which appropriated, under certain circumstances, a fifth of the revenues of the sequestrated livings for the maintenance of the wives and children of the ejected pastors, were measures of justice and charity which the Episcopalian restorers would have done well to imitate. But, when due notice has been taken of the ordinances by which the Parliament sought to mitigate the hardships inflicted by its ecclesiastical policy on innocent women and children, it still remains an indisputable historic fact, that the proceedings against scandalous and contumacious ministers were cruelly fruitful of destitution and penury in the clerical order.

But if the proceedings of the Parliament, during its contest with Charles the First, against Royalist incumbents and unquestionably scandalous ministers were in some cases harsh and cruel, what must we say of the wholesale ejectment of non-conforming ministers in 1662? In defence of the earlier expulsions it can be honestly urged, that they took place in the heat of a frightful contention; that a large proportion of the deprived clergy were men whose removal from their spiritual offices was demanded by religion and decency; and that the least offensive of the other part of them were violent and extreme politicians, whom the government was justified in silencing for the sake of public tranquillity and the success of the popular cause. No such pleas can be advanced in behalf of the evictions which took place under the Act of Uniformity. Of the two thousand ministers whom that equally harsh and unwise measure drove from the service of the Church, there was not one who had disgraced his calling. They had done their duty faithfully to their nation and their God. Many of them were scholars and writers of great learning and ability. Many of them were politicians of unassailable loyalty to the House of Stuart. All of them were ready to maintain the established government; and by their preference of what they conceived to be their duty, before what they could not fail to see would conduce to their worldly interests, all of them demonstrated their possession of that severe conscientiousness which is the most valuable of all moral qualities in a national priesthood. No humane and intelligent Churchman of the present day can, without mingled anger and shame, reflect on the treatment which those men endured. Had the interests of the Church, had the success of the episcopal system, required their expulsion and ruin, our grief for their wrongs would not be without consolation. But whilst the secure establishment of episcopacy could have been effected by arrangements that would have retained them in their places and yet put no constraint on their consciences, the Church was deeply injured by the loss of their services at a crisis when the national life stood in especial need of moral and religious instruction. But it is not the purpose of this chapter to expatiate on their virtues or to denounce their oppressors. On the present occasion it is enough to notice the addition which accrued from their persecution to the indigence of the clerical order. Driven from their homes, and compelled to earn precarious subsistences—as schoolmasters, ushers in schools, secretaries, clerks, booksellers' hacks, or preachers to secret associations of Dissenters—they still retained their clerical quality. They were ejected ministers, but their misfortunes could not undo the fact that they had been educated and ordained to fill spiritual offices. Most of them were married men; and, when most of the ejected husbands

Part III.—Clerical Women.

and fathers had perished prematurely of hard labour and insufficient food, their penniless wives and forlorn offspring belonged to that rapidly increasing army of clerical women and children, whose distresses stirred compassionate observers in every part of the kingdom.*

To alleviate the clerical distress which had increased with alarming rapidity during the civil disturbances, certain benevolent persons, with the Protector's sanction and encouragement, established the association familiarly designated the 'Sons of the Ministers,' by which they endeavoured to confer on the indigent orphans of clergymen a small amount of nurture and education, and to afford pecuniary relief to clerical widows. The first sermon in behalf of this charitable undertaking was preached in old St. Paul's cathedral on November 8, 1655, by Mr. George Hall, minister of St. Botolph's. On the restoration of episcopacy, together with the re-establishment of the Stuart rule, the clergy, dropping the term 'ministers' from the title of the charity and putting 'clergy' in its place, were at pains to relieve an excellent foundation of the signs of what they regarded its disgraceful origin. On July 1, 1678—the thirtieth year, according to Royalist computation, of Charles the Second's reign—the crown granted a charter to the Corporation for the Relief of the widows and children of the Clergy when the society had been in existence just three and twenty years; and henceforth it became the fashion of the friends of the Charity, in sermons and after-dinner speeches at its annual festivals, to speak of the institution

---

* In illustration of one of the political results of clerical marriage, it is well to observe that, but for the influence of clerical wives and children on the ministers who disapproved of episcopacy, the clerical secession of 1662 would probably have numbered far more than two thousand pastors. In his notice of the Rev. Richard Hawes, M.A., an ejected minister of Leintwardine, Herefordshire, Dr. Calamy remarks, in 'The Nonconformists' Memorial,' 'When the Bartholomew Act came out, such was Mr. Hawes's moderation, that some apprehended he might have conformed, particularly one of his neighbour-ministers, Mr. C——y of W——t, who complained that he was like to stand alone on that side of the county, being so bent against yielding to any of the terms required, that it were but to read some small part of the Popish Prayer-book (as he termed the Common Prayer), that he declared he would sooner suffer himself to be torn in pieces. However, when they both went together to the bishop, this man (overcome by the importunities of his wife) soon yielded: but to his death detested what, for lucre-sake, he practised, always declaimed against it, and never thrived afterwards.'

as a thing that had sprung directly from Charles the Second's royal munificence to the Church, for which his father had endured martyrdom.* Even at the present time, when there is a growing disposition on the part of Churchmen to render justice to the Long Parliament and Cromwell's government, it is usual for clerical advocates of the corporation to attribute its creation to the restored monarch. Whether the annual festivals of the charity were celebrated with banquets during the Commonwealth I am unable to say, but in 1674 we find sixteen stewards appointed to promote the interests of the Charity by bringing to

* Writing in 1733, the author of 'A Compleat List of the Stewards, Presidents, Vice-Presidents, and Treasurers, belonging to the Royal Corporation for the Relief of the Poor Widows and Children of Clergymen,' speaks of the charitable corporation as erected by Charles the Second, and with notable inconsistency mentions events in the career of the institution which occurred during that monarch's exile, and in the years which intervened between his restoration and 1678. 'His late majesty King Charles the Second,' says the writer of this sketch, 'did, in the thirtieth year of his reign (July 1, 1678), erect a corporation for the relief of poor widows and children of clergymen; which corporation hath from time to time been endowed by the charity of well-disposed persons with a revenue now amounting to about two thousand pounds per annum. This revenue, great as it is, and vastly redounding to the honour of the pious benefactors, one of which alone some time ago bequeathed to the corporation the sum of 18,000*l.*, is nevertheless far insufficient to answer the pressing wants, for the relief of which this corporation was established. For there are commonly near six hundred widows of clergymen, who have been left so entirely destitute of all subsistence as to apply yearly for relief to this corporation; and it has been observed, that the number of poor persons so applying has greatly increased. The number of clergymen in England may be computed to be about twelve thousand, their widows applying for charity about six hundred, which is about one in twenty. *But when it is considered that there are five thousand livings (including donations and perpetual curacies) not exceeding fifty pounds a-year, and of these two thousand not exceeding ten pounds a-year*, it will not appear so strange, that of clergymen's widows one in twenty should come to want; or that from among the other clergy (chiefly) in forty years' time, a subsistence for them should be raised of two thousand pounds a-year. But besides, these six hundred poor widows have generally large families of children depending on them; and the number of such miserable orphans, from the certificates given in to the corporation, have been computed to amount to at least two thousand. From whence it appears, that in order to allow each of these six hundred poor widows with their families, for their whole subsistence, but ten pounds a-year, it would require an annual revenue of at least six thousand pounds; that of two thousand pounds, wherewith this corporation is at present endowed, though applied with the exactest care and fidelity, not being hitherto capable of affording to each more than three pounds yearly: a sum much smaller than many of the meanest poor receive, especially if they have families to take care of.'

the annual meeting persons likely to contribute liberally to the inadequate funds of the corporation. Probably the first annual festivals of the 'Sons of the Clergy' gave rise to our modern fashion of subsidizing the funds of benevolent institutions by means of subscriptions collected at charity dinners.

The little which the corporation of the Sons of the Clergy could effect for the alleviation of clerical distress was lamentably disproportionate to the magnitude of the evil which it vainly endeavoured to remedy. Every year saw an increase in the number of miserable applicants for the alms of the association: and, as time went on, the appeals by which the applicants urged their claims became more and more eloquent of destitution and despair. Moreover it was known that the charity afforded no palliation whatever to the miseries of the most numerous class of clerical paupers—the clerical widows who, without possessing the means to educate their offspring or even the means of bare subsistence, were placed slightly above that condition of extreme destitution which furnished more candidates for the bounty of the corporation than it was able to relieve. The clerical widow with several children and a sure income of $30l$, $20l$, or even $10l$ a year was in a less deplorable state than the several hundreds of absolutely destitute widows of clergymen: but still her lot was one of miserable and hopeless indigence.

Affairs had passed from bad to worse, when a clergyman, more thoughtful and sagacious, and more earnest in benevolence, than most of his kind-hearted contemporaries, struck out a notable plan for applying a remedy to the spring and source of the mischief. In these days when we delight to commemorate our national heroes with festivals and statues, our social reformers should render due honour to William Assheton, who unquestionably deserves a high place amongst the benefactors of his species. A doctor of divinity and rector of Beckenham in Kent, the Reverend William Assheton was in his day a personage of considerable influence, as well as a man of remarkable ability. As domestic chaplain of his Grace the Duke of Ormond he came occasionally in contact with people of fashion and aristocratic rank: but his claim to be remembered gratefully by the present generation is found in the services which entitle him to be called the Originator of modern Life Assurance. Painfully considering the sorrows and sufferings of the clerical widows and orphans, and penetrating beneath the repulsive surface of the social trouble in search for the hidden causes of the evils which stirred his compassionate nature, this gentleman—whose name is mentioned in no biographical dictionary—was not long in discovering the obscure source of, and the only remedy for, the greater part of the misery over which humane ladies and gentlemen were daily shedding futile tears. The source of the evil was social improvidence or want of the right machinery for provident action: the remedy was mutual hand-in-hand co-operation. Mr. Assheton saw that the clerical widows and children were the widows and children of men who had for the most part enjoyed incomes beyond their absolute wants: that notwithstanding the narrowness of their means the deceased clergymen had saved small sums from their yearly receipts, and hoarded them as a provision against adversity: that the greater part of the misery endured by their widows and orphans might have been obviated had these same deceased clergymen together with the more fortunate of their order, made common cause against misfortune, and combined to assure a certain modest measure of material prosperity to their families. The more that Mr. Assheton thought about the matter, the surer he was that, to secure his wife against indigence in case he should die before her, any clergyman would gladly pay any obtainable sum of money into a common fund on which in case of his death she could have a claim for proportionate assistance. In short, Mr. Assheton hit upon a rude scheme of life assurance, whereby the clergy should be enabled to provide for their widows.

In these days when London contains scores of Life Assurance offices with agents established throughout the provinces, Mr. Assheton's scheme may appear a simple matter to thoughtless persons who need to be told that it is just as difficult to originate and put in practice a plan of social reform, as it is easy to extend and profit by its arrangements when it has once been put in operation. And Mr. Assheton's suggestion possessed in a very high degree the merit of originality, although it sprung from an attentive consideration of the principles of Ship Insurance and Fire Insurance, and merely aimed at applying to the disastrous consequences of death preventive measures similar to those by which merchants had for generations protected themselves against losses by storms at sea, and London householders, since the recent fire of 1666, had provided against losses by conflagration.

The scheme, as it took its first form in the innovator's mind, was this,—to find or form a company that would undertake to pay an annuity of 30*l*, a-year to every clergyman's widow whose husband should, before attaining the age of sixty years, pay into its fund of insurance a sum of one hundred pounds. In case the insurer outlived his wife, the hundred pounds would remain the property of the company, and there would be no claim upon its exchequer in consideration of the money so paid in anticipation of a contingency that, since the execution of the agreement, had through death passed out of the list of possibilities. The projector anticipated that a considerable proportion of the clerical wives, for whose possible widowhood provision had been thus made, would pre-decease their provident husbands; and he calculated that the profits accruing to the company from such cases would enable the company to pay the annuities in other cases where the wives of clerical insurers should outlive their husbands by many years. Instead of limiting the amounts for which insurances should be effected to annuities of thirty pounds, Mr. Assheton contemplated the probability of provident husbands wishing to purchase contingent annuities of sums greater or less than thirty pounds.

But he was of opinion that, whatever the amount of the contingent annuity so purchased, the sum paid for it should be in the proportion of a hundred pounds for every thirty pounds of annuity. The man, who wished to secure a contingent annuity of 300*l*. to his wife, should be enabled to do so by an immediate cash payment of one thousand pounds; on the other hand the poor and provident pastor, who could command no more than 50*l*., might with that sum purchase a contingent annuity of 15*l*. The obvious defect of Mr. Assheton's scheme was that its rate of insurance was the same for men of twenty-one years of age and men who were in the sixtieth year of life; and it seems that this defect cannot be accounted for on the supposition that young insurers were in his opinion morally bound to do more in the cause of co-operation than older insurers. He was ready to stipulate that every insurer should on effecting his bargain with the company be of such an age that the company might have some chance of benefit from its compact with him. It seemed to him unreasonable that a very old man, tottering on the verge of the grave, should be allowed to buy for a hundred pounds a contingent annuity for the benefit of a young and healthy wife who might survive him by half-a-century. But so long as insurers were between the ages of twenty-one and sixty, it appeared to him that young and old should purchase the benefits of co-operation on the same terms; and it speaks much for the general ignorance of the statistics of mortality, that, when the projector's scheme was put in operation, the commercial speculators upon it were so far of his opinion that, whilst declining to do business to the same amount with old as with young insurers, they still consented to do business on one uniform rate with insurers of various ages.

Having in the first instance devised his scheme of Life Insurance, at the instigation of a fervent desire to alleviate clerical distress, Mr. Assheton soon saw that it was not more applicable to the needs of ecclesiastical persons than of laymen. In allusion to the insecurity of their worldly positions, clerical wives were ordinarily spoken of as dependent on 'steeple-house jointures.' If the clergyman's wife lost her hold on the church through her husband's death, she straightway dropt in the social scale. A squire or yeoman could settle on his wife a permanent interest in his real estate; but a parson usually had no estate apart from his ecclesiastical preferment, and his ability to provide for his conjugal partner was limited by the uncertainty and necessary shortness of his tenure of life and living. The wives of landed proprietors were women with jointures on real estate; the wives of parsons had nothing but 'steeple-house jointures,' *i. e.* participation in their husbands' life-interests. But the same, urged Mr. Assheton, might be said of the wives of many lawyers, doctors, merchants. 'And not only Churchmen,' he wrote, 'but also all other orders of men, may receive the benefit of this proposal. There are several physicians, lawyers, merchants, traders, &c., who, during their own lives, are either men of competent estates or have the credit to be thought so, and consequently their wives are suitably maintained. But at their deaths, their wives (as well as those of the clergy), are sometimes left in a mean, if not indigent condition. For as a Churchman's preferments are only for his life, so neither can a physician practise nor a lawyer plead in the other world. I have, therefore, sometimes wondered why the clergy should be upbraided with steeple-house jointures, since the wives of other professions are in this respect as liable to be exposed as the clergy.'*

Yet further, on consideration he saw that his scheme of Life Assurance might be of great convenience and service to gentlemen of landed estate, who, by the general usage of the time, were required to settle incomes on their wives, in case of their widowhood, in the proportion of £100 per annum for every £1000 which the ladies brought to their husbands. ' A. B., possessed of an estate in land,' urged Mr. Assheton, ' of 300l. per annum, proposeth marriage to C. D. whose portion is 3000l. For which portion, according to the custom of England, she expects a jointure of 300l. per annum. Which, being the whole of A. B. his estate (and which, perhaps, is not only charged with the payment of debts, but also portions for younger children) cannot conveniently be all settled as a jointure without the ruin of the family in the next generation, especially should C. D. marry to a second husband . . . Now with what ease are all difficulties met by this proposal? For by paying 1000l. to the Mercers' Company, his wife is jointured in 300l. per annum. He hath 2000l. to answer other occasions. And his land is cleared, to be enjoyed by his eldest son, even during his mother's life.'

Of course Dr. Assheton's proposal was ridiculed by dull wits as the fanciful suggestion of a crack-brained projector. Like nearly every inventor or original thinker before or since his time, the doctor was derided as a quack and impostor, and encountered many a rebuff from sapient gentlemen who, speaking with the authority of *practical* knowledge, assured him that no *practical* man of business would pay an hour's serious attention to his fantastic device for interfering with Providence and

* *Vide* 'A Full Account of the Rise, Progress, and Advantages of Dr. Assheton's Proposal (as now improved and managed by the Worshipful Company of Mercers, London) for the Benefit of Widows of Clergymen and others, by settling Jointures and Annuities at the rate of Thirty per cent.' (1700.)

putting an end to poverty. He laid his plan before the managers of the 'Corporation of the Clergy', as persons specially concerning in the work which it was designed to accomplish: but they 'held themselves incapable to accept his proposal!' He solicited attention from the Governors of the Bank of England, who decided that they were not in a position to take up his scheme. After these rebuffs, he went before a general court of the Mercers' Company, on Friday, Nov. 11, 1698, and entreated them to enter the business of life assurance in accordance with his proposals. Fortunately the rulers of the company saw the prudence and soundness of the scheme, which they forthwith acted upon, after amending it in certain particulars.

Pledging the rents of their large landed estates as security for the fulfilment of their contracts with insurers, the Mercers entered on business as life assurance agents. Limiting the entire amount of subscriptions to 100,000*l.* they decided that no person over sixty years of age should become a subscriber; that no subscriber should subscribe less than 50*l.*—*i.e.* should purchase a smaller contingent annuity than one of 15*l.*; that the anunity to every subscriber's widow or other person for whom the insurance was effected should be at the rate of 30*l.* for every hundred pounds of subscription. It was stipulated that subscribers must be in 'good and perfect health at the time of subscription.' It was decided that all married men of the age of thirty years, or under, might subscribe any sum from 50*l.* to 1,000*l.*; that all married men, not exceeding sixty years of age, might subscribe any sum not less than 50*l.* and not exceeding 300*l.* The company's prospectus further stipulates 'that no person that goes to sea, nor soldier that goes to the wars, shall be admitted to subscribe to have the benefit of this proposal, in regard of the casualties and accidents that they are more particularly liable to.' Morover it was provided that 'in case it should happen that any man who had subscribed should voluntarily make away with himself, or by any act of his, occasion his own death, either by duelling, or committing any crime whereby he should be sentenced or put to death by justice: in any or either of these cases his widow should receive no annuity, but upon delivering up the company's bond, should have the subscription money paid to her.'

The bond by which the Mercers obliged themselves to pay to 'such person or persons, as by his last will and testament' every subscriber should direct and appoint 'to receive the annuity accruing from his subscription,' was drawn thus:—
'We, the Wardens and Commonalty of the Mercers of the City of London, do acknowledge to have received of . . . Inhabitant in the Parish of . . . in the . . . of . . . the sum of . . . which he hath subscribed for the benefit of such person or persons as the said . . . by his last will and testament shall direct and appoint, during the natural life of . . . his now widow, aged . . . years, the daughter of . . . of . . . in the . . . of . . . in case he dies before her. And we do promise and oblige ourselves, and our successors, in case the said . . . shall dye (except in such manner as is excepted in the general proposal made by us for payment of the annuities to widows) to pay unto such person or persons as the said . . . by his last will and testament shall direct, during the natural life of the said . . . his wife . . . yearly, free of all taxes and charges, being after the rate of Thirty Pounds per cent. per ann. of the said . . . his subscription, at the two usual feasts of the annunciation of the Blessed Virgin Mary, and St. Michael the Archangel. The First Payment to be made on the First of the said Feast Days that shall happen Four months or more after the Decease of the said . . . the person or persons being so entitled, producing such his, her, or their title, together with this obligation, and due certificates of the Death of the said . . . and the life of the said . . . To the which payment we bind ourselves and our successors firmly by these presents. In testimony whereof we have hereunto affixed the seal of the said Company the . . . day of . . . in the year of our Lord.'

The success which attended the Mercers' operations was so decided that it soon gave rise to companies specially created to secure the public against some of the calamitous consequences of death. In 1706, the Amicable Life Assurance Office—usually, though, as the reader has seen, incorrectly, termed the *first* Life Insurance Office—was established in imitation of the Mercers' Office. Two years later, 'The Second Society of Assurance,' for the support of widows and orphans, was opened in Dublin, which, like the Amicable, introduced numerous improvements upon Dr.

Assheton's scheme, and was a Joint-stock Life Assurance Society, identical in its principles with, and similar in most of its details to, the modern Insurance Companies, of which there were in London as many as one hundred and sixty in the year 1859.

CHAPTER VI.

ELIZABETH'S TWELFTH INJUNCTION.

NO observer of England's social story can fail to remark the wide difference between the clerical homes of the present century and the clerical homes of the earlier generations of the Reformed Church, or can fail to be struck by the completeness with which the results of sacerdotal marriage have falsified the gloomy predictions of the Churchmen who foretold that grave evils would ensue from the abolition of the ancient laws which denied the blessings of matrimony to the priestly order.

Conceded reluctantly as an objectionable alternative that would afford society an escape from the inconveniences and iniquities of ecclesiastical celibacy, sacerdotal marriage was granted as a means for the avoidance of atrocious sin, rather than as an aid or instrument for the attainment of positive virtue. The experience of its effects upon the character of the clergy and the moral life of the nation, during Edward the Sixth's brief and distracted reign, had done so little to weaken and dissipate the popular prejudices against so needful a change, that, when the privilege of marriage was for a second time expressly accorded to ecclesiastics, it was guarded with provisions and restrictions expressive of the fear prevalent amongst the Reformers that it would be more productive of scandals and embarrassments than of social health and spiritual edification. Whilst the Catholic majority of the realm declared their disgust at what they regarded as a shameless avowal of the unholy appetites of the heretical priests, the influence of ancient usage and conservative preference for old ways to new fashions, induced a considerable proportion of the Protestant minority to regard the hazardous experiment with a disapprobation not altogether devoid of abhorrence.

Whilst the statesmen who had insisted most strongly on the

advisability of the innovation were by no means without secret misgivings as to its consequences, the most liberal and farsighted divines of the period, who had enforced their arguments in favour of sacerdotal wedlock by taking wives in defiance of law which rendered their conduct felonious, were far from imagining all the beneficial consequences that eventually accrued to their order from the abolition of the celibatic system. Indeed, the Elizabethan Englishman would have been regarded as ripe for the horn and star of a Bedlamite who had ventured to prophesy that sacerdotal matrimony would, in course of time, contribute largely to the influence, wealth, prestige, stability, and holiness of the clerical order. And yet such a prediction would have been fulfilled by what has been the condition of our national clergy for several generations.

On the other hand, it must be admitted that events have, to a certain limited extent, sustained the judgment of those advocates of celibacy who, in the heat of the marriage controversy, maintained that by burdening the clergy with the costly care of offspring, wedlock would in certain respects diminish their efficiency and zeal, and, together with their willingness, would lessen their ability to contribute to the maintenance and education of the indigent laity.

In accordance with the spirit of admonitions and ordinances issued in the times of her brother and father, Elizabeth, in the first year of her reign, commanded her beneficed clergy to contribute a certain proportion of the revenues accruing from their preferments to the education of poor scholars at grammar-schools and the universities. Notwithstanding the love of worldly pleasure, and the habits of indulgence which prevailed amongst certain kinds of ecclesiastics in every period of the Medieval Church, society had always cherished the theory, that the priest held his preferment in trust for the benefit of the poor, the sick, the aged, and the ignorant, to whose wants he was bound to minister out of the surplus of income that remained to him after the satisfaction of his natural wants and reasonable desires. Like most other fine and pleasant theories, this conception of sacerdotal responsibility and obligation was not severely put in practice; but it was something in behalf of general morality and clerical dutifulness that the theory was never altogether lost sight of, and that the priest whose conduct rendered no recognition to its requirements was deemed a social defaulter, and did not venture to justify deliberately his shortcomings. The true priest might live out of his tithal and other emoluments; but, for whatever he took beyond his living and spent on personal enjoyment, he would one day be called to terrible account.

Recognising this universal obligation of holders of benefices, Queen Elizabeth in her twelfth injunction (1559) urged, 'and to the intent that learned men may hereafter spring the more, for the execution of the premises, every Parson, Vicar, Clerk, or beneficed man within this Deanery, having yearly to dispend in Benefices and other promotions of the Church an hundred pounds, shall give 3*l.* 6*s.* 8*d.* in exhibition to one scholar in either of the universities, and for as many C.li, more as he may dispend, to so many scholars more shall give like exhibition in the University of Oxford or Cambridge, or some grammar-school, which after they have profited in good learning, may be partners of their Patron's Cure and charge, as well in preaching, as otherwise in executing of their offices, so may, when time shall be, otherwise profit the commonweal with their counsel and wisdom.' That this injunction was generally acted upon—in many cases, perhaps, reluctantly and parsimoniously, but still with an appearance of honest compliance, for many years after its promulgation, we may safely infer from what is known of the ways of the period, and from the frequent mention which Elizabethan clerical biography makes of the munificence exhibited to poor scholars, by clergymen possessing no highly lucrative preferments, as well as by the wealthy magnates of the ecclesiastical order.

In the assistance which Jewel received from Parkhurst, and the aid which Jewel conferred on Richard Hooker we have instances of the manner in which this kind of help was given to poor students in the later years of Henry the Eighth, the days of Edward the Sixth, and the time of Elizabeth. On entering Merton College in 1539, the fourteenth year of his life, John Jewel was received with paternal kindness and cherished with fatherly munificence by his tutor, John Parkhurst, who on Elizabeth's accession was elevated to the see of Norwich. In 1544, when Jewel took his M.A. degree, the cost of his commencement was paid by Parkhurst, who at that time held the rectory of Cleve, in Gloucestershire, in the parsonage of which valuable preferment it was his wont to entertain with characteristic hospitality the poor students whom his patronage fostered. It is recorded of this benevolent clergyman that he rarely dismissed his student-guests until he had given them presents, wherewith to cover the expenses of their return to Oxford, and aid them in continuing their studies at the University. 'What money, I wonder, have these miserable, beggarly Oxonians!' he exclaimed, one morning playfully, on entering the chamber in which a party of these guests had passed the previous night beneath his roof; and, as he spoke, the light-hearted host seized 'their pitifully lean and empty' purses, and 'stuffed them with money till they became both fat and weighty.' Another of Jewel's benefactors, at a later period of his earlier career, was Curtop, a fellow of Corpus Christi College, to which house Jewel migrated from Merton, who for some time allowed the future Bishop of Salisbury forty shillings a-year.

In due course, when Jewel, after enduring the privations and miseries of exile, had risen to be a chief of the newly-established Church, he repaid the goodness of his early patrons by extending to indigent scholars such help as Parkhurst and Curtop had awarded to him in his time of need. One of the most notable recipients of his bounty was Richard Hooker, for whose maintenance and education the bishop set apart an annual donation during the seven years prior to his entry at Oxford; and, when the future defender of the Anglican polity had become a student of Corpus Christi, his patron's college, the prelate continued to contribute towards his support, and to foster him with parental solicitude. One of the last, if not the very last, of the interviews which Hooker had with this generous protector was the occasion when the bishop lent the Oxford scholar a walking-stick, which he humorously called a good and serviceable horse. 'I have sent for you, Richard, to lend you a horse which hath carried me many a mile, and, I thank God, with much ease.' The bishop added, 'Richard, I do not give but lend you my horse; be sure you are honest, and bring my horse back to me at your return this way to Oxford. And I now give you ten groats to bear your charges to Exeter; and here is ten groats more, which I charge you to deliver to your mother. Tell her I send her a bishop's blessing with it, and beg the continuance of her prayers for me. If you bring my horse back to me, I will give you ten more to carry you on foot to the College; and so God bless you, good Richard!'

So long as the clergy were unmarried and childless, it is clear that their obligation to contribute towards the maintenance and education of poor scholars was fruitful of benefit to the laity in whose ranks alone could be found the appointed objects of clerical benefaction,—of benefits, moreover, that would naturally be withdrawn to a great extent from the laity by a change which would in due course give rise to an abundance, if not an excess, of such objects of ecclesiastical bounty within the lines of the clerical class. Nor are the clergy in any degree blameworthy because on coming to have children of their own geniture they ceased to expend on the sons of laymen the means which were required for the sustenance and culture of their own offspring. Even in the days of clerical celibacy, and in the time before the clergy had generally availed themselves of their newly acquired privilege of marriage, it was deemed just and in every way appropriate that rich incumbents, in selecting recipients of their alms from the vast multitude of indigent boys, should be influenced by personal affection and considerations of private interest. Naturally and rightly, in choosing their poor scholars from a crowd of candidates for help, they gave their preference to the children of kindred and close friends,—the boys of a poor sister or brother, before the boys of parents to whom they were bound by no domestic ties. If therefore it was right and commendable in them thus to help their collateral relations and private connexions before they extended patronage to persons outside their familiar circles, it was no less decent and natural in them to prefer their own children before all other applicants for help.

No doubt the laity suffered somewhat from this transference of eleemosynary support from their offspring to children of clerical parents; but it cannot be said that the change affected society prejudicially, or that it tended to defeat the main object of Elizabeth's twelfth injunction,—the purpose of which was not the education of laymen's children in preference to the sons of the clergy, but the supply of a sufficient number of persons competent to discharge the functions of the priesthood. It might indeed be fairly urged that, far from doing society any incidental injury, this transference of patronage must have resulted in uniform good to the country by causing the clergy to select for objects of their educational care persons whose moral and intellectual welfare their natural instincts would impel them to cherish to the utmost.

But, though it would be most absurd to charge the clergy with culpable neglect of their duty to the laity because, on having families of their own to provide for, they generally ceased to support other persons' children at the grammar-schools and universities, the question may fairly be raised whether affluent incumbents, without children of their own to educate, are not still morally bound by the ancient obligations of their order to contribute yearly a proportion of their ecclesiastical emoluments to the higher education of their neighbours' children? On the present occasion I neither answer nor raise this question; but I may observe, that those who would answer it in the negative cannot, even in these days of general enlightenment and culture, fairly insist that the obligation to cherish poor scholars has ceased *because* there is an abundant supply of persons qualified by other means to minister to the spiritual needs of the community.

Again, it is certain that for whatever loss the poorer sections of the laity sustained for a time from this withdrawal of clerical alms they received a speedy and abundant compensation in the influences of the clerical homes to supply whose wants the transference of bounty was effected.

CHAPTER VII.

THE MODERN CLERICAL HOME.

THOUGH Lord Macaulay ludicrously underrates the social quality of the wives of our clergy in Elizabethan England and throughout the seventeenth century, it cannot be denied that during what may be termed the period of ecclesiastical insecurity and clerical poverty,—the days when agriculture was comparatively unproductive and a large proportion of our wealthier ancestors could not believe in the permanence of the Anglican settlement,—the women of our clerical families were upon the whole decidedly inferior in extraction and culture to the wives of the laymen with whom the beneficed clergy associated on terms of personal equality.

Together with the general growth of popular confidence in the durability of the Anglican establishment, and with the increase of material prosperity in the clerical order, clergymen however found it more and more easy to ally themselves in marriage with the families of the gentry. During the Interregnum, from causes to which allusion has already been made, the social status of the clerical wife greatly improved. And on the re-establishment of the ecclesiastical system and order, for whose dignity and privileges Charles the First was much more of a martyr than Englishmen of the present day are prone to think, the clerical ladies of the kingdom rose with the fortunes of episcopacy to a far higher place in social esteem than any they had ever before attained to. Clarendon alluded with surprise and regret to the few instances which had occurred in his time of clergymen finding their brides in aristocratic families, and the Cavalier historian regards such instances as strongly illustrative of the disturbance which the civil troubles had effected in social relations and sentiments.

But had he lived to the close of the seventeenth century with unimpaired faculties he would have taken a juster view of the occurrences which provoked his astonishment; and, enlightened by the rapid increase of the number of such cases of feminine eccentricity, he would have interpreted them rightly as evidences of the growing respect for the Church, and as proofs that even in the ranks of a fastidious and conservative aristocracy social opinion had got the better of its old prejudices against clerical marriage.

It is also a matter of certainty—established beyond question by the pedigrees of gentle families and the literature of domestic annals—that throughout the earlier years of the eighteenth century, the status of our clerical women continued to improve with even greater rapidity than the political power and social dignity of other ecclesiastical persons; although Lord Macaulay, with an astounding blindness to the purposes of satire, and a still more extraordinary ignorance of the artistic devices by which it achieves its ends, has the mingled hardihood and obtuseness to argue, from a pungent passage in Swift's 'Advice to Servants,' that the wives of our beneficed clergy in George the Second's time, in cases numerous enough to affect the esteem in which their class was held, were dishonoured waiting-women whom stewards would have disdained to wed.*

Throughout the eighteenth century the clerical profession grew in favour with the aristocracy, as the ancient Catholic families disappeared and were replaced by families of the Protestant commonalty, who after acquiring wealth in commerce and other secular vocations invested their acquisitions in land, intermarried with the old squirearchy, and rose to rank amongst the territorial houses of the kingdom. Prudential motives also co-operated with the prohibitions against simony to raise the social status of the clerical order, by inducing the younger sons

---

* As I should be sorry to do injustice to so great an authority as Lord Macaulay, I quote his exact words:—' Even so late as the time of George the Second, the keenest of all observers of life and manners, himself a priest,' Dean Swift, 'remarked that, in a great household, the chaplain was the resource of a lady's maid whose character had been blown upon, and who was therefore forced to give up hopes of catching the steward!!!' Surely Lord Macaulay must have been a lineal descendant of the country gentleman who used to read 'Gulliver's Travels' once every year, in the firm belief that it was literally true!

of territorial families to qualify themselves to discharge the routine duties, and receive the steadily increasing emoluments, of livings which patrons were forbidden to sell and clergymen were enjoined not to buy.

Using the exact words of her brother's injunction against simoniacal practices, Elizabeth in the first year of her reign issued the following order;—' Also, to avoid the detestable sin of simony, because buying and selling of benefices is execrable before God, therefore all such persons, as buy any benefices, or come to them by fraud or deceit, shall be deprived of such benefices, and be made unable at any time hereafter to receive any other spiritual promotion; and such as do sell them, or by any colour do bestow them for their own gain and profit, shall lose their right and title of patronage and presentment for that time, and the gift thereof for that vacation, shall appertain to the Queen's Majesty.'

That in spite of prohibition livings were extensively sold and purchased in the seventeenth and eighteenth centuries, there is no need to observe; but the open and methodical traffic in ecclesiastical preferments, which is so noticeable a feature of clerical life at the present time, is a thing of quite recent origin. Our ancestors' general forbearance from the practice of simony was mainly due to their respect for law, and their superstitious abhorrence of arrangements which they had been trained to regard as abominably sinful; but without detracting from the merit of their usual abstinence from reprehensible dealings in clerical patronage, I may remark that their temptation to disregard the orders against simony was far weaker than the temptation to which patrons and clerks of our own time no less generally succumb. Until agricultural improvements had doubled, and in some cases quadrupled twice over, the tithal dues of incumbents, an ordinary living was no such source of income that clergymen with money in their pockets, or capitalists ready to lay out money for the advantage of their ordained sons, should be eager in competing for it in open or secret market; and it was not until the rapid growth of our material prosperity, from the development of commerce and the industrial arts, had produced a large number of persons anxious to become purchasers of ecclesiastical offices, that clerical patronage was a commodity saleable at high rates. Whilst buyers in the market were few, and those few would give only low prices for the article of forbidden traffic, the ecclesiastical patron was not to be credited with any high degree of virtue who, preferring the good opinion of his neighbours to a small acquisition of worldly gain, preferred to appoint a friend or a friend's child to a post which it was beyond his power to sell for a considerable sum.

On the other hand, so long as the patrons generally refrained from selling their presentations, the clergy were much less strongly tempted than they are at the present time to acquire preferments by simoniacal purchase. Before simony became general in the Reformed Church, the decidedly able and meritorious clergyman usually obtained a living before he had been many years in orders. No doubt there were then, as now, worthy pastors who remained curates all their days; but it cannot be questioned, that in the time when livings were almost universally given away, instead of being sold, the fairly educated, intelligent, well-mannered young clergyman had every reason to believe, as well as to hope, that before he had entered middle life he would acquire a parsonage and a living by the unbought favour of a patron. The same cannot be said of the professional chances of the average curate at the present time, when young clergymen, entertaining conscientious scruples against simoniacal dealings, are soon taught that they must either set aside their scruples and make the ordinary arrangements for the purchase of a living, or must make up their minds to go unbeneficed to the grave.

But long before the patron condescended to seek, or seeking could have found, a safe and lucrative market for his ecclesiastical patronage in the public auction-room, he derived pecuniary advantage from his advowsons by educating his younger sons for the clerical profession and appointing them to his vacant benefices. As soon as a prudent squire had thus dealt with his preferments, his example was speedily followed by his county neighbours; and hence arose the system under which the livings in the gift of a landed proprietor became to be regarded as appanages for the provision of his younger sons. The heir of a county estate looked forward to the time when he should reign in the ancestral hall, whilst his younger brothers prepared themselves at college to hold the family livings—to perform service in their churches on Sundays, and mingle with their old county neighbours on week-days. Under this system a class of gentlemen, corresponding to the aristocratic medieval monks, began to take orders in the Reformed Church early in the seventeenth century; and, though they may not have become a very important element of clerical life till after the Restoration, their number was considerable when George Herbert startled and scandalized his aristocratic acquaintance by announcing his intention to retire from court and adopt the habit of an ecclesiastic.

That the church was not in all respects a gainer by this accession of gentle priests it is needless to observe; but it is certain that their presence in the clerical order tended greatly to enhance the dignity of clerical ladies. Marrying in the ranks which gave them birth, they brought to their rectories and vicarages wives who were gentlewomen, equal in birth and culture to the first ladies of their shires. Of two sisters, connected in blood with the best families of a county-side, one would marry a squire, the other would become the bride of the squire's clerical brother; and though their sisterly intercourse might be disturbed by jealousies and bickerings, arising from differences of material endowment and influence, their marriages helped to accelerate the fusion of the lay gentry and the richer clergy.

It was remarked with more of satirical pungency than of profound discernment by the Dutch Mandeville that woman's natural weakness and cowardice caused her to regard with especial favour two classes of men,—the soldiers who had power to shield her from bodily assailants, and the priests to whom she attributed the ability to defend her against ghostly enemies. Without overloooking its injustice and fallaciousness, we may admit that the facts which induced the philosopher to utter this sarcastic judgment are conspicuous amongst existing social phenomena. Admiration of their physical courage and prowess still inspires ordinary women to exalt the members of the military service above the followers of all other secular vocations; but their esteem for martial men is frigid in comparison with the feelings of mingled reverence and affection which they cherish for ecclesiastics. In ball-rooms and other scenes of frivolity, the soldier no doubt commands a larger measure of feminine homage and approval than the priest; but away from places of trivial diversion the wearer of the clerical habit enjoys, so far as woman's opinion is concerned, a manifest superiority over the wearer of the brilliant uniform and flashing sword.

This feminine preference of the clergy to laymen is notably illustrated by the matrimonial successes of the clerical order. In every rank of existing English society, from the higher grades of the aristocracy to the obscure grades of the prosperous middle classes, clergymen are more successful suitors for woman's love than any other kind of men of the same rank and degree of affluence. Of course this peculiar influence of clerical persons is counteracted and modified by other influences, which are productive of results that might induce a hasty critic to deny, that it is in any degree operative in those patrician circles where the lay-holders of vast ancestral estates and bright historic titles, in the absence of spiritual competitors similarly endowed with wealth and rank, are never or very seldom surpassed in their pursuit of woman's affection by ecclesiastical rivals. Rank, wealth, and titular distinctions are social forces great enough to overcome the peculiar endowments by which the sacerdotal class asserts its power over the intellect and affections of women. But it may be confidently averred, that if the men of our highest aristocracy were to contract a fashion of taking holy orders and discharging the functions of the national priesthood, so that a half of the temporal peerage should become ecclesiastical personages, the peers thus invested with the sanctity and powers of the sacerdotal order would speedily be found more influential over the women of the high nobility than the peers who should continue to be laymen.

Against this view it may be remarked that the wives of spiritual peers are seldom women of noble extraction. To which objection the obvious replications are—that our bishops ordinarily marry when they are comparatively humble persons, having no better social status than the less affluent of the untitled gentry: that on reaching the episcopal bench they are seldom of a marriageable age or at liberty to choose wives in the social class to which they have been elevated: and that, notwithstanding the high respect in which the episcopacy is held, the ordinary Anglican bishop—holding no distinctions and privileges which he can transmit to his descendants, enjoying no rank apart from that which came to him with his office, and possessing no wealth which approaches in value to the riches of a fairly prosperous lay noble—is in some respects so far less favourably placed than the average secular peer, that, even when he seeks a bride after his elevation to the bench, he cannot be said to prosecute his suit, under conditions of perfect or approximate equality with any well-endowed member of the hereditary aristocracy who may be his rival.

But on withdrawing his attention from the wealthiest and most powerful personages of the high aristocracy, and surveying the lower grades of our exalted classes, from the houses of the chief nobility to the families of the untitled territorial gentry, no observer can fail to remark the numerical importance of their clerical members. After noting the numerous cases where the representative of a patrician house, or chief of a gentle stock, is an ecclesiastical dignitary or clerk in holy orders, he is struck by the large proportion of gently descended women— mentioned in the genealogical dictionaries of aristocratic families—who are recorded as the wives of clergymen. No doubt the majority of these ladies, in marrying priests, became the wives of men of their own social degree; but a fact which forcibly demonstrates the favour exhibited by aristocratic damsels for the clerical order, is the great number of priests—bearing names that testify to the humility of their extraction—who are mentioned in our books of the Peerage, the Baronetage, and the Landed Gentry, as the husbands of women who would have never condescended to marry country attornies, or country doctors. Probably most of these unions of high-born girls with priests of lowly parentage were at first disapproved strongly, and at last sanctioned reluctantly, by the ladies' parents; but a daughter's *mésalliance* with a poor clergyman of obscure descent is an annoyance to which aristocratic parents reconcile themselves with comparative ease,—with all the more ease, because by their command of ecclesiastical patronage they can at a small sacrifice, or with no sacrifice at all, put her husband in a comfortable and dignified position. The case is different with the high-born girl who has set her affections on a briefless barrister, an unsuccessful physician, an unendowed civil servant, or a meritless artist. The preferments of the law cannot be bestowed on barristers until they have proved their fitness for them by acquiring the confidence of clients; a physician must be the architect of his professional fortunes; the prizes of the Civil Service can be won only by patient discharge of duty; the honours of art are not at the distribution of ministers of state. But a clergyman can be provided for without difficulty by parents who can get the ear of a lord chancellor, or have interest with ecclesiastical patrons, or are themselves the holders of clerical patronage. A girl's marriage with a poor parson does not, therefore, involve her permanent exclusion from society, if he is a man of decent character, with enough ability to discharge the routine duties of a country rectorate. The earl's daughter who elopes with her brother's tutor may give society a shock by her imprudence, and for a season she may be talked against as a terrible example of filial undutifulness: but ere long her husband's promotion to a good living or a fat canonry rehabilitates her in social esteem, and places her in a secure, though modest, position, from which she may hope to rise to better things.

Whilst parents of the superior classes allow their daughters to marry clergymen, in consideration of the value and attainableness of ecclesiastical preferments, parents of the inferior classes are ambitious of clerical alliances for their girls, out of regard for the distinction which attaches, in the humbler of the middle grades, to a clergyman's wife. The amount of wealth that steadily flows to the clerical order through the action of this particular ambition is enormous. In our large cities this tendency of newly acquired riches is very observable. The prosperous tradesman or small merchant, who would regard his daughter's marriage with a thriving man of business as no affair for exultation, and who would refuse his consent to her marriage with a struggling doctor unable to make a settlement upon her, is well pleased to give his only girl, with her fortune of ten or twenty thousand pounds, to a clerical incumbent whose private fortune would not furnish his bride's drawing-room, and whose professional income does not exceed an average curate's stipend. The girl, he argues, has enough for herself and children; and, though she won't have a rich husband, she will be a rector's wife. Setting aside the fortunes made by our great bankers and merchant princes, I am disposed to think, that of the wealth realized and accumulated during the last two generations in this country by enterprise in commerce and the industrial arts at least one-third has flowed to the clerical order through the wedding-ring. Whilst our recently enriched families send a considerable proportion of their sons to the universities, in order that by entering the church they may ascend from the rank of trade to the grade of gentry, the daughters of these same families are also educated for the clerical sphere. In the circles of petty provincial gentility, the richer girls, with fortunes that render them especially attractive and place them above the necessity of selecting fairly affluent suitors, almost invariably fall to curates or clergymen with small benefices.

In the middle classes, especially the middle classes of the provinces, the conspicuous matrimonial successes of the clergy occasion not a little discontent and irritation in the breasts of laymen who sometimes are heard to account, by suggestions neither generous nor just, for the comparative disesteem in which they are held by the fair sex. It is asserted that the clerical successes are due to fortune-hunting on the part of the ordained suitors, and a paltry yearning for parochial gentility on the part of the ladies who are said to be too often ready to sacrifice much of their material prosperity, and many of their best chances of domestic happiness, to attain the position and social homage which belong to a rector's or vicar's wife. The nature of this double accusation is revealed by the ring of animosity which attends its utterance. Since money, as a source of power and enjoyment, is a thing to be desired, there is surely no reason why the clergy should not take all honourable means to acquire it; and though they may not be altogether innocent of the love of gain imputed to them by their acrimonious censors, the happiness and thorough domestic harmony which almost invariably prevail in clerical homes forbid us to believe, that sordid motives are productive of a larger proportion of clerical than of lay marriages. On the other hand, though the girls of our middle classes may not be perfectly guiltless of snobbishness, it is difficult to believe that a miserable thirst to participate in clerical gentility can account for their decided preference for ecclesiastical admirers.

A far more reasonable way of accounting for the preference, is the supposition that the clerical intellect, style, and office have certain qualities by which the average girl, in every grade of English society, is agreeably and decidedly affected,—in fact, that her nature is more thoroughly in unison with the ecclesiastical than any other kind of masculine nature. A consideration of the circumstances and necessary results of feminine education, and of the principal differences between ecclesiastics and laymen, inclines me to adopt this hypothesis. In spite of all that has been lately urged about the growth of neology and scepticism within the clerical order, it cannot be questioned that the average clergyman is an orthodox theologian, that he is a rigid teacher of the doctrines of the church, and that he sincerely believes all that he teaches. On the other hand, it cannot be denied that there is a considerable amount of heterodoxy prevalent amongst laymen; that, though there never was a time since the sixteenth century, when educated laymen were more reverentially and seriously disposed than they are at the present, the intellect of the laity and the intellect of the clergy have not, during the present generation, been in perfect harmony upon matters pertaining to religion. To a certain extent the average layman and the average ecclesiastic are set asunder, and the same gulf which separates the layman from his spiritual neighbours divides him also from his countrywomen.

That there is a considerable amount of sceptical restlessness and commotion within the ranks of my countrywomen I am well aware. Some years since one of my friends, who had recently published an article in the 'Westminster Review,' received a letter from a lady, asking for further information respecting some points raised in his essay. A correspondence ensued between the reviewer and the lady; and in one of her letters, she said, 'I have now told you my real name. You know that I am the wife of a clerical dignitary who is regarded by England as one of the ablest and most zealous defenders of

Part III.—Clerical Women.

orthodox opinion. That you must keep my secret I need not impress upon you, when I tell you that my husband has not a suspicion that I do not share his opinions. My dear and incomparably good husband is happy in his faith; and I would not disturb it by so much as a whisper of truths unknown to him.' But this lady, so mercifully considerate for her poor husband, was unquestionably an eccentric clerical wife; for although Strauss's 'Life of Jesus' found its first English translator in a woman of noble intellect, and Theodore Parker's works have found their best editor in another of my countrywomen, I am convinced that the educated Englishwomen, who have any leaning towards the conclusions of modern scepticism, do not exceed a few hundreds. The girls of England, and the women of England are with a very few exceptions altogether guiltless of religious heterodoxy. By her mother in the nursery, her governess at home, her teachers at school, her pastors at church, the English girl reared within the pale of the church is carefully trained to believe, feel, inquire, pray *with* the national priesthood; and when her preliminary education terminates with the ceremony of confirmation, she goes out into the world a carefully grounded and enthusiastic believer of all that the church teaches. And very soon she finds a want of harmony between herself and a considerable proportion of the laymen of her acquaintance. Her non-clerical brothers and male cousins frighten her by their significant silence even more than by their rash speeches. Imputing to *all* laymen the state of mind *which* she has detected in a *few* of them, she is disposed to shrink from them in her serious moments. There is a gap betwixt her and them. But she has no such secret fear and distrust of the clergy whom she encounters. The good men, whom she has been trained to regard reverently, think as she thinks. And it is this harmony between her intellect and the clerical thought, which makes her confide in the pastors of her church,—and disposes her to prefer for her husband a poor clergyman to a rich layman.

Clerical marriage has contributed to the stability of the Anglican church in a way never imagined by the framers of our ecclesiastical polity; and especially has this result followed from the matrimonial alliances of the clergy with the newly enriched families of the country,—the first and most notable consequence of those unions being a great increase of the number of ecclesiastical patrons, each of whom is substantially interested in preserving the system under which he has acquired patronal rights. The open and methodical simony of the present day, a practice which, however bad in theory, is attended with none or only few of the pernicious effects which would have resulted from it in the days when it was prevented as well as denounced—may at least be defended as beneficial to the church, by continually redistributing the patronage of the establishment amongst the individuals best qualified to protect it from spoliation, and by continually widening and deepening the foundations of personal interest on which the political fabric of the church was originally built. Every rich man who by the marriage of his daughter with an unbenefied clergyman is induced to purchase the advowson of a living, or any amount of patronal power over an ecclesiastical benefice, binds himself to sustain the establishment in which he may be said to obtain proprietary rights. And so in like manner, every well-to-do family of the kingdom, which thus becomes specially interested in the welfare of the individuals sheltered under a single parsonage, conceives a warmer attachment to the entire ecclesiastical system of which that parsonage is a part.

But a still more important consequence of clerical marriage is its effect on those clerical homes which are such prominent features of our rural life, and which more than any other element of our national prosperity fill the intelligent visitor from a continental country with surprise and envy. The tourist, unfamiliar with the ways of England, is apt to form erroneous conclusions from the magnitude and pictorial adornment and evident luxury of the abodes of our rural clergy. Wherever he goes, the inquiring visitor to our shores observes throughout the land dwellings which he is likely to mistake for the homes of territorial personages; and on learning that these mansions, standing in landscape gardens and flanked with noble timber, are the rectories and vicarages of village cures, he not unfrequently falls into the error of egregiously exaggerating the revenues of an ecclesiastical establishment which affords such imposing residences to country ministers.

Only the other day I was reading a Frenchman's narrative

of English country life, in which the writer expatiates on the magnificence of our emparked rectories, and after setting forth their appointments—their green-houses and pleasure-gardens, their stables and coach-houses—attributes the existence and maintenance of such sumptuous establishments to tithal revenues. Had he remained longer in England before he wrote about it, he would at least have had time to ascertain that the superior livings of most of our English counties have been overbuilt by incumbents whose yearly incomes greatly exceeded their annual ecclesiastical emoluments, and whose superfluous wealth came to them in a large proportion of cases through marriage with opulent women. He might have learnt that notwithstanding the amplitude and occasional extravagance of our parochial endowments, they would fail to produce those evidences of affluence which distinguish the provincial rectors of England from the peasant-priesthood of French departments; that the wealth of our clergy depends less on their preferments than on their private resources; and that their private resources are more often the results of matrimonial enrichment than of inheritance from opulent ancestors.

Of the influence of the prosperous clerical home on the rural parish in which it is situated it would be difficult to speak with excessive praise. Much is often said of the good effects wrought by the personal character and exertions of the country rector who, in the customary absence of the territorial magnates of his district, discharges the functions of a benevolent squire, no less than the duties of a spiritual adviser, to the peasantry of his parish; but though I cordially concur in the praise universally bestowed by intelligent laymen on the zeal, efficiency, and beneficial labours of our country clergy, I am disposed to regard the influence of the average clerical household as scarcely less conducive to our national health than the influence of the average pastor. In the purely agricultural parish, in which there are no resident gentry outside the rectory garden, the clerical home is often the one social power which softens the manners, elevates the minds, and mitigates the distresses, of a rude and indigent community. From its kitchen, timely aid flows to the sick villagers who would, but for its christian care, be left altogether to the harsh and unfeeling ministrations of the poor law. Its inmates are the comforters of the aged, and the voluntary instructors of the infantile population. Of incalculable value also is the clerical home as a school of manners to the offspring of petty farmers and small tradesmen, of ignorant artisans and boorish labourers. The pleasant arts, the graceful courtesies, the dress and refined ways of the ladies of the parsonage are imitated—always awkwardly, sometimes with touches of grotesque exaggeration—by the women of the lowly households that look to their 'betters' for guidance on matters of decorum and taste, no less than on matters of opinion and duty. Sometimes the young ladies of a rectory in a wild and primitive district are heard to speak disapprovingly, and even with irritation, of the quickness with which their new fashions of toilet and diversion are parodied rather than copied by their humble imitators in the village street, and the kitchens of adjacent farmsteads. But instead of wishing to repress this imitative habit, they should regard its results as gratifying proofs and significant demonstrations of their influence upon their humble neighbours. The rustic hoydens and serving-girls who copy their parson's young ladies in such matters as crinolines and bonnets, ribbons and hair-stuffers, strive also to imitate their gentle voices and winning modes of address, their reverential demeanour in church and good humour to the world.

Whilst rendering this grateful recognition to the influence of the clerical home, I do not forget that its pleasant and serviceable qualities are not without attendant disadvantages; that the refinements and luxurious dignity of our rectories are largely accountable for what has been already termed the weak point of our ecclesiastical system—the church's imperfect hold on the affections of the working-people who more readily open their hearts to the comparatively humble ministers of the Nonconforming congregations than to the aristocratic priesthood of the Established Church. Nor am I unaware that in rural districts —more especially in provincial towns, where the clerical is only one, and sometimes not the preponderating, element of cultivated society—jealousies, and petty household contentions, and miserable parochial feuds are continually arising from the antagonistic action of the lay and clerical forces of the local community. But every beneficial system has its weaknesses

Part III.— Clerical Women.

and attendant evils; and no dispassionate observer of modern English life can question that when the most had been made of the shortcomings and wrongdoings of the clerical home, they are few and trivial in comparison with its virtues and noble services.

Nor is it foreign to the purpose of this chapter to remark how exactly the labours and ministerial activity of the women of our clerical homes correspond to the services which the professedly religious women of past time rendered to medieval society. Like the nuns of feudal England, the wives and daughters of our clergy relieve the poor, comfort the aged, sustain the sick, and teach the young. Under the superintendence of their husbands and fathers they discharge the functions which the more devout and zealous nuns of Catholic England discharged under the surveillance of a celibate priesthood. This historic parallel between the inmates of the old nunneries and the women of our modern parsonages is all the more worthy of consideration because, in their zeal to establish sisterhoods of religious ladies in imitation of the ancient deaconesses and medieval nuns, some of our ecclesiastical reformers often represent that the church in recent days has altogether neglected to avail itself of the ministerial abilities of devout christian women. That every large English city has an abundance of work for these new sisterhoods, and that some of the modern associations of religious women have in these later years demonstrated practically their power to render good service to the church, it is needless to remark: but whilst paying proper homage to the devotion and usefulness of the Protestant sisters, it is well for us to remember that in our rural districts—where the clerical home is a dominant social power—the clergy have long had a full measure of feminine co-operation.

PART IV.—OLD WAYS AND NEW FASHIONS.

CHAPTER I.

GOD'S HOUSE THE PEOPLE'S HOME.

IGNORANT of the uses to which sacred edifices were formerly put, and of the secondary ends for which they were erected, numerous modern writers arguing on false assumptions have formed, from the magnitude and number of our medieval churches, very erroneous estimates respecting the populousness of our country in past time. Assuming that the buildings were raised solely for the requirements of public worship, that they were designed for the accommodation of none but the persons ordinarily dwelling in their immediate vicinities, that their habitual frequenters were provided during celebrations of divine service with only a bare sufficiency of room, and that the average congregation of a parish church was very nearly as large an assembly as the place could entertain, the framers of these computations, using the amount of church-accommodation as a measure of population, have represented that the number of our medieval ancestors did not fall much short of the number of persons that would have nearly filled all their churches at the same time. On the fallaciousness of these calculations there is no need to speak at great length; but they are noteworthy, in that they serve to show how far we have lost sight of the inferior aims of our old church-builders, and of what may be termed the social theory of medieval Christianity.

The glory of God and the promotion of true religion were the first objects of the pious builders of our old Gothic churches;

but the same considerations, which induced the chiefs of the ecclesiastical system to sanctify human labour by encouraging clerical persons to bestir themselves in every department of secular industry, inspired them with an ambition to exalt and purify all human interests by controlling and fostering them, under the roofs and within the walls, which piety had reared and the Church consecrated for the worship of the Triune Deity. In the earliest period of our Christian story, when the conflict between Pagan error and the True Faith was still in progress, every material church was the asylum of converts,—the home in which they congregated for physical comfort as well as for spiritual edification; the place in which they sought congenial refreshment after toil, and enjoyed intercourse with pilgrims from distant communities of believers. The Lord's Temple was the Christian's home;—especially was it the home of the Christian who was too poor to provide himself with a private dwelling, and had no place but the House of Prayer in which to seek shelter from the frosts of night and lay his weary head. From the commencement of the parochial system till its completion, each new church was fashioned and ordained for the creature's comfort as well as the Creator's honour. The same spirit animated our ecclesiastical rulers in later times, who, far from thinking that a church was desecrated by arrangements which made it a scene of social diversion and a place for the transaction of honest affairs of secular business, were of opinion that its sacred purpose was observed, and its spiritual usefulness enhanced, by every homely and not absolutely irreverent usage that encouraged people to enter its walls gladly and leave them gratefully,— every custom that stimulated the ordinary citizen's gratitude for the existence of Lord's Houses,— every practice that led him to regard his parish church as an institution no less convenient and beneficial to his worldly concerns than advantageous to his eternal interests.*

---

* In Wilkins's 'Leges Anglo-Saxonicæ Ecclesiasticæ' the reader, in the several injunctions against profanation of churches and their application to secular purposes, may find abundant testimony that the familiar use of the Christian temples resulted, at an early period of our Christian history, in indecorous practices demanding correction. The same laws and injunctions are also evidence that our ancestors of the later generations of the Saxon period, so far

At a time, when we regard any introduction of secular interests within the walls of our churches as an act of impiety, when for good and sufficient reasons we forbid our temples to be used for any but religious purposes and spiritual ends, and when in our commendable zeal to protect our holy places from profanation we attach such sanctity to their very precincts as to think them no fit spots for mere diversion, the foregoing facts should be borne in mind. For through neglect to give them due consideration and their proper place amongst the data of England's social story, the modern reader is apt to form a wrong estimate of our ancestors' piety, when he finds them using their churches for objects which devout persons of our own day dismiss from their thoughts so soon as they have entered a place of Christian worship.

In feudal England, besides being temples for divine worship and schools of religious instruction, our churches were used for purposes of an altogether secular nature. They were halls for social intercourse, receptacles for articles of merchandize, storehouses for worldly treasure, buildings in which courts of justice were held, and places for periodic markets and fairs. In London and the minor cities, in rural towns and even in parishes which comprised no town, the ordinary Englishman of

as their reverential care of sacred places is concerned, aimed at a puritanical strictness that contrasts strongly against the practices of the Norman-English. Ælfric says, 'Non est bibendum, nec hæreticorum more ludendum, nec manducandum in ecclesia nec inutilia verba ibi dicenda sunt; sed orandum est quoniam domus orationis ipsius est quia Salvator expulit e sancto templo omnes qui in hæresibus suis fabulantur, et dixit ita domus mea vocata est domus orationis.' Like the precisians of Elizabethan England, and all their devout descendants of the present time, the more enlightened and pious Anglo-Saxons of the tenth and eleventh centuries maintained that God's house should be preserved for prayer and religious exercise; but their protests against its abuse demonstrate that it was abused. So also, in like manner, Eadgar enacts :— ' Docemus etiam ut presbyteri ecclesias custodiant cum omni veneratione ad ecclesiasticum ministerium et ad purum servitium et ad nullas alias res ; neque sit aliquid inutile ibi neque in vicinia. Non permittantur vana colloquia nec vanæ actiones, neque indecora compotatio, neque unquam alia vanitas, neque intra ecclesiæ sepem canis aliquis veniat, neque porcorum plures quam quis regere possit.' It is in the highest degree noteworthy how, on three most important points of religious usage— intra-ecclesial interment, jealous care for the sanctity of churches, and strict observance of the Lord's day—we have decided to imitate our forefathers of the Saxon period.

the Plantagenet period sauntered daily to church, to pray for a few minutes and amuse himself for a full hour.

In his parish church the loiterer, if a townsman, saw the wares of wealthy tradesmen,—if a countryman, he saw the agricultural produce of neighbouring farmers, stowed away in sacks and cases, and marked with the names of the persons who had confided their property to the ecclesiastical authorities for safer custody than could be obtained for precious commodities in private buildings. From this customary use of the bodies of churches, every place of worship afforded its habitual frequenters the same security against thieves which in these times we derive from strong closets furnished with patent locks, and the establishments of those agents who gain their livelihood by taking charge of chattels deposited in their warehouses. The dealer who had on hand more goods than he could conveniently keep in his own premises, packed them in chests, and sent them to his parish church. The thrifty householder pursued the same course for the safe keeping of his superfluous money and chattels. In this way the space and weather-tight roof of a country-church were of especial service to producers and dealers in wool and other valuable products that could be stowed closely against the walls of the sacred building. For the room and guardianship thus accorded to wool-packs and boxes of treasure the incumbents of churches received small payments of money from the owners of the property,—sums which, without being burdensome to the depositors, amply remunerated the depositaries for the slight pains which it cost them to protect from sacrilegious hands the property thus confided to holy guardianship. That the authorities of churches had no great difficulty in discharging their trust the reader will perceive on learning that the thief, who stole aught of the goods thus committed to the priesthood, was guilty of sacrilege—the crime to which the superstitious sentiment of medieval society attached such infamy and terrible consequences that it was seldom perpetrated, even by men inured in sin and capable of every other kind of iniquity.

The use of churches as courts of justice was universal in feudal England. The consistorial courts were for centuries held in places of worship; and, though much of the business of these courts pertained strictly to the interests of religion, a still greater proportion of their transactions were altogether of a secular nature. The most famous of our consistories, the Court of Arches, derived its name from the peculiar architecture of the Church (St. Mary-le-Bow, London) where it was held. The trials of the earlier Lollards and the later martyrs of the sixteenth century, whether presided over by bishops in person or episcopal commissaries or Royal commissioners, usually took place in cathedrals or other important churches. The commissioners, appointed to try Ridley and Latimer for heresy, opened their proceedings at Oxford in the divinity school, but they continued them in the university church, St. Mary's, where their judicial seat was ' a high throne well trimmed with cloth of tissue and silk.' It was before this same ' solemn scaffold ten feet high, with cloth of state very richly and sumptuously adorned,' that Cranmer was arraigned on the charges that resulted in his martyrdom. Placed ' at the east end of the said church at the high altar ' this judgment-seat was so made that bishop Brooks, ' the Pope's legate, apparelled in pontificalities, and representing the pope's person, might sit under the sacrament of the altar.' Against the gorgeously arrayed judges, placed on high with the sacrament of the altar over their heads, Foxe puts the prisoner on trial in strong contrast. ' And thus,' says the martyrologist, 'these bishops being placed in their pontificialibus, the bishop of Canterbury was sent for to come before them. He, having intelligence of them that were there, thus ordered himself. He came forth of the prison to the church of St. Mary, set forth with bills and glaves for fear he should start away, being clothed in a fair black gown, and in his hand a white staff: for as he was now left only to the stay and succours of virtue and learning, which, after the loss of all his worldly honours and dignities, only remained to him : so appointed he himself thereafter.'

Down to quite recent times the business of our ecclesiastical courts was performed in churches : and when the ordinary work of a spiritual tribunal was removed from the cathedral or other church, in which the judges had previously sat for generations upon generations, to a convenient court-house on unconsecrated ground, its sittings continued to be opened formally in the sacred building, beneath whose roof counsel were no longer permitted to rail and wrangle. Even now this use of churches has not been altogether relinquished. For instance, the commissary court of Surrey still holds sittings in the church of St. Saviour's, Southwark: and any of my London readers who are at the small pains to visit that noble church, during a sitting of the Commissary's court, may ascertain for himself that, notwithstanding our reverence for consecrated places, we can still use them as chambers of justice. The court of course is a spiritual court: but a great, perhaps the greater, part of the business transacted at its sittings is of an essentially secular kind.

But it was not only for the business of the consistories that our churches were used in old time as courts of law. There is abundant evidence that manorial courts were held in places of worship; and it is probable that this practice originated with those remote manorial lords, the churches on whose estates had been raised by their own devout munificence or by the pious liberality of their immediate ancestors. It is also a matter of certainty that secular courts, such as justices' sessions, were very commonly held in churches throughout the strictly feudal period of our story and long after the Reformation. One of the ecclesiastical innovations which rendered Archbishop Laud so odious to the Puritans of Charles the First's time was his attempt to put an end to the practice of holding lay-tribunals in consecrated places. At his trial the managers of the Primate's prosecution charged him with illegal conduct in 'calling some justices of the peace into the high commission, for holding the sessions at Tewkesbury in the churchyard, being consecrated ground, though they had licence of the bishop, and though the eighty-eighth canon of the Church of England gives leave that temporal courts or leets may be kept in the church or churchyard.' To this charge the primate answered, ' that no temporal courts ought to be kept upon consecrated ground; and that though some such might upon urgent occasions be kept in the church with leave, yet that is no warrant for a sessions where there might be trial for blood.' The primate, having thus stated his notion of the fitness of things, and admitted its repugnance to the long established usage of the country, further urged that he had not acted criminally in striving to keep off profanation from the churches.

Even more repugnant to our reverential sentiment than this

ancient application of churches to the convenience of litigants and lawyers, is the manner in which our feudal ancestors permitted the sacred edifices to be used as markets and bazaars. On hearing for the first time that the body of some majestic cathedral, specially endeared to us by pious associations, was the spot where the forefathers of the surrounding town's-people periodically assembled to bargain at hucksters' stalls and enjoy all the excitements of the market or fair, our impulse is to exclaim against the frivolity and godlessness of those who could thus desecrate so fair and sublime a temple. But on recalling what were the secondary objects for which churches were built, and on remembering that the grand social purpose of medieval Christianity was to exercise a sanctifying influence on all human labours and interests, we are enabled to control our righteous indignation and appreciate charitably the motives of the pious ecclesiastics, who looked on with approval whilst workmen raised, beneath their cathedral's vaulted roof, the wooden stalls for the coming fair—and who, whilst the frolic and traffic were at the height of their activity, moved complaisantly to and fro amongst clamorous buyers and sellers, watching the eager throngs of boys and girls with benevolent amusement, and gazing approvingly at the gambols of the morris-dancers and the stages of the miracle-players.

To reconcile our minds still further to this riotous and unseemly use of a Christian church, and to see how the members of a Christian community came thus to abuse it without any deliberately profane intention, we must recall the position which the rulers of our chief sacred edifices held in feudal society. The bishop in his cathedral city, the abbot in his abbey-town, closely resembled in secular matters any lay-baron or wealthy manorial lord. Within the limits of his jurisdiction the abbot, apart from his spiritual functions, exercised powers identical with those of a secular noble. Dwelling in the centre of a large ecclesiastical estate he was surrounded by a population that owed him fealty and regarded him as their patriarch. The chief farmers and traders of the district were his tenants; the people of the town looked to him for patronage and government —their industries, like the very dwellings which they held on lease from the abbey, having proceeded from the influence of

Part IV.—*Old Ways and New Fashions.* 343

the minster and the college of which he was the chief. When the inhabitants of the surrounding country flocked to his town, they came to the home of their social chief, and it devolved on him to provide for their discipline and entertainment—especially at seasons of periodic festivity, when they came in extraordinary numbers to enjoy the diversions of his petty capital, and to contribute to its prosperity. As a dignitary of the church, he entertained them in the vicinity of his minster, encouraging his dependants to do their business under the shadow of its walls, and seek their repose and innocent recreation beneath its roof. And what the bishops, aided by their cathedral clergy, and the abbots, assisted by their monks, accomplished in this respect for the towns built near cathedrals and abbeys, the incumbents of small market-towns and inferior parishes achieved amongst their congregations.

Again, to get a satisfactory view of the chief social conditions which resulted in the hurtful custom of holding fairs in the temples of worship, the reader must bear in mind that most of the chief markets at which our feudal ancestors transacted so large a proportion of their commercial business, had their commencement in the periodic gatherings of the people to celebrate the anniversaries of the days on which their churches were dedicated to God's service. On the conversion of the Saxon tribes to Christianity, their Paganalia, or feasts in honour of deities and heroes, were reformed and changed into festivals of thanksgiving for the blessings of Christian light. The heathen riot was exchanged for a religious observance. Thus instituted, the wake or feast of dedication was an occasion on which the frequenters of each particular church came together for social intercourse under the control of their clergy, and besides coming themselves they drew with them many of their friends from adjacent parishes. When the church was a building of more than ordinary importance, or stood in a populous district, the number of persons who flocked to its annual celebration was considerable, and the individuals thus brought together by religious excitement or social sympathy made their meeting for a pious purpose, subservient to their temporal engagements. To provide for the assembly, special preparations were made by victuallers and hostelers: and when the operations of sutlers and purveyors for the crowd of jubilant worshippers had once imparted an air of jocund briskness and commercial enterprise to the proceedings of the Encænia, the mundane characteristics of the festival soon put its religious origin out of sight. The wake became a bazaar, where people of all ages and both sexes congregated for pleasure and gain much more than for spiritual edification: and after its nature had been thus altered, the clergy continued to control its action and derive pecuniary profit from its humours.

For the proper celebration of their wake the inhabitants of a market-town contributed with labour or gifts to the embellishment of their church. For the comfort and refreshment of holiday-makers, booths of canvas and green boughs were raised in the church-yard. Dealers in earthenware and cutlery, venders of artificers' tools and implements of husbandry, lay packmen and friars engaged in peddlery, dames seeking purchasers for home-spun linen and dairy produce, fixed their stalls in lines upon the sacred ground. On the outskirts of the field would appear lots of sheep and farm-horses, greyhounds, and trained hawks, offered for sale by the breeders and jobbers of the district. Whilst gaily-attired throngs passed up and down the avenues betwixt the lines of stalls, chaffering with dealers and jesting with one another, the music of the fife and bagpipe would be audible in the drinking-booths, where stout yeomen congregated to drink malt-liquor and haggle over samples of corn. Mountebanks, mimers, jesters, ballad-singers, and morris-dancers added to the noise and merriment of the scene.

In fine weather, the holiday-makers enjoyed themselves in the open air; but when rain fell, the motley assembly sought shelter in the church, whither the spenders of money were quickly followed by the caterers of amusement. The frequency with which the wakers of humid England were thus driven by rain and wind from the precinct to the interior of the church soon resulted in the erection of stalls, and the exhibition of sacred or profane interludes, under the very roof of the consecrated building. And in many cases—as in old St. Paul's and other cathedrals in populous cities—the stalls, erected in the first instance for special occasions and removed immediately after their temporary objects had been achieved, were permitted to remain and become the nuclei of continual bazaars. In churches possessed of famous shrines, that attracted large numbers of visitors throughout the year, these permanent fairs were permitted and encouraged by the clergy, who maintained that they were conducive to the convenience and well-being of the public. And whilst the clergy defended an irreverent practice, from which the chapters of cathedrals and the incumbents of parish churches derived considerable emolument, the laity sanctioned it by the alacrity with which they used their church-bazaars as pleasant places for a morning gossip or a midday promenade.*

That medieval opinion saw nothing reprehensible in this application of the naves of churches to secular objects is demonstrated by the terms in which Archbishop Stafford, in the reign of Henry the Sixth, enjoined a stricter observance of Sundays and other chief holidays. As we have already intimated, and in a subsequent chapter shall more precisely show, our feudal ancestors were comparatively free from Sabbatarian notions respecting the Lord's day. Every now and then the student of ecclesiastical affairs in feudal times sees an archbishop or other leader of the church confounding the Christian Sunday with the Jewish Sabbath, and witnesses a fitful agitation to make the national observance of Sunday resemble the Israelitish manner of keeping the Seventh Day; but such confusion of two different institutions was infrequent amongst our priests of old time, who usually concurred in regarding the first day of the week as an appropriate time for social mirth and activity.

The Sunday of Catholic England was a day for feasting and pomp. In the twenty-eighth year of Edward the Third, it was

---

* A volume might be filled with passages from old writers, illustrative of the irreverent familiarity with which our ancestors used their churches. Speaking of the profanations which Thomas Cranmer, whilst primate, exerted himself to suppress, Strype says, ' Sacred places, set apart for divine worship, were now greatly profaned; and so, probably, had been before by profane custom : for in many churches, cathedral as well as other, and especially in London, many frays, quarrels, riots, bloodsheddings, were committed. They used also, commonly, to bring horses and mules into and through churches, and shooting off hand-guns, making the same, which were properly appointed to God's service and common prayer, like a stable or common inn, or rather a den and sink of all un-Christiness.'

ordained that wool-staplers should forbear to exhibit their wools on Sundays and solemn feasts: but though this injunction implies that the religious sentiment of the period disapproved of men who followed their ordinary avocations on the holy days, there is abundant evidence that the Sunday in ancient England was no such day of general rest as it gradually became after the Reformation. In the middle of the fifteenth century there was, however, a notable attempt on the part of high ecclesiastics to relieve the Lord's Day of that excess of worldly jollification which the Wycliffian reformers had loudly denounced in the previous century. And in furtherance of this endeavour Archbishop Stafford in 1444 decreed throughout his province ' *ut nundinæ ac emporia in ecclesiis aut cœmeteriis, diebusque Dominicis atque festis, præterquam tempore messis, non teneantur;*—*i. e.* that fairs and markets should no more be kept in churches or churchyards on the Lord's days and other holy days, except in time of harvest.' Had the sentiment of devout persons generally condemned the custom of holding fairs in churches, the reforming Primate would unquestionably have forbidden the objectionable practice: but, notwithstanding his desire to restore holy things to their proper honour, he merely prohibited the holding of markets in churches at times not lying within seasons of harvest, and, whilst distinctly permitting such markets in harvest-time, tacitly sanctioned the use of churches for secular traffic on ordinary days throughout the year.

CHAPTER II.

CHURCH PLAYS AND CHURCH ALES.

AT the risk of shocking some of my devout readers, it is right to observe that the theatre and the church are found in close alliance in feudal England, that our national drama had its rise in the national cathedrals, and that, whilst the best of our medieval dramatists were scholarly divines, their plays were put on the boards and performed by actors, who, if not themselves clerks in orders, followed the histrionic art under the patronage of important ecclesiastics. And in the days when the services of the church were celebrated in a tongue unintelligible to the vulgar, when the humble laity could seldom read the words of the Gospel, and when comparatively instructed persons rarely saw a copy of the Scriptures, it can be readily believed that simple folk derived the greater part of their imperfect knowledge of the Saviour's story and mission from the sacred interludes presented to them at wakes and festivals. That the doctrines of the miracle-plays and mysteries of the Catholic writers and mimics were widely and deeply influential with the common people in the sixteenth century, we know from the manner in which Bishop Bale endeavoured to counteract them by Protestant dramas in the same style of art.

One of the bishop's dramatic achievements is, 'God's Promises: A Tragedye or Interlude. Manyfestyng the Chefe promyses of God unto man by all ages in the old laws, from the fall of Adam to the incarnacyon of the Lord Jesus Christ. Compyled by Johan Bale, A.D. MDXXXVIII.' One of the actors in this marvellous drama is ' Pater Cœlestis;' and it forcibly illustrates human inconsistency that Bale, who never wearied of ridiculing the impostures of the roods and denouncing the irreverent nature of pictorial representations of the Trinity, should have had the hardihood — with difficulty we refrain from adding the indecency — to put an impersonator of the Heavenly Father on a theatrical stage. A still more remarkable piece of pious irreverence is the same prelate's ' Brefe Comedy or Enterlude of Johan Baptystes preachyng in the wyldernesse, openynge the craftye assaultes of the hypocrites, with the gloryouse Baptyme of the Lord Jesus Christ. Compyled by Johan Bale. Anno MDXXXVIII.' In this singular piece the actors are Pater Cœlestis, Joannes Baptistes, Publicanus, Pharisæus, Jesus Christus, Turba Vulgaris, Miles Armatus, and Sadducæus. Of the devices, employed for its representation, the most outrageous was a mechanical contrivance which produced a semblance of the Holy Ghost descending in the form of a dove. ' *Descendit tunc*,' runs one of the stage-directions of the interlude, ' *super Christum Spiritus Sanctus in columbæ specie, et vox patris de cœlo audietur hoc modo*.' In this play ' Pater Cœlestis' does not appear personally, as he does in ' God's promises.' That we may understand the religious life of our ancestors it is necessary to ponder on these things, repugnant and absolutely horrifying though they are to our devotional feelings. The disquiet and anger that I experience in relating them warn me that I must urge the reader to remember that John Bale was no flippant wit or profligate derider of sacred things, but a pious prelate whose zeal for religious reform nearly cost him his life, and compelled him to seek safety in exile during the Marian persecution. The excellent purpose which he had in producing this, in one respect, revolting play is declared in the epilogue which, in the printed copies of the drama, is uttered by the Prolocutor, Balœus. The last three verses of the epilogue are these:

' The ways that Johan taught, was not to weare harde clothynge,
To say longe prayers, nor to waundre in the desart,
Or to eate wylde beasts. No, he never taught soch thynge,
Hys mynde was that faythe should puryfy the heart.
My ways (sayth the Lord), with mennys ways have no part.
Mannys ways are all thynges, that are done without fayth,
God's ways is hys worde, as the holy scripture sayth.

If ye do penaunce, do soch as Johan doth counsell.
Forsake your olde lyfe, and to the true fayth applye;
Washe away all fylthe, and folowe Christe's gospell.
The justyce of men is lust and hypocrisie,

> A work with fayth, an outwarde vayne glorye,
> An example here, ye had of the Pharysees,
> Whom Johan compared to unfruteful wythered trees.
>
> Give care unto Chryst, let mennys vayne phantasyes goe,
> As the father bad, by hys most hygh commaundement,
> Heare neyther Frances, Benedict, nor Bruno,
> Albert no Domynyck, for they newe rulers invent.
> Beleve neyther Pope, nor Prest of hys convent,
> Folowe Christe's Gospell, and therein fructifye,
> In the prayse of God, and hys son Jesus glorye.'

An act of convocation, passed by Henry the Eighth in 1536 after the abolition of the Papal authority, ordained that every church should hold its feast of dedication on the first Sunday of October in each year, instead of on the day of its patron saint.* The avowed object of this act was to reduce the number of religious festivals, which, it was urged, were so frequent throughout the kingdom, as to interfere with business by withdrawing humble people too much from their labour, and keeping them in a state of almost continuous riot. But though the framers of the act may have sincerely wished to amend the manners of the lower orders, it is almost needless to remark that the measure was designed quite as much to lessen the influence of Papal traditions as to promote morality and orderliness.† The enactment, like most legislative measures for ecclesiastical reform, failed to meet with general compliance. As obedience

---

* Embodied in the act that ordered this great modification of ancient usages is an apology for the change, which is worthy of attention. 'And sith the Sabboth-day,' runs the act, ' was ordeyned for man's use, and therefore ought to gyve place to the necessitie and behove of the same whan soever that shall occurre; mouch rather any other holy institute by man. It is therefore by the kyngs hyghnes auctority, as supreme head in earth of the Church of Englande, with the common assent and consent of the prelates and clergy of this his realme in Convocacyon lawfully assembled and congregate, among other thynges decreed, ordeyned and established,— First, that the feest of Dedicacyon of the church shall in all places throughout this realm be celebrated and kept on the firste Sonday of the moneth of October for ever, and upon none other day.' The terms of the foregoing apology help us to realise the light in which our ancestors regarded the holy days of the Church.

† That the inconvenience, stated to have resulted in Catholic times from the excessive number of religious festivals, was an actual embarrassment, and no mere imaginary grievance invented by the Reformers to serve as a pretext for doing away with the Papal saints, the reader may infer from the admissions of Catholic writers. In his memorial for a resettlement of the country within the

to its requirements would have deprived the feasts of the presence of strangers from adjacent parishes, and have put an end to the opportunities which the wakes had hitherto afforded humble people of exchanging hospitable courtesies with distant neighbours, social opinion declined to adopt the proposed change. But on this delicate point there was gradually effected between authority and populace a compromise which gained for the former all that it really had at heart, and reserved for the latter all that it cordially cared to retain in the long established wakes. Whilst the clergy and magistrates refrained from insisting that the feasts of dedication should all be held on the same Sunday, the people were content that the wake of each church should be transferred from the anniversary day of its saint to the Sunday following the saint's day. By this arrangement the minds of simple folk were weaned from their superstitious attachment to the Catholic saints, and at the same time no check was put on their sociable dealings with friends in contiguous parishes.

Out of our ancestor's social use—or, as some readers may prefer to say, out of our ancestor's riotous abuse—of the medieval churches arose those congenial meetings on consecrated ground at which fellow-parishioners came together to combine charitable effort with bodily indulgence and the delights of neighbourly intercourse. If in the old feudal days a quarrel

---

lines of Papal authority, Parsons the Jesuit says (1596):—'A calendar is to be drawn out and agreed upon for holy-days that are to be observed in England; few and well kept were much better than many with hurt of the commonwealth and dissolution of manners. It is no small temporal loss for poor labouring men, that live and maintain their families upon the labours of their hands, to have so great a number of vacant days as in some countries there be, whereby the poor are brought to great necessity, and the realme much hindered in things that otherwise might be done, and corruption of manners much increased. For remedy of the first, (I mean besides Sundays) let it be considered, whether this moderation, amongst others, might not be admitted, that some days had only obligation to hear mass, and that afterwards they should work, and that nothing should be taken from labouring men's wages for the time spent in hearing of mass: so that this loss would fall only upon the richer sort, that are better able to bear it. Holydays might be for half a day only, to wit, for the forenoon, and that after dinner every man should work; and that this should not be left to any man's proper will to work or make holydays at his pleasure: for that many, out of idleness, would play, and induce others to do the same; but only the order set down should be inviolably kept.'

Part IV.—Old Ways and New Fashions. 351

about some matter of parochial politics arose amongst the inhabitants of a township, or if a choleric householder fell out with his ancient comrades on a private matter, the dispute was often terminated by a love-meeting and love-feast in the parish church. Through the kindly mediation of mutual friends, the disputants were brought together in the house of prayer, and after joining hands and offering a few words of supplication to their favourite saints, they pledged one another in cups of ale in the church or its precincts, before returning to their houses all the happier for the cheering drink and the termination of their feud.

Similar in nature to these meetings for the reconciliation of foes, were the periodical congregations of fellow-parishioners at Church-ales, Clerk-ales, and Bid-ales.

The Bid-ale was a charitable device analogous to the balls, dinners, and raffles, which are now-a-days held for the aid of benevolent institutions or impoverished persons. When an Englishman in old time failed in business, or through some catastrophe was plunged in unexpected poverty, his neighbours were wont to subscribe a purse for his benefit or send him presents of food and drink. The sympathetic housewife would give a bag of meal or a basket of eggs; the farmer would furnish a bushel of malt or a joint of pork. Some of the contributors would give in kind, others in money. In these times such gifts would be for the poor man's immediate use. But our ancestors had peculiar ways: with the presents thus showered upon him the bankrupt was expected to make a feast or 'ale,' to which he would bid his comrades and acquaintance,—it being understood that every one of the guests would pay to the host a sum of money for his share of the banquet for which his generosity had helped to supply the materials. The sum which the ale-giver received in his character of host was the fund on which he renewed his fight with the world.

The Clerk-ale was a feast provided in the same manner, and paid for by feasters who had previously contributed materials for its making, the pecuniary proceeds of the entertainment being designed for the augmentation of the parish-clerk's inadequate salary. Explaining the nature and etiquette of Clerk-ales in his defence of Church-feastings, Bishop Pierce remarked in Charles the First's time, 'For in poor country parishes, where the wages of the clerk are but small, the people, thinking it unfit that the clerk should duly attend at church and gain nothing by his office, send him in provision, and then come on Sundays and feast with him, by which means he sells more ale, and tastes more of the liberality of the people, than their quarterly payment would amount to in many years.'

Of the Church-ale, often called the Whitsun-ale from being generally held at Whitsuntide, it is necessary to speak at greater length, for it was a far more important institution than the Bid-ale or the Clerk-ale. The ordinary official givers of a church-ale were two wardens who, after collecting subscriptions in money or kind from every one of their affluent or fairly well-to-do fellow-parishioners, provided a revel that not unfrequently surpassed the wake in costliness and diversity of amusements. The board, at which everyone received a welcome who could pay for his entertainment, was loaded with good cheer; and after the feasters had eaten and drunk to contentment, if not to excess, they took part in sports on the turf of the churchyard, or on the sward of the village-green. The athletes of the parish distinguished themselves in wrestling, boxing, quoit-throwing; the children cheered the mummers and morris-dancers; and round a may-pole, decorated with ribbons, the lads and lasses plied their nimble feet to the music of fifes, bagpipes, drums, and fiddles. When they had wearied themselves by exercise, the revellers returned to the replenished board: and not seldom the feast, designed to begin and end in a day, was protracted into a demoralizing debauch of a week's or even a month's duration.*

Describing the manner in which these revels were sustained in Elizabethan England, Carew in the 'Survey of Cornwall'

---

* Referring to the riot and debauchery that frequently attended the celebration of Church feasts, even to the defilement and desecration of holy places, Henry the Eighth, after assuming the supreme government of the English Church, enjoined that no 'Christian person should abuse the same' (*i.e.* churches) 'either by eating, drinking, buying, selling, playing, dancing, or with other profane or worldly matters. For all soberness, quietness, and godliness, ought there to be used.' But in the sixteenth century it was easy for authority to publish edicts against ancient usages, and just as difficult to compel universal obedience to the new orders.

Part IV.—Old Ways and New Fashions.

says: 'two young men of the parish are yearly chosen by their last foregoers to be wardens, who, dividing the task, make collection among the parishioners of whatsoever provision it pleaseth them voluntarily to bestow. This they employ in brewing, baking, and other acates against Whitsontide: upon which holidays the neighbours meet at the church-house, and there merrily feed on their owne victuals, contributing some petty portion to the stock, which, by many smalls, groweth to a meetly greatness: for there is entertayned a kind of emulation between these wardens, who, by his graciousness in gathering, and good husbandry in expenditure, can best advance the churches profit. Besides, the neighbour-parishes at those times lovingly visit each one another, and this way frankly spend their money together. The afternoons are consumed in such exercises as olde and young folke (having leisure) doe accustomably weare out the time withall. When the feast is ended, the wardens yield in their account to the parishioners: and such money as exceeded the disbursement is laid up in store, to defray any extraordinary charges arising in the parish, or imposed on them for the good of the country, or the prince's service: neither of which commonly gripe so much, but that somewhat still remayneth to cover the purse's bottom.' In his 'Anatomie of Abuses,' 1585, Stubbs* records that some of the money raised by these revels was devoted to the needful repairs of the church, to the enrichment of it with service-books and sacramental vessels, and to the cost of washing 'surplesses for Sir John, and such other necessaries.'

From other and less prejudiced informants, however, we

---

* Stubbs says, 'In certaine townes, where drunken Bacchus beares swaie, against Christmas and Easter, Whitsondaie, or some other time, the church-wardens of every parishe, with the consent of the whole parishe, provide half-a-score or twentie quarters of mault, whereof some they buy of the churche stocke, and some is given them of the parishioners themselves, every one conferring somewhat according to his abilitie; which maulte being made into very strong ale or bere, is sette to sale, either in the churche or some other place assigned to that purpose. Then, when this is set abroche, well is he that can gete the soonest to it, and spend the most at it. For this kinde of practice they continue sixe weekes, a quarter of a yeare, yea, halfe a yeare together. That money, they say, is to repaire their churches and chappels with, to buy bookes for service, cuppes for the celebration of the Sacrament, surplesses for Sir John, and such other necessaries.'

learn that the pecuniary proceeds of Church-ales were largely useful in providing for aged indigence and putting out orphans as apprentices. In many a parish, in post-Reformation times, the Church-ale was serviceable in this way to the extent of obviating all need to levy church-rates and poor-rates. In his 'Wiltshire Survey,' John Aubrey assures us that during his grandfather's time 'there were no rates for the poor' of the important parish of Kingston St. Michael, for whose wants an adequate provision was made by the Whitsun Church Revels.' That these revels were derived from the Agapæ, or Love-Feasts of the early Christian churches, the antiquary makes no doubt; and he tells us that amongst the amusements provided at them for the younger people, were 'dancing, bowling, and shooting at butts,' of which sports the parochial elders were grave and attentive spectators.

In the earlier centuries of feudal England, the Church-ales, Clerk-ales, and even Bid-ales, for the benefit of particular individuals, were held in the churches, like the Feasts of Dedication or Wakes, which were the most ancient and important of all the secular-religious merry-makings.* But in the interval between the rise of the Wycliffian agitation and the final abolition of the Papal authority, our forefathers exhibited their respect for growth of Puritanical sentiment by providing in many rural parishes houses in the vicinity of the churches, where the eating and drinking could be carried on without doing violence to the feelings of those precisians who were of opinion that the Lord's House was an inappropriate place for hilarious entertainments. In Elizabethan England these Church-houses, as our ancestors called them, were numerous. In Worsley's History of the Isle of Wight, mention is made of 'a house called the Church-house, held by the inhabitants of Whitwell, parishioners of Gatcombe, of the lord of the manor,' which

* Amongst the Church-feastings of our ancestors, funereal banquets—for the entertainment of mourners at obsequies—were by no means the least frequent, or the least riotous. 'Margaret Atkinson, widow,' runs a passage in Strype's edition of Stowe's London, 'by her will, October 18, 1544, orders that the next Sunday after her burial there be provided two dozens of bread, a kilderkin of ale, two gammons of bacon, three shoulders of mutton, and two couple of rabbits, desiring all the parish, as well rich as poor, to take part thereof, and a table to be set in the midst of the church, with everything necessary thereto.'

Part IV.—Old Ways and New Fashions. 355

dwelling the holders granted, in 1574, to one John Brode by a lease, which contained this condition : 'Provided always, that, if the Quarter shall need at any time to make a Quarter-ale, or Church-ale, for the maintenance of the chapel, it shall be lawful for them to have the use of the said house, with all the rooms, both above and beneath, during their ale.' Speaking of North Wiltshire in the following century, John Aubrey says, 'In every parish is (or was) a Church-house, to which belonged spits, crocks, &c., utensils for dressing provision. Here the housekeepers met and were merry, and gave their charity.' But though these Church-houses became general, the wakes and minor revels continued to be held within the walls of some churches long after the Reformation, in parts of the kingdom where the gentry and populace held tenaciously to old ways. Writing in 1585, Stubbs states precisely that the malt liquor provided for the Church-ales and minor revels, no less than the drink brewed for wakes, was broached, drawn, and sold within the walls of churches.

In the Book of Anglican Canons ('Liber quorundam Canonum Disciplinæ Ecclesiæ Anglicanæ'), promulgated in 1571, churchwardens are specially enjoined to disallow the holding of feasts, drinking-parties, banquets, and public entertainments within the walls of churches. '*Æditui convivia, symposia, cœnas, ac invitationes publicas in templis celebrari non patientur.*' This prohibition is of itself evidence of the frequency with which such repasts and merry-makings were held *in* churches during the first thirteen years of Elizabeth's reign. The publication of this order must have increased the number of Church-houses; and it is probable that it caused the inhabitants of Whitwell to provide themselves with a Church-house by the stipulation already noticed in their lease of a dwelling to John Brode. I am inclined to think that most of the Church-houses alluded to by Aubrey had their origin in the requirements of the canon entitled, 'Æditui Ecclesiarum ac alii selecti.' But that the canon did not immediately effect its purpose of withdrawing the ales and other feasts from all the churches of the country, we have the evidence of Stubbs and later witnesses. Another object of this same canon was to suppress the fairs and markets which, in defiance of previous and repeated prohibitions, were still held on Sundays. The canon further enjoined churchwardens to drive all beggars and vagabonds from the churchyards and church-porches, and to prevent all peddlers from following their trades in the same places, or anywhere else, on Sundays and festal days, during hours of Divine service. 'Non patientur ut quisquam ex circumforaneis istis tenuibus, ac sordidis mercatoribus, qui aciculas ac ligulas, ac crepundia, ac res viles ac minutas circumferunt ac distrahunt, quos pedarios, aut pedalarios appellant, proponat merces suas vel in cœmeteriis, vel in porticibus Ecclesiarum, aut uspiam alibi diebus festis, aut dominicis, interim dum peragitur pars aliqua sacri ministerii, aut habetur sacra concio; nec ut mendici aut errones, quibus nulla certa sedes, toto illo sacrorum aut concionum tempore hæreant in cœmiterio vel in porticu, sed mandabunt, ut aut ingrediantur aut discedant.'

Though the removal of the feasts from churches to church-houses was an important concession to Puritan opinion, it failed to reconcile the Sabbatarian reformers to revels that were held on the Lord's Day; and the controversial literature of Elizabeth's reign, and the earlier half of the seventeenth century, abounds with evidence of the disapprobation with which the precisians regarded these festal desecrations of the days which they spent in fasting, prayer, and solemn meditation. To suppress these profane festivities was one of the chief objects which the Puritans proposed to themselves in the way of social reform; and though Queen Elizabeth bore them no goodwill, she was inclined to support them in their attempt to purge the Sunday of the most flagrant of its customary desecrations. In the 38th year of her reign, the justices assembled at Bridgwater ordered the total suppression of church-ales, clerk-ales, and bid-ales, and this order was signed by Popham, her lord chief justice. The same order was renewed three years later. Even in the reign of James the First, the first promulgator of the 'Book of Sports,' this prohibition was repeated at Exeter without causing any commotion beyond the particular district in which the feasts were suppressed. But in the days of Elizabeth and James, things could be done against the privileges and powers of the clerical order, which it was not safe to repeat in Charles the First's time, after Laud had risen to the chief place in the

Part IV.—Old Ways and New Fashions. 357

hierarchy. For their boldness in repeating the order for the suppression of the Sunday revels, whilst they were officiating as judges on the Western Circuit, Chief Justice Richardson and Baron Denham were sharply called to order by the Primate, who maintained that, as secular judges, they had exceeded their functions in dealing with a question that pertained altogether to the spirituality. Wakes and ales were religious institutions, and, though some correction of their abuses might be required, the lay tribunals had no right to stir in the matter. Whatever reform was needed with respect to these sacred and edifying jollifications on the Lord's Day, the archbishop, in the exercise of his office, and the bishops, by means of their consistories, could effect; but no lay-judge should be permitted to usurp the functions of the priesthood.

This was the Archbishop's way of looking at the case; and poor Sir Thomas Richardson, on appearing at the Council to render an account of his outrageous proceedings against the Church, was rated in round terms for his insolence by the Primate, and was required to revoke his own order. 'I was well-nigh choked by his lawn-sleeves,' said the humiliated Chief Justice, on escaping from the council-chamber, when recounting to the Earl of Dorset the treatment which he had endured at his Grace's hands. Having snubbed the lay-judge, Laud forthwith wrote for further information to Pierce, bishop of Bath and Wells, respecting the Sunday frolics; and Bishop Pierce could give no information against a system that encouraged the gentry and commonalty to celebrate their Sundays with drunkenness, gluttony, dancing, gambling, and profane music.* The question of wakes became a party-question; and a squabble of sermons and pamphlets ensued between the Puritans and Laudian Clergy,—the Puritans maintaining that half the social iniquity of the country was distinctly traceable to the

* The favourite arguments of Charles the First's High-church clergy in defence of the old Church revels and Sunday sports, were the same as those used by the Elizabethan Catholics against the Reformers who required a Sabbatarian observance of the Sunday. In his 'Memorial,' already quoted, the Jesuit Parsons (1596) says, 'The old exercises of England for parishes to meet together upon holydays at the church-houses, church-yards, and other such places, and there to disport themselves honestly, for the avoiding irkness or worse occupations at home, is not evil, but to be continued, avoiding all the excesses or abuses that

Sunday revels: and the Clergy insisting that the revels were things of sacred origin, that they were greatly conducive to the temporal and spiritual welfare of the humbler people, and that their suppression would be an humiliation to the Church and an injury to the whole commonwealth. Here and there an enlightened incumbent ventured to side with the Sabbatarians, and to declare that wakes and ales and all other Sunday riotings were sinful against God, and unspeakably hurtful to the morals of all classes of men who indulged in them. But these bold priests were not numerous, and the bishops found but small difficulty in silencing them. When Mr. Theophilus Bradbourne, the Suffolk parson, published his 'Defence of the Most Ancient and Sacred Ordinance of God, the Sabbath Day,' he was called to order promptly and with such effect that he gave the defenders of ales no more trouble. 'The poor man,' as Fuller quaintly observes, 'fell into the ambush of the High Commission, whose well-tempered severity so prevailed with him, that he became a convert, and conformed quickly to the Church of England.' That the arguments of the Puritans were altogether free from sins against good taste and the errors of deficient learning, no critic of the present day is likely to represent; but so far as reasoning, knowledge of history, and common sense are concerned, they got the better of their opponents. But the bishops had the verdict of authority and fashion. The 'Book of Sports' was republished: the men and women of the cavalier gentry encouraged the artisans and peasantry to make Sunday their day of weekly frolic, and supported the ancient institution of the country by themselves taking part in the Sunday dances and games round the parish may-poles.

If the Rebellion and the rule of 'the saints,' may be commended for nothing else, we have reason to be thankful to them for rendering the English Sunday what it still remains, a day of

may be therein, which were commonly accustomed to be great: but the thing itself, I mean that meeting and entertainment of mirth, worketh divers good effects, as by the want thereof in some other countries has been noted; for it holdeth the people in contentment, and maketh friendship of one man with another, and of one parish with another; and when they are joined together any good instruction or exhortation may be made unto them, if the curate or any spiritual man will take the same in hand.'

Part IV.—Old Ways and New Fashions. 359

rest from secular toil and vulgar pleasure,—a tranquil day for prayer and meditation, for religious study and the exercise of Christian benevolence. The Parliament, that abolished the crown and the bishops, shifted the wakes and ales from Sundays to ordinary days, and, driving the roisterers from the churches and church-yards to the market-squares and other profane places, ordained that the ancient festivals should no longer be held in the precincts of houses devoted to sacred worship. And though Charles the Second's restorers undid nearly every good thing that had been accomplished during the Rebellion and the Commonwealth, they had the good sense to refrain from reviving the Sabbatarian controversy by another republication of the 'Book of Sports.' Left to the action of time, the Sacred Feasts and Church Fairs—the Wakes and Revels and Ales—of the seventeenth century, have gradually dwindled and dropped into such insignificance and disrepute, that even the superior servant-girls of our provincial towns would scorn to lower themselves by dancing at village hoppings.

The social use of the churchyard, however, purified of old excesses and abuses, may be said to have continued in rural parishes to the close of the last, and even to the beginning of the present century. ' A country-fellow,' Addison observed in 'Spectator' 112, 'distinguishes himself as much in the churchyard as a citizen does upon the Change, the whole parish politics being generally discussed in that place either after sermon or before the bell rings. My friend, Sir Roger, being a good churchman, has beautified the inside of his church with several texts of his own choosing: he has likewise given a handsome pulpit cloth, and railed in the communion-table at his own expense . . . The fair understanding between Sir Roger and his chaplain, and their mutual concurrence in doing good, is the more remarkable because the very next village is famous for the differences and contentions that rise between the parson and squire; and the squire, to be revenged on the parson, never comes to church. The squire has made all his tenants atheists and tithe-stealers: while the parson instructs them every Sunday in the dignity of his order, and insinuates to them, almost in every sermon, that he is a better man than his patron. In short, matters are even come to such an extremity that the squire has not said his prayers either in public or private this half-year; and that the parson threatens him, if he does not mend his manners, to pray for him in the face of the whole congregation.' Of this social use of the churchyard, good instances may still be found in our rural districts.

END OF THE FIRST VOLUME.

LONDON:
STRANGEWAYS AND WALDEN, PRINTERS,
28 Castle St. Leicester Sq.

www.ingramcontent.com/pod-product-compliance
Lightning Source LLC
Chambersburg PA
CBHW020314240426
43673CB00039B/805